The Contemporary Cath

The Contemporary Catholic School:

Context, Identity and Diversity

Edited by

Terence H. McLaughlin,
Joseph O'Keefe S.J.
and Bernadette O'Keeffe

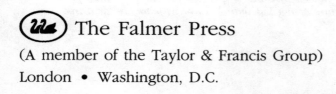 The Falmer Press

(A member of the Taylor & Francis Group)
London • Washington, D.C.

UK	The Falmer Press, 1 Gunpowder Square, London, EC4A 3DE
USA	The Falmer Press, Taylor & Francis Inc., 1900 Frost Road, Suite 101, Bristol, PA 19007

First published in 1996

A catalogue record for this book is available from the British Library

Library of Congress Cataloging-in-Publication Data are available on request

ISBN 0 7507 0471 3 cased
ISBN 0 7507 0472 1 paper

Jacket design by Caroline Archer

Typeset in 10/12pt Garamond by
Graphicraft Typesetters Ltd., Hong Kong.

Printed in Great Britain by Biddles Ltd, Guildford and King's Lynn on paper which has a specified pH value on final paper manufacture of not less than 7.5 and is therefore 'acid free'.

Contents

Contents

Chapter 1

Setting the Scene: Current Realities and Historical Perspectives

Terence H. McLaughlin, Joseph O'Keefe S.J. and Bernadette O'Keeffe

This volume is designed to contribute to the research effort which is needed if appropriate forms of analysis and enquiry are to be brought to bear on the many issues which arise concerning the contemporary Catholic school. Written by contributors from both sides of the Atlantic, and from a number of different disciplinary backgrounds and points of view, these essays tackle a number of the central questions which confront Catholic schools today.

The volume arises in part from a conference on 'The Contemporary Catholic School and the Common Good' which was jointly organized by the Von Hügel Institute at St Edmund's College in the University of Cambridge and Boston College which was held at St Edmund's in July 1993. The conference featured Professor Bryk from the University of Chicago as its main speaker and included participants from the UK, Ireland and the United States concerned with questions of Catholic education, including educational practitioners and policy makers, as well as theologians, philosophers, sociologists and psychologists working in the academic study of education and in educational research. A number of the papers presented at the conference are included in this book, together with additional papers especially commissioned by the editors.

The themes of context, identity and diversity are prominent throughout the volume. We shall consider briefly each of these themes in turn.

Context

It is necessary to provide some general and historical background relating to the context of contemporary Catholic schools on both sides of the Atlantic. The two contexts differ in a number of significant respects. In England and Wales, for example, Catholic schools enjoy considerable support from public funds in a way inconceivable in the United States. In the US, the term 'Catholic school' embraces the higher education sector, whereas in England and Wales the

Catholic element of the higher education sector is small and there are no Catholic universities. In this volume we shall be confining attention to Catholic institutions of learning for students up to the age of 18. Before looking in more detail at some comparative statistics relating to Catholic schools in England and Wales and in the US, we offer a historical perspective from which they can be viewed.

Historical Context of Catholic Schools in England and Wales

In a review of the roots of the emergence of the post-Reformation English Catholic community, Hornsby-Smith identifies four distinct strands. First, 'recusant Catholics', those Catholics who can trace the continuity of their Catholicism from pre-Reformation times. The term recusant was used to refer to Catholics who were subject to penal taxation and fines because of their refusal to attend Anglican services. There are an estimated 650,000 successors of 'recusant' Catholics in England and Wales who can trace their Catholicism to the pre-Reformation period (Hornsby-Smith, 1987, pp. 23–4). These 'Old Catholics' for the most part were members of the aristocracy; landowners together with their tenants and defendants.

A second strand in the growth of the post-Reformation Catholic Church was conversion. Between 1900 and 1960, it was estimated that there were 740,000 adult conversions to Catholicism in Britain (Hornsby-Smith, 1987, p. 23). A significant number of converts were influenced by Newman. In 1952, converts over the age of 14 reached a peak and accounted for 10.2 per cent of all baptisms (Spencer, 1975). More recently, the 1978 study of Roman Catholic opinion estimates that approximately 11 per cent of Catholic adults are converts (Hornsby-Smith, 1987, p. 24).

Third, Irish immigrants made a vital contribution to the growth of the Catholic community. For more than a century, Irish immigration was one of the most important factors in the Catholic revival. Cardinal Manning, writing in 1890, noted that eight-tenths of the Catholic population in England were Irish. However, the Irish Catholic factor had been important long before the immigration which followed the famine (Gwynn, 1950, p. 266). The number of Irish priests who had come to minister before the Hierarchy was restored increased greatly when new parishes were created which literally laid the foundations of the subsequent progress (Gwynn, 1950, p. 289). Bishop Ward, writing some twenty years later about the Catholic revival, makes the point that Irish immigration after the famine:

> . . . affected the future of Catholicism in this country more than the Oxford Movement, for it was the influx of Irish in 1844 and the following years which made our congregations what they are . . . Up to that time, English Catholics relied for the building of their churches almost solely on the donations of the few hereditary Catholics and others of

the upper classes; after Irish immigration, it became possible to build from the pennies of the poor. Many missions owe their very existence, including serviceable churches and schools, to the large Irish congregations. (Gwynn, 1950, p. 270)

In general, the Irish Catholics settled initially in specific areas, particularly in London and crowded northern cities and they were subject to marked religious and racial discrimination. Throughout the nineteenth century, large sections of the Catholic community continued to face hardship, insecurity and powerlessness born out of poverty and economic insecurity. The newly built churches and schools were central to their lives insofar as they nurtured a sense of identity and group solidarity. Those nineteenth century Irish immigrants brought to the Church in Britain more than their deeply rooted faith. Their peasant, rural (foreign) origins contrasted starkly with the educated aristocratic and landowning 'old English' Catholic stock. A reflection of the class structure in the wider society became manifest in the body of the Catholic community.

Fourth, a large number of Catholics who were born in countries outside the British Isles, enlarged the Catholic community. The greatest numbers came from Italy and Poland. It is estimated that there are now over 100,000 Catholics from Africa, West Indian and Asian countries. Estimates suggest that there are about 460,000 second generation immigrants in the population as a whole whose origins lie outside of the British Isles (Hornsby-Smith, 1989, pp. 86–7).

The year 1850 was critical for Catholics in England and Wales. Not only was the Hierarchy restored, but it was a time when the Bishops had 'all but everything to do' as Hughes notes:[1]

They had to provide everywhere the urgently needed priests, and churches, and schools — and these schools, in that age when for poor men's children there were no schools save those which religious bodies built and maintained, were not only the security that education should be centred round the knowledge of God, but they were sole means of instructing the working classes in the rudiments of reading and writing. (Hughes, 1950, p. 4)

Additionally, the bishops in seeking to defend the faith against 'old bitter calumnies' confronted the need to tackle the widespread prejudice, ignorance and misunderstanding of Catholic beliefs and practices. Hughes refers to Greville's comments on the prevailing climate: 'While everything else is in a constant state of change, Protestant bigotry and anti-Catholic rancour continue to flourish with undiminished intensity, and all the more from being founded on nothing but prejudice and ignorance, without a particle of sense and reason' (Hughes, 1950, p. 4).

By the middle of the nineteenth century, Catholic schools already existed for educating the children of the upper classes. These schools, apart from a few exceptions, were long standing and flourished on the Continent in Penal Times. They were single sex schools founded by religious teaching orders. For their existence, these schools had to depend on school fees and endowments thus largely limiting their intake to pupils whose parents could afford them. Many of these schools had a considerable number of non-Catholic pupils.

State intervention in Catholic education was introduced in 1847 when the State gave a grant to the Catholic Poor School Committee which was set up to help with the founding of Catholic schools. The grant signified an important point in the history of Catholic schools as it implied a recognition that the Catholic school sector was an integral part of the national provision of state maintained education. In the following quarter of the century, Catholics built 439 churches and the number of priests virtually doubled to 1,634. A momentum to build and maintain a system of elementary schools was generated. Whereas in 1851 there were 99 elementary Catholic schools with a pupil population of 7,769, by 1874 there were 1,484 schools and 100,372 pupils (Hughes, 1950, p. 20). As Beales notes, the bishops were single-minded on the 'schools question'. So much so, he observes that: 'Whereas the story of Catholic second-ary education is the story of the Religious Orders, that of the primary schools for the masses is the story of the Bishops to the extent which makes the two parts of the picture delineable separately without doing violence to the whole' (Hughes, 1950, p. 367). Despite the formidable constraints on Catholics, pion-eers of Catholic elementary education set up schools for educating and (later) clothing and (still later) apprenticing poor Catholic children. The policy of the Secretary of the Poor School Committee, Thomas William Allies (1853–90) was based on three maxims: 'There can be no sound education without religion. As is the teacher so is the child. As is the trainer so is the teacher' (Hughes, 1950, p. 372).

From their inception, Catholic elementary schools were established on a parochial basis and controlled by the parish priest or a religious teaching order, and set out to preserve the religious culture between parish, school, and home, which assisted the Church in its mission of 'preserving the faithful' in a world sheltered from alien influences.

The consistently declared policy of providing a place for every Catholic child in a Catholic school derived from Canon 1374 which simply stipulated that policy, but as Sharratt notes, this question was also coloured by the tone of Canon 2313 which prescribed excommunication for a Catholic who entered a 'mixed marriage' with the intention of educating children outside the faith. The link between the two — education and marriage 'suggested a deliberately self perpetuating process of social enclosure' (Sharratt, 1977, p. 130). Not sur-prisingly, the past tensions and suspicions which bequeathed a long legacy of mistrust between Catholics and the wider society led the Catholic Church to pursue a separatist policy of Catholic education. The bishops were single-minded in their attempt to maintain a religious subculture against perceived threats of an increasingly secular society and what they saw as an emerging secular state school system. As a result, the Church carried out its educational role in relative isolation from the wider state maintained education system. The pursuit of a separate Catholic school system and the emphasis on religious endogamy was a major mechanism by which the Catholic community maintained its group identity.

Increased financial support was given when the Elementary Act of 1870 established a national educational system. However, the issue of state funding for denominational schools, both Anglican and Catholic, was surrounded by ideological storms of conflict and sectarian bitterness.[2] Nevertheless, there was general agreement that no education, whether provided by the State or the Churches could be regarded as complete without instruction in the Christian religion. The disagreement was over the content of the instruction.

The basic claims of the Catholic Church for a separate school system and control over the religious curriculum and moral teaching were based on the natural rights and duties of parents to have their children educated according to their consciences; and a civic right in respect of financial justice, in the sense that the education of a child should not cost a Catholic parent relatively more than parents who sent their children to other schools.

The partnership between the Catholic Church and State was advanced by the Act of 1902, which formed the basis of what has become known as the 'dual system' of Church and County schools.[3] By 1920, the Catholic community in England and Wales had grown to over two million. By this time, Catholic schools were educating some 400,000 children. Importantly, this period ushered in a growing acceptance of Catholic educational claims for publicly funded Catholic education.

The 1944 Education Act did much to build a climate of common interest and a strong sense of partnership. It marked a new relationship between the Catholic Church and State by bringing both partners into a single publicly funded national education system. It was the end of passionate intensity after decades of strident opposition. Religious teaching in Catholic schools continued to be both instructional, in the sense of teaching pupils the Catholic faith and 'ecclesiastical' so as to encourage pupils to become full and participating members of the Catholic Church. The Act facilitated the building up of the Catholic schools sector and as Hastings observes, the Act 'raised them educationally without submerging them religiously' (Hastings, 1986, p. 422). It put an end to a much declared principle expressed by opponents of Church schools that there should be no denominational teaching in schools provided for by public money.

The 1944 Education Act made possible the objective of the Catholic bishops to establish a network of schools, initially at primary level, but later at secondary level with a minimum of encroachment on the Church's autonomy. In 1974, the Catholic school population peaked with almost half a million children attending primary schools. An additional 352,642 pupils were receiving their education in Catholic secondary schools.[4]

The history of Catholic elementary schools is one of self-help, of enormous financial commitment and immense striving in pursuit of a Catholic school sector. Expansion, progress and achievement were painstakingly won by generations of Catholics. The Catholic Church invested vast resources, personal and financial, in the development of a system of Catholic primary and secondary schools within the state maintained sector. However, despite its enormous commitment, by the mid 1960s only 60 per cent of Catholic children had access to a Catholic school.

In the late 1950s, the breaking up of the old working class Catholic culture, when the younger generations moved out of the inner cities to the suburbs and new housing estates, was an important factor contributing to change in the hitherto flourishing Catholic community. The changes initiated by the 1944 Education Act were themselves symptomatic of wider and deeper currents within society at large. Greater social mobility, a lessening of deference in the face of authority and an enlargement of horizons in many directions has characterized the post-war experience. The growth of secular institutions offered the kinds of social, recreational and communal satisfactions previously provided in the local parish. The sense of loyalty to geographically definable institutions centred upon the parish church were weakened progressively by such changes. The post-war period witnessed the emergence of a 'new Catholic middle-class', upwardly mobile from its working-class roots as a result of post-war expansion of educational and occupational opportunities especially among second and third generation Irish Catholics (Hornsby-Smith, 1987, p. 79).

With their particular history, sense of identity and community support, Catholic schools have entered a new era of education provision. Increasingly, Catholics are turning their attention to the ways in which Catholic schools in this new phase of their history should respond to contemporary challenges brought about by the sweeping and wide ranging changes in the education system initiated by the 1988 Education Reform Act and developed in subsequent legislation.

The 1988 Education Act established a legal framework for publicly funded schools to become Grant Maintained (GM) Schools. The new legislation is intended to provide greater diversity of schools within the publicly funded system, more autonomy to schools and increased choice for parents. Essentially, schools are empowered to exercise their right to opt out of the control, funding and administration of Local Education Authorities (LEAs) to be controlled, funded and administered directly by central government. GM schools therefore remain part of the state system. Schools responding to the invitation to become Grant Maintained have been offered attractive financial incentives. Grant Maintained schools receive a greater proportion of funding than they would under LEA arrangements for delegation of budgets and an increased chance of capital improvements. Catholic schools are also eligible to 'opt out' without prejudice, it is claimed, to their Catholic character. A most obvious incentive for Catholic schools to 'opt out' is that all capital works are 100 per cent funded from public money, eliminating the 15 per cent contribution which has to be found by Catholic schools under LEA control. At the end of 1994, 128 Catholic schools were Grant Maintained bringing to an end a unified policy of voluntary aided Catholic schools within the LEA system. The policy of Grant Maintained schools has been controversial, and Catholic Bishops and educational authorities have voiced their opposition to the policy in general, and as it applies to Catholic schools. With regard to the latter there is a concern that the 'opting out' of Catholic schools will affect episcopal control over particular institutions and over the planning of Catholic school provision as a whole.

Historical Context of Catholic Schools in the United States

In most histories of the United States, Catholics arrived on the scene in a significant way only with the large wave of European immigrants in the latter half of the nineteenth and early-twentieth century. In reality, Catholic education was established in New Spain (Buetow, 1970, pp. 4–10) and New France (Desjardins, 1981, p. IV). There were no Catholics of any sizable number in the Dutch, Swedish and English colonies, except for Maryland. And even in Maryland, by the end of the seventeenth century 'Catholicism became a distrusted and persecuted religious sect' (Dolan, 1985, p. 84). It is indisputable that Catholics remained on the margins of mainstream American culture because

> Catholicism was not only an immigrant religion, but an immigrant religion coming into a culture which, for a number of historical reasons, was antipathetic to Catholicism. Therefore, this particular immigrant religion was faced with the dilemma of becoming American enough to survive in the new society and remaining Catholic enough to maintain its allegiance to the world-wide Roman Catholic faith. (Greeley, 1967, p. 19)

While Catholics fared better in the more tolerant religious atmosphere of the new American republic, as witnessed by the opening of Georgetown in 1788, their small numbers — 1.1 per cent in 1790 — made them insignificant (O'Gorman, 1987, p. 11).

Two major waves of immigration swelled the Catholic population of the US from 500,000 in 1829 to 8,000,000 in 1884 (Buetow, 1970, p. 112). The immigrants were largely Irish and German. In 1850, almost 60 per cent of all Roman Catholics were foreign-born (O'Gorman, 1987, p. 12). The second wave, from 1885 to the time of World War I, raised the Catholic population to 17,735,553 in 1920. These new arrivals, for the most part semi-skilled workers or peasants who sought work in the cities, came from southern and central Europe or from a still impoverished Ireland (Buetow, 1970, p. 167). By the end of the second wave of immigration, anti-Catholicism rose to a fever pitch.

In the early nineteenth century xenophobia took on a more religious focus for three reasons. First, most of the eighteenth century immigrants were Protestants from Ireland or Germany, but in the nineteenth century economic conditions in Europe prompted Catholics to migrate. Second, resurgent evangelical

Protestantism replaced the more tolerant deism of the previous generation. Third, Catholicism itself was more militant as it reeled from the effects of the Enlightenment and the revolutionary upheaval that followed. North American Protestants eyed with suspicion the re-establishment of the Roman Catholic hierarchy in Britain and the Netherlands (Glenn, 1988, p. 68). In Oregon, for example, the majority believed that the State had a right to demand that every child spend sufficient time in American institutions of learning '. . . to inoculate it with the fundamentals of Americanism' (James, 1983, p. 65). Extending the metaphor, Catholicism and non-Anglo ethnicity were diseases; public schools were the cure.

Both blatant forms of anti-Catholicism and more subtle forms of exclusion existed in the common schools (Smith, 1967, p. 695). Put simply, public did not mean secular; Protestant beliefs were taken as facts. Timothy Smith summarized the situation well:

> By their establishment and control of both public and private schools, churchmen stamped upon neighborhoods, states and nation an inter-denominational Protestant ideology which nurtured dreams of personal and social progress. By the mid-nineteenth century, leading citizens answered that Americanism and Protestantism were synonyms and that education and Protestantism were allies. (Smith, 1967, p. 687)

The Protestantism of the common schools was often explicit, especially regarding the scriptures. Horace Mann, considered the Father of American Public Schools, considered the Bible to be the book of every Christian and thus all-inclusive. In fact, the Catholic laity rarely read the Scriptures and, when they did, they used the Douay-Rheims edition, a significantly different version than the King James edition used by the Protestants. In Philadelphia, Bishop James Kenrick was denied his request that the Douay version be given to Catholic children in the public schools. In 1844, the Bible controversy led to bloody riots (Jorgenson, 1987). Nonetheless, Mann felt that 'the Bible was allowed to speak for itself . . . what could be more fair or reverent?' (Glenn, 1988, p. 169). Furthermore, 'those who opposed this view were enemies of the State' (Jorgenson, 1987, p. 135). At the end of the nineteenth century the Bible was read in all common schools in Delaware, New Jersey, Georgia, Massachusetts, New York, Iowa, Indiana, North and South Dakota, 87 per cent of the schools in Pennsylvania, and in 'most of the schools' in the other states (Smith, 1967, pp. 14–15).

The Bible was not the only text that helped to socialize public-school children into a Protestant religious sensibility. McGuffey readers were 'handbooks of the common morality, testaments to the Protestant virtues which a half-century of experience had elevated into the culture-religion of the new nation' (Smith, 1967, p. 695). Noah Webster's *American Spelling Book* taught more than orthography. His stated goal was to 'enable teachers to instill into their [students] minds, with the first rudiments of language, some just ideas of religion, morals and domestic economy' (Webster, 1816, p. 5). Alexis de Toqueville, in his famous visit to the United States, remarked that although the various denominations differed in worship, they preached 'the same moral law in the name of God' and that this moral law could be taught in the common schools (De Toqueville, 1958, p. 314). Lloyd Jorgenson labels this morality a uniquely 'Anglo-Saxon conception of righteousness' (Jorgenson, 1987, p. 258). According to David Tyack,

> The result was a society permeated with a religious purpose. Education demonstrated this evangelical Protestant influence: both sectarian schools and public education were part of a pervasive Protestant crusade. Schools and churches were allies in the quest to create the Kingdom of God in America. (Tyack, 1966, p. 448)

Catholics, the only numerically significant non-Protestant group in the United States, became the focus of the religious struggle in American schools. Unable to find a home in the educational institutions of the majority population, they moved toward the formation of their own schools. As a result, 'the characteristic American pattern became an essentially neutral though Protestant-flavored public sector with a large Catholic subsociety with its own institutional expressions' (Glenn, 1988, p. 256).

Official church documents portray unqualified support for institutional expressions of a religious subsociety. The fourteen archbishops and sixty bishops in attendance at the Third Plenary Council of Baltimore mandated that every parish should erect a school within two years of the promulgation of the council's decrees, that any pastor who is negligent in doing so be removed from office and that all Catholic parents were bound to send their children to parochial schools, except in cases where it was not possible:

> Near each church, where it does not exist, a parochial school is to be erected within two years from the promulgation of this Council, and it is to be maintained *in perpetuum*, unless the Bishop, on account of grave difficulties, judges that a postponement may be allowed. (Buetow, 1970, pp. 152–3)

Some Catholic leaders, like Archbishop John Ireland of Saint Paul, wanted to build bridges to the larger US culture but the majority, convinced of the intransigent anti-Catholicism of public schools, opted for segregation. The debate among the bishops ended by 1892 and the majority opinion prevailed (Sanders, 1981, p. 134). Bishop Bernard McQuaid of Rochester typifies the attitude that won out; he saw schools as protective walls. In order 'to protect children from the "wolves of the world" who were destroying countless numbers of the unguarded ones' he committed the Church to building those walls and, he added, 'if the walls are not high enough they must be raised, if they are not strong enough, they must be strengthened.' Indeed '. . . a clearer statement of the Catholic fortress mentality would be hard to find' (Dolan, 1985, p. 273). In fact, the hopes of the bishops were never fully met. In 1884, 37 per cent of Catholic parishes had schools, in 1891, 44 per cent. The figure dropped to 35 per cent in 1896 and then it began to grow until the collapse of the system in the mid-1960s. In 1967, 56 per cent of US parishes maintained a school (McCluskey, 1968, p. 86). By the end of the 1980s that percentage dropped to slightly less than 40 per cent (Kealy, 1989, p. 279).

Catholic schools grew at different rates and to a different extent according to local circumstances. The dioceses of the mid-west, with their large German populations, had more Catholic schools per capita than the dioceses of the east coast where the Irish predominated (McCluskey, 1968, p. 86). There was variation within dioceses too. In Boston, for example, there was a higher per capita percentage of schools in the French-Canadian-dominated Merrimac Valley than in Irish-dominated Boston (Sanders, 1985). Indeed, 'the professedly, even officially, ethnic Catholic school offered a more familiar environment than could the public school' (Sanders, 1981, p. 126).

In the nineteenth century, three types of Catholic schools developed on the grounds of social class (O'Gorman, 1987, p. 16). First there were classical academies, usually run by religious orders. The second type of school was modelled after the benevolent schools run by charitable institutions funded by the State. These included orphanages run by religious orders of women. The third type became the paradigm of Catholic schools in the twentieth century: parochial schools for all. In the early years of the century, the high schools played a predominant role as 'transitional institutions, providing an effective passage for immigrant parents and their children as they adapted to the American environment'. By mid-twentieth century, where the schools had 'once permitted themselves to serve as an arm of the ethnic community and of the poor, they had become an expedient conduit for the expression of mobility aspirations' (Fass, 1989, p. 219).

Until the mid-1960s, Catholics balanced political assimilation with religious distinctiveness. The social mobility and ethnic assimilation of Irish and German Catholics, the influx of southern and eastern European immigrants and the resurgence of anti-Catholicism after World War I prompted Catholics to demonstrate that their religion was compatible with true Americanism (O'Gorman, 1987, p. 28). Pius X's condemnation of modernism in 1907 and the Americanism controversy undoubtedly forced US Catholics to prove that they could be productive citizens in modern society. A new assimilationism represented '. . . a break with the image of Catholic education as a fortress defending ethnic and religious enclaves from a dangerous and hostile environment. In contrast, it stressed the public character and responsibilities of Catholic education' (O'Gorman, 1987, p. 25). From the beginning of the century until the mid-1960s Catholics separated the sacred and the profane, the theological and the political. Catholic schools were still a fortress, the wall built by people like Bishop Bernard McQuade to protect children from the 'wolves of the world'.

In 1967 Andrew Greeley claimed that the Roman Catholic community in the United States changed from being the 'garrison church of the Counter-Reformation to the open church of the ecumenical age' (Greeley, 1967, p. 301). The election of an Irish-Catholic to the presidency in 1960 was a watershed event. The income level and educational attainment of Catholics also increased considerably. Robert O'Gorman, writing in the late 1980s, claims 'ours is no longer a poor, insolvent, non-cash available population . . . the mean incomes of Catholics have risen dramatically since the time of an earlier immigration' (McCready, 1989, p. 221). In a 1987 study, George Gallup noted the 'stunning momentum' of the Catholic Church (Gallup and Castelli, 1987, p. 2).

The stunning momentum of US Catholics was not only social, economic and political; it was also spiritual. In the mid-1960s the Church itself, the last vestige of the siege mentality, underwent dramatic change. Catholics were ready for renewal. Robert Bellah explains:

> The period 1930–60 was a kind of culmination of a long process of institution building and self-help. The Church, still a minority, but long the largest single denomination, grew in confidence as the majority of its constituents gained middle-class respectability. An educated and thoughtful laity was thus ready to respond to the new challenges the Second Vatican Council opened up in the early 1960s. (Bellah *et al.*, 1985, p. 238)

The focal question of the 1960s is the focal question of the 1990s. In the mid-1960s, Mary Perkins Ryan noticed the demise of the 'old climate' in which there existed a Church 'intent on self-preservation, spending its efforts to hold its own, to preserve, to fight off attacks, to centralize authority, and to maintain order within the ranks'. The 'new climate' was marked by a diffusion of responsibility, unity without uniformity, inculturalization, openness and freedom (Ryan, 1964, pp. 167–9). Fortress schools were no longer necessary; middle-class, assimilated Catholics had no attacks to fight off.

The fortress of Catholic education, the wall built to protect a religious minority group of low-income immigrants, crumbled. Because of internal and external changes, the outsiders became insiders; the minority blended in with the majority. In his comparison of burgeoning Evangelical schools with declining Catholic schools, James Hunter claimed that, because '. . . a pluralistic and secular America has become a more comfortable place to live for the majority of Catholics, church-sponsored schools are no longer needed as a refuge from a hostile public system' (Hunter, 1988). Though many are calling for a return to past defensive models and rigid opposition to majority culture, ethnic assimilation and upward mobility make a return to the past unlikely.

An important recent development has been the alliance between the official leadership of Catholic schools at the United States Catholic Conference (the public policy wing of the National Catholic Conference of Bishops), the National Catholic Educational Association and the Republican Party (McDonald, 1995) on the question of public funding of Catholic schools. In addition, Catholic

Table 1.1: Total Catholic population in England and Wales and the United States — 1994

	England and Wales	United States
Total population	50,430,000	257,970,516
Catholic population	4,413,165	59,858,042

Source: Catholic Directory of England and Wales 1994. US Catholic Directory, 1994. Figures in England and Wales are based on estimates of Catholic population (not weekly Mass attendance) by parish clergy. These figures are generally thought to be an underestimate of the Catholic population.

leadership has publicly espoused free-market models of parental choice in schools (O'Keefe, 1995). These alliances create a serious conflict between Catholic teachings on solidarity with the poor and the radical individualism inherent in most school choice schemes.

The Context of the Catholic School in England and Wales and in the United States

We present the situation in which US and English and Welsh Catholic schools currently find themselves in relation to four sets of descriptive statistics for 1994.[5] These relate to the total Catholic population, the numbers of Catholic schools, the numbers of pupils being educated in Catholic schools and the nature of the teacher population of the schools. Because of the complexity of the two educational systems, precise comparative figures are difficult to provide in some cases (for example, the exact definition of primary and secondary schools is not explored).

Table 1.1 provides an outline of the Catholic population of England and Wales and the United States.

Table 1.2 gives the comparative statistics for numbers of Catholic schools in England and Wales and the United States.

In England and Wales, Catholic schools form part of both the publicly funded and independent sectors. 92 per cent of all Catholic schools are in the public sector. In this sector, Catholic schools in the traditional partnership with Local Education Authorities have all running costs and 85 per cent of capital costs covered by public funds, whilst those who leave this partnership to become 'Grant Maintained' have all costs met from the public purse. Catholic schools in the independent sector are financed through endowments and school fees, in the same way as private schools in the United States.

In the United States, all Catholic schools are in the private sector and cannot be directly supported by public funds. Of the elementary schools, 83.5 per cent are parochial (financed and administered by the local parish but sometimes subsidized by central diocesan funds and private benefactors) 10.3 per cent interparochial, 2.3 per cent diocesan (under the direct administrative and fiscal control of the diocesan Superintendent of schools) and 3.9 per cent private (usually owned by a self-perpetuating board of trustees, founded by a

12

Table 1.2: The total number of Catholic Schools in England and Wales and the United States — 1994

	England and Wales	United States
Catholic Schools	2,464[1]	8,345
Primary	1,954 (79.3%)	7,114 (85.2%)
Secondary	443 (18.0%)	1,231 (14.8%)
Primary/Secondary	67 (2.7%)	—

Source: Statistics in above and following tables for England and Wales from Catholic Education Service and for US from Brigham 1994.
Notes:
[1] Includes schools in the Independent and in the publicly funded sectors.
[2] In addition to the above statistics for England and Wales there are also three Catholic nursery schools catering for 176 pupils and fourteen special schools. These latter schools cater for 1,146 pupils with special educational needs.

religious order that sometimes continues to provide personnel, and recognized by the local bishop as Catholic). Among high schools, 11.5 per cent are parochial, 12.8 per cent interparochial, 34.8 per cent diocesan and 40.9 per cent private. Among all schools, 35 per cent are in urban areas, 12 per cent inner-city (in low-income, ethnic minority neighborhoods), 31 per cent suburban and 22 per cent rural. 7,860 schools are coeducational, 285 are all female and 205 are all male.

Table 1.3 provides statistics for pupils in Catholic primary and secondary schools in England and Wales. The statistics for the United States are for pupils pre-K-12 (up to the age of 18).

Table 1.4 outlines the percentage of non-Catholic pupils in Catholic schools.

The decline in births and falling pupil numbers have affected all schools in England and Wales, including Catholic schools. Between 1984 and 1994, 15 per cent of Catholic schools were closed. The proportion of pupils who are Catholics attending Catholic schools is declining. In 1974, 8,068 (1.6 per cent) of pupils in Catholic primary schools were non-Catholics and 8,579 (2.4 per cent) of pupils in Catholic secondary schools. In 1994 the comparable figures were 45,346 (10.6 per cent) for Catholic primary schools and 49,078 (16.1 per cent) for Catholic secondary schools.

Some Catholic schools have voiced reservations as to their ability to maintain a Catholic ethos in a school which includes a significant non-Catholic pupil population. Such concerns have on occasion given rise to the view that current practice conflicts with the aims and objectives of the original Trust Deeds, leading to school closure and the dispersal of staff and pupils.

In England and Wales, the numbers of teachers in Catholic schools who are not Catholics have increased significantly since 1974. In 1974 1,855 (9.8 per cent) of primary teachers were non-Catholics and 72,277 (35.6 per cent) of secondary teachers. In 1994 the number of non-Catholic teachers had risen to 2,039 (12.1 per cent) in primary schools and 7,439 (41.1 per cent) in secondary schools. These figures relate to publicly funded Catholic schools. In 1994, non-Catholic teachers in independent Catholic schools accounted for 43.5 per

Terence H. McLaughlin, Joseph O'Keefe S.J. and Bernadette O'Keeffe

Table 1.3: *Catholic pupils in Catholic Schools — 1994*

	England and Wales	United States
Total pupil population	7,329,990	*49,661,000
Pupils in Catholic schools	790,711 (10%)	2,567,845 (5.29%)

*Source: Schaub and Baker, 1994.

cent of all teachers. Concerns expressed over the emergence of large numbers of non-Catholic teachers centre on a perceived dilution within the school of that distinctiveness which requires a solely Catholic teaching staff. But the *Memorandum on the Appointment of Teachers* (The Bishops of England and Wales Education Commission, 1974) generously acknowledges '. . . with gratitude the devotion and service given by many non Catholic teachers.'

In the United States, there are no statistics on the per cent of non-Catholic teachers. Among full-time staff, 88.2 per cent are lay (71.5 per cent women and 16.7 per cent men) and 11.8 per cent are not (9.1 per cent are sisters, 1.1 per cent priests, 1.6 per cent brothers). It was not always thus; in 1980 73 per cent of Catholic school teachers were lay; in 1960, 26.2 per cent; in 1920, 8 per cent (Brigham, 1994). In the past, members of religious communities could contribute extensively to these schools at little cost. Today, they need a full salary to support the large number of elderly and infirm members of their religious communities. Lay people must be paid a living wage, and in too many Catholic schools their remuneration is shockingly inadequate. Rising personnel expenditures have had a serious detrimental impact on the schools. The marked decline over the years of the numbers of clergy and members of religious orders teaching in Catholic schools is also apparent in England and Wales. In 1970 they accounted for 13.1 per cent of all teachers whereas in 1994 they accounted for only 2 per cent of all teachers in Catholic schools.

Information on the ethnicity of pupils varies by country. For example in the United States, pupils are categorized using the racial categories of the US Department of the Census. In 1994, 10.7 per cent of the pupils were identified as Hispanic, 8.4 per cent African-American, 4 per cent Asian and 0.6 per cent native American. In England and Wales comparative statistics are not currently available.

Identity

One of the most central features of the contemporary Catholic school is a concern with its precise identity. What exactly is the distinctive role and purpose of the Catholic school? Who does it serve and why? These issues are inseparably connected to fundamental questions of interpretation concerning the nature of Catholicism itself.

Conflicting interpretations of the identity of the Catholic school can be illustrated by two extracts from recent church statements about education.

Table 1.4: The percentage of non-Catholic pupils in Catholic Schools — 1994

	England and Wales	United States
Non-Catholics in primary schools %	45,346 (10.6%)	231,142 (11.6%)
Non-Catholics in secondary schools %	49,078 (16.1%)	98,492 (16.8%)

Working together with our colleagues, every Jesuit ministry can and should promote justice in one of the following ways: (a) direct service and accompaniment of the poor; (b) developing awareness of the demands of justice and the social responsibility to achieve it; (c) participating in social mobilization for the creation of a more just social order. Each Jesuit ministry should work to deepen its particular implementation of our full mission of faith and justice, which can only be enriched by efforts to dialogue and inculturate more effectively. (Documents of the 34th General Congregation Society of Jesus [Jesuits], March 1995)

First, truth exists, it has been revealed by God, and men and women can discover and understand it. Second, truth is not an abstraction, but a person, Jesus Christ. Third, we encounter the truth, Jesus Christ, most fully in the Catholic Church. Fourth, we must share the truth with the world. (*In the Beginning, the Word*, Pastoral Letter of J. Francis Stafford Archbishop of Denver, March 1995)

Though these two statements emanate from one faith community, the context of the statements is vastly different. The first was written by Jesuits from around the world convened in a General Congregation to chart the future of the order in the midst of declining personnel and dwindling resources. The second was written by an American Archbishop seeking to give direction to the schools in his local archdiocese. However, both of these statements were written and promulgated at the same time in history on the same topic: the fundamental identity of Catholic educational institutions. The statements are not necessarily contradictory; nonetheless, diversity of texture and tone are unmistakeable. This is reflected in the wide ranging debate about how the distinctiveness of the Catholic school is to be understood; a debate which runs through many of the contributions to this volume.

Diversity

The reality and importance of diversity is of crucial importance for the contemporary Catholic school. There is diversity within Catholicism itself. There is also a marked diversity within the population of Catholic schools. Some pupils are committed and practising Catholics, others are 'lapsed' or are Catholic only in name. Increasingly Catholic schools admit pupils from other faith backgrounds and none, particularly in areas of deprivation. This requires appropriate educational response from Catholic schools, for they cannot conduct 'business as usual' without taking account of their varied constituencies. Nor can the Catholic school, if it is to have a role in relation to the marginalized, and to the common good more generally, ignore the diversity that is characteristic of the wider society, not least ethnic and cultural diversity.

Overview of the Book

The first section of the book is concerned with matters of context. Anthony Bryk offers an overview of the central findings of his recent empirical study into Catholic school in the US. This research supports earlier research findings that, compared to US public schools, Catholic schools have a more positive effect upon the achievement of students (particularly those from minority and disadvantaged backgrounds) and that this effect is independent of other variables. The research claims that, at a time when the public school system in the United States is increasingly dominated by the values of the market place, a radical individualism and the pursuit of economic reward, Catholic schools offer to American society as a whole an alternative', more humane vision of how secondary schooling might be organized. The features of successfully functioning Catholic High Schools identified by Bryk and his associates include a focused and constrained academic programme (with an emphasis on academic achievement for all), a communal organization, highly committed teachers who play an 'extended' role in relation to pupils, decentralized governance and a shared sense of moral and educational values (an 'inspirational ideology') which articulates the work and life of the school. Among the lessons for educational institutions in general which Bryk draws from his analysis is caution about the value of a 'market place' approach to educational reform, and the need for morally enriched educational debate and practice. One of Bryk's most prominent theses, reflected in the title of his book, is the contribution which Catholic schools make to the public good as a whole. For Bryk, therefore, the public has a 'strong stake' in the preservation of Catholic schools. In his chapter, Bruce Cooper elaborates on the public significance of such schools and contrasts the US attitude to the public funding of Catholic schools with that found in England and Wales. He outlines the various obstacles which have arisen in relation to the provision of public funding for US Catholic schools, and suggests ways in which they can be overcome or ameliorated. This is necessary in Cooper's view if vulnerable Catholic schools are to be saved and their public benefits reaped. From the perspective of England and Wales, Richard Pring outlines and criticizes the philosophy of educational reform which has been espoused by recent Conservative governments with its emphasis upon the metaphor of the educational market, and indicates its fundamental incompatibility with the principles of a Catholic philosophy of education. The impact of these reforms on

Catholic schools is brought to life in Gerald Grace's discussion of the dilemmas faced by Catholic headteachers in England and Wales. On the one hand, Heads must sustain the market position of their schools as reflected in public examination results, but on the other, they must respond in the light of Catholic principles to the call to serve the needs of less able pupils. The notion of the 'common good' features strongly in the contributions of Bryk, Cooper, Pring and Grace. In the final chapter of this section, David Hollenbach SJ explores from a philosophical perspective how education rooted in the Catholic tradition can contribute to the advancement of the common good in societies characterized by pluralism. One of the central elements of this contribution is the contra-individualistic emphasis of Catholic social thought, (describable as 'personalistic communitarianism') which includes a concern for justice. One of the key educational tasks which Hollenbach derives for Catholic schools from this tradition is that of contributing to the effort to 'reweave the fabric' of an increasingly fragmented society into a 'unified whole'. In the light of the public significance of tasks such as these for Catholic schools, Hollenbach joins Bryk and Cooper in arguing that the law relating to the public funding of Catholic schools in the US needs to be re-thought.

The next section of the volume is concerned with issues of identity, focused on the question 'What makes a school Catholic?' In a theological exploration of this question, Thomas Groome argues that the distinctive features of Catholicism itself should constitute the distinctiveness of the Catholic school. The eight such features he identifies are translated into educational implications and imperatives. John Haldane, approaching the question as a philosopher, is concerned to emphasize that the distinctiveness of Catholic identity is partly but essentially constituted by authority and dogma, and that the primary function of Catholic schools is to transmit the 'essential doctrines and devotions' of Catholicism. He criticizes the 'inspirational ethic' identified by Bryk and his associates as distinctive of Catholic schools on the grounds that it inadequately embodies these distinctively theological elements. In his chapter, Terence McLaughlin explores the contours of a distinctively Catholic conception of education with reference to a contrasting influential conception of public education, which is based on contemporary agnosticism about substantial conceptions of the good. Alan McClelland delineates a distinctively Catholic philosophy of education with particular reference to statements and documents from various Church sources, and to the notion of 'wholeness'. In the final chapter in this section, James Day explores issues of identity from the perspective of a clinical psychologist. He explores the tensions which arise between on the one hand the publicly stated norms and values of the Church and its educational institutions and on the other the actual experiences and reactions of individual pupils. He draws attention to the potentially damaging disassociation which can occur between the two, which he illustrates by case studies from his experience as a counsellor, and appeals for Catholic schools to recognize the value of, and the need for, dialogic considerations to be given salience in moral education.

The third section of the volume is concerned with questions of diversity. Joseph O'Keefe SJ provides evidence which illustrates the rate of closure of Catholic schools in deprived urban areas in the US. He develops a case for seeing provision for the needs of the poor and the fostering of diversity as crucial aspects of the vocation of Catholic schools, and ends his discussion by outlining an agenda which educational policy makers should address in relation to these matters. Writing in the context of England and Wales, Leela Ramdeen develops an argument which insists that Catholic schools should take seriously issues of multiculturalism and racial equality. This is reinforced by Richard Zipfel, who, in his contribution, focuses the questions at stake in two questions which he poses to Catholic schools: 'Who do we serve?' and 'What do we offer?' In his chapter, Paul Hypher describes the background to the consultation on 'Catholic Schools and Other Faiths' which has just been completed at the request of the Bishops Conference of England and Wales, and outlines some of the central considerations which were addressed. Michael Barnes SJ outlines a theological background for the proper understanding of the relationship between Catholicism and other faiths. Drawing upon certain developments in the post Vatican II thinking of the Church, he indicates how the dual tasks of dialogue and proclamation confront both the Church and the Catholic school in relation to other faiths. In a chapter based on first hand teaching experience in the institution concerned, Vincent Murray discusses the reality of the experience of interfaith dialogue at St Philip's Catholic Sixth Form College in Birmingham, and offers a critical perspective on the forces which led to the closure of the college in its present form.

The final section of the volume is concerned with the future of the contemporary Catholic school. In a contribution from the US, Catherine Lacey RSCJ outlines the distinctive benefits arising from the network of relationships between teachers forged in an initiative related to teacher renewal for teachers in the Sacred Heart schools. Peter Hastings describes his experience as the headteacher of a Catholic secondary school in Warwickshire, England, and insists that such schools cannot avoid promoting an open critical attitude to matters of faith on the part of pupils. James Gallagher SDB, formerly director of the Catholic national project for religious education in England and Wales, shares a similar commitment to the importance of openness and cautions against an approach to religious education which is not based on a realistic appraisal of the nature and level of the actual religious understanding and beliefs of pupils. The section ends with a chapter by two of the three editors which indicates a research agenda for the contemporary Catholic school on both sides of the Atlantic.

Notes

1   There separate hierarchies of bishops exist for the purposes of ecclesiastical administration in the British Isles; one for England and Wales, one for Scotland, and one

for Ireland. Northern Ireland falls within the jurisdiction of the Irish bishops. These differing hierarchies reflect different histories and religious and legal contexts.

2   In the years leading up to 1870, the initiative in the development of English public elementary education was undertaken by voluntary Anglican, Non-Conformist and Catholic voluntary societies. The Forster Act of 1870 set up Board schools to 'fill the gaps' in the denominational voluntary educational provision. The religion of the Board school was non-denominational whereas in Church schools it was 'Church related'.

3   The 1902 Act established what is now known as the Dual System. It refers to the arrangement whereby County schools (formerly known as Board schools) and Voluntary schools or denominational schools became part of one public maintained system.

4   Church schools within the publicly funded system were divided into two categories, 'aided' and 'controlled'. Whereas Church of England schools opted for both voluntary controlled and voluntary aided status, Catholic schools insisted upon the greater degree of independence provided by voluntary aided status. Voluntary controlled schools gave reduced rights for the Churches, but freed them from all financial obligations. The Local Education Authority was made responsible for staff appointments (except in the case of 'reserved teachers' who were appointed for the purposes of giving denominational religious instruction), the curriculum and pupil admissions. Denominational religious instruction was to be given to those children whose parents requested it. Any other religious instruction had to be based on an 'agreed syllabus' (i.e., a syllabus judged acceptable to Christians of different denominations). Voluntary aided schools became the responsibility of the governors. The Act enabled such schools to provide denominational religious instruction and denominational worship. Although the Local Education Authority became responsible for the all the running expenses of Voluntary aided schools, a financial contribution from the Churches was required. The Churches were responsible for meeting half the cost of capital expenditure (i.e., new school buildings, improvements, and external repairs), and the remaining half of the cost was met from public funds. This public contribution was increased from 50 per cent to 75 per cent in 1959; to 80 per cent in 1967; and to 85 per cent in 1975.

5   It must be made clear that statistics provided in this chapter relating to Catholic schools in England and Wales do not include Scotland. After 1872, the situation for Catholic schools in Scotland differed from that in England.

References

ADVISORY GROUP ON THE CATHOLIC CHURCH'S COMMITMENT TO THE BLACK COMMUNITY (1986) *With You in Spirit*, London, The Print Business.

BEALES, A.C.F. (1950) 'The struggle for schools', in BECK, G.A. *The English Catholics 1850–1950*, London, Burns Oates.

BECK, G.A. (1959) (Ed) *The English Catholics 1850–1950*, London, Burns Oates.

BELLAH, R.N., MADSEN, R., SULLIVAN, W.M., SWIDLER, A. and TIPTON, S.M. (1985) *Habits of the Heart*, New York, Harper and Row.

BRIGHAM, F.H. (1994) *United States Elementary and Secondary Schools 1993–1994: Annual Statistical Report on Schools, Enrollment and Staffing*, Washington, National Catholic Education Association.

BRYK A.S., LEE, V.E. and HOLLAND, P.B. (1993) *Catholic Schools and the Common Good*, Cambridge, Harvard University Press.

BUETOW, H. (1970) *Of Singular Benefit: The Story of US Catholic Education*, New York, MacMillan.

CONVEY, J. (1992) *Catholic Schools Make a Difference: Twenty-five Years of Research*, Washington, DC, National Catholic Educational Association.

Cook, E.B. (1893) *The Nation's Book in the Nation's Schools*, Chicago, Women's Educational Union.

De Toqueville, A. (1958) *Democracy in America*, New York, Vintage Press.

Desjardins, J. (1981) *An Historical Notice on the Collège de Québec*, Collège Ste-Marie et Eglise du Gésu, Montréal, n.p.

Dolan, J. (1985) *The American Catholic Experience*, New York, Image Books.

Durkheim, E. (1956) *Education and Sociology*, (Trans. Fox, S.D.) Free Press, New York and London.

Fass, P.S. (1989) *Outside In: Minorities and the Transformation of American Education*, New York, Oxford University Press.

Gallup, G. and Castelli, J. (1987) *The American Catholic People*, New York, Doubleday.

Glenn, C.L. (1988) *The Myth of the Common School*, Amherst, MA, University of Massachusetts Press.

Greeley, A. (1967) *The Catholic Experience*, New York, Image Books.

Gwynn, D. (1950) 'The Irish immigration', in Beck, G.A. *The English Catholics 1850–1950*, London, Burns Oates.

Hastings, A. (1977) *Bishops and Writers: Aspects of the Evolution of Modern English Catholicism*, Wheathampstead, Anthony Clarke.

Hastings, A. (1986) *A History of English Christianity 1920–1990*, London, SCM.

Hornsby-Smith, M.P. (1986) 'The Immigrant background of Roman Catholics in England and Wales: A research note', *New Community*, **13**, 1, *Spring-Summer*, pp. 79–85.

Hornsby-Smith, M.P. (1987) *Roman Catholics in England: Studies in Social Structure since the Second World War*, Cambridge, Cambridge University Press.

Hornsby-Smith, M.P. (1989) *The Changing Parish: A Study of Parishes, Priests and Parishioners after Vatican II*, London, Routledge.

Hornsby-Smith, M.P. (1991) *Roman Catholic Beliefs in England: Customary Catholicism and the Transformation of Religious Authority*, Cambridge, Cambridge University Press.

Hughes, L.S.H. (1950) 'The English Catholics', in Beck, G.A. *The English Catholics 1850–1950*, London, Burns Oates.

Hunter, J.D. (1988) 'Catholic schools and Christian academies', *Wall Street Journal*, 8 March.

Hunter, J.D. (1988) 'Evangelical schools in growth, Catholic schools in decline', *Wall Street Journal*, 8 March.

James, T. (1983) 'Questions about educational choice: An argument from history', in James, T. and Levin, H. (Eds) *Public Dollars for Private Schools*, Philadelphia, Temple University Press.

Jorgenson, L.P. (1987) *The State and the non-Public School*, Columbia, MO, University of Missouri Press.

Kealy, R. (1989) 'Collision course: Clergy and laity on Catholic schools', *Chicago Studies*, **28**, 3, November.

Kosmin, B.A. and Lachman, S.P. (1993) *One Nation Under God: Religion in Contemporary American Society*, New York, Harmony.

McCluskey, N. (1968) *Catholic Education Faces its Future*, New York, Doubleday.

McCready, W.C. (1989) 'Catholic Schools and Catholic Identity: Stretching the vital connection', *Chicago Studies*, **28**, 3, pp. 217–231.

McDonald, D. (1995) 'Toward full and fair choice: An historical analysis of the lobbying efforts of the leadership organizations of the Catholic school in pursuing federal tax-supported choice in education 1972–1992', Unpublished doctoral dissertation, Boston College.

O'Gorman, R.T. (1987) *The Church that Was a School: Catholic Identity and Catholic Education in the United States since 1790*, Monograph on the History of Catholic Education in the United States written for the Catholic Education Futures Project.

O'Keefe, J. (1995) 'School choice: A Jesuit perspective', Paper presented at the Annual

Meeting of the American Association of Colleges of Teacher Education, 13 February, Washington, DC.

RYAN, M.P. (1964) *Are Parochial Schools the Answer?*, New York, Holt, Rinehart and Winston.

SANDERS, J.W. (1981) 'Roman Catholics and the school question in New York City: Some suggestions for research', in RAVITCH, D. and GOODENOW, R.K. (Eds) *Educating an Urban People: The New York City Experience*, New York, Teachers College Press.

SANDERS, J.W. (1985) 'Catholics and the school question in Boston: The Cardinal O'Connell years', in SULLIVAN, R. and O'TOOLE, J. (Eds) *Catholic Boston: Studies in Religion and Community 1840–1970*, Boston, Archdiocese of Boston.

SCHAUB, M. and BAKER, D. (1994) *Serving American Catholic Children and Youth: A Study of the Number of School Age Children Enrolled in Catholic Schools and Parish Religious Education Programs*, Washington, United States Catholic Conference.

SEBRING, P.A. and CAMBRUN, E.M. (1992) *A Profile of Eighth Graders in Catholic Schools*, Washington, DC, National Catholic Educational Association.

SHARRATT, B. (1977) 'English Roman Catholicism in the 1960s', in HASTINGS, A. (Ed) *Bishops and Writers: Aspects of the Evolution of Modern English Catholicism*, Hertfordshire, Wheathampstead.

SMITH, T.L. (1967) 'Protestant schooling and American nationality, 1800–1850', *Journal of American History*, **57**, March.

SPENCER, A.E.C.W. (1975) 'Demography of Catholicism', *The Month*, April.

TYACK, D. (1966) 'The Kingdom of God and the common school: Protestant ministers and the educational awakening in the West', *Harvard Educational Review*, **36**, Fall.

WEBSTER, N. (1816) *The American Spelling Book, Containing an Easy Standard Pronunciation Being the First Part of a Grammatical Institute of the English Language to Which is Added an Appendix Containing a Moral Catechism and a Federal Catechism*, Boston, n.p.

Part 1

The Context of the Contemporary Catholic School

Chapter 2

Lessons from Catholic High Schools on Renewing our Educational Institutions

Anthony S. Bryk

During the 1980s, a spate of research studies and newspaper stories chronicled the unusual effectiveness of Catholic high schools. These accounts claimed that Catholic schools do a better job of engaging students in schooling, have lower dropout rates, and produce higher levels of academic achievement, especially for disadvantaged students (see Coleman, Hoffer and Kilgore, 1982; Greeley, 1982; Coleman and Hoffer, 1987). Moreover, Catholic schools use only very modest fiscal resources to produce these desired outcomes. Although these reports have been subject to rigorous critique and considerable reanalysis, the basic pattern of results has been sustained.

Promoting greater equality of educational opportunity has been a major theme in educational policy over the past several decades. Catholic high schools appear to be 'doing something right' in this regard. Curiously, however, there has been little rigorous examination of the internal operations of Catholic high schools and how their organization might actually produce these desired outcomes. *Catholic Schools and the Common Good* (Bryk, Lee and Holland, 1993) represents the culmination of almost ten years of inquiry on this topic. Our findings are based on intensive field work in seven purposefully selected school sites, analyses of extant national databases on US high schools (both Catholic and public), and an exploration of the history and tradition which forms the distinctive character of these institutions.

I begin by summarizing what we have learned from our investigations about how Catholic schools manage simultaneously to:

- achieve relatively high levels of student learning;
- have this learning more equitably distributed with regard to race and class than in the public sector; and
- sustain high levels of teacher commitment and student engagement.

I then turn to a more general discussion of the implications of these findings for renewing US educational institutions.

Anthony S. Bryk

What We Have Learned about the Functioning of Effective Catholic High Schools

A Focused Academic Programme

Our initial reason for undertaking a study of the internal organization of Catholic high schools was to better understand the factors contributing to what Coleman, Hoffer and Kilgore (1982) reported as the 'common school effect' found in these schools. Stated simply, these researchers had concluded that the personal background of students and their families (e.g., ethnicity and social class) had less influence on subsequent academic achievement in Catholic than in public schools. Formally, we describe this phenomenon as Catholic schools having a 'more equitable social distribution of achievement'. The first phase of our research sought to try to understand better what factors might contribute to this desirable outcome. We eventually learned that the curricular organization of school plays a key role in this regard.

The central tenet of the academic organization of the Catholic high school is a core curriculum for all students, regardless of their personal background or future educational plans. This curriculum is predicated on a proactive view among faculty and administrators about what all students can and should learn. Required courses predominate students' study plans with electives limited in their content and number. Some students may begin the curriculum at a more advanced level and proceed in more depth, but the same basic academic goals apply for everyone. Although some tracking occurs, potential negative effects are moderated by school policies that allocate limited fiscal and human resources so that all students make satisfactory progress. At base, integrating these structures and policies, is an active institutional purpose — to advance a common education of mind and spirit for all.

How schools should properly respond to differences in student background is a central organizational problem in education. In principle, initial differences among students can either be amplified or ameliorated as a result of subsequent school experiences. The constrained academic structure in Catholic high schools acts to minimize the subsequent effects on student learning of these initial differences. In contrast, the modern comprehensive public high school has a highly differentiated academic structure in which students exercise considerable discretion over course taking. Our results clearly indicate that such school structures amplify initial social differences among students and culminate in a less equitable distribution of achievement.

We present in our book detailed statistical evidence, including a number of complex analyses, to substantiate this claim. Some of our simplest results, however, are also most powerful in this case. Consider, for example, the gap in achievement between minority and white students. At sophomore year in high school, minority students are scoring behind their white classmates in both public and Catholic schools. The size of this 'minority achievement gap' in mathematics, for example, is about a third smaller in Catholic than in public schools. In large part, this difference reflects the fact that minority students in Catholic schools are somewhat more advantaged than their minority counterparts in the public sector. Of most significance for our argument is what happens to these students over the last two years of high school. In the public sector, the 'minority achievement gap' grows larger by senior year; in Catholic schools it shrinks in size. That is, student achievement becomes more socially differentiated over time in public schools, but becomes more homogeneous within Catholic schools.

The effects of a larger school size also bear particular note. In general, Catholic high schools are relatively small. Very few Catholic high schools enroll more than 1,500 students, with the average around 500 to 600. Although we found no effect of school size on average achievement levels, size does have a strong impact on the degree of instructional differentiation that occurs within schools. Quite simply, it is easier to create a more varied academic programme in a large school. The limited fiscal and human resources generally found in small schools tend to preclude this. Although instructional differentiation is not a necessary consequence of a larger school size, size does act as a facilitating factor. When accompanied by a dominant public educational philosophy that views individual differences in ability and interest as the organizing principle for determining the subject matter to which students are exposed, the observed results are not surprising.

The first piece of our investigation, regarding the nature of the academic organization of schools and the consequences that flow from this, now seemed clear to us. We reached this understanding in 1986, about three years into our efforts. The obvious policy implications of this work — increased academic standards for all — caused us to worry a bit. Dropout rates, particularly in urban schools, were already very high. Would raising academic standards just exacerbate these problems? As we were considering this issue, new evidence appeared from Coleman and Hoffer (1987) which suggested that such was not the case in Catholic schools. In fact, Catholic schools had much lower dropout rates than expected given the nature of their enrolments. And again, these schools seemed especially effective with disadvantaged students.

Our own field work also raised several related puzzles. We had observed very high levels of teacher commitment in the schools we visited. Discussions about merit pay proposals to stimulate greater teacher productivity were quite commonplace at that time. The underlying micro-economic assumptions here, however, could not explain what we had observed. On average, Catholic high school teachers in our field sites were paid about 75 per cent of prevailing local public school wages. While a persuasive 'just wage' argument can be made for greater Catholic school teacher salaries, it was very clear from our field observations that economic incentives were not driving teacher behaviour.

Similarly, we had observed relatively high levels of student engagement in classroom instruction which we judged as rather ordinary. Many professional educators argue that a more relevant curriculum and more stimulating instruction are needed to enhance student engagement in learning. While such developments may be highly desirable, the basic premise behind their arguments — an appeal for more immediate rewards from learning — was certainly not producing the student engagement that we had observed in Catholic high school classrooms.

Perhaps most significant in all of our field work was the pervasive talk among teachers, principals, and students about their school being a community. As field researchers who had recently spent a considerable amount of time in public high schools, this language and accompanying practices of community appeared quite distinctive. Trying to make sense of these disparate observations and trying to understand better what it means to talk about a 'school as a community' became the motivating concerns for the second phase of our research.

Communal Organization

Our field investigations indicated that the focused academic programmes found in Catholic high schools are embedded within a larger social organization of the school as a community. We came to conclude that this communal structure is formed around three core features. First is an extensive array of school activities which provide numerous opportunities for face-to-face interactions and shared experiences among adults and students. The common academic programme described above is a major contributor in this regard. There are also numerous school events — athletics, drama, liturgy, and retreat programmes — which engender high levels of participation and provide more informal occasions for interactions among students and adults. These activities afford opportunities to deepen attachments among current school members and to create connections with those who came before and those who may come after. School rituals can be especially powerful in helping to connect the current social group to a larger tradition.

Second are a set of formal organizational features that enable the community. Chief among these is an extended role for teachers. Teachers are not just subject-matter specialists whose job definition is delimited by the classroom walls. Rather, they are mature persons whom students also encounter in the hallways, playing fields, in the school neighbourhood, and sometimes even in their homes. In the numerous personal interactions that occur among adults and students outside of classrooms, many opportunities are afforded for expressions of individual concern and interest.

Collegiality among teachers is also important in this regard. Catholic school faculty spend time with one another both inside and outside of school. These social interactions serve as a resource for school problem-solving and contribute to adult solidarity around the school's mission. In such contexts, school decision-making tends to be less conflictual and more often characterized by mutual trust and respect.

The relatively small size of Catholic high schools provides a significant advantage here too. The coordination of work in larger organizations typically imposes demands for more formal modes of communication, and encourages increased work specialization and more extensive bureaucratization. In contrast, a smaller school size facilitates personalism and social intimacy, both of which are much harder to achieve in larger contexts.

Third, and crucial for communal school organization, are a set of shared beliefs about what students should learn, about proper norms of instruction, and about how people should relate to one another. Underpinning this educational philosophy in Catholic high schools are a set of general moral beliefs about the person and society and the role of schools to advance social justice. This distinctive organizational purpose marks contemporary Catholic schools as post-Vatican II institutions. (This topic will be discussed in more depth below.) At this juncture, my main point is that this set of shared beliefs establishes a common ground which orders and gives meaning to much of daily life for both faculty and students.

Building on our field observations, we used analyses of a national survey on US high schools (the *High School and Beyond* data and especially information from the *Administrator and Teacher Survey*) to bring empirical specificity to these ideas and to test hypotheses about the effects of communal organization on those who work and learn in such schools. Our statistical analyses indicated powerful effects of communal organization on both students and teachers. In schools with a strong communal organization, fewer problems with classroom disruptions, class cutting, absenteeism and dropping out were reported. Teachers were more likely to express a greater sense of efficacy and satisfaction with their work and staff morale was higher. Moreover, these effects exist in both the public and Catholic sectors. That is, public schools with a strong communal organization have levels of student engagement and teacher commitment similar to those found in the Catholic sector.

Thus, a second strong theme had now emerged from our research. The basic social organization of the high school as a community has substantial social and personal consequences for both teachers and students. Thinking about these results led us toward two more questions: How did Catholic schools come to be organized in this way? What helps to maintain this distinctiveness? Up to this point, our research had focused primarily on the practices and structures that organize life inside Catholic high schools. These new questions broadened our attention toward concerns about external control. More specifically, they focus subsequent inquiry on the role of an inspirational ideology and decentralized governance. We came to conclude that two major organizational control mechanisms, ideology and markets, interact in complex ways to both guide and anchor the work in Catholic high schools.

We had inquired about Catholic school governance issues during our original field work and they will be addressed in a subsequent discussion in this chapter. But the questions about the role of ideology were new. Like the focus on communal school organization, a focus on ideology was not a part of our original investigation but rather had emerged from reflections on our field observations. Thus, in 1988, we launched our third major strand of research work on the social and intellectual history of Catholic schools.

Anthony S. Bryk

An Inspirational Ideology

At the crest of Catholic school enrolment in 1965, serious questions were raised about continuing a separate Catholic school system. Many Catholics had successfully entered mainstream American life and the need for a separate school system was no longer apparent. Vatican II, in proclaiming a new role for the Church in the modern world, however, created such a purpose. The charter for Catholic schools shifted from protecting the faithful from a hostile Protestant majority to pursuing peace and social justice within an ecumenical and multicultural world. Each school would seek to enact the image of a prophetic Church. While thoroughly engaged in American culture, the aims, organization, methods, and daily life of Catholic schools sought to offer a strong countervailing image — a distinctive vision of democratic education for a post-modern world.

Two important ideas — personalism and subsidiarity — shape life in Catholic schools. Personalism calls for humaneness in the hundreds of mundane social interactions that comprise daily life. Key to advancing personalism is an extended role for teachers that encourages staff to care about both the kind of person students become as well as the facts, skills, and knowledge they acquire. Moreover, personalism is a communal norm for the school — the kind of behaviour modelled by teachers and held out as an ideal for students. As such, personalism is valued not only because it is an effective device to engage students in academic work, but also because it signifies a moral conception of social behaviour in a just community.

Similarly, subsidiarity means that the school rejects a purely bureaucratic conception of an organization. Clearly, there are advantages to work place specialization, and it is hard to imagine the conduct of complex work without established organizational procedures. Subsidiarity, however, claims that instrumental considerations about work efficiency and specialization must be mediated by a concern for human dignity. Likewise, decentralization of school governance is not chosen purely because it is more efficient, although it does appear to have such consequences. Nor is it primarily favoured because it creates organizations that are more client-sensitive, although this also appears true. Rather, decentralization is predicated on a view about how personal dignity and human respect are advanced when work is organized around small communities where dialogue and collegiality may flourish. At root is a belief that the full potential of persons is realized in the social solidarity that can form around these small group associations.

In a related vein, subsidiarity also makes a claim on the policy-making activities of higher-level institutions. For the Catholic Church, a commitment to subsidiarity means that dioceses and religious orders see their role as enhancing the function of local institutions where they currently exist and promoting the development of new institutions in response to new needs. Rather than regulating human activity under the homogenizing norms of a central bureaucracy, the role of external governance is to facilitate and stimulate collective local action. In the simplest of terms, the central norm of higher levels of government is to 'Educate rather than regulate'.

At base here is quite a different language for discussion about education. It is a language which encourages students to engage questions about the kind of persons they should become and the kind of society we should want. It is a language that also makes important demands on schools; fostering such moral reflections requires that schools themselves must be moral communities.

Decentralized Governance

A fourth distinctive feature of Catholic high schools is decentralized governance. The specific arrangements vary from school to school, depending upon the nature of school ownership (parish, diocesan or private). In reality, the 'Catholic school system' is a very loose federation. Virtually all important decisions are made at individual school sites. To the best of our knowledge, no current efforts to promote decentralization in the public sector approach this level of school-site autonomy.

Externally, Catholic high schools, like all private schools, are subject to market forces. These market effects were quite apparent in the 1970s, when parents spurned Catholic schools that adopted such then-popular innovations as an expanded personal development curriculum. As a result, these reforms never took deep root in Catholic schools. Market influences can also be seen in Catholic school history. For example, many immigrant Catholic parents aspired that their children should become something more than just 'hewers of wood'. These collective aspirations are part of the reason why vocationalism was never taken up strongly in the Catholic sector. Today, market forces contribute to the relatively low dropout and expulsion rates in Catholic high schools. Since most schools are not over-enrolled, they have an institutional interest in holding students in order to balance their budgets.

Nevertheless, the control of Catholic school operations involves considerably more than market responsiveness to clients. Many important observations about these schools cannot be reconciled in these terms. Market forces, for example, cannot explain the broadly shared institutional purpose of advancing social equity. Nor can they account for the efforts of Catholic educators to maintain inner-city schools (with large non-Catholic enrolments) while facing mounting fiscal woes. Likewise, market forces cannot easily explain why resources are allocated within schools in a compensatory fashion in order to provide an academic education for every student. Nor can they explain the norms of community that infuse daily life in these schools.

In sum, four key features combine to create a distinctive Catholic school life. A focused academic life is embedded within a larger communal organization. Taken together, these two features create an engaging social institution for both adults and students that produces a more equitable social distribution of achievement. Undergirding this institutional life is a combination of an inspirational ideology that nicely co-exists with a decentralized governance and market influences.

Some 'Larger Lessons' from Our Analyses of Catholic High Schools

Educational Markets as a Basis for Improvement

After a century and a half of strong public support for a publicly controlled and managed educational system, advocacy for greater parental choice within an expanded educational market has become widespread. We have already noted that some aspects of Catholic school operations are influenced by market concerns. We have also described how the spirit of Vatican II has catalyzed dramatic changes in Catholic schools over the past twenty years. Taken together, these two control mechanisms — ideology and markets — jointly shape the operations of Catholic schools. Vatican II ideals inspire human action, and the market acts as an empirical lever. Absent either one, the contemporary Catholic school would surely be a very different institution.

Consequently, it would be inappropriate to assume that a new system of education, just because it was market-driven, would produce effects similar to those found in Catholic schools. In this regard, there is a ruse to be dispatched. Popular arguments for a system of market controls in education commonly employ a micro-economic explanation that bears little relation to the ideas about schools-as-communities which have been discussed. Under this micro-economic view, stimulating teachers' entrepreneurial motives would make schools more efficient service providers. This conception of teacher thinking and behaviour is quite antithetical, however, to the social foundations of a communal school organization. Although individual entrepreneurship may fuel economic development, it rings less true as a basic motivation for processes of human betterment. There is simply no evidence that such motives currently play a role in motivating teachers in Catholic schools. More generally, it is difficult to envision how unleashing self-interest becomes a compelling force toward human caring.

These observations are important because so much of the current rhetoric about privatization and choice can be traced to the recent studies on public and private schools. A clear understanding of these findings is very important. Specifically, many of the positive effects found in Catholic schools are not characteristic of non-Catholic private schools. For example, the more equitable social distribution of achievement, or 'common school' effect, that occurs in Catholic schools, does not typify other private schools. Similarly, the reduced dropout rates and unusual effectiveness of Catholic high schools for at-risk youth are not characteristic of private schools in general (Coleman and Hoffer, 1987). The special effectiveness of Catholic girls' schools also does not appear to generalize across the private sector as a whole.[1]

Advocates of choice have argued that 'effective organizational practices' are more likely under a market system because such practices are currently more prevalent in private schools which benefit from a higher degree of school autonomy. While this is a valid public–private comparison, it is also important to recognize that, within the private sector, some of the so-called 'effective organizational practices' are actually more prevalent among non-Catholic than Catholic private schools. However, the positive student outcomes described above do not generally occur in these non-Catholic private schools (Chubb and Moe, 1990).

In short, extant research clearly indicates differences among private schools in both their internal organization and their outcomes. These findings raise doubts about any blanket claim that a move toward greater privatization will ensure better consequences for students. In our view, much more attention is required to the actual content of the values operative in schools and to the consequences which derive from these values.

Fundamental to the operations of Catholic schools are beliefs about the dignity of each person and a shared responsibility for advancing a just and caring society. These aims are formally joined in an educational philosophy that seeks to develop each student as a 'person-in-community'. Not surprisingly, this educational philosophy aligns well with social equity aims. Moreover, when such understandings meld to a coherent organizational structure with adequate fiscal and human resources, desirable academic and social consequences can result. Absent this particular value system, however, a very different pattern of effects seems likely.

The School as a Voluntary Community

As an alternative to describing a school 'as a market-responsive firm' we offer the idea of a school 'as a voluntary community'. The notion of a school as a voluntary community synthesizes three important features of Catholic high schools.

First, a communal organization, as described earlier, structures daily life within the school. Second, each school possesses a relatively high degree of autonomy in managing its affairs. This autonomy is important because much of the rationale for activity within a communal organization relies on traditions and local judgments. Such schools simply do not meet the criteria and operating principles of centralized bureaucracies, where standardization is seen as an organizational imperative and particularisms as imperfections needing redress.

Third, the voluntary association of both students and teachers with the school marks individual membership. Implicit here is the idea that participation in a particular school is not an inalienable right. While Catholic school faculty go a long way toward helping students and working with parents, reciprocity is also expected. Students who seriously or chronically violate community's norms must leave. Similarly, faculty who do not share the school's beliefs and commitments usually move on as well, mostly by their own choice. Because membership involves an ongoing exercise of free will, individuals are less likely to interpret school life as coercive and are more likely to express the personal sentiment, 'This is *my* school.'

This notion of membership in a school community, in turn, licenses a different form of social relations among parents and professionals. Rather than 'the contract' which formalizes market-place interactions or 'the client and interest politics' of the public bureaucracy, a set of fiducial commitments are at the core of the voluntary community. The importance of these trust relationships is readily manifest in school life. Effective teaching makes personal demands which leave teachers vulnerable — literally, 'I put *myself* on the line each day.' To maintain such commitments, teachers need support both from their colleagues and from parents. That is, a considerable measure of trust is required among all participants to sustain engaging teaching (see Cohen, 1988).

Thus, the internal life of Catholic schools benefit from a network of supportive social relations, characterized by trust, that constitute a form of 'social capital'.[2] In this regard, voluntary association functions as a facilitating condition. Trust accrues because school participants, both students and faculty, choose to be there. To be sure, voluntary association does not automatically create social capital, but it is surely harder to develop such capital in its absence.

Our investigation of Catholic schools suggests that schools formed as voluntary communities induce important institutional and personal consequences. On the organizational side, a voluntary community enjoys a base of moral authority. The commitment from both teachers and students to a particular school makes moral authority possible, since such authority depends on the consent of those influenced by it. The presence of moral authority is important because, as noted earlier, much of what happens in schools involves discretionary action. Great effort may be required within public bureaucracies to secure basic agreements on issues which are intrinsically judgmental. In contrast, much of the effort expended on such matters can be redirected toward the actual work of schooling in a voluntary community. Moreover, many potentially contentious issues never develop into conflicts, since communal norms define a broader realm of 'what is appropriate here'. Further, because these communities value social interactions which are respectful and civil, when disagreements do occur, participants assume good intentions all around. This is quite different from the suspicion, fear, and distrust which often afflicts the interest politics surrounding public education.

A base of moral authority also helps to guide the work of individual adults. The latter is particularly important because autonomous action characterizes much of teaching. A major policy lesson of the 1960s and 1970s is that the behaviour of teachers is relatively impervious to direct regulation. In part, this reflects the relatively private nature of teaching — typically an individual adult working with a group of students behind a closed door. Also significant is that the craft of teaching involves complex and spontaneous judgments. Because such decisions draw substantially on personal experiences, beliefs, and values, the normative standards of a voluntary community help to naturally order these judgments (see Clark and Peterson, 1986).

For all participants, personal experiences in a voluntary community have inherent meaning above and beyond their instrumental value. Communalism is an ethical end where members derive personal support from others with whom they share this commitment. Students who participate in this type of schooling derive more from their education than just something to be endured now in order to get a good job in the future. Similarly, teachers' efforts in such environments involve more than earning an income to support out-of-work activities. Likewise, school administration takes on a distinctive character, where tending to the meaning-inducing quality of school life is a deliberate aim, on a par with concerns about the efficient organization of instruction. In such contexts, the managerial ethic of the bureaucracy is tempered by a personalism more characteristic of the family.

In sum, many desirable personal and institutional consequences derive from the organization of schools as voluntary communities. Nevertheless, we reiterate our doubts that the specific consequences found in Catholic high schools would appear more broadly should a market-based system of schooling emerge in America. In particular, without commitment to the specific values operative in the Catholic sector, we suspect that neither the quality of internal life found in these schools nor the more equitable social distribution of achievement would result. Rather, a market system seems likely to produce a highly differentiated set of schools, where educational opportunities would be even more inequitably distributed among individuals and communities than is already the case. We are reminded of Max Weber's famous prediction that, 'Capitalism stripped of its religious imperative is a cloak of steel, a cage of iron.' A market system of schools, absent a vital moral imperative, would likely enact this image.

The High School as a Bridging Institution

Our research demonstrates that disadvantaged children can benefit from attending Catholic schools. The particular combination of organizational structure, social behaviour, beliefs, and sentiments found in Catholic high schools constitutes a distinctive approach to the education of the disadvantaged. This approach can be summarized in the idea of 'school as a bridging institution'.

The philosophy of a bridging institution is dialogical. On one side is an empathetic orientation toward children and their families which is grounded in an appreciation of the dignity of each person without regard for outward appearances, customs, or manners (see Coles, 1987). The school welcomes all who want to come, and it conveys to parents and children a sense of security, personal well-being, and engagement. On the other side is a clear recognition of the demands of contemporary middle-class American life for which the school consciously seeks to prepare these children. From this perspective, the school is of value to disadvantaged students because it is culturally different. Specifically, school staff aim to provide an education that will enable each student to develop the knowledge, skills, dispositions, and habits necessary to function both effectively and critically in modern democratic society.

The tasks of the bridging institution involve constant tensions. While sensitive to the mores of family and community, it must also challenge behaviours and attitudes clearly at odds with the child's progress in school. While social idealism is a source of inspiration, the school and its students must also live in this world. While the school espouses a caring community, it also operates within a larger culture which values hard work, delayed gratification, and material success. While schools are committed to systematically preparing students with the intellectual and social competencies required for functioning in contemporary middle-class American life, they also seek to hone a critical consciousness toward social life as it should be.

Staff in a bridging institution seek to nourish and validate the best of family and community ties while also providing a link to a very different world. The transitions are difficult both for those individuals who seek to ford it and for those institutions which seek to act as bridge. To be sure, the Catholic schools we studied were far from perfect in this regard. These concerns, however, were very alive in the conversations among school staff, and a collective moral voice made claims on school participants to act.

As we begin to think about urban schools in these ways, we are reminded that all schools undeniably act as agents of socialization. This socialization role is especially salient in the inner city where the formation of a two-class society appears immanent. If real educational opportunities are to be afforded students who live in 'underclass' neighbourhoods, students must have access to schools with strong institutional norms. In the Catholic schools that we studied, these norms were central to the schools' effectiveness in educating disadvantaged youth. Our findings link to a growing body of evidence that suggest that the disadvantaged in our society benefit most from such strong institutions. For the disadvantaged, more than anyone else, must rely on the expertise, good intentions, and efforts of societal institutions for advancement. Anything less may resign large number of students to a permanent underclass.[3]

This line of analysis raises questions about whether Americans can obtain such moral aims as equality of educational opportunity without an enlivened moral discourse about the aims and methods of schooling. Public educational policy has instead searched for instrumental levers to advance moral purposes. In the recent past, bussing programmes, magnet schools, and individual educational plans have served as such levers. Now school improvement plans, accountability systems, and markets are offered as solutions. To be sure, different organizational arrangements can facilitate different consequences. Ultimately, however, it is school values, norms, and traditions that influence the selection of 'appropriate structures' and create meaning for participants within whatever structure they happen to confront. Whatever specific reform initiative we choose to pursue, it will eventually be enacted by individuals in schools, each of whom draws on his or her own personal beliefs yet operates within a larger context where moral conversation holds a very uncertain status.

Role of Religious Understanding in Contemporary Schooling

More generally, these observations direct our attention to the role of religious understandings in contemporary schooling. Past discussions about this topic have tended to flash around such highly visible events as Bible reading, school prayer, and crèches at Christmas. For several decades now, efforts have vigorously sought to banish all such symbols from schools, and counter-efforts have arisen in their defense. To be clear, the central issue to us is not the presence or absence of these activities in schools. For some, these symbols have meaning; for many others, they do not. Much more important in our view is the quality of the interior life that schools foster in their students, the voices of conscience they nurture or fail to nurture. In this sense, *all* education conveys religious understandings; that is, a set of beliefs, values, and sentiments which order social life and create purpose for human activity.[4] These may be comprehensive ideals which ennoble the person and reach out broadly to others, or they may narrowly focus only on advancing material self-interest.

In terms of the Catholic schools we studied, school life comprises a tradition of thought, rituals, mores and organizational practices that both invites students to reflect on this systematic body of thought and to immerse themselves in a communal life that seeks to live out its basic principles. The aim of this type of schooling is to nurture in students the feelings, experiences, and reflections that can help them apprehend their relations to all that is around them — both the material world and the social world, both those who have come before and those who will come after.

Isn't this what education should be about? Isn't this what we should want for all our children? At root here is a fundamental question: What in the postmodern age is 'education for democracy?' The 'Catholic answer' involves a melding of the technical knowledge and skill to negotiate an increasingly complex secular world, with a moral vision which points this skill toward a more convivial and humane society, and a voice of conscience that encourages each student to critically pursue the vision.

Revitalizing the public conversation about this question is essential to all Americans, whether young or old, whether they have children in school or not. Life in a free society presumes broadly shared commitments to basic principles of truth, justice, and human compassion. So much of the livability and vitality of a free society depends on the 'right living' of its people. In its absence, we are less secure and less free. Ultimately these are questions about what kinds of hopes, aspirations, and visions we offer our children about the kind of society we should be.

Implications for Current Efforts at School Improvement

In most general terms, our research began as a search for the key organizational elements in Catholic high schools that produce the desired outcomes observed there. As this scientific work proceeded, we gradually added a second focus on the 'public theology' at work in these schools, on the nature of their institutional vision and the sources of hopefulness that ground these communities' vitality and inspire human effort. We are convinced that if we are to have a renewed public philosophy for education in America — one that is capable of ennobling the work of faculty and staff and firing the hearts and minds of young people — it must involve more serious dialogue between the instrumental and evocative realms that interweave to create school life.

As we turn to focus specific attention on the 'Catholic lessons' for improving urban schools, I am reminded of the two central characters, Lafeyette and Pharaoh, in Alex Kotlowitz's *There are No Children Here*. In our field visits to Catholic schools, we were told about students enrolled in those schools whose home environment and community context were like Lafeyette's and Pharaoh's — chaotic, precarious, and often beyond their parents' control. We are convinced that many urban children like this can learn in an educational environment which combines a strong press toward academic work with a caring ethos that demands personal responsibility and the good efforts of all participants. In fact, it is not clear to us that public schools can better serve disadvantaged children who want to learn and also encourage larger proportions of the students to share these aims unless many more schools are transformed along lines similar to those found in Catholic schools.

We see these ideas as particularly timely in the context of many diverse efforts now underway to reinvent urban public education. As we move to transform our large public school systems into systems of publicly supported schools, there is now more space for new schools, organized like Catholic schools, to emerge. Specifically, in the context of current efforts to break up large public high schools into smaller 'schools-within-a-school', there are opportunities now to create more schools where a deliberately formed academic and social life create strong educative institutions for the disadvantaged.

In my current work, I am now deeply involved in efforts to promote school reform and school improvement in Chicago Public Schools. Through the Center for School Improvement at the University of Chicago, which I direct, we are engaged in a wide range of activities, from promoting comprehensive restructuring in a small number of very disadvantaged Chicago elementary schools, to leadership development programmes for school principals, to an extended array of research projects concerning the unfolding of 'School Reform: Chicago Style'. This research activity has led us into more formal collaborations with other researchers around the city and to form a new organization, the Consortium on Chicago School Research, which I also lead. The Consortium seeks to promote an integrated programme of analytic work focusing on the implementation of school reform, assessing reform's progress over time, and, more generally, supporting school improvement efforts. Participants in the Consortium share a commitment to direct their research toward the improvement of local practice.

On occasion, people have asked me, 'How do you reconcile your empathetic account of Catholic schools with your current work on improving urban public schools?' In most conversations, support for Catholic schools is typically posed as in opposition to public education. In my view, however, discussions about the future of Catholic and public schools in our major cities are really all of one fabric. The core threads that ties them together are a massive need in our cities for strengthening and recreating vital local institutions and a larger public policy to support such local institution building.

Catholic schools are strong local institutions. They have evolved out of a complex political history involving both internal conflicts within a multi-ethnic American Catholic Church and a need to respond to the external hostilities confronted by Catholic immigrants in a Protestant dominated America. In the mix of these political conditions with a distinctive Catholic ideology, a vital philosophy of institutional subsidiarity and its support for local institutions emerged.

Chicago's school reform, which seeks to weaken central office control and reorient the connections of school professionals back toward their local communities, also embraces a commitment to institutional subsidiarity. To be sure, this legislation is far from perfect, and I am still a serious skeptic in some respects. Nevertheless, as I have had opportunities to observe its effects, both up close in school communities and more generally across the system, I have come to appreciate some of its distinctive strengths.

The core idea here is quite simple. We live through our institutions. Many analyses of the problems of contemporary urban life point to the gradual erosion of local institutions — economic, religious, social — which make communal life possible. The aim of Chicago school reform is to build stronger school–community institutions. This is the only large scale school reform initiative that directly seeks to link the problems of urban school improvement to the larger need for urban community development. It is hard to envision renewal of urban life without a massive, sustained commitment to such institution building.

It is this same logic which ultimately led me to conclude that the public has a strong stake in the preservation of Catholic schools. These are vital institutions often located in very troubled neighbourhoods. It is hard to comprehend how the continued loss of these institutions can mean anything but a further erosion of urban life. At base here, I return to the principle of subsidiarity. We need to preserve vital local institutions such as urban Catholic schools, strengthen institutions that are currently troubled such as many of our public schools, and more generally promote local institution building of all kinds.

Catholic Schools and the Common Good

Finally, what about the future of urban Catholic schools? The fiscal pressures on these schools continue to mount. Despite the best efforts of all involved, we will surely see more urban school closings in the next few years.

Contemporary Catholic schools are very different from those of thirty years ago. They now educate a very broad cross-section of Americans of diverse race, ethnicity and social class. They accomplish this with very modest fiscal resources and in the process extend significant educational opportunities to many. Instruction is not narrow, divisive, or sectarian, but rather is informed by a generous conception of democratic life in a post-modern society. Moreover, many of these schools are located in very disadvantaged communities and constitute an important resource to their communities. It is observations such as these which lead us to conclude that Catholic schools serve the common good and the public has a stake in their preservation.

Notes

1   In addition to the research reported in Chapter 9, Riordan (1985), using NLS72 data, also found positive effects on achievement for Catholic girls' schools. A report on recent field research in progress, however, (Lee and Marks, 1991) suggest that this pattern may not be generally characteristic of other non-Catholic schools. Should these findings be sustained by further analyses, they would confirm other evidence about private schools as a set are a very diverse enterprise with few generalizations appropriate for the entire set.
2   Coleman (1987) introduced the idea of social capital in the context of describing Catholic high schools as functional communities. His explanation, however, was located external to the school in the structure of relationships among parents and their children. We agree with Coleman that Catholic high schools benefit from a form a social capital but we locate that capital in the relations among school professionals and with their parent communities.
3   The idea of an underclass has been developed by Wilson (1987), and subjected to considerable debate and scrutiny in an edited volume by Jencks and Peterson (1991). In brief, Wilson argues that economic and demographic forces reshaped many of our urban centres during the 1970s, creating a distinct separate underclass. We are now witnessing a secondary consequence of this phenomenon, as the children of the underclass are increasingly entering the public school system. Thus, what began as an economic and demographic problem (e.g., the movement of jobs and institutions to the suburbs) may now be beginning to manifest itself as a cultural issue.
4   This conception of religious understanding is based on Paul Tillich's claim that religion is the ultimate concern which informs all other activity in one's life. See Tillich, (1957). This idea is elaborated by Gamwell (1986) with the notion that religious understanding is a comprehensive ideal for human life. A similar concept is used by Booth (1985) in his analysis of the truncated rhetoric employed in modern science.

References

BOOTH, W.C. (1985) 'Systematic wonder: The rhetoric of secular religions', *Journal of the American Academy of Religion*, **53**, pp. 677–702.
BRYK, A.S., LEE, V.E. and HOLLAND, P.B. (1993) *Catholic Schools and the Common Good*, Cambridge, Harvard University Press.
CHUBB, J.E. and MOE, T.M. (1990) *Politics, Markets and America's Schools*, Washington, DC, Brookings Institution.

CLARK, C.N. and PETERSON, P.L. (1986) 'Teachers' thought processes', in WHITROCK, M.C. (Ed) *Handbook of Research on Teaching*, 3rd ed. New York, Macmillan, pp. 255–96.

COHEN, D.K. (1988) 'Knowledge of teaching: Plus que ça change . . .', in JACKSON, P.W. (Ed) *Contributing to Educational Change*, Berkeley, CA, McCutcheon, pp. 27–84.

COLEMAN, J.S. (1987) 'The relations between school and social structure', in HALLINAN, N.T. (Ed) *The Social Organization of Schools: New Conceptualizations of the Learning Process*, New York, Plenum.

COLEMAN, J.S. and HOFFER, T. (1987) *Public and Private High Schools: The Impact of Communities*, New York, Basic Books.

COLEMAN, J.S., HOFFER, T. and KILGORE, S.B. (1982) *High School Achievement: Public, Catholic, and Private Schools Compared*, New York, Basic Books.

COLES, R. (1987) *Dorothy Day: A Radical Devotion*, Reading, MA, Addison Wesley.

GAMWELL, I. (1986) 'Religion and reason in American politics', in LOVEN, R. (Ed) *Religion and American Public Life*, Mahwah, NJ, Paulist Press.

GREELEY, A.M. (1982) *Catholic High Schools and Minority Students*, New Brunswick, NJ, Transaction Books.

JENCKS, C. and PETERSON, P. (Eds) (1991) *Urban Underclass*, Washington, DC, Brookings Institution.

KOTLOWITZ, A. (1991) *There Are No Children Here*, New York, Doubleday.

LEE, V.E. and MARKS, H.M. (1991) 'Which works best?: The relative effectiveness of single-sex and coeducational secondary schools', Paper presented at the Annual Meeting of the American Educational Research Association, Chicago, IL, April.

MOLES, O.C. (1988) *High School and Beyond: Administrative and Teacher Survey (1985)*, Data file users' manual, Washington, DC, Office of Educational Research.

NATIONAL CENTER FOR EDUCATION STATISTICS (NCES) (1982) *High School and Beyond 1980 Sophomore Cohort First Follow-up (1982)*, Data file user's manual, Washington, DC, National Center for Education Statistics.

NATIONAL CENTER FOR EDUCATION STATISTICS (1984) *Bulletin*, February.

NATIONAL CENTER FOR EDUCATION STATISTICS (1987) *Digest of Educational Statistics*, Washington, DC, Government Printing Office.

RIORDAN, C. (1985) 'Public and Catholic schooling: The effects of gender context policy', *American Journal of Education*, **5**, pp. 518–40.

TILLICH, P. (1957) *Dynamics of Faith*, New York, Harper and Row.

WILSON, J.T. (1987) *The Truly Disadvantaged*, Chicago, University of Chicago Press.

Chapter 3

National Crisis, Catholic Schools and the Common Good

Bruce S. Cooper

In the inner-cities of the United States today, ill-educated children live in drug-infested, dangerous, even deadly, conditions. Babies are killed by stray bullets in shoot-outs between rival gangs or irate neighbours, and 65 per cent of all live births in large cities are of children born to unwed minority mothers under the age of 18. The number of children killed in New York City and Washington, DC, for example, has reached epidemic proportions, to a point where the life expectancy of young people in the world's poorest countries (Bangladesh, for example) exceeds that of babies born into American inner-city neighbourhoods. An African-American male living in an urban community is ten times as likely to die before reaching age 25 as a white male in the United States.

And urban public schools are often no better. Jonathan Kozol, in comparing rich and poor communities, found 'savage inequalities'. He reported that after many years 'when I visited Morris High [School], most of the conditions were unchanged. Water still cascaded down the stairs. Plaster is still falling from the walls. Female students tell me that they shower after school to wash the plaster from their hair. Entering ninth grade children [around age 15], I'm told, read about four years behind grade level' (Kozol, 1991, p. 100). Violence was so pervasive that a system strapped for textbooks and xerox paper was prompted to buy 2,300 pairs of handcuffs for the NYC's 1,000 public elementary and secondary schools, to allow security guards to restrain student transgressors (Kozol, 1991, p. 118). In New Jersey, the state department of education has 'taken over' urban districts (Patterson, Jersey City, Elizabeth) because of the appalling conditions in these urban school districts, and the inability of local education authorities to manage the schools under their control. When one combines the violence, inhumanity, and death, with the low test scores, high truancy and dropout rate, and the high turnover of teachers, one has school systems in crisis in the urban United States.

Importantly, Catholic schools in the American inner-cities have confronted the problems of urban life — drugs, violence, crime and low achievement — and have succeeded in making a difference for these disadvantaged students. This chapter argues that the willingness of the Roman Catholic community in the United States to support inner-city non-public schools for the poor (and non-Catholic) students establishes their commonweal function and justifies their receiving some public financing and support.

Catholic Schools and Public Funding: Two National Perspectives

The plight of children in the American inner-cities indicates a society under extreme strain. It calls for a national effort to counter a threat to the survival of a moral, just, and liveable society: in short, a threat to the common good. Although Catholic schools in the United States have a potentially vital role to play in relation to these problems their contribution is often overlooked and unappreciated.

The US Government has isolated religiously-sponsored schools as 'private' and as having no part in the national effort to improve education for the poor. In its view, 'public' schools contribute to the public or common good while private schools are primarily vehicles for personal and individual interest. This identification of the public school with the common good and the separation of the private school from the public sphere means that somehow the public schools are part of the 'social contract' and the private schools are not. In contrast, virtually all other modern nations treat public and private schools in this respect rather more evenhandedly. (See Sherman, 1993; Cooper and Doyle, 1985).

Cibulka and Boyd (1989) recognized that policies affecting private schools are inherently moral and value-laden, and help to determine the qualities of a moral and just society — issues strongly related to concepts of the common good. 'How to draw the invisible line between public and private, then, or whether to honor it at all, is a matter of ideology and the social interests behind these ideologies . . . Even apart from ideologies, however, national traditions have led to quite different organizational arrangements. Further, these arrangements are not fixed over time, but have evolved to accommodate changing national and international circumstances' (ibid., p. 1).

Often those who separate public from private in the United States cite the Bill of Rights, which states that the Government should neither establish an official religion nor prohibit the 'free exercise' of religious preferences. The First Amendment does not ban governments from giving families resources (much like food stamps, the GI Bill, and Tuition Assistance plans) and allowing the family to 'buy' the services from a public or a private provider.

In contrast to the United States, in England and Wales religious schools (mainly Roman Catholic and Church of England schools) are not only to be found in the 'independent' or 'private' sector of schooling but are also a prominent part of the publicly funded education system. They are therefore seen as part of the national educational effort, and as having an acknowledged role to play in relation to the common good.

In England and Wales around a third of students attend a church school within the publicly financed system. Unlike religious schools in the 'independent' sector, parents pay no tuition and almost all the financial needs of the school are met from public funds. These schools are therefore not 'private' in the American sense at all. They provide within the public system diversity and choice for parents at no additional cost. All programmes, teacher salaries, and resources available to the state-owned schools accrue to these schools. In fact, Catholic school teachers are on the national pay scale — unlike in the United States where parochial school teachers are paid considerably less than local public school teachers. These schools remain the property of the Church. In return for some financial responsibilities (relating mainly to capital expenditure), the Church has some degree of control over such matters as the curriculum of religious education and the appointment of teaching staff.

In the United States, however, the governments (federal, state, and local) have isolated the religiously affiliated schools — even though, ironically, the United States is among the modern world's most actively religious societies. American policy-makers have purposely excluded religious schools from their strategies and have even tried to ban forms of religious instruction and practice, prayer, and even religious singing at assemblies in public schools ('Jingle Bells' was in; 'Silent Night, Holy Night' was out). Only recently were students even allowed to hold meetings at school for religious purposes (e.g., Bible study clubs) and only children can legally lead graduation prayers (not ministers, rabbis or teachers).

The roots of this anti-religious attitude go back to the mid-nineteenth century when public education gained control over public funding. In New York, for example, Bishop John Hughes had received steady public subsidies for Catholic schools for twenty years. Once this ended, the Church determined to provide a free, available Catholic education to every Catholic child, as part of the cost of running the local parish (see Lannie, 1968; Lee, 1967). From then on, the public school groups sought successfully to direct all public funds to public schools, cutting parochial schools out of the process for nearly a century. The state-owned (public) schools therefore took over the general education of students.

The Government and the Church have in fact been working in opposite directions. State and local governments have pressed the official position that only state-owned schools are entitled to perform public tasks with tax support, while some Catholic church leaders have, in supporting near universal education for all Catholic children in church-run schools, expanded the role of Catholic education into public life.

The Public Value of Catholic Schools

Catholic schools have been seen by some as a needed antidote to the expanding public school monopoly. As Buetow explained in *Of Singular Benefit*:

. . . it is historically and otherwise demonstrable that Catholic education has given education in the United States a temper of wisdom, contributed a needed examination of ultimate goals and aims, provided
challenging concepts of personal formation, supplied stimulation in
many areas, contributed greater profundity than most other educators
to true foundations of such virtues as citizenship and patriotism, and
donated resources and services of countless thousands of dedicated
personnel to United States communities across the land. (Buetow, 1970,
p. 380)

Nowhere was the role of Catholic education more critical than in the
cities, where poor families suffered economic privation and had few educational options. The more Catholic schools accepted the challenge of educating
the urban poor, and the more 'public' their function became, the more they
needed government help to offset the costs. Sadly, just when inner-city Catholic
(and some other religious schools) were desperately needed to off-set the failure of city school systems and the decline of urban life, these private religious
schools were closing down — a crisis within a crisis in the United States (Cooper
and Dondero, 1991).

Educational experts in the United States have tended to define educational problems as primarily technical (how to raise standards and improve test
scores) or as social (how to overcome the deficits of broken homes, shoddy
neighbourhoods, crime, and dislocation) and have excluded religious-affiliated
schools from the public solution. Unlike Britain, reformers in the United States
have avoided — even rejected — the moral dimension of the problem and
have overlooked the remarkable contribution of religious schools (particularly
schools run by Roman Catholic, Lutheran and Seventh-day Adventist communities) to the education of the poor.

Bryk, Lee and Holland (1993) state the advantage of Catholic schools best.
These schools are effective with many children but particularly with the poor
because of the school's personal commitment to children, to peace and justice,
and to a living Catholic social ethic. Bryk *et al.* further explain:

Underpinning these organizational tenets is a vital Catholic social ethic.
First is a belief in the capacity of human reason to arrive at ethical truth.
An immediate implication of this belief is that education must aim to
develop in each person the critical consciousness which enables and
motivates this pursuit. The Catholic school's emphasis on an academic
curriculum for all is one direct consequence of this stance. Moreover,
such an education involves nurturing both spirit and mind, with equal
concern for what students know and whether they develop the disposition to use their intellectual capacities to affect a greater measure of
social justice. This is the Catholic conception of an education of value
for human development and democratic citizenship. (Bryk *et al.*, 1993,
pp. 23–4)

Coleman, Hoffer and Kilgore (1982) earlier found similar evidence that Catholic schools do better for these inner-city children from poor, minority homes because the schools offer high 'social capital' in their being embedded in consensual, supportive, and caring communities (i.e., the parish and neighbourhood).

This sociological analysis was bolstered by the socio-political findings of Chubb and Moe (1990) who, using the same data set (*High School and Beyond*), determined that complex democratic demands from diverse constituencies put such overpowering political pressure on school systems that large school district bureaucracies emerged which tended to over-regulate and over-control urban public schools. And Bryk *et al.* (1993), using organizational analysis, confirmed Coleman, Kilgore and Hoffer, and Chubb and Moe's conclusions: that Catholic schools are freer, leaner, smaller, and more focused, leading to better attainment by students. Hence, sociological, political, and organizational analyses all point to the same conclusion: Catholic schools work.

Yet, rather than being hailed as paradigms, if not paragons of the best practices of American schooling — strong values, clear mission, strong commitment, narrow but academically demanding curriculum, less tracking and separation, and high expectations for all —, the USA has systematically isolated, denigrated, and ignored its inner-city parochial schools, watching them merge, close, and diminish to the breaking point where some leaders wonder whether these schools will survive at all. While the public schools receive between $5,000 and $9,000 per pupil in the larger cities, the parish schools can only charge $1,200 to $1,800 per student and try to raise the remaining money (about $1,000 per student) from church donations, private contributions, and a profusion of fund-raising projects.

Catholic School Decline in the US

The 1980s saw the continued slow decline by attrition of many inner-city parochial schools, not withstanding their importance to the poor. Even though James S. Coleman and colleagues discovered parochial schools high in 'social capital' and more effective in helping the impoverished in comparison to many urban public high schools, Catholic schools were themselves low in financial capital — and mergers and/or closings were common.

Catholic schools increased in number and size steadily, sometimes dramatically, between 1880 and the mid-1960s and have declined more or less ever since. The peak year was 1964, with some 5.66 million students enrolled in over 13,000 Roman Catholic schools nationwide. The 1980s saw a 20 per cent drop in enrolments and a 8.8 per cent dip in numbers of schools. Research shows that a large number of the school closings were in cities, often of schools serving low-income, minority pupils. But even middle-income schools were hit hard in the last few decades, as the costs of Catholic education rose and competition from public schools increased.

Between 1965 and 1980, for example, the total private school enrolment went from 6.369 million to 4.876 million students, a dip of 23 per cent. The Catholics, meanwhile, declined by 43 per cent during this period while other types of private school student grew from 0.795 million to 1.769 million students, or a jump of 123 per cent. Then, between 1980 and 1989, data shows a somewhat different pattern, with Catholic school enrolment declining by 18 per cent (from about 3.1 million to 2.5 million), while non-Catholic private school pupil populations grew by 57 per cent (from 1.770 to 2.780 million in nine years), bringing up the total enrolments in private schools nationally from 4.875 million in 1980 to 5.34 million in 1989 or plus 9 per cent in nine years.

Finally, there has been a total drop in private school pupils between 1965 and 1989. Again, Catholic schools have declined most: by 54 per cent, from 5.574 million to 2.551 million pupils in twenty-four years. Meanwhile, schools sponsored by other groups (e.g., Lutheran, Jewish, Quaker, Seventh-day Adventists, Greek Orthodox, and 'independent') have increased during this same period, from 0.795 million to over 2.55 million: a rise of 221 per cent. Because of the Catholic school decline, the overall number of children in the United States attending all kinds of non-public schools dipped from 6.369 million in 1965 to around 5.312 million in 1989: a reduction of 17 per cent.

One may draw several conclusions from these data. First, one can assume that the growth in non-Catholic schools (+57 per cent), typically more expensive and more middle-class, indicates continued concern about the public system. Parents with resources were availing themselves of the 'choice' which the affluent have long had: to select a private school in communities where public schools are in trouble because of strikes, racial problems, declining quality and test scores, violence, or other factors.

Second, as the courts enforced bans on school prayer and religious practice in public schools, a growing number of families abandoned public education, establishing a vital, fast-growing 'Christian' school sector, or kept their children home for Christian 'home schooling', rather than risk, in their terms, endangering the souls of their youngsters in 'Godless' ('value-free') and 'secular humanist' public schools.

Third, private (usually Catholic) schools which attend mainly to poor students found the 1980s a difficult period, with steady declines every year of around 2 to 3 per cent. Such small, consistent drops probably reflect an attempt on the part of bishops, pastors, and other Catholic leaders to minimize the damage of school closings by careful planning and, where possible, the merger of two (or even three) costly schools into one that is more viable.

Public Funding and US Catholic Schools: Recent Developments

The major reason most often given for not aiding parochial schools from public funds is a legal one. Direct grants in aid are probably not constitutional under the ban against the Government 'establishing' religion. But aid to children and their families is legal, as the Mueller decision determined. As long as the 'Church' (schools) and the 'State' (education departments) are not directly entangled, then the justices seem to think that subsidies through the family as consumer are legal.

Government policy in the United States has systematically isolated religious schools, even from broad-based federal programmes for the poor, such as 'Chapter 1'. Between 1965 and 1985, a modest amount of federal money was used to hire public school teachers to give remedial help to poor, underachieving students in private and parochial schools. No money was given to religious schools directly, as part of the political deal cut between President Lyndon B. Johnson and the Catholic bishops. Instead, additional federal money went to local public school authorities to buy additional books and equipment to be 'loaned' to parochial schools with poor students, and to hire additional public school teachers who visited the parochial schools to teach underachieving students there.

However, in 1985, the case of *Aguilar v. Felton* pressed by 'civil liberties', public school, and anti-Catholic groups was successful in removing from the premises of private schools all public school personnel hired to provide remedial services there. Rather elaborate and ridiculous arrangements were made to transport children to 'neutral' or public school sites, or expensive mobile vans were driven to the private schools to house remedial classes.

Even small attempts to give grants-in-aid to poor families to buy this guaranteed federal remedial help were trounced by Congress, which was influenced by unified lobbying by teachers unions, school administrators, civil liberties, and other liberal-Democratic groups. These groups would rather waste millions of dollars transporting children or educating them in expensive vans than give a few dollars to families of students in private schools for these critical catch-up reading, writing, and math services. When Chapter 1 came up for re-authorization in 1988, the Republicans proposed a number of local option vouchers (LOVs) which would have allowed the passing of resources directly to parents in parochial schools if the District could not reasonably and economically provide federally supported services to students in religious schools.

Two rather modest and sensible bills were introduced to extend federally guaranteed services to poor and underachieving children attending parochial schools: one called CHOICE (Children's Option for Compensatory Education Act of 1986) and the other, AEA (American Excellence Act of 1987). The United States Congress roundly rejected these rather limited aid bills which might have benefited the needy children much more than the Catholic schools. The CHOICE bill had several unique features to overcome the legal and political resistance to public aid to children in parochial schools. As Cooper (1988) explained about the abortive bill, 'If a locality cannot serve private school students well, it can use "the issuance of educational vouchers" (Section 555.a) for poor, underachieving school children' (p. 177). The two potential laws went far to accommodate the concerns of anti-parochial school aid factions — but not far enough.

First, the legislation would have been aimed at the poorest and least achieving students — a kind of focused categorical aid. These schools might have sought 'general' direct aid, though this would surely have been stricken down by the courts as helping to Establish religion.

Second, the legislation puts aid to parochial schools in the form of a voucher or euphemistically a 'compensatory Education certificate' (CEC), a means for helping children not schools. This removed the Government from dealing directly with the religious schools. Third, both bills allowed the authorities to determine whether poor, private school children should receive a voucher or CEC.

Fourth, if state constitutions for any reason prohibits publicly funded vouchers for students to attend religiously affiliated schools, then the proposed law provided a 'bypass' provision by which funds can be set from the federal Government to the Catholic schools, circumventing the State and local authorities.

These laws, like most others in the United States, would have narrowly directed small amounts of money to particularly needy children, to teach them basic skills. Since this money was already ear-marked for parochial school pupils anyway, why would the Democratic Party and others resist these bills and others so actively? The answer is political: the public school system, jealous of 'its money', guards against any funds going to any children, no matter how poor and under-performing, simply and only because these pupils exercise their constitutionally supported right to practise their religion.

Thus, the First Amendment, designed to further citizens religious rights, was actually twisted to prevent public money from reaching children for guaranteed secular services.

America's Catholic schools did not benefit from the interest in 'privatization' of education in the 1980s. As we have seen, direct attempts to help poor children in Catholic schools were foiled by the public school lobby (e.g., the National Educational Association (NEA) and the American Federation of Teachers (AFT)) and the Democratic Party, all of which resisted attempts to 'privatize' public funding for private education in the US. Although many reformers at the federal level seemed to worship the special qualities of private schools in theory, they were unable to help these schools in practice.

Several states, however, including Minnesota and Wisconsin, made some modest efforts to aid non-public schools. For example, Minnesota passed the most extensive school choice plan in the nation: parents could transfer out of district, select regional magnet schools, and apply for state tax breaks for using private schools. And in Wisconsin, some 400 Milwaukee children were funded to attend private, non-sectarian schools under a state law pressed by state representative Polly Williams, a black Democrat. Even this very modest effort, however, has run into a few snags.

First, the enabling law for this Wisconsin experiment was attached inappropriately to a general state appropriations law, an illegal act in the state. Second, one of the participating private schools in Milwaukee has already asked to be released from the plan, since it wishes to affiliate with a religious group. Despite these minor glitches, however, these experiments hold promise, as we shall suggest below.

Public Funding for US Catholic Schools: Prospects for the Future

It seems the smaller the enrolment in Catholic schools, the greater their threat to the monopolistic public schools. The enigma is how to aid Catholic schools without (1) raising the wall of legal separation between religion and the State, (2) endangering the independence of private schools under state support, and (3) inciting the anti-private, anti-Catholic forces which lobby viciously against any aid to private schools. No one since President Lyndon B. Johnson (1963–8) has been able to build the necessary coalition between private and public school constituencies, liberal and more conservative groups, to get the direct aid passed.

One of the most interesting recent developments has been the suggestion by John Coons and colleagues that black students be permitted to attend parochial schools under a federal, court-ordered desegregation order (a response to the *Jenkins v. State of Missouri* court decision declaring the schools to be racially segregated) which created a massive 'magnet school' choice plan in Kansas City, Missouri. Since real racial balance is difficult or impossible to attain within this city (given that the public school population is 80 per cent African-American and Latino), Coons and others filed a brief in federal court to permit black parents and their children to choose among local, integrated parochial schools, a position not well received by the federal judge Clark.

Most black parents in Kansas City, Missouri, had found it difficult to exercise choice since so few white pupils were available to desegregate the city's schools; hence, white applicants could go to any public school of choice while Blacks had to wait for the right racial balance (i.e., for more Whites to apply). Hence, Coons and colleagues questioned this situation and the following conditions:

- making black children wait for places dependent on white enrolments;
- denying minority students their first choice;
- bussing them into white suburbs; or
- moving them across town to find white pupils for an 'integrated education'.

They asked of the judge: Why not take advantage of the high-quality, integrated, private schools that were available right in the community, that are willing to take poor black children, and can educate them for half the cost of the public system? Their plan has been rejected thus far, however, since public systems — afraid to lose their students — have exerted considerable influence

— to block it. Nevertheless, the debate about this plan suggests that parochial schools may have promise as a way of helping inner-city public schools, furthering racial and social integration (desegregation), and expanding choice for the nation's poorest, most deprived children.

Another promising tactic might be to make Catholic schools publicly 'public'. Chemerinsky (1989), points a direction for giving private schools a major role in seeking a just, moral, and literate society. As major contributors to the public good, they are indeed 'public' in the best sense (see Bryk *et al.*, 1993).

The Case for Public Funding

The strongest argument for federal, state, and local aid for Catholic schools is the 'public one', that these schools are fulfilling several critical 'public functions' all at once: offering help to those least successful in school, at very low cost, and without much recognition (and some scorn). Catholic schools possess a combination of successful characteristics and qualities that sometimes draw attacks from the public schools establishment (especially when tax money is involved):

New by Being Old

Catholic schools stand by old values and thus become highly 'modern' in a society where children need structure, direction, and responsibility. In a society often distracted by the fear of offending someone's (anyone's) values, Catholic schools stick by their beliefs. As educators in the public schools struggle with moral and ethical issues — trying to solve social and personal problems without appearing to take a moral stand — Catholic schools start off with their beliefs, and the rest follows. At times when home, community, and church were intact, the school could afford to be 'value neutral', if not bland, and it worked. Now, with the home in decline (65 per cent of children born in the nation's largest cities are born to young mothers and into homes without fathers), these 'kids of kids' find themselves raised by grandparents or by mothers too young to provide good homes. Some would argue that schools take on this familial role.

Challenging by Being Modest

Catholic schools are attacked any time they ask for help from government, whether at the national, state, or local level. Even when Catholic schools in Kansas City offered to take poor and minority children — left out of the public school's magnet school admissions procedure — the judge refused for fear of crossing the imaginary line between 'Church' and 'State'. Catholic and other non-public schools are rarely recognized for the jobs they do: educating millions of students at no real cost to the public. The nature of the attacks would lead one to assume that the fewer Catholic schools exist, the more the public school interests attack choice and private education.

Effective by Being Simple

Catholic schools have been found effective as models of high 'social capital' (strong community support centred in the parish structure) and as places where 'autonomy' seems to work as compared to the bureaucratic public system. Their simplicity is both organizational and curricular. Catholic schools have a one-track curriculum: all students take algebra, compared to only 60 per cent in public schools, mainly because the Catholic schools cannot afford to offer 'streams' of courses (remedial math, general math, consumer math, or business math) as many larger, richer public schools do. Research has found that the clearest determinant of students continuing on to further and higher education was whether pupils had access to algebra (and thus to physics and chemistry, higher mathematics, such as geometry, trigonometry, and calculus). Catholic schools might have offered all these 'levels' of math and science if these schools had the money. But offering one type of math is all these schools can afford. And it seems to work: better to have students to struggle through algebra than to 'breeze through' watered-down math for years and be cut out of advanced academic work.

Endangered by Being Dedicated

Catholic schools run the risk of going out of business in many cities because they refuse to abandon the difficult task of educating poor, minority students; these schools refuse to move to the suburbs where the job is easier and the clients are wealthier.

When we add up all the accomplishments and problems facing Catholic schools in the United States, a number of ironies, painful and poignant emerge:

- In one of the western world's most religious nations, public help to religious schools is limited and even forbidden in some locations.
- Catholic schools are successful because they are unashamedly religious and moral; qualities which disqualify them from receiving public help.
- In schools that work for the poorest and toughest students better than many public schools, the public system would rather fail these students than hand them over to Catholic schools (through voluntary subsidies and transfers).

- Public school choice schemes are endangering Catholic schools which cannot easily compete with these new tuition-free public 'schools of choice' or public Magnet Schools.

Thus, models of choice are losing out because the public system is using the 'private' approaches of recruitment, meeting client needs, specializing, and operating in a semi-autonomous manner. The more 'private' the public schools become, the more they lure students away from the other, real 'private' and parochial schools.

England and Wales, meanwhile, presents an interesting contrast to the United States. Roman Catholic and other religious schools have taken their rightful place in the national educational service system and participate in the national educational effort as full partners. Catholic schools must compete within the public system but do so as full co-equals, not as second class participants defined 'out' of the public debate.

The Future

American Catholic schools do not have to be isolated and forlorn. The American Catholic bishops (see National Catholic Welfare Conference, 1961) defined the role and rights of religious schools in the nation through principles still relevant in the USA today:

1 Education in church-related schools is a public function which, by its nature, is deserving of governmental support.
2 There exists no constitutional bar to education in church-related schools in a degree proportionate to the value of the public function it performs.
3 The parent and child have a constitutional right to choose a church-related educational institution meeting reasonable state requirements . . .
4 Government in the United States is without power to impose upon the people a single educational system in which all must participate. (ibid., p. 437).

The way ahead seems clear in Britain: religious schools will continue to play an essential role in the education of children within the publicly funded system. In fact, new kinds of religious schools are seeking to join that system, including those sponsored by the growing Islamic community. In time, the Government will take these schools into the fold, awarding them full funding for operations and a percentage of the construction costs.

The way is not so clear in the United States. A range of plans have been tried, from tax breaks to grants and scholarships (vouchers), from charter schools to 'baby' Basic Educational Opportunity Grants (BEOGs) as proposed by (New York-Democrat) Senator Daniel Patrick Moynihan as a means of granting poor children a scholarship to religious elementary and high schools, much as the Government supports attendance at church-related colleges and universities.

Nations have many education problems and limited resources. To squander away an economical, effective, and available category of school, is at best foolish and at worst perverse. The United States for mainly political reasons is refusing to aid religiously affiliated schools and thus endangering the effective urban Roman Catholic school. These schools seem to work for children who need good education the most: the poor, the African-American and the Hispanic students, for whom traditional public schooling has often failed. Catholic schools seem to have the right balance of caring and kindness, mixed with structure, rules, rigor, and fixed values and norms.

Some school reformers believe that a loose, 'progressive' atmosphere is best for these students. But for children from fractured homes and violent neighbourhoods, the comfort of attending a school where 'you know where you stand' is critical. Their small size, strict rules, tight and focused curriculum, and most important, their safety make the urban Catholic school an ideal place for poor children (see Bryk *et al.*, 1993; Coleman and Hoffer, 1987).

The Catholic Church has made a commitment to work in, and support, poor neighbourhoods with their schools, even when many Catholic parishioners have moved away and remaining resources are tight. Since the poor cannot pay sufficient tuition to offset the costs and make few major financial gifts, these parish schools have struggled to keep tuition affordable, buildings open, enrolments up, and costs down. But increasingly, these schools are closing or merging, endangering schools that work best.

The United States, in comparison to Britain, has defined most private and parochial schools 'out' of the problem and thus out of the 'solutions' to the woes of urban education, refusing to subsidize their work. Public opinion leaders continue to define the mission of parochial schools as private, even when Catholic schools fulfil the clearly 'public' function of successfully educating the urban poor. Without some way of helping low-income families to afford a Catholic education, if they want one, the Catholic schools will face more closings and the inner-city family will have fewer choices and options.

The issue here is a moral one. Great Britain has embraced the religious school as a vital component of its national education service — supporting them fully and well. The United States has turned itself inside out to exclude private, religious schools from its 'system'. The losses to society, children, and education, resulting from this split ('wall of separation') between private schools and the public good, are best illustrated, as we have seen in this analysis, in the losses to the education of America's growing ethnic, urban, underclass.

State (public) schools seem to have failed to educate the urban poor: the drop-out rate is often over half; violence is high and rising; poor performance continues; and the costs have doubled in just ten years to no avail. Catholic schools, where they survive, have a strong record: 95 per cent of New York

City's Catholic high school students graduate and 85 per cent go on to college and university, most on scholarships. These Catholic schools are orderly, focused, inexpensive, and effective, becoming as Bryk *et al.*, explain, the New Public Schools (see also Coons, 1981, pp. 91–106). But how long will they survive? If the closings and mergers continue, we may enter the twenty-first century with few or no parochial schools in our inner-cities, and families there will have less choice, voice, and opportunity, and no viable competition for state schools (leading to even poorer performance in public education).

We must save our Catholic schools, and like the British, find a useful place for them within the 'maintained' sector. No other 'models' of education work so well — for public schools have greater problems trying to be avowedly religious and moral, a key ingredient to ending the urban school crisis. Surely, in some states or at the national level, a voucher, tax break, grant-in-aid, or some other option will pass into law. But will it come in time to save beleaguered urban Catholic schools? We have faith that cities and their governments will recognize the common good value of religious-related schools and support them.

A former United States President did: 'Of all the dispositions and habits which lead to political prosperity, religion and morality are indispensable supports.' George Washington in his 'Farewell Address' continued to explain:

> In vain would that man claim the tribute of patriotism who should labor to subvert these great pillars of human happiness, these firmest props of the duties of men and citizens. . . . And let us with caution indulge the supposition that morality can be maintained without religion. Whatever may be conceded to the influence of refined education on minds of peculiar structure, reason and experience both forbid us to expect that national morality can prevail in exclusion of religious principle.

References

BUETOW, H. (1970) *Of Singular Benefit: The Story of US Catholic Education*, New York, Macmillan.

BRYK, A.S., LEE, V.E. and HOLLAND, P.B. (1993) *Catholic Schools and the Common Good*, Cambridge, MA, Harvard University Press.

CHEMERINSKY, E. (1989) 'The Constitution and the private school', in DEVINS, N.E. (Ed) *Public Values and Private Schools*, London, Falmer Press.

CHUBB, J.E. and MOE, T.M. (1990) *Politics, Markets, and America's Schools*, Washington, DC, The Brookings Institution.

CIBULKA, J.G. and BOYD, W.L. (1989) 'Introduction: Private schools and public policy', in CIBULKA, J.G. and BOYD, W.L. (Eds) *Private Schools and Public Policy: International Perspectives*, London, Falmer Press.

COLEMAN, J.S., HOFFER, T. and KILGORE, S. (1982) *High School Achievement: Public, Catholic, and Private Schools Compared*, New York, Basic Books.

COLEMAN, J.S. and HOFFER, T. (1987) *Public and Private High Schools: The Impact of Communities*, New York, Basic Books.

Coons, J.E. (1981) 'Making schools public', in Gaffney, E.M. Jr. (Ed) *Private Schools and the Public Good: Policy Alternatives for the Eighties*, Notre Dame, IN, The University of Notre Dame Press.

Coons, J.E., Clune, W. and Sugarman, S.D. (1970) *Private Wealth and Public Education*, Cambridge, MA, Harvard University Press.

Cooper, B.S. (1988) 'The uncertain future of national educational policy: Private schools and the federal role,' in Boyd, W.L. and Kerchner, C.T. (Eds) *The Politics of Excellence and Choice in Education*, London, Falmer Press.

Cooper, B.S. and Dondero, G. (1991) 'Survival, change, and demands on America's private schools: Trends and policies,' *Educational Foundations*, **5**, 1, Winter, pp. 51–74.

Cooper, B.S. and Doyle, D.P. (1985) 'Nonpublic schools, worldwide', in the *International Encyclopedia of Education*, 1st ed., London, Pergamon Press.

Doyle, D.P. and Cooper, B.S. (Eds) (1989) *Federal Aid to the Disadvantaged: What Future?*, New York, Falmer Press.

Greeley, A.M. (1981) 'Catholic high schools and minority students,' in Gaffney, E.M. Jr. (Ed) *Private Schools and the Public Good: Policy Alternatives for the Eighties*, Notre Dame, IN, University of Notre Dame Press.

Estelle, J. (1987) 'The public/private division of responsibility for education: An international comparison', *Economics of Education Review*, **6**, pp. 1–14.

Estelle, J. (1989) 'Public and private education in an international perspective,' in Boyd, W.L. and Cibulka, J.G. (Eds) *Private Schools and Public Policy: International Perspectives*, London, Falmer Press.

Kozol, J. (1991) *Savage Inequalities: Children in America's Schools*, New York, Crown Publishing.

Lannie, V.P. (1968) *Public Money and Parochial Education: Bishop Hughes, Governor Seward, and the New York School Controversy*, Cleveland, The Press of Case Western Reserve University.

Lee, J.M. (Ed) (1967) *Catholic Education in the Western World*, Notre Dame, IN, University of Notre Dame Press.

Levy, D. (Ed) (1986) *Private Education: Studies in Choice and Public Policy*, New York, Oxford University Press.

National Catholic Welfare Conference, Legal Department (1961) 'The constitutionality of the inclusion of Church-related schools in federal aid to education,' *The Georgetown Law Journal*, **50**, 2, Winter, pp. 421–39.

Sherman, J.D. (1983) 'Public finance of private schools: Observations from abroad,' in James, T. and Levin, H.M. (Eds) *Public Dollars for Private Schools: The Case of Tuition Tax Credits*, Philadelphia, Temple University Press.

Vitullo-Martin, T. and Cooper, B.S. (1989) *The Separation of Church and Child: The Constitution and Federal Aid to Religious Schools*, Indianapolis, The Hudson Institute.

Wells, A.S. and Biegel, S. (1993) 'Public funds for private schools: Political and first amendment considerations,' *American Journal of Education*, May.

Willms, J.D. (1985) 'Catholic school effects on academic achievement: New evidence from the high school and beyond study,' *Sociology of Education Review*, **58**, pp. 98–114.

Chapter 4

Markets, Education and Catholic Schools

Richard Pring

Introduction

The British Government's 1992 White Paper, 'Choice and Diversity' (Department for Education, 1992), provides a framework for the future of the educational system. It claims to be a radical departure from earlier arrangements in important respects, and indeed it is. Behind these proposals is a set of ideas which together could be said to constitute a coherent philosophy of education. I believe this philosophy to be mistaken. I believe, too, that it is not compatible with those understandings which are basic to a distinctive Catholic idea of the purpose and nature of schools.

Philosophy might seem a generous description of what is said in that White Paper, but I use it in the sense of Chesterton, quoted by Haldane in this volume:

> Every education teaches a philosophy; if not by dogma then by suggestion, by implication, by atmosphere. Every part of that education has a connection with every other part. If it does not all combine to continue to convey some general view of life it is not education at all. (p. 126)

'Choice and Diversity' does represent a coherent set of ideas, characterized by the use of key words that have their own distinctive and interconnected logic; and these ideas do, 'by suggestion, by implication, by atmosphere' embody an idea of human motivation and human nature, of the common good, of the relation of the individual to society and of the purpose of education in promoting both individual welfare and the common good.

I believe that these ideas are mistaken — mistaken in the sense that the underlying notion of the 'common good' is indefensible within the social and ethical philosophy that should underpin Catholic education. If what I say is true, then we have cause for worry about the steps that some Catholic schools are taking.

I shall, therefore, in this chapter do the following:

1 make explicit the ideas represented by 'Choice and Diversity';
2 pick out the dominant aspects of these, namely, the concept of market and of the connected sense of the common good;
3 examine critically the adequacy of that language, and of those ideas, for describing education and its organization; and
4 indicate how these considerations affect our understanding of a distinctively Catholic education.

Choice and Diversity

The White Paper set out a new framework for schools — no mere tinkering with the present arrangements, no focus on specific parts of the system only, but a utopian plan which would transform a system of education that is thought to be fundamentally flawed.

The key interconnected ideas which give form or structure to the framework are five: quality, diversity, choice, school autonomy and accountability.

- **Quality** refers to standards in learning. These standards are related to explicit 'performance indicators' by which they are measured and thereby ranked at different levels — hence, a National Curriculum with explicit attainment targets pitched at progressively more difficult levels. Quality, therefore, is identified with reaching preconceived outcomes which can be measured and made public. A system of 'quality control' (testing) and 'quality assurance' (inspecting) ensures that judgments of quality are available to a wider public for their use.
- **Diversity** refers to the range of provision arising from the freedom 'which all schools now have . . . to take decisions reflecting their own priorities and circumstances in a way that was not possible a few years ago under the bureaucratic rule of local government' (ibid., sec. 1.16).

  It is characterized by a system which contains, at the secondary level, Local Authority and Grant Maintained schools, City Technology Colleges, state supported and independent private schools, grammar and secondary modern schools, even a Burger King school, sixth form and further education colleges. All of these are supported from different modes and rates of public funding. In this way, quality is promoted by a range of provision to reflect different means by which that quality might be acquired — and, indeed, defined. Independent schools, not constrained by the National Curriculum and the national assessments, and City Technology Colleges, having a special relationship with the business world which sponsors them, are able to spell out different criteria of quality.
- **Choice** refers to the opportunities now provided by that diversity.

Remember that to choose rationally there have to be several things to choose from which roughly serve the same purpose, and those things have to be accurately labelled so that the choice is an informed one. The national assessments provide the labels, and the parents are supposed to do the choosing. 'Parents know best the needs of their children — certainly better than educational theorists or administrators, better than our mostly excellent teachers' (ibid., sec. 1.6).

The justification for the ability to choose is threefold. First, freedom to do what one thinks best or wants seems to be a *prima facie* good. Second, the customer knows best. Third, in so choosing, the receiver of the service keeps the providers on their toes — thereby enhancing the quality of provision.

- **Autonomy** refers to the status of the providers of the service. They, the schools, should be responsible for providing the service, where 'responsible' entails deserving of blame when the quality of service is poor. The autonomous institution cannot pass the buck to someone else — the politicians and bureaucrats, competing schools or external circumstances. Autonomy entails moral responsibility. And there are no others one can rely upon to help one out of a mess. One lives or dies by one's own decisions.

- **Accountability** refers to two things: the obligation of the school to give an account of what it has done, so that the recipient of the service might exercise choice more freely, and openness of the school to be evaluated on the basis of that account. Hence, schools are now obliged to publish details of their curriculum, attendance, truancy and test scores.

These key ideas hang together in a coherent 'philosophy' of how schools should be run and how they should relate to those who make use of them, namely, the children, or the parents on behalf of the children. Schools are providers of a service, which is both public and private. It is public insofar as everyone is obliged by law to make use of it. But it is essentially private in that it is concerned with improving the prospects and personal well-being of each pupil. And the individuals themselves or their parents are in the most privileged position to judge that. I am the one who can best judge what is good for me — not the professional, not the administrator. Hence, the schools in effect relate to individuals, all seeking their own good out of the service. Each individual, as recipient of the service, is 'in the driving seat', in contrast with the previous arrangement whereby the local authority determined where one should go and the teacher, as the professional in charge, determined what one should do when one got there.

However, if the recipients of a service (which is for their personal good) are to be 'in the driving seat', they need to know about the details of that service and whether it is successful; they need to be able to hold the school to account for when it fails to live up to expectations and to 'exit' from the school if they are not satisfied. To hold the school to account requires accurate and objective information — one cannot otherwise make rational decisions about the well being of one's children. And to exit from the school where one is dissatisfied requires diversity of provision — one must have something different to go to. The weight then is put on individual choice and on the provisions necessary for that choice to be a rational and realistic one.

In such a system of autonomous providers, each of which is to serve the personal needs of the recipients, regulations are required to ensure that the recipient gets a fair deal. And indeed that is the Government's main job. It sets the framework within which schools can act autonomously. It ensures that the recipients of the service get the information necessary for making rational choices. It promotes the conditions, namely, diversity of provision, which make choice possible and which enables the recipient to register a protest if dissatisfied. That then is the role of the Government — maximizing individual choice and providing the framework for it.

Of course, the Government has not been entirely consistent with its philosophy because, in providing a very detailed framework, it has curtailed choice. It has said to parents that their choice must include the attainment targets of the National Curriculum — although it is possible for them to avoid that if they go private (and the Government makes that possible by subsidizing the private sector through the Assisted Places Scheme).

Individualism, choice, subservience of the providers to the purchaser, the Government as the regulator of the process to ensure maximum choice and a fair operation of it, the common good arising out of the aggregate of individual choices within a framework set by a benign government — that is the 'philosophy' enshrined within the White Paper. It not only affects practice through the regulations which have arisen from it; it affects how we think about practice through the ideas which it embodies.

Concept of the Market and of the Common Good

There has been much criticism of the Government's policy on the grounds that it is dominated by the metaphor of the 'market'. The market is said to depict the relations between teacher and learner in a particular way — namely, as a relation between provider and consumer — which is inappropriate. It represents a shift in language about education, and about the relation between teacher and learner within education, which seems to distort that relationship and misdescribe the educational process.

I want, therefore, in this section to explore how far the market is an accurate way of describing the new relations which I have described and which the Government is promoting.

First, it is argued that the market is a useful metaphor because it reflects a set of relationships which have not always prevailed in education but which might and should prevail if educational goals are to be realized. Thus the school, and the teachers in that school, provide a service to a set of individuals.

As with any service, the recipients are the best judges of whether that service meets their needs or wants. There is always the chance that the service might be sloppy or off target. There is a need, therefore, to provide a way in which the recipients can demonstrate dissatisfaction, mainly by taking their custom elsewhere. The argument, underlying the Educational Reform Act of 1988 and the White Paper, is that in the past the recipients of the educational service have not had the opportunity to protest in the most appropriate manner, unless they were rich enough to pay for private education. The learners got what they were given — the teachers and their employers were 'in the driving seat'. The same could be extended to Church schools. In a fairly authoritarian Church the recipients were not allowed to patronize the non-Catholic alternatives. Under the new arrangements that has changed. The recipients can object through availing themselves of the new opportunities provided by open enrolment and Grant Maintained schools. The providers must meet the wishes of the clients, otherwise they will lose the income necessary to stay open. 'Market' is contrasted with top–down planning; it represents consumer power as against bureaucratic power.

Second, the metaphor of the market emphasizes the importance of choice and the conditions for the exercise of rational choice. Imagine the archetypal market, a set of fruit and vegetable stalls. The customer is able to examine the different fruits, their quality and their prices. They can decide whether they want several cheap apples or one excellent one — or, indeed, given the prices, whether to buy oranges instead. Prices are kept down because otherwise the customer will purchase elsewhere; but quality is kept up because otherwise the customer will not purchase at all. Fashions change for all sorts of reasons; the interest in bananas gives way to the interest in kiwi. Thus, since the customer knows best, the merchant has to be sensitive to changes in taste and fashion. Choice requires different items to choose from, but, to be rational in choice, the chooser needs basic information about those items: the cost and the quality.

Third, 'the market' assumes the importance of competition in obtaining maximum benefit. Thus, in order to sell the product to the choosy purchaser, providers will strive to out-do the other providers in establishing lower prices or higher quality products. Furthermore, given the 'positional good' granted by a good education (by that I mean the credits obtained by education which can be swapped for good jobs and social position), then the recipient will compete with other potential recipients for the limited number of high quality products. In the fruit market they come early in the morning; in education they study harder or pay higher fees for attendance at the most prestigious schools or universities.

Fourth, the 'perfect market' assumes that people will look after their own self-interest, indeed pursue their own self interest. If they choose not to go to the market in time to get the best fruit, then that is because they prefer to stay in bed. Early rising is a price not worth paying. Students similarly may choose immediate pleasure to the postponement of pleasure necessary for winning the educational competition — that is their choice. The market enables them to take that kind of responsibility.

These then seem to be the characteristics of educational processes and the ideal educational framework picked out by the market metaphor. Education is a commodity which can be bought or sold like any other commodity. It is much in demand because of the 'positional good' it can purchase. Since people are motivated by pursuing their own interest, there will always be a demand for the commodity. Teachers are there simply to provide it and thus to provide a service that people, in the light of their understanding of their own interests, ask for. What is needed for people to be able to choose wisely or rationally is simply the right kind of information about the quality of the commodity and about the price one has to pay for it. The Government's responsibility is mainly to ensure the proper framework for these market forces to operate fairly, namely:

- schools, so that no one will be prevented from receiving an education;
- choice of schools, so that people can act on their judgment about the relative values of the services provided; and
- accurate information about the schools, so that, in the light of their values and desires, parents or students can be rational in their choices.

Furthermore, beneath this way of conceiving the relationship between teacher and learner are certain assumptions of a philosophical kind about society and the nature of individuals within that society, about what is worthwhile and how we decide what is of most worth, about expert knowledge and access to that knowledge, about the processes of learning and how those processes might be evaluated. Thus, the world is the aggregate of individuals who are motivated chiefly by the pursuit of their own self-interest. Only they, in the final analysis, know what is good for them — there are no experts in educational ends. But, in the light of that self-knowledge, each individual needs accurate information about the public services which lead to that personal fulfilment. Such knowledge relates to quality of the service and to its cost, both of which can be objectively measured and clearly stated. Does it provide a product at a cost or sacrifice that makes it worthwhile? The teachers simply provide those services; their knowledge is essentially technical, an expertise in delivering the means not in determining the ends to be served. The common good is essentially the aggregate of the individual goods, and is achieved by everyone pursuing his own self-interest. Not all can succeed as well as the others. But in trying to beat the others, all will gain more of what is wanted.

Critique of 'the Market Philosophy'

There are three criticisms I want to make of the 'market' as a suitable metaphor for the educational system or of educational relationships, although it is important also to bear in mind the weaknesses of the educational system to which the introduction of the market metaphor has served to draw our attention. Educational discourse is necessarily permeated with metaphor. But the problem with any metaphor is that, whilst being appropriate to the situation in some respects, it none the less distorts it in others. In this case there is more distortion than appropriateness.

On the other hand, we must be careful in what we mean by saying that it distorts. That could mean that it simply does not fit things as they really are. Or it could mean that it does not fit things as ideally as they should be. Things, as they are, change under the influence of the metaphors used, and thus what once was an inappropriate description becomes increasingly an appropriate one. Language changes how we perceive reality and to that extent reality changes. That sadly is what is happening and the reality of, and relationships within, schools increasingly change to fit the language borrowed from what once were very different worlds — of business, of commerce, of material exchange.

Decrease in the Benefits for All

An assumption behind creating market conditions for the distribution of educational opportunities is, not that it is worthwhile in itself, but that it is the most suitable mechanism for delivering an improved distribution of education for everyone. There are links here to the *laissez-faire* economic theory which argues that if everyone seeks to maximize his or her wealth, everyone will benefit because of the trickle down effect — richer people demand more services or have to invest their money. Similarly, the selfish pursuit of one's own positional good by some will benefit everyone insofar as the schools will improve their performance for everyone to attract an increasing number of potential purchasers. The total is more than the sum of the parts.

There is a limited justification for saying this. Thus, in the absence of certain market features, namely, a range of provision from which parents might choose, the dissatisfied parent cannot demonstrate dissatisfaction in the most significant way — namely, by removing the child and sending him or her elsewhere. Schools should be responsive to parental concerns and there is a danger of bureaucratic planning which simply gets it wrong. Thus, talk about the market is often a reaction to insensitive top–down planning and the assertion that parents should be partners in the education of their children — with a penalty clause attached to those schools that resist this.

Nonetheless, the market is severely limited as a model for 'delivering' education even within a social context in which all individually seek the best positional good for their own children and in which schools, now acting autonomously within this market economy of schooling, seek their best advantage *vis-à-vis* the other schools. Separate parents seeking the optimal positional good for their respective children will seek a system of schooling which puts them at an advantage over other children — let us say, a selective system in which the majority is sure to fail. The child of parent A (in, say, going to the selective grammar school) will gain more than if the children of the two families remain together (in, say, the non-selective comprehensive) but the child of parents B may lose disproportionately, losing interest and self-confidence and possibly turning in his or her disappointment to crime. A's improved positional good might be more than overshadowed by a decrease in overall good of A and B put together, which indirectly will then affect A (more money has to be spent on crime prevention, for example). Thus, in opting out of LEA control, certain schools gain financially but others lose out and the overall good amongst the schools is less. Indeed, this is empirically the case. Opted out schools are now in a position to select parents, and thus exclude those who normally would have gone to that school. The pursuit of positional good by one leads to the denial of positional good to others, and the schools, having to respond to the individual's pursuit of positional good, is not able to assess what the overall good is for all potential participants. In other words, cooperation might lead to the greatest good of the greatest number, but the pursuit of the individual good in a competitive system will likely lead to a position which benefits some without reference to the effect on others — and thus to a deteriorated situation from the point of view of both the loser and the dispassionate bystander. These considerations are clearly relevant to a society which is increasingly divided between the materially successful and the failures who, in their aliena-tion and disillusionment, threaten that material success. Surely, the fact that the prison service is the fastest growing industry in Britain is evidence, though by no means proof, that the pursuit of individual positional good without reference to the wider social effect does not necessarily lead to the greatest aggregate of benefits and furthermore creates the conditions in which the beneficiaries themselves are threatened.

This is exacerbated by the problem of what is referred to as the 'prisoner's dilemma' (Jonathan, 1990). Thus two prisoners, A and B, are kept separately in prison, convicted of a minor crime but suspected of a major one. Each has been sentenced to two years in respect of the minor crime. If convicted of the major crime as a result of their owning up, they both will get six years. If, however, one is convicted of the major crime as a result of the other's confes-sion, then he will get ten years, but the other, by telling, will be let off lightly — one year only. Hence the choice for prisoner A is: Should he confess or not? If neither confesses, then both will get only two years — the maximum good as far as the two are concerned. If A confesses and B does not, then A gets only one year but B gets ten — good for A but disastrous for B and, overall, much less satisfactory than the first situation. If both confess, then both get six years — better for A than when, in not confessing, he is caught through the confessions of B. What should A do in seeking his best interest whilst being prevented from cooperation with B? Both the interests of each and the overall best position is for both to cooperate in not confessing. But in the absence of the framework for cooperation, the safest position is to confess, with the result that the best overall position is not attained.

Translate this analogy to the pursuit of school self interest through 'opting out' of the democratically accountable Local Educational Authorities which, through strategic planning, were able to provide a service according to the wider community interests and to the needs of the least well off. School A realizes that the best possible position is for everyone to remain within the Local Authority. However, school A realizes that if school B 'opts out' and school A does not, then school A will be worse off. Hence, school A 'opts out', putting itself as a result of certain financial incentives at an advantage over school B — better off than if school B had 'opted out' first, but in the long run worse off than if the two had remained together.

The analogy also explains why parents often reluctantly send their children to private schools. They are put in a position of competing individualism in which the way to defend the positional good of their own children is to subscribe to a system in which the overall social good from which they would otherwise benefit thereby deteriorates. No one can deny the social divisiveness of the system.

The point is that the market model of individuals all pursuing their own respective interests leads not to an improvement of the general good but only to an improvement of the positional good of some *vis-à-vis* other competitors and also to a deterioration of the overall situation, which could affect A detrimentally *vis-à-vis* the previous non-market situation.

Misconception of Education

A more fundamental criticism must be directed against the underlying concept of education, which is reflected in the use of language. Thus, to conceive of education as a commodity to be bought and sold, as a positional good which can be swapped for social and economic advantage, ignores what might be regarded as the intrinsic value which is attributed to the activities and to the processes which the word 'education' picks out. Education refers to those activities concerning the development of the mind — the capacity to think intelligently, to engage imaginatively with problems, to behave sensitively and with empathy towards other people. It is essentially concerned with the life of the mind, and thus with how each person learns to participate actively in the traditions of intellect, imagination and behaviour that we have inherited. A policy of educational provision would reflect what these different traditions are, what public forms of understanding we need to master to make sense of the world both physical and social, and what we need to do to enter into these forms of understanding — how best we might acquire them through learning.

Therefore, a more appropriate metaphor than 'the market' is that of Oakeshott (Oakeshott, 1989) who likens education to the initiation into the conversation which takes place between the generations of mankind in which the new generation hears and is introduced to the voice of poetry and of philosophy, of science and of history, of art and of religion. These are the voices through which we have come to understand what it means to be human — one might say the conversation, always continuing, through which that humanity has been defined.

The role of the teacher in such initiation is one of mediating particular stages of that conversation and to help the neophyte, as it were, get on the inside. To that extent the teacher is an authority, and education, at least at the beginning, is not a democratic affair. The philosophy of choice for those who are in a state of ignorance, and whose tastes remain unformed, is empty.

Distorted View of Human Nature and the Relation of the Individual to Society

Perhaps, however, the most important defect in the market metaphor and the underlying educational philosophy is the assumption they make about human nature and the relation of the individual to others and to the State. The kind of educational arrangements one makes and the content of that education presuppose a view, a theoretical position, about what makes people tick and what is worthwhile pursuing. Behind all education is an idea of human nature, and that idea can be, and often is, an impoverished one.

Education is, as Richard Peters argued (Peters, 1966), the initiation into worthwhile activities — into those kinds of knowing, understanding, appreciating, imagining and doing, which have value. For that reason, educational arguments are at root ethical ones, arguments about the life worth living, the personal qualities and virtues worth acquiring, the knowledge and understanding which will best serve the learner in seeking out what is valuable. But the answers to those searches and questions must lie in a view of what it is to be human. People with very different views about human nature will arrive at very different educational philosophies. For example, those who, within a particular religious tradition, are convinced that human nature is essentially corrupt, will not espouse the child-centred ideas of Froebel or Pestalozzi. Those who believe that people are but complicated machines will see no wrong in reprogramming them to function more effectively within the overall social system. Those who think that people act only from self-interest will welcome a market system which regulates that pursuit of self-interest. Those who argue that the intellect is a fixture we are born with, largely unaffected by learning, will no doubt want a system of education which differentiates between those who are intelligent and those who are not. And those who, sceptical of any objective arguments for deciding what is humanly desirable, will no doubt wish to leave questions of what is worthwhile to the customer or client, not to those who claim to be experts within an educational tradition.

Of course, our understanding of human nature changes as insights are gained through advances in science or developments in the arts or arguments in philosophy and in theology. But that does not mean that at any one time we can be freed from our commitment in practice, whether intelligently engaged in or not, to a philosophical position. Both the aims of education and the processes of teaching and learning, through which those aims are achieved, involve a set of ideas which can be articulated, criticized, improved or rejected. And, in so doing, one comes back to those ethical considerations which reflect what it means to be human.

Similarly at stake is the relation of the State and the wider community to individual improvement through education. If there is no such thing as society, only an aggregate of individuals, then the pursuit of positional good is more significant than the apprenticeship to the values and activities of one's wider community. Enterprise becomes an important virtue. Competition rather than cooperation provides the social and economic background to the formulation of educational aims and programmes. And the State becomes the regulator of the ensuing competitive activities.

Certainly, the application of the market metaphor to education does reflect a distinctive view of human nature and of how that individual human relates to the regulator of that market, the State. Taken to its logical conclusion, the source of what is worthwhile lies in the tastes of the consumers, not in the traditions of educational thinking which have evolved through the ages — the product of the conversations between the generations of mankind of which Oakeshott speaks. The authority of the teacher in matters concerning what is worth learning gives way to the authority of consumer choice or of those who, empowered by the State, are able to impose what they think should be taught. That search for meaning, that engagement in argument, that enjoyment of discovery, that struggle to gain insight, which characterize the transaction which takes place between teacher and learner, give way to the attainment of measurable outcomes and behaviours. The useful replaces the intrinsically worthwhile, performance indicators replace the judgment of educated persons. And the attempt to understand which is exercised by each of us in different ways, with different degrees of success and at different speeds, is scored high or low on a standardized measure which makes a mockery of that attempt. Indeed, those who have to struggle are no longer welcome — not selected by schools which now have the power to select or excluded by schools which want to make themselves attractive to the consumer, because these pupils will not perform well against the public indicators of success.

Conclusion: Catholic Education

It requires little argument to demonstrate that the Christian tradition, as that has been articulated through the Catholic Church, portrays a distinctive view of human nature and, therefore, of the qualities and values, knowledge and understanding that are worth acquiring. To that extent one would expect a distinctive philosophy of education and distinctive educational practices. Furthermore, that philosophy would define the proper relation between those responsible for that education and the State.

Negatively, it is difficult to see how that philosophy could be compatible with what is spelt out in 'Diversity and Choice'. As Bryk (Bryk *et al.*, 1993) so well argue:

> the control of Catholic school operations involves considerably more than market responsiveness to clients. Many important observations about these schools cannot be reconciled in these terms. Market forces cannot explain the broadly shared institutional purpose of advancing social equity or account for the efforts of Catholic educators to maintain inner-city schools (with large non-Catholic enrollments) whilst facing mounting fiscal woes. Likewise, market forces cannot easily explain why resources are allocated within schools in a contemporary fashion in order to provide an academic education for every student. Nor can they explain the norms of community that infuse daily life in these schools. (ibid., p. 300)

The qualities or virtues — of charity and humility, of caring for those less well endowed, of awe in the wonders of creation, of confidence in the human spirit, of the treatment of each person as of equal value — which are part and parcel of that Christian tradition, however much individual Christians may fail in them, are more than moral exhortations. They reflect a view of human persons, sinful but redeemed, humbled but with a sense of dignity, weak but with strength to persevere. The list of virtues associated with that distinctively Christian form of life do not include 'enterprise' and 'entrepreneurship' — which is not to say they are wrong, only that they have not the place in the quality of life worth living which many others would attribute to them.

Certainly the place of the intellect — its formation and its perfection — would have a prominent place, but the meaning of that might be somewhat different. First, certain voices — those of religion and of morality — would play a more prominent place in the conversation between the generations, helping the young learner to define what it is to be human. And, those voices would draw upon a theological tradition too often ignored. Second, the relation of intellectual formation to the quality of living, of theorizing to practising, of thinking to doing and to feeling would be central, because such a Christian philosophy of education would be for the formation of the whole person, not just the intellect.

Furthermore, the Christian school would look with suspicion upon the control of education by those who seek to impose learning objectives from outside. What authority have they, from outside the Christian account of what it means to be human, to define the quality of life worth living? And the school would reject the treatment of education as a commodity to be purchased for the purpose of obtaining some positional good. It simply is not that sort of thing.

Since each person is of equal value and equally deserving of recognition, then it is difficult to see how the Catholic school could reject people on grounds of inability, poverty, social background or ethnicity. Such attributes are irrelevant to the value of each person, and thus personal dignity should not depend upon them. Indeed, it is a central job of the school to generate that sense of personal worth on the basis of values which do not depend upon the contingencies of life here and now.

Finally, the relation of the individual to the community — the obligations of service that one owes to it, the respect for members of that community irrespective of personal faults, the recognition of the interdependence of each other within that community — would be an essential element in that Catholic philosophy.

These are but sketchy points with which to conclude. What is so surprising is that, despite the money and energy spent to build and to maintain Catholic schools, so little thought has been given to the philosophy of Catholic education. That is explicable possibly when the prevailing philosophy was not antagonistic towards the personal and social values represented by Catholic education. That, alas, is no longer the case as individualism replaces community, consumer demand determines what is of value, competition replaces cooperation, utility replaces the 'best that has been thought and said'. Diversity and choice are justified in terms of client satisfaction.

References

BRYK, A., LEE, V. and HOLLAND, P. (1993) *Catholic Schools and the Common Good*, Cambridge, Harvard University Press.

DEPARTMENT FOR EDUCATION (1992) *Diversity and Choice: A New Framework for Schools*, Cm. 2021, London, HMSO.

JONATHAN, R. (1990) 'State education service or prisoner's dilemma', *British Journal of Educational Studies*, **38**, 2.

OAKESHOTT, M. (1989) 'Education: Its Engagement and its Frustration', in FULLER, T. (Ed) *The Voice of Liberal Learning: Michael Oakeshott on Education*, New Haven and London, Yale University Press.

PETERS, R. (1966) *Ethics and Education*, London, George Allan and Unwin.

Chapter 5

Leadership in Catholic Schools

Gerald Grace

Catholic Schools in many societies are working in social, political and ideological conditions which challenge fundamentally their distinctive educational mission and their historical educational commitments. In these present contexts, a Catholic conception of education as primarily moral and spiritual, concerned with principled behaviour and focused upon community and public good outcomes faces a major challenge from New Right conceptions of education which are aggressively market orientated and individualistic in approach.

While some formulations of New Right ideology celebrate the importance of traditional spiritual and moral values in education, the advance of a competitive market culture in schooling, supported by other New Right agencies, is in many ways inimical to the development of such values. In other words, educational reform, wherever it is significantly influenced by New Right ideology is characterized by contradictions and Catholic education is caught up in these contradictions.

Leadership in Catholic education as represented by headteachers and school principals, governors, trustees and school board members and the Catholic hierarchy itself clearly has a strategic role to play in the maintenance of the distinctive character of Catholic education. It can be argued that such educational leaders have a responsibility to maintain and to reinvigorate Catholic culture in education as an alternative to the worst excesses of market culture in the wider educational system. There is a fundamental tension, in the realm of education at least, between Catholic values and market values. Catholic values in education insist upon the primacy of spiritual, moral and ethical understandings of the good life and of the good society. For Catholic education, academic achievement is not an end in itself but an enterprise serving a larger purpose. Catholic education cannot therefore operate as if pupils and students can be regarded as 'inputs' and educational achievements regarded as 'output'. It cannot accept the radical proposition of New Right agencies and ideologues that education is a commodity in the market place (see Grace, 1994), and therefore legitimately subject to the full impact of market forces.

In addition to changes arising from New Right ideological initiatives, Catholic schools in many settings face other major issues relating to changing

cultural and social mores, demographic movements and economic and financial constraints. In an examination of these challenges much more needs to be
known about the current mission and effectiveness of Catholic schools and the
ways in which Catholic school leadership is responding to the many dilemmas
which contemporary conditions generate.

What follows is an attempt to illuminate some of these issues, using existing research studies and the findings of a recently completed inquiry in England
(see Grace, 1995). The Catholic headteachers who cooperated in this research
inquiry shared the responsibilities of school leadership with their school governors and with the diocesan authorities. Nevertheless, the day to day pressure
of leadership responsibilities and the associated moral, ethical and professional
dilemmas focused upon the position of the headteacher. From small, rural infant
schools to large urban comprehensive schools, Catholic headteachers were at
the meeting point of Catholic values and of market values, of Catholic culture
and morality and of pluralistic challenges to these.

Catholic Schools, Leadership and the Common Good

Bryk *et al.* (1993, p. 301), in a major study of the culture of Catholic schooling
in the USA, have argued that such schools are informed by 'an inspirational
ideology' which makes them qualitatively different from public (state) schools.
This inspirational ideology celebrates the primacy of the spiritual and moral
life; the dignity of the person; the importance of community and moral commitments to caring, social justice and the common good. Vatican II, in the view
of Bryk *et al.*, produced not only a new role for the Church in the modern
world, but a new conception of the Catholic school and of Catholic education
in which enhanced importance has been given to respect for persons, active
community and a strong social ethic of citizen responsibility in a national and
an international sense. The argument of *The Catholic School and the Common
Good* is, among other things, that Catholic schools are culturally and morally
distinctive as educational institutions:

> Two important ideas shape life in Catholic schools, making them
> very different from their organizational counterparts in the public sector:
> Christian personalism and subsidiarity. Christian personalism calls for
> humaneness in the myriad of mundane social interactions that make
> up daily life . . . it signifies a moral conception of social behaviour in
> a just community . . . subsidiarity means that the schools rejects a purely
> bureaucratic conception of an organization . . . Decentralization of
> school governance is not chosen purely because it is more efficient
> . . . rather decentralization is predicated in the view that personal dig-
> nity and human respect are advanced when work is organized in
> small communities where dialogue and collegiality may flourish. (Bryk
> *et al.*, 1993, pp. 301–2)

Gerald Grace

These at least are the commitments of the formal inspirational ideology of the new Catholic schooling in America, although the extent to which these virtues are actually realized will, it is acknowledged, vary from school to school.

The critical agents for the translation of these formal commitments into lived school experience are, in the view of Bryk *et al.*, the school principals. Catholic school principalship in America has been strongly influenced by the spiritual and moral capital of the various religious orders which have provided most of the leadership positions until recently.[2] There are therefore also qualitative differences in the nature of school leadership:

> Although much of the work of Catholic school principals is similar to that of their public school counterparts, we conclude that the nature of school leadership has a distinctive character here. Both public and Catholic school principals value academic excellence and students' educational attainment. For principals in Catholic schools, however, there is also an important spiritual dimension to leadership that is apt to be absent from the concerns of public school administrators. This spirituality is manifest in the language of community that principals use to describe their schools and in their actions as they work to achieve the goal of community. (ibid., p. 156)

Although lay Catholics are increasingly taking over school leadership positions, such lay principals are the heirs of a tradition of spirituality established by religious orders and it is not uncommon for them to have received their own education and professional formation in institutions provided by such orders.

The distinctiveness of Catholic schooling culture and of its educational leadership has been commented on, in a variety of contexts, by Hornsby-Smith (1978), Flynn (1985), Egan (1988), Angus (1988), O'Keeffe (1992) and McLaren (1993). In all cases these analyses have noted the tensions and dilemmas which occur when Catholic schooling values (which are themselves in a process of change) encounter situations of rapid social, cultural and ideological change. The Catholic schooling system has been historically relatively insulated in various ways from the changes in secular culture in America, Australia and Britain. Catholic schools in these societies were constructed as defensive citadels for minority communities anxious to preserve the transmission of the Faith and of its spiritual and moral codes and symbols. How this relatively insulated educational tradition is responding to the challenges of individualism, competitiveness, new managerialism, market culture and the commodification of knowledge is a matter of considerable research interest. For McLaren (1993) the issues are clear:

> It is crucial that we continue to explore how Catholic schooling, by virtue of its ineffably vast and unique universe of signifying structures, plays a fundamental role in the socialization of students [p. 254]. A pedagogy that is not grounded in a preferential option for

the disempowered and disenfranchised — 'the wretched of the earth' — only transforms students into vessels for the preparation of new forms of fascism and a grand epic of destruction [p. 290].

In referring here to the preferential option for the poor, McLaren is emphasizing the historical commitment of Catholic schooling to the service of poor immigrant and ethnic minority communities and to its particular mission in inner-city localities in a number of societies. However, the Catholic population in various contexts has become more prosperous and socially differentiated over time so that the mission of Catholic schooling is less focused and unitary than it once was. As Catholic schools respond to contemporary market values in education and to the issues of institutional survival which they generate, a conflict of values is likely to result. Stated in the starkest form, it could be argued that there is little market yield or return for schools which continue to operate a preferential option for the poor. In a market economy for schooling the imperatives of visible and measurable success, financial balance and good public image all combine against commitment to 'customers' who are lacking in both cultural and economic capital. How will the leaders of Catholic schools respond to this dilemma? Will headteachers and school principals work to maintain the integrity of Catholic schooling values and commitments in the new market place for education? Will they be able to balance moral purpose and institutional survival?

In a recently completed research study in England I have investigated Catholic leadership responses to contemporary challenges. The thirty-four Catholic headteacher accounts which were generated during the fieldwork for this study represented the responses of fifteen headteachers in the north-east region and nineteen working in other regions. These headteachers were asked, with varying degrees of explicitness, to indicate their responses to the changing culture of English schooling in relation to the 'special mission' of the Catholic school. In order to provide the appropriate value framework in which these responses could be located, the participants were invited to make explicit, as school leaders, their understanding of the distinctive objectives and commitments of Catholic schooling.

The Special Mission of the Catholic School

Writing of Catholic schooling, Bryk *et al.* (1993, p. 279) have asserted that 'the underlying values of the institution — shared by its members — provide the animating force for the entire enterprise'. This formal position was endorsed by all of the Catholic headteachers but from a research viewpoint what was more significant was the way in which these Catholic school leaders articulated and defined 'the underlying values'. The predominant view was that the special mission of Catholic schools was expressed in three interrelated features i.e., Gospel values, the teachings of Christ and the nurture of community. These features were articulated by primary and secondary school headteachers:

- We represent the only 'face of Christ' for many pupils. We are the new Church — and possibly the Hope of tomorrow . . . (against) a vast depressive value-for-money culture being focused on our pupils. Catholic schools are about evangelization and mission. They are about community . . . 'our' school is a protector of the real values. RC schools must uphold such commitment. (Male Secondary Head) (63)[3]
- The special mission of a Catholic school is to have Christ at the centre of all we do in school and to give the pupils in our care opportunities to take part in spiritual growth . . . in a living, worshipping community . . . I firmly believe it is my prime responsibility to keep God at the heart of our school, permeating everything. (Female Primary School Head) (64)

In these terms, the underlying values of Catholic schooling were defined formally by many of the headteachers in this inquiry. However, all of them recognized that this was a *discourse of mission*. The realization of this mission was not straightforward but dependent upon their own leadership qualities; support from parents, governors and the parish; the commitments of teachers, not all of whom were Catholics; the response of pupils, many from nominally Catholic homes and an increasing proportion from non-Catholic backgrounds. At the same time some of the headteachers believed that wider social, cultural and ideological changes in English society were antithetical to the special mission of Catholic schools.

In addition to the prime value commitments already indicated, many of the participants saw a social ethic of 'serving others' as central to the mission of the Catholic school. In many accounts this social ethic was implicit in the strong discourse and imagery of educational community and wider community. In other accounts, it was explicitly referred to:

- To find God in all things and to serve others are at the heart of what we try to do. (Male Secondary Head) (72)
- To provide an overtly Christian education within an overtly Christian environment and with particular concern for the 'poor' (of all types). (Male Secondary Head) (76)
- The total development of individuals to full potential — spiritual, intellectual, social, moral, physical. It is not self-fulfilment but the development and use of our gifts to serve God through others. (Male Secondary Head) (73)

There was a division of opinion among the Catholic headteachers participating in this study as to whether or not the realization of the special mission of the Catholic school was becoming more difficult to achieve in contemporary conditions. Some headteachers took the view that the challenges which Catholic schools faced had resulted in more explicit discussion and clarification of underlying values and mission and that the schools were stronger in their identity from these processes. An enhanced culture of partnership with governors, parents and the parish was also seen to have reinvigorated and empowered the schools in respect to their spiritual and moral purposes. A sense of confidence existed among some of these Catholic school leaders who believed that the defined spiritual and moral commitments of Catholic education were attractive to a wide constituency of parents i.e., not only to Catholic parents.

Other headteachers were less confident that their schools were actually realizing their special mission in terms of real effects upon the beliefs and practices of their pupils. They recognized considerable contemporary impediments to the successful translation of formal mission into lived practice. For these headteachers such impediments were located both within Catholic schools and in the wider society.

The participants however, whether confident or less confident on this issue, were largely in agreement that Catholic school leaders faced a whole range of moral, ethical and professional dilemmas of a kind not encountered by their predecessors. These dilemmas ranged from the specifics of individual moral behaviour to wider cultural, structural and political issues. Taken together they provided considerable challenges to Catholic headteachers as school leaders.[4]

Catholic School Leadership and Changing Moral Codes

Referring to a new culture of religious and moral teaching in Catholic schools, Bryk *et al.* (1993) have argued that:

> The spirit of Vatican II has softened Catholic claims to universal truth with a call for continuing public dialogue about how we live as people . . . This principle implies a very different conception of religious instruction. In contrast to the pre-Vatican II emphasis on indoctrination in the 'mind of the Church', contemporary religion classes now emphasise dialogue and encounter. Drawing on systematic Christian thought, teachers encourage students to discuss and reflect on their lives . . . (Bryk *et al.*, 1993, p. 302)

While many liberal Catholic educators and school leaders have welcomed this greater openness about religious and moral questions, this new culture also generates its own problems and dilemmas. In a pluralist and secular society, the existence of an absolute and clear-cut religious and moral credo provides an anchor for teaching and for moral decisions. Where the credo is less absolute and clear-cut, the dilemmas for teachers and parents become more challenging. This situation is no longer about the application of an absolute moral code to a given human situation. School leaders, teachers and parents have to engage in principled moral reasoning about different human dilemmas in which some degree of personal autonomy and situational adjustment is expected by the participants.

At the level of the Catholic school, leadership on these complex issues is looked to from the headteacher, among others. The headteachers in this study had encountered dilemmas of moral behaviour relating to pupils, parents and teachers. They were aware that some form of moral leadership was expected from them but they were now more uncertain than in the past about the nature and direction of that moral leadership.

Many of the dilemmas which the headteachers faced arose from a disjuncture between official Catholic moral teaching and the mores of contemporary society:

- The gap between traditional Catholic images of 'the family' and the reality of children's experience of single parents, violence, abuse, crime. (Female Primary School Head) (66)
- Increasingly, Catholic staff are divorced, separated or living together. As a leader of a Catholic community where do I draw the line between the Church's teaching and my compassion as a Christian? (Female Infant School Head) (75)

While it was open to these Catholic headteachers to try to displace such sharp moral dilemmas to the school governors, the priest or school chaplain or to religious education teachers and pastoral care staff, their own professional conception of school leadership prevented this from being an easy way out. The community of school parents who might have been looked to as a source of support in coming to a reasoned and consensual position on these moral dilemmas was not an unproblematic ally. Parents' own double standards and disagreements about the appropriate 'Catholic' response to particular situations were complicating factors. In particular, some headteachers noted that community, partnership and dialogue approaches to trying to resolve difficult moral and behavioural situations were being threatened by parents' more assertive use of legal procedures:

Parents' knowledge of, and awareness of, their legal rights is in conflict with the concept of working together and ideas of mutual support and reconciliation. (Female Primary School Head) (66)

It became apparent during the course of this study that 'community' as a central value and symbol of Catholic schooling was under attack from the ethic of possessive individualism, from market forces and from a customer culture reinforced by quick recourse to legal procedures.[5]

In his ethnographic study of the conservative Catholic school of St Ryan, McLaren (1993) noted that:

In essence, the teacher defined — in fact, *created* — a moral order. The parameters that defined Catholic behaviour were thus drawn up and the students now had a criterion with which to judge subsequent behaviour as right (Catholic) or wrong (non-Catholic). (McLaren, 1993, p. 107)

These certainties were no longer available to the Catholic headteachers participating in this study. Both the spiritual and moral orders of the schools were now open to discussion and dialogue among pupils, parents and teachers. For most of the research participants, who were lay Catholics rather than priests or religious, spiritual and moral leadership in these circumstances was demanding. They were aware of their own professional needs for staff development and support in dealing with changing moral codes. Such support was looked for in courses provided by the Diocese, the Catholic Education Service and professional organizations such as The Association of Catholic Schools and Colleges.[6] The headteachers recognized the strategic importance of 'good priests' and 'good school chaplains' in assisting them to find a basis for dealing with the moral dilemmas of school leadership. In these cultural support networks, Catholic headteachers had access to resources for dealing with the challenges of moral leadership and in this sense they were in a relatively stronger position than their colleagues in state schools.

Bernstein (1990, p. 149) has suggested that 'Christianity is less a religion of certainty (faith cannot be taken for granted, it must be continuously won) than a religion of ambiguity and paradox'. The culture of traditional Catholicism had been constructed to reduce ambiguity and paradox by the strong framing of its teaching. Post Vatican II Catholicism has resulted in greater realizations of ambiguity and paradox in moral codes. Leadership in Catholic schools has therefore involved headteachers in a continuing struggle with these ambiguities.

Catholic Schools and Community: Admissions and Exclusions

As Christians we aim to create a loving, worshipping community where joys and sorrows, successes and set-backs will be shared . . . We aim to provide a curriculum permeated by the Gospel spirit . . .

This statement, taken from the mission document of one of the participating Catholic schools in this inquiry, represents important elements of the 'inspirational ideology' of Catholic schooling. A high aspiration for the creation of a loving and worshipping community is set forth as the educational ideal to be worked for.

On trying to realize this ideal in their particular school settings, Catholic headteachers had to face many impediments and dilemmas. Among these were the difficult issues of school admissions and exclusions. Such issues were fundamental to the constitution and nature of the Catholic school as a community. Admission decisions regulated who might be allowed to join the community and to benefit from its academic, spiritual and moral culture. Exclusion decisions involved painful decisions about temporary or permanent 'excommunication' from the school community.

Dilemmas of admission related to conflicts in wishing to be 'open' to the Catholic communities and to other faith communities in the locality without weakening the Catholic ethos of the school.[7] While this was the ostensible issue, it also encoded a whole range of other issues relating to the social class and ability characteristics of pupils and issues of race and ethnicity. In other words a tension existed between a relatively open and comprehensive policy on school admissions and an awareness that certain amounts of selectivity by faith commitment, social class and ability level would be in the long term interests of the school in a competitive market for schooling.

The disjunctures between the principles of formal mission statements and the realities of admissions policies were clear to a number of the participants:

- When rejecting admissions applications are we displaying Gospel values? (Male Primary School Head) (67)
- Coping with increasing numbers of SEN pupils in mainstream school (especially behavioural/emotional needs) creates much tension and moral dilemma. We are under-resourced and inappropriately trained and skilled to cope. The mission is under threat. (Female Secondary Head) (82)
- Preference in admissions at Year 7 is sometimes given to the most able rather than the most deserving, in order to maintain good results. (Male Secondary Head) (77)

If dilemmas of admissions exercised the moral and professional conscience of Catholic school leaders, issues of exclusion from school were even sharper. Catholic headteachers could find themselves torn between a 'prodigal son/daughter' imperative with its implications of forgiveness and reconciliation and a responsibility to the whole community imperative with implications for firm discipline and hard decisions if necessary. The act of exclusion has powerful symbolic and cultural meanings within Catholic schooling. To the extent that such schools explicitly represented themselves as loving and caring communities permeated by Gospel values, the act of pupil exclusion, as an act of apparent rejection, was discordant with this value culture. Catholic schools in general have an educational culture strongly marked by ritual and symbolic forms derived from the symbolic capital of Catholicism as a religion. Permeating such schools in the practice of the faith is a discourse and an imagery of fall and reconciliation, of sin and forgiveness, and of justice and mercy. But just as the Catholic Church has rituals of inclusion and acceptance but also rituals of exclusion and rejection, so too do Catholic schools. The modern and enlightened practice of both the Church and the schools has been to place the emphasis upon the former, but the latter still exists and may be used if the circumstances require it.

Some of the Catholic headteachers in this study were finding that the circumstances in their school and localities were requiring the serious consideration of exclusion despite the negative spiritual, moral and cultural associations which it carried. With the removal of certain forms of traditional disciplinary sanction in Catholic schools, the act of exclusion had taken on a new significance but at the same time challenged school leaders who claimed that community informed by Gospel values was a defining feature of Catholic education. Because such headteachers had a keen awareness of this dissonance and because they realized that most cases for the exclusion of individual pupils arose out of wider interpersonal and social difficulties in the life of such pupils, they encountered moral and professional dilemmas. These dilemmas were sometimes compounded by pressure brought to bear upon headteachers by groups of parents or groups of teachers who claimed that the exclusion of certain pupils was necessary for the common good of the school. In these circumstances such headteachers felt a leadership responsibility as the guardian of the school's moral and spiritual integrity in making judgments about individual deviance and the common good:

- Exclusions are a very difficult area especially for Roman Catholic schools because by exclusion we put a child out of our pastoral care and the Church itself is 'opportunity for forgiveness'. However there is also the claim of Justice and Peace for others in the community, other pupils and the staff. Staff feel that we don't support them if we hold on to their problems. (Female Secondary Head) (82)
- There is a danger of casting a child adrift. Those excluded often lack parental support/control in any case. (Male Secondary Head) (78)
- The dilemma is care for the individual pupil versus showing the pupil that there must be boundaries . . . There is the dilemma of the racial imbalance in exclusions (e.g., black pupils are 10 per cent of the school population but 20 per cent of exclusions). (Male Secondary Head) (76)

Even within the confidential and confessional context of the research inquiry, headteachers were silent on some issues which were known to be real problems in their schools and localities. For the sample of schools, drug-taking was a paradigm case of headteacher silence. The sample of Catholic schools was a national one (albeit small) including major metropolitan areas as well as small town and rural areas. Despite this wider social and cultural constituency it is remarkable that very few references were made to racial or ethnic issues as one which posed dilemmas for Catholic school leaders. The explicit acknowledgment of the racial imbalance in pupil exclusions in an urban Catholic school, given in account (76) broke this culture of silence.

The culture of silence on racial issues in the participating Catholic schools might be explained in various ways, including the stance that for Catholic headteachers there is 'no problem here'.[8] However, as O'Keeffe (1992) notes:

Gerald Grace

The demographic changes which have taken place in British society are manifested in all aspects of British life including the pupil population of Catholic schools . . . Catholic schools face the need for development of good practice in multicultural education, the adoption of anti-racist stances and the demands of a multi-faith intake. (O'Keeffe, 1992, pp. 42–3)

It seems improbable that Catholic urban schools are insulated from problems of locality racism or institutional racism and therefore another explanation for the silence on these issues might be that Catholic headteachers find it a discomforting issue. Official Catholic teaching is quite clear that racism, in all its forms, offends against Christian values, ideas of community and respect for persons, and Catholic schools have been exhorted to generate an educational ethos which resists racism. The relative silence of the Catholic school leaders on this issue does however suggest that there must be more than exhortation if an effective anti-racist stance is to become a priority commitment for Catholic headteachers.

Catholic Schools and Community: Grant-maintained Status

The Education Reform Act 1988 and Education (Schools) Act 1992 have set in train a transformation of our school system. They have created more choice and wider opportunities as a springboard to higher standards. Central to this has been the development of school autonomy, both within schemes of local management and increasingly as GM (grant-maintained) schools outside local government. (White Paper, 1992, par. 3.1, p. 19)

The official discourse of the government White Paper, 'Choice and Diversity: A new framework for schools' (1992), made it quite clear to all governors, parents and headteachers that a strong political imperative existed to encourage maintained schools to opt out of local government jurisdiction and to choose 'autonomous' grant-maintained status. To add economic incentives to these political imperatives, parents and governors were assured in 1993 that the grant-maintained school 'received extra money to reflect its particular circumstances and responsibilities compared with other schools' (DFE, 1993, p. 5) and in 1994 large scale newspaper advertising was undertaken by the Department for Education with headings such as 'Three-quarters of grant-maintained secondary schools have employed additional teachers' (*The Guardian*, 1994, 4 February) and 'The majority of grant-maintained schools have increased spending on books and equipment' (*The Times Educational Supplement*, 1994, 4 February).

For Catholic school governors and parents, the financial incentives associated with the option for grant-maintained status constituted a particular form of educational temptation. As Simon and Chitty (1993) noted:

The most decisive of financial inducements so far offered lies in capital grants (for new buildings etc.). Several years' experience have now
made it abundantly clear that schools becoming GMS have been treated
far more generously than county schools. In 1991 for instance GMS
schools got an average four times as much in the way of capital grants
than mainstream county schools . . . (Simon and Chitty, 1993, p. 44)

As the Catholic community in England and Wales has significant financial
responsibilities for the capital costs of the Catholic schooling system, the grant-
maintained option became a major focus for debate in the 1990s. For some
Catholics the grant-maintained option appeared to be a form of manna from
heaven, providing extra resources to build upon and expand the excellences
of Catholic education. For other Catholics, the financial inducements were the
equivalent of thirty pieces of silver, encouraging Catholic schools to abandon
community values for individual self-interest.[9] In other words, the Catholic
educational community in England was deeply divided as to what course of
action would be in the best interests of the pupils, the future of Catholic schooling and of the integrity of its special mission.

In order to give educational leadership in this contested situation, the
Catholic hierarchy through the agency of the Catholic Education Service gave
its formal response to the White Paper. This response took up the moral and
professional dilemma of common good versus individual self-interest and
implicitly criticised the GMS option for advancing the latter:

We do not in principle oppose increased independence and self management for schools. However, the GM option is more than this. It
intensifies financial and curricular inequalities between schools and
creates new inequalities. It also supposes that schools derive their
strength from their own autonomy, without any sense of having a
wider responsibility (the common good). Moreover there is no reason
to believe that the growth of the GM sector will do other than undermine the financial viability and reputation of those schools which
remain outside the GM sector. (CES, 1992, p. 7)

The official discourse of the Catholic hierarchy, although coded in diplo-
matic forms, made it clear that they had grave reservations about the autonomous
advantages of grant-maintained schools and perceived serious moral dilemmas
arising from conflicts between Catholic community values and the values of
the GMS option.[10] However, as James Arthur (1994a, 1994b) has demonstrated,
Catholic parents and school governors in England were not prepared to accept
the voice of the hierarchy as the definitive voice on this issue. Some parents
and governors took the view that it was for Catholic parents by a democratic
process of balloting to adjudicate the GMS option in particular localities and
for particular schools. The ideology of parent power had produced some
significant transformations within Catholic schooling culture. In a culture which

had been historically characterized by deference to the teachings and advice of an ecclesiastical hierarchy on matters spiritual, moral and social, the 1980s and 1990s had produced a more assertive and differentiated Catholic community.

The headteachers of Catholic schools were caught up in this struggle between hierarchical counsel and parental assertion, and in the dilemmas arising from conflicts between a construct of special mission as community values and a construct of special mission as providing the best educational resources for Catholic pupils.

The most characteristic response of the participants was a recognition of the moral and professional dilemmas posed by the GMS option without much indication of how they, as school leaders, thought that these dilemmas should be resolved:

> The option of GMS presents a major philosophical dilemma. If a school opts out, does it benefit to the detriment of others; if the school stays with the LEA are the pupils not receiving their due desserts? (Male Secondary Head) (40)

Many of the Catholic headteachers, while fully recognizing the moral dilemmas posed in the option for grant-maintained status, also recognized the power relations in which such a decision was structurally located. If the authority of the Catholic hierarchy had been opposed by groups of parents and governors on this issue, then the authority of the headteacher as school leader could similarly be challenged if the head was explicitly opposed to such a change. The dilemma for the headteachers was that they were aware of expectations for leadership on this major policy issue and yet they were cautious about giving such leadership if this meant expressing an authoritative professional and moral stance. Formally, this was a decision for the parents and therefore it was possible to say that constitutional leadership involved facilitating the correct procedures for parental decision-making rather than articulating a personal professional preference.

Catholic educational leadership in the 1980s and 1990s in England has had to face, once again, fundamental dilemmas between notions of the common good and of autonomous advantage. These dilemmas have been crystallized particularly by the specific policy issue of grant-maintained status and by a general increased salience of market values in schooling. The Catholic community appears to have been as divided on these issues as the non-Catholic constituency. In the most recent review of these divisions, James Arthur (1994a) concludes:

> The Church's dispute with both government and some of its own members can be located in the differing interpretations of parental rights. The government's stress on parental involvement and choice gives predominance to 'the market' and emphasises individual rights over the rights of the community as a whole. By contrast, the Church's

distinctive mission places greater emphasis on the right of the whole Catholic community in determining the future of Catholic schools. The Church does not recognize that the rights of parents and pupils already placed in Catholic schools can override the rights of the whole Catholic community. (Arthur, 1990a, p. 188)

There are considerable theoretical paradoxes and contradictions which are generated by this situation. On the one hand, an essentially hierarchical leadership claims to speak for the good of the whole Catholic community on educational policy matters. On the other hand groups of school governors and parents claim through the process of a ballot to be the democratic voice of the community on a key issue such as grant-maintained status. Objections to the validity and legitimacy of both sets of claims can be made. What is missing in this contested area of educational policy is the active democratic involvement of the whole Catholic community informed by a balanced representation of the arguments.[11] Without such involvement, Catholic headteachers as school leaders find themselves, in general, trapped in a network of contradictions.

Catholic Values and Market Values

Bryk *et al.* (1993) have argued that Catholic schools in the USA have historically been engaged in a cultural struggle to balance market concerns (critical to survival) with Catholic values (critical to mission). In other words, Catholic schooling in America has been powerfully shaped both by the influence of market forces and by the influence of an inspirational ideology of Catholic schooling. The sensitivity of American Catholic schools to market values has been the inevitable result of receiving no financial support from public funds. American Catholic schools, unlike their English counterparts, have not been culturally and financially insulated from the market and they have had to demonstrate a responsiveness to clients in a competitive situation. However, Bryk *et al.* (1993) concluded in their major research inquiry:

> Even so, the control of Catholic school operations involves considerably more than market responsiveness to clients. Many important observations about these schools cannot be reconciled in these terms. Market forces cannot explain the broadly shared institutional purpose of advancing social equity or account for the efforts of Catholic educators to maintain inner-city schools (with large non-Catholic enrolments) while facing mounting financial woes. Likewise, market forces cannot easily explain why resources are allocated within schools in a compensatory fashion in order to provide an academic education for every student. Nor can they explain the norms of community that infuse daily life in these schools. (Bryk *et al.*, 1993, p. 300)

The detailed research reported in *Catholic Schools and the Common Good*, while it celebrates the balance achieved between market and mission in Catholic schooling, concludes in sombre terms. Contemporary conditions in America are beginning to demonstrate that market forces, market values and the inexorable circumstances for institutional survival and financial solvency are threatening the historical mission and values of Catholic schooling.

For English Catholic schools in the maintained sector of education this encounter with market forces and market values is a much more recent phenomenon, an experience of the 1980s and 1990s. Previously insulated to a large extent from market forces by state and diocesan funding, by the historical loyalty of local Catholic communities, and by large pupil enrolments resulting from large Catholic families, Catholic schools were the possessors of a relatively autonomous zone of influence. Within this autonomous zone, Catholic school leaders could articulate a distinctive mission and set of Catholic values independently of market culture and market values.

The critical question for Catholic school leaders in new circumstances is: can a balance be found between Catholic values and market values, or will market forces begin to compromise the integrity of the special mission of Catholic schooling? Can Gospel values survive in the face of a more direct relationship with the market place?

McLaughlin (1994) has argued that there are important moral limits to the extension of market culture into schooling. Among these are considerations about the generation of civic virtue and about the provision of fair educational entitlements for all pupils. Given the centrality of both of these considerations to Catholic social and moral teaching, it is an implication of McLaughlin's argument that central elements of market culture are in conflict with Catholic values in education.

A minority of the Catholic headteachers involved in this inquiry were confident that, with appropriate school leadership, the integrity of Catholic values in education could not only be maintained but extended in its range of influence:

- Heads of Catholic Aided schools might experience fewer dilemmas here than County colleagues . . . The apparent decline of moral and spiritual functions in schools might explain why Church schools are quite attractive to a wide community. (Male Secondary Head) (40)
- There is support from parents for a stance which is overtly counter to the prevailing market values. Parents do want good exam results but not at all costs and an education which is balanced and Christian has attractions. (Male Secondary Head) (72)

This confident minority of headteachers took the view that not only were the spiritual and moral resources of Catholic schooling strong enough to resist possible corruption or pollution by market values in education but that, ironically, these moral resources were being recontextualized as potent market assets in the competitive appeal for parental choice of schools in a wider constituency.

In other words, demonstrable moral leadership would ensure the success of Catholic schooling in the new conditions of the educational market place.

While not denying that Catholic schools had moral and spiritual strengths which could be viewed as assets in a competitive situation of parental choice, the majority of the headteachers had reservations and dilemmas about the impact of market values upon the special mission of their schools:

- Catholic values and market values appear to be ever in conflict — an obvious example is the funding available for religious education and for spiritual and moral experiences e.g., residential courses. (Female Secondary Head) (69)
- I would rather see the school shrink in size but remain true to its ideals and faith commitment. I do not see a child as £1,000 through the school gate. (Male Primary School Head) (42)
- Catholic schools really must keep the explicit link between Christ and person-centred education . . . How do we square our vocational vision of pupils as persons, with the market vision of economic units? How does this affect our treatment of special educational needs? How does this affect our admissions policy? (Female Secondary Head) (82)

For the Catholic headteachers who took seriously those aspects of the special mission of Catholic schools which related especially to service to the poor and the disadvantaged there were dilemmas. Such headteachers realized that a new set of strategies known as 'playing the market' was emerging among some school leaders in their localities. In essence, playing the educational market involved selecting the most able pupils from educationally supportive homes in order to maximize the output of measurable success on league tables of performance.[12] In this way, a public image of an 'excellent', 'successful' or 'effective' school could be constructed and the cultural capital of success once acquired could be further strengthened. Failure to engage in this market strategy could lead to a school's decline and to the creation of a 'sink school' image.[13]

The moral dilemma for educational leaders (as opposed to simply managers) was constituted by a recognition that 'playing the market' made it much more difficult to serve the poor and the powerless. Success could be achieved with the poor and the powerless but at a greater cost in terms of time, resources, staff commitment and educational support. It was precisely the questions of 'cost' and 'cost effectiveness' which were preoccupying all headteachers in the market conditions for schooling.

Challenges for Contemporary Catholic School Leaders

Catholic school principals and headteachers are being exhorted to defend the historical commitment of Catholic schooling to the service of disadvantaged

Gerald Grace

communities in America and in Britain. McNamee (1993) in reviewing the challenges for Catholic schools in the USA, concludes:

> What can Catholic schools do to meet current and future challenges presented by Hispanics, new immigrants and the poor? First, the Church must make a commitment to increase the access of these special populations to Catholic schools. (McNamee, 1993, p. 17)

As this study has shown, the growing influence of market culture upon Catholic schooling makes the realization of this educational ideal more difficult than in the past. Also, as a result of wider cultural and religious change, it is much less certain that 'the Church' as an entity can make such a commitment in an era of devolved school-site management and of increased parental choice and assertion.

In a similar way, O'Keefe in his contribution to this volume argues that:

> In the United States today, schools for the poor present a powerful challenge to the Catholic community. (p. 177)

Despite an analysis which calls for a new belief in education for the common good, O'Keefe is forced to acknowledge 'the reluctance of white, middle class suburban Catholics to see themselves in communion with poor, urban minorities.' (p. 179)

In Britain, John Haldane has argued that:

> Catholic education must establish a social conscience as well as one concerned with individual well-being . . . the first task for a Catholic philosophy of education is to identify the good. The social good is only a part of that but it is a sufficiently large and central part to justify making it a focus of attention . . . (Haldane, 1993, pp. 11–12)

At the same time as he sets this mission for Catholic education, Haldane recognizes that liberal individualism is politically and ideologically in the ascendant in Britain and elsewhere rather than forms of social communitarianism with commitments to the social good.

These are the fundamental dilemmas and challenges for Catholic school leaders in contemporary conditions. While there have always been tensions between the educational pursuit of the common good and the educational pursuit of individual interest, these tensions have at least been held in a position of ideological balance. There has been an educational settlement or compromise based upon a recognition that both common good and individual interest have their legitimate claims in educational theory and practice. The ideological changes of the 1980s and 1990s, in particular the influence of New Right agencies in both America and Britain, have broken that historical settlement by in effect denying the existence of constructs such as 'society' or of 'common good'.

The apparent triumph of liberal individualism as a decisive political, economic and cultural doctrine and its implementation in terms of educational policy and practice provided the majority of Catholic headteachers in this study with the greatest challenge they had yet faced in their careers as school leaders. These headteachers might look for guidance or leadership to 'the Church' on these contested matters, but in a post-modern age what 'the Church' was and what its voice on these issues might be lacked the definition and certainties of the past. There were therefore no *ex cathedra* statements or absolute moral codes which could give instant guidance on these social, cultural and professional dilemmas.[14]

Notes

1 This chapter is a revised version of Chapter 9 in my book, *School Leadership: Beyond Education Management*, London, Falmer Press, March 1995.
2 Bryk notes that 'the majority of principalships in Catholic high school (61 per cent in 1988) still come from religious orders, an arrangement that provides schools with some distinct benefits' (p. 157).
3 Numbers in brackets refer to the research account code.
4 It must be noted here that the participating headteachers represented a very limited sample of the Catholic school system in England and Wales which consists of 1886 primary schools and 407 secondary schools. Catholic provision is approximately 10 per cent of the public education service (Catholic Education Service data).
5 However, it is important not to romanticize concepts of community in schooling. Community can be appropriated for oppressive and unjust processes and recourse to legal and bureaucratic procedures may be necessary in the interests of justice for individuals.
6 It can be noted that all of these agencies are giving much more attention in the 1990s to courses on school leadership rather than simply school management and that such courses are addressing spiritual, moral and value issues in Catholic schooling.
7 This major dilemma permeated many of the headteacher accounts. Demographic changes were affecting Catholic schools and school closures were becoming a feature of the system (356 schools closed between 1978 and 1991). The percentage of Catholic teachers in Catholic secondary schools has fallen from 66 per cent in 1978 to 58 per cent in 1991. Non-Catholic pupils have increased from 3 per cent of the school population to 14 per cent in 1991 (Catholic Education Service data).
8 The 'no problem here' response is characteristically given in schools and localities which have no significant ethnic diversity or in situations where it is claimed that racism may feature in the community but not in the school.
9 This classic phrase was used by some headteachers during the course of this inquiry.
10 The Catholic response can be compared with the much stronger criticism of grant maintained policy emanating from the Muslim community in Britain. *The Times Educational Supplement* for 1 July 1994 carried a front page report under the heading 'Muslims condemn "unfair" GM Policy'. Leading Muslim educators argued that 'it's not acceptable and it's not Islamic to disadvantage the majority for the benefit of the privileged minority'.
11 Despite a Vatican II discourse of involvement of the 'whole people of God' in the life of the Church, active democratic involvement is radically at odds with the hierarchical and authoritarian traditions of Catholicism.

12 These strategies are indicated by a growing discourse in education using constructs such as 'the major players' or 'the stakeholders'.
13 As one head noted, 'once a school is on a downward spiral it is going to be much more difficult than in the past to build it up'. His argument was that the removal of LEA support and greater dependence on market forces would cause this difficulty.
14 The categorical teaching of Catholicism on the regulation of sexual behaviour can be contrasted with a much greater degree of ambiguity on social, economic and political matters.

References

ANGUS, L.B. (1988) *Continuity and Change in Catholic Schooling*, London, Falmer Press.
ARTHUR, J. (1994a) 'Catholic responses to the 1988 Education Reform Act: Problems of authority and ethos', in FRANCIS, L. and LANKSHEAR, D.W. (Eds) *Christian Perspectives on Church Schools*, Leominster, Fowler Wright Books.
ARTHUR, J. (1994b) 'Parental involvement in Catholic schools: A case of increasing conflict', in *British Journal of Educational Studies*, **42**, 2, June, pp. 179–90.
BERNSTEIN, B. (1990) *The Structuring of Pedagogic Discourse: Class, Codes and Control*, Vol. 4, London, Routledge.
BRYK, A., LEE, V. and HOLLAND, P. (1993) *Catholic Schools and the Common Good*, Cambridge, MA, Harvard University Press.
CATHOLIC EDUCATION SERVICE (1992) *A Response to the White Paper*, 24 September.
DEPARTMENT FOR EDUCATION (1992) *Choice and Diversity: A New Framework for Schools*, ('White Paper' July) Cm.2021, London, HMSO.
DEPARTMENT FOR EDUCATION (1993) *Grant Maintained Schools: Questions Parents Ask*, November, p. 5.
EGAN, J. (1988) *Opting Out: Catholic Schools Today*, Leominster, Fowler Wright Books.
FLYNN, M. (1985) *The Effectiveness of Catholic Schools*, Homebush, St Paul Publications.
GRACE, G. (1994) 'Education is a public good: On the need to resist the domination of economic science', in BRIDGES, D. and McLAUGHLIN, T.H. (Eds) *Education and the Market Place*, London, Falmer Press.
GRACE, G. (1995) *School Leadership: Beyond Education Management*, London, Falmer Press.
HALDANE, J. (1993) 'A Prolegomenon to an unwritten Philosophy of Education: Catholic Social Teaching and the Common Good'. Paper presented to the Conference, *The Contemporary Catholic School and the Common Good*, St Edmund's College, Cambridge, July 1993.
HORNSBY-SMITH, M. (1978) *Catholic Education: The Unobtrusive Partner*, London, Sheed and Ward.
McLAREN, P. (1993) *Schooling as a Ritual Performance: Towards a Political Economy of Educational Symbols and Gestures*, London, Routledge.
McLAUGHLIN, T.H. (1994) 'Politics, markets and schools: The central issues', in BRIDGES, D. and McLAUGHLIN, T.H. (Eds) *Education and the Market Place*, London, Falmer Press.
McNAMEE, C. (1993) 'Catholic schools in the US: Perspectives and developments', Paper presented to the 'Contemporary Catholic School and the Common Good' Conference, St Edmund's College, Cambridge, July.
O'KEEFFE, B. (1992) 'Catholic schools in an open society: The English challenge', in McCLELLAND, V.A. (Ed) *The Catholic School and the European Context*, Hull, University of Hull.
SIMON, B. and CHITTY, C. (1993) *SOS: Save Our Schools*, London, Lawrence and Wishart.

Chapter 6

The Common Good, Pluralism, and Catholic Education

David Hollenbach S.J.

The effort to clarify the contribution of Catholic education to the common good stands in a rich tradition. Catholic thought has long held that the common good is the overarching end to be pursued in social and cultural life. Since education is the activity through which culture is sustained and developed, the success or failure of a society to realize its common good will be largely dependent on what transpires in its educational endeavours.

In the United States today, however, reflection on the role of education in the pursuit of the common good confronts an apparently ever-growing challenge — the fact of pluralism. In a pluralist society, people hold diverse understandings of the meaning and purpose of human life. They disagree about the value that can be realized in their life together in interpersonal relationships, in work and economic activity, and in politics. They disagree even more markedly about the larger questions of meaning that are addressed by religions or competing comprehensive philosophies of life. A pluralist society, by definition, is one in which there is disagreement about the meaning of the human good. This leads some to conclude that the idea of the common good and the reality of pluralism are utterly incompatible. In such a context, the pursuit of the common good and reflection on the role of education in encouraging it may seem like a futile task. The difficulty is heightened by the fact that the long-standing awareness of pluralism that has been historically characteristic of American self-consciousness is increasing today, not decreasing. Even more daunting is the challenge of reflecting on how one out of the many religiously distinctive communities in the United States — in this case the Roman Catholic community — can serve the common good of all people. Finally, if one adds to this picture the view of Catholicism as a distinctly divisive force in American culture, a view that has been influential through much of the country's largely Protestant history and that is very much alive today, the problem verges onto the terrain of the impossible.

Despite these large obstacles, this essay will argue that the time is opportune for fruitful exploration of the possible contributions of education rooted in the Catholic tradition to the advancement of the common good. The time is also ripe for action that aims to actualize these possibilities. There are two reasons for such a hope. First, some of the most urgent cultural and social problems in the United States today seem highly resistant to solutions built on individualistic presuppositions. The need for stronger bonds of social solidarity and for efforts to attain a greater degree of shared moral vision is increasingly being urged as a prerequisite if these problems are to be understood and addressed. Second, the Roman Catholic tradition possesses some distinctive resources that can be brought to bear on these challenges. During the period leading up to the Second Vatican Council and following after it, the Catholic tradition has been engaged in efforts to develop these traditional resources in ways that make them usable in the context of acknowledged pluralism. Continuation of the process of retrieving and adapting these resources holds promise of enabling Catholic education to make a distinctive contribution to the renewed pursuit of the common good today.

The Problem: Pluralism or Social Conflict?

The problems that call for a more communal, less individualistic orientation today are both social and cultural. Socially, we face an array of issues that make the need to address the interdependence of persons on one another increasingly evident. A very partial list of such issues would include: the continuing crisis in American cities brought recently — and briefly — to the headlines by the riots in South Central Los Angeles; the chaos in family life and sexual relationships in an age of single parenthood and of AIDS; the obstacles posed to the reform in the provision of health care by business-as-usual, interest-group politics; the serious dangers posed by environmental degradation regionally and globally; the clashes of 'identity politics' within the United States and of national cultures on a more global scale; the lack of even an approximation of economic justice in a world where the very notion of a domestic economy seems anachronistic.

In the background of these social issues stands the cultural question of the values that inform people's ability and willingness to live in ways that contribute to addressing these issues in a positive way.

One example drawn from this list will serve to illustrate the growing salience of the idea of the common good in the renewal of American public life today: urban poverty. The quality of life in American cities is marked by economic deprivation, homelessness, unemployment, and frightening drug-related violence. The inner cores of many large American cities are increasingly isolated from surrounding suburbs economically, racially, and culturally. We seem to have made little progress in addressing urban social and economic conditions that in 1968 led a National Advisory Commission on Civil Disorders (the 'Kerner Commission') to conclude that 'Our nation is moving toward two societies, one black, one white — separate but unequal.'[1] Though the black middle class has grown and its economic status has improved during recent decades, the isolation of the urban poor from the rest of society has worsened and their economic condition declined to an alarming degree (see Wilson, 1987). The civil unrest in South Central Los Angeles during 1992 only served to remind us how much remains to be done if we are to address the continuing plight of the urban poor. But the short-lived attention to urban problems stimulated by the Los Angeles upheaval suggests that the nation is unprepared to make efforts to address these problems that are commensurate with their seriousness.

This lack of response can be explained at least in part by the fact that most people live in neighbourhoods that isolate them from people of significantly different social-economic backgrounds. This isolation is due, on one level, to the apparently impersonal forces of the real estate market. These market dynamics, however, are sustained by zoning laws and other boundaries that are the result of political choice rather than geography. Anthony Downs has argued that the social-economic hierarchy of neighbourhoods is founded on two moral principles accepted by most Americans. Americans appear to believe, first, that every household has the right to live in a neighbourhood populated largely by other households approximately like itself, and, second, that each neighbourhood has the right to protect the quality of its life, its environment, and its property values by excluding groups of people that would significantly diminish these (Downs, 1981, 1991). Downs states that these principles of homogeneity and self-protective exclusion do not extend to the legitimation of racial discrimination. Nevertheless there can be little doubt that other criteria for the desired form of homogeneity have indirect racial consequences as well as the obvious direct impact effect of economic and class stratification. In Downs' view, these criteria ought to be challenged despite the fact that they appear to be accepted as morally legitimate by the majority of Americans. Such a challenge can arise only within a moral framework that expands the understanding of community beyond that of homogeneous groups of the like-minded or those who are similarly situated economically. Such a challenge will be dependent on the development of an understanding of the common good that reaches beyond the boundaries of existing groups.

That, however, is the rub. In the face of numerous problems that bedevil our complex social world, the need for a stronger sense of community is very much alive among those with the education and leisure to contemplate the realities of the larger society around them. But the problems seem so huge that the quest for community is easily deflected into relatively manageable realms such as networks of friends and others who are enough like oneself for commonalities to be established comparatively easily. This point has been made in a book that has become something of a *vademecum* in discussions of individualism and community in recent years, *Habits of the Heart* by Robert Bellah and four co-authors (Bellah *et al.*, 1985, p. 335). It argues that many Americans recognize today that they cannot go it alone in the face of the complexities of contemporary life. They need some sense of connection in their lives if they are to find meaning and a sense of both direction and control. But *Habits of the Heart* also describes an unfortunate and arguably pathological result of some of the efforts to find community today. The quest for community among suburbanites often leads to the development of 'lifestyle enclaves'. People in such enclaves find and express their identities through linkages with other persons with 'shared patterns of appearance, consumption, or leisure activities . . .' These relationships are based on sharing some feature of private rather than public life. They 'do not act together politically' as citizens of a polis and they 'do not share a history'. Rather, they act as friends together in a kind of club. So they are not likely to translate their need for community into ways of thinking and acting that are capable of addressing issues such as the divisions between core cities and suburbs. In fact the need for community, when expressed in lifestyle enclaves, can have exactly the opposite effect. It can lead to the construction of walls and moats, in the form of bigger and better malls and tougher zoning ordinances that are designed to strengthen the locks that protect the privileged from those who are different.

Bellah *et al.* contrast such an enclave with a community in the stronger sense described by Aristotle as the *polis*, or by Cicero as the *res publica*, which can be translated the 'public thing', the 'commonwealth', or the 'commonweal'. These strong communities are places where people are truly interdependent on each other through their participation in, discussion concerning, and decision-making about their common purpose. Such strong communities are, therefore, political communities, where people make decisions about the kind of society they want to live in together.

A case can be made, therefore, that in the United States citizenship has itself become a problematic concept in our time and we are experiencing an 'eclipse of citizenship' (Pranger, 1968; Walzer, 1970, pp. 203–28). The low percentage of Americans who exercise their right to vote is the most visible evidence for this. This is caused in part by a lack of confidence that individual people can have any meaningful influence in a political society as vast as ours. Many people, including many in the middle class, feel politically powerless. E.J. Dionne, in a book tellingly titled *Why Americans Hate Politics*, argues that this alienation from citizenship can be attributed to the fact that current political discourse fails to address the real needs of communities (Dionne, 1991). This failure is itself partly the result of the fact that interest-group politics is frequently incapable of even naming the social bonds that destine us to share either a common good or a 'common bad'. Politics is perceived as a contest among groups with little or no concern for the wider society and its problems, for example suburbanites versus the urban 'underclass'. Lifestyle enclaves seem the only form of communal connection realistically available.

This tendency was discussed at some length in the United States Catholic bishops' 1986 pastoral letter, *Economic Justice for All*. Following a line of analysis that has become almost routine in the social theory of modernization, the bishops noted the deep structural causes for the contemporary devaluation of citizenship. Modern societies are characterized by a division of labour into highly specialized jobs and professions. Individual lives are further fragmented by the way family life, the world of work, networks of friendship, and religious

community are so often lived out in separate compartments (National Conference of Catholic Bishops, 1986). In the words of Bellah and his co-authors,
contemporary American culture is a 'culture of separation'. It is increasingly
difficult to see how our chopped-up segments of experience fit together in
anything like a meaningful whole. 'The world comes to us in pieces, in fragments, lacking any overall pattern' (op. cit., p. 277). This fragmentation can
undermine the sense of overall purpose in the lives of individual persons,
leading to a seemingly endless quest for one's own identity (Berger *et al.*, 1973,
pp. 77–8). Because of the complexity and high degree of differentiation characteristic of modern social existence, individuals lack a readily intelligible map
by which they can locate themselves and chart their course through life. Such
preoccupation with personal identity makes it very difficult to see how the
kinds of lives we lead make a difference for the common good of the whole
community. Lack of public discussion of the common good in turn generates
a heightened sense that individuals are powerless over the larger social forces
that shape their lives. It also helps explain the prevalence of single-issue styles of
political action among many who do continue to see politics as a sphere open
to at least some influence. Thus at the very time that it has become increasingly
difficult to sustain a vision of the common good, doing so is more urgently
important if we are to sustain democratic practices.

Is Tolerance Enough?

The standard prescription in much political and educational thinking when
faced with the diversity of groups and value systems in the United States has
long been an appeal for the growth of the virtue of tolerance. Tolerance is a
live-and-let-live attitude that avoids introducing conceptions of the full human
good into political discourse. This is the prescription of the eminent political
theorist and moral philosopher, John Rawls. Rawls recommends that we deal
with the fact of value-pluralism by what he calls 'the method of avoidance'. By
this he means that in political life 'we try, so far as we can, neither to assert
nor to deny any religious, philosophical or moral views, or their associated philosophical accounts of truth and the status of values.' (Rawls, 1987, pp. 12–13).
This appeal hopes to neutralize potential conflicts and to promote democratic
social harmony. But it may ironically have the effect of threatening democracy
through alienation and anomie. A principled commitment to avoiding sustained
discourse about the common good can produce a downward spiral in which
shared meaning, understanding, and community become even harder to achieve
in practice. Or, more ominously, when the pluralism of diverse groups veers
toward a state of group conflict with racial or class dimensions, pure tolerance
can become a strategy like that of the ostrich with its head in the sand.

It is not my intent to appeal simply to fear of violent social conflict as a
motive for resuscitating concern for the common good in American education. Urban unrest remains a simmering threat today, to be sure. But the more
fundamental issue is the question of whether we need some basic consensus on

social and moral values if we are to address problems ranging from the inner city to the global environment. Recovery of confidence that we both need and can attain a shared understanding of the lineaments of what a good life together might be is an urgent necessity in pluralist democracies today.

According to this analysis, the basis of democracy is not the autonomy of atomistic individuals. Participation in democratic life and the exercise of real freedom in society depend on the strength of the communal relationships that give persons a measure of real power to shape their environment, including their political environment. As John Coleman has argued, the commitment to democracy as it is understood in recent Catholic thought rests on 'a presumptive rule about where real vitality exists in society' (Coleman, 1982, p. 226). This presumption is that solitary individuals, especially solitary individuals motivated solely by self-interest and the protection of their rights to privacy, will be incapable of democratic self-government. Democracy requires more than this. It requires the virtues of mutual cooperation, mutual responsibility, and what Aristotle called friendship, concord, and amity (see Aristotle's *Nicomachean Ethics*, 1,167a, b).

Of course Aristotle knew that there were limits to how wide a circle of friends one might have, as he knew there were limits to the size of a city-state. Today we are acutely aware that a nation as vast and diverse as the United States cannot hope to achieve the kind of social unity that might have been possible in the Athenian *polis*. While it might be true that the virtues of mutual cooperation, responsibility, and friendship can exert positive influence in small communities governed by town meetings, in clubs, and in churches that share a common vision of the final good and meaning of life, we hardly expect this to occur on a national much less the international level.

But here the paradox of modernity once again becomes vividly visible. As the scale and diversity of society tempts us to conclude that community is achievable only in private enclaves of the like-minded, our *de facto* technological, political, and economic interdependence is also growing stronger each year. This fact cries out for conscious acknowledgment and for a renewed commitment to our moral interdependence. Stress on the importance of the local, the small-scale, and the particular must be complemented by a kind of solidarity that is more universal in scope. This wider solidarity is essential if the quest for community is to avoid becoming a source of increased conflict in a world already riven by narrowness of vision. Commitment to small-scale communities with particular traditions and ways of life must be complemented by a sense of the national and the global common good and the need for a vision shaped not only by particularist traditions but by hospitable encounter with traditions and peoples that are different.

The Catholic Tradition of the Common Good

The tradition of Catholic social thought, especially as it has developed over the past century, is positioned to make a significant contribution to the recognition of the importance of both small-scale and wider forms of community. It is particularly noteworthy that several commentators from outside the Catholic tradition have commented upon this. William Lee Miller, in his sprightly review of the role of religion in American public life, has wondered whether the late twentieth century might not be a moment when the Catholic tradition's long commitment to the idea of human interdependence in community might not be just what is needed for the well being of the American republic as it faces a complex and uncertain future. American culture has historically been oriented in a strongly individualistic direction by both its Protestant and Enlightenment sources. Miller observes that Catholicism possesses resources that both Protestantism and secular liberalism lack that can help shape a response to both the challenges and opportunities of a world that needs a stronger sense of life being bound up with life if it is to flourish in a way that befits the dignity of human beings. He calls this solidaristic vision 'personalist communitarianism':

> Something like such a personalist communitarianism is the necessary base for a true republic in the interdependent world of the third century of this nation's existence. And the Roman Catholic community is the most likely single source of it — the largest and intellectually and spiritually most potent institution that is the bearer of such ideas. (Miller, 1986, pp. 288–9)

Miller's appeal to the resources of the Catholic tradition of the common good is echoed by other Protestants, by several Jewish thinkers, and by some with a more secular mindset (Douglass, 1986; Strain, 1989; Lutz, 1986; Gannon, 1987; and Green *et al.*, 1989, pp. 180–4).

This personalistic communitarianism is based on the recognition that the dignity of human persons is achieved only in community with others. To paraphrase John Donne's words, no person is an island. This understanding of the human has biblical roots in the notion of covenant — the fact that God called Israel precisely as a *people*, not as individuals one at a time. It also has Greek roots in Aristotle's understanding that the human being is a social or political animal (*zoon politikon*), whose good is essentially bound up with the good of the polis. This understanding of the person has direct implications for the way freedom is understood. Freedom's most important meaning is positive, the ability to shape one's life and environment in an active and creative way, rather than the negative state of privacy or being left alone by others. For the ancient Greeks, privacy was a state of deprivation, a fact echoed in the etymological link of privacy and privation in English. Similarly, the biblical understanding of freedom, portrayed in the account of the Exodus that is so central in liberation theology today, is not simply freedom from constraint but freedom for participation in the shared life of a people. Liberation is *from* bondage *into* community. As the US bishops put it, in the Bible 'being free and being a co-responsible community are God's intentions for us' (National Conference of Catholic Bishops, 1986, No. 36). To be sure, freedom from oppression demands that persons' dignity and rights be protected from infringement by other people, by society, or by the State. Freedom in its most basic form is freedom from oppression. But freedom will be understood in a truncated way if its meaning is understood only as the negative immunity that protects one from interference by others. Individualistic isolation is finally a prison, not a liberation. The Catholic tradition's appreciation of this fact is most relevant to the problems faced by American society and culture today.

Pope John Paul II has stressed this social dimension of freedom in his frequent discussions of the moral basis of democracy. Catholicism, of course, has often been regarded with justifiable suspicion in discussions of democracy because of its history of opposition to democratic movements in the modern era. Since the Second Vatican Council, however, the Catholic Church has become one of the strongest advocates and agents of democratization visible on the global stage today (see Huntington, 1991, pp. 29–42). In his role as advocate of democratic government, John Paul II has been critical of ideas of democracy based on individualism and on strictly negative understandings of freedom. His philosophical analysis echoes that of some of the founders and framers of the American experiment in its insistence that the success of democracy over the long haul is dependent on the virtues present in the citizenry. The Pope's argument resembles the founders' particularly in its explicit stress on the essential link between the life of virtue and commitment to the common good.

This linkage is most evident in John Paul's frequent discussion of what he calls 'the virtue of solidarity'. This will not be found on the classical lists that include prudence, justice, temperance and fortitude. Nevertheless, the fact that it belongs there is evident from the Pope's definition. He calls solidarity 'a firm and persevering determination to commit oneself to the common good; that is to say to the good of all and of each individual' (John Paul II, 1992). For Christians, such a commitment is rooted in the commandment of love of neighbour. Thus in the Pope's theology, 'Solidarity is undoubtedly a Christian virtue ... [There are] many points of contact between solidarity and charity, which is the distinguishing mark of Christ's disciples (cf. Jn 13:35).' It is a recognition of one's neighbours as fundamentally equal because they are 'living images of God, redeemed by the blood of Jesus Christ and placed under the permanent action of the Holy Spirit' (John Paul II, 1992, p. 40). The promotion of the common good therefore flows from the heart of Christian faith. It is intrinsic to it, not an optional secular extension of the proper life of the Christian community.

At the same time, solidarity as the Pope understands it is not far removed from the virtue that Aristotle called 'civic friendship' or 'civic amity' (Aristotle, op. cit.). Precisely as commitment to the common good, the virtue of solidarity ought to link Catholic Christians with the larger community of non-Catholics, non-Christians, and non-believers. This virtue is attainable by men and women without an explicit faith. Indeed John Paul II expresses the hope that all people, 'whether or not they are inspired by religious faith, will become fully aware of the urgent need to *change* the *spiritual attitudes* which define each individual's relationship with self, with neighbor, with even the remotest human communities, and with nature itself'. Such a change in attitudes arises from recognition of 'higher values such as the *common good*' (John Paul II, 1992, p. 38). Thus the effort to nurture this virtue of solidarity not only has distinctively Christian warrant in theology but is also proposed as a worthy and in fact essential task in a secular, pluralistic context.

Justice: Prerequisite for a Good that is Common

Further, the linkage of solidarity and commitment to the common good with the demands of Christian charity should not be mistaken as limiting this virtue to the domain of affectivity. It is surely the case that the moral transformation of persons envisioned by the Pope is a matter of a change of heart away from individualistic concern for the private good to a more social concern for the good of the larger community. But solidarity 'is not a feeling of vague compassion or shallow distress at the misfortunes of so many people both near and far'. Rather it is a hard-nosed recognition of the reality of human interdependence, 'sensed as a *system determining* relationships in the contemporary world, in its economic, cultural, political, and religious elements, and accepted as a moral category' (ibid.). This more systemic view of the meaning of the virtue of solidarity puts it in direct continuity with Thomas Aquinas's understanding of the orientation of all virtues to the promotion of justice, and through the promotion of justice to the enhancement of the common good.

For Aquinas, the premier moral virtue is justice, which directs a person's actions toward the good of fellow human beings. Because all people are both individuals and also participants in the common life of the civil community, the advancement of their good must be directed not only to their private good but to the good of the community as well. Thomas Aquinas calls the concern for the common good of the community 'general justice'. He contrasts it with 'particular justice', the virtue that specifies obligations to individuals. The obligations of general justice can be contrasted with the obligations, for example, of individual parents to the good of their children or the duties of identifiable employers to protect the good of their employees by paying a just wage. These latter concerns are of course indispensable in any life that is virtuous. But they are not the whole of virtue, just as the duties of justice toward one's children or employees are not the whole of justice. When one possesses the virtue of general justice one's actions will be habitually directed toward the good of the larger community of one's fellow human beings. Justice, then, is the virtue of good citizens. Echoing Aristotle, Thomas Aquinas wrote 'that the virtue of a good citizen is general justice, whereby a person is directed to the common good' (Thomas Aquinas, *Summa Theologiae*, q. 58, art. 6). The achievement of the common good requires a citizenry nurtured in ways that enable them both to understand the meaning of justice in society and to work for its achievement.

David Hollenbach S.J.

Thus it should come as no surprise that John Paul II enumerates some of the most pressing issues that pertain to the pursuit of social justice in his discussion of the virtue of solidarity. For example, he states that solidarity is a moral bond of responsibility of more influential persons for those who are weaker. It is a bond that links the poor with each other in asserting their needs and rights in the face of the inefficiency or corruption of public officials. It is opposed to every form of imperialism, hegemony, greed, or unrestrained quest for power. It is the path to both peace and genuine economic development (John Paul II, 1992, pp. 38–39). This strong language is further intensified when he lists some of the manifestations of human sinfulness that are directly opposed to solidarity. These include: trampling upon the basic rights of the human person; attacks and pressures against the freedom of individuals and groups; racial, cultural, and religious discrimination; violence and terrorism; torture and repression; arms races and military spending that divert funds that could be used to alleviate misery; the increasing inequality of the rich and poor. All of these phenomena divide persons and communities from each other and undermine human solidarity on a social, structural level. In the Pope's words, 'The overwhelming power of this division makes the world in which we live a world shattered to its very foundations' (John Paul II, 1984, pp. 432–58).

An adequate and precise discussion of the full meaning of justice, of course, would be a immensely complex undertaking. The issue can be somewhat simplified for present purposes, however, by noting that in their 1986 pastoral letter on economic questions the United States Catholic bishops offered this definition of the bottom-line demands of justice. They said 'Basic justice demands the establishment of minimum levels of participation in the life of the human community for all persons.' Or put negatively, 'The ultimate injustice is for a person or group to be treated actively or abandoned passively as if they were nonmembers of the human race' (National Conference of Catholic Bishops, 1986, p. 77). The US bishops call this exclusion 'marginalization' — exclusion from social life and from participation in the common good of the human community.

Unjust exclusion can take many forms, as justice can take many forms. There is political marginalization: the denial of the vote, restriction of free speech, the tyrannical concentration of power in the hands of a ruling élite, or straightforward totalitarianism. It can also be economic in nature. Where persons are unable to find work even after searching for many months or where they are thrown out of work by decisions they are powerless to influence, they are effectively marginalized. They are implicitly told by the community: we don't need your talent, we don't need your initiative, we don't need *you*.

This general normative perspective could be made concrete by a survey of the extent to which people are excluded or left behind in the life of the nation and throughout the world today. For example, over eight million people are looking for work in the USA but unable to find it. Over thirty million Americans live below the official poverty line. One out of every four children under 6 and one out of every two black children live in poverty. One-third of all female-headed families are poor. During a ten year period, one-fourth of all Americans fall into poverty during at least one year and must turn to an inadequate and degrading welfare system for support. Beyond our borders at least 800 million persons live in absolute poverty and nearly half a billion persons are chronically hungry. This despite fruitful harvests worldwide, and a food surplus in the US that is driving down prices and causing bankruptcy for large numbers of American farmers.[2]

When citizens acquiesce in this situation when remedial steps could be taken, injustice is being done. One can hardly think of a more effective way to deny people any active participation in the economic life of society than to cause or allow them to remain unemployed. Similarly, persons who face hunger, homelessness, and the extremes of poverty when society possesses the resources to meet their needs are treated as non-members. Citizens who permit or abet such conditions when effective action could be taken to change them for the better fail to exercise their responsibility toward the common good. As Michael Walzer puts it with respect to meeting the basic material needs of the underclass: 'Men and women who appropriate vast sums of money for themselves, while needs are unmet, act like tyrants, dominating and distorting the distribution of security and welfare' (Walzer, 1983, p. 76). In the same way, the hungry and homeless people in this nation today are no part of anything worthy of being called a commonwealth. The extent of their suffering shows how far we are from being a community of persons. The willingness of citizens to tolerate such conditions and even take actions that perpetuate them shows how far we are from an effective commitment to the common good in this nation.

Against the background of this normative understanding of justice and the common good, the fear that introducing substantive notions of the human good into our public life will be divisive and lead to intolerance seems rather quaint. We live in a dangerously divided nation and world. If we are to make a beginning in the task of securing even minimal justice, we need to confront these divisions, not avoid or 'tolerate' them. The chief problem in explicating an adequate concept of justice in our society today is not the different conceptions Americans have of what makes for full happiness or what private 'life-plans' are worth pursuing. The problem is that many would prefer not to reflect on what it means to say that marginalized people are members of the human community and we have a duty to treat them as such.

Consequences for Education

The difficulty of specifying how citizens might respond to this duty is very obvious. Does commitment to the common good really mean that each of us is responsible for the well being of all our near and distant neighbours throughout the world — for everybody? This is clearly not possible. Individuals, at least when acting one at a time, are simply incapable of shaping the quality of community life on such a vast scale, ranging all the way from the nearest of our neighbours to the persons half way around the globe. Rather, whatever the more specific duties of civic virtue or civic friendship or solidarity may be, they are necessarily mediated and specified through our roles as citizens, our roles as economic agents, our positions of responsibility on the job, the location that we have within a particular geography, and so on. One of the most important of the roles through which this responsibility is exercised is the role individuals and the community at large play in the sphere of education.

The link between education, virtue, and the common good was made explicit in the writing of a recent representative of the Catholic tradition, John Courtney Murray. In the 1950s, Murray argued that concern for the common good translates directly into concern for the moral substance of public affairs. The relevance of this concern to education is clear from the fact that, as Murray put it, 'the great "affair" of the commonwealth is, of course, education' (Murray, 1960, p. 9). He understood education in a capacious sense:

> It includes three general areas of common interest: the school system, its mode of organization, its curricular content, and the level of learn-ing among its teachers; the later education of the citizen in the liberal art of citizenship, and the more general enterprise of the advancement of knowledge by research. (ibid.)

Education, in its many forms and dimensions, therefore, shapes the values that become operative in the public affairs of a republic by helping to shape the virtues and character of its citizenry. Put negatively, worries about the quality of public life in a democracy lead directly to worries about the whole process by which one generation prepares its progeny to assume their responsibilities as citizens. This is the entire undertaking of education broadly conceived. Education in virtue is education that guides the development of students in ways that enable them to become good citizens, men and women dedicated to the service of the common good.

The discussion of the understanding of the common good presented in this chapter suggests that the Catholic community possesses a long tradition that, in its renewed contemporary form, positions it to make a potentially unique contribution to education of this sort. The appropriation of this tradi-tion by those involved in the educational project is a prerequisite first step for the realization of this potential. The Church as a whole has a critical role to play in enabling present and future teachers — parents first of all, but also teachers in formal school settings — to learn and appreciate this tradition. Catholic universities also have an essential role to play in educating these future teachers. These universities should also be places where the research into the contemporary challenges and opportunities for a broader commitment to the common good as well as the deeper cultural and philosophical resources for creative response is undertaken. These challenges and resources touch the entire educational undertaking in its curriculum, its mode of pedagogy, its patterns of organization and administration, and, above all, its intellectual and moral substance.

The realization of this potential contribution by the Catholic community is already well underway in Catholic schools, as the research of Anthony Bryk, Valerie Lee, and Peter Holland has shown (Bryk *et al.*, 1993). Bryk, Lee and Holland have also suggested that the endeavours underway in Catholic schools can provide suggestive models for how public schools might more effectively serve the common good. Some of the responses to Bryk, Lee, and Holland have questioned whether their study takes sufficient account of the need to preserve the distinctive religious identity of Catholic schools. This is indeed a serious question and needs to be dealt with in depth. In this context, it can only be observed that preservation of Catholic identity and the service of the common good of a pluralist society ought to be allies, not adversaries. Historical circumstances are surely imaginable where the fidelity of the Catholic community to its authentic tradition might call for direct resistance to, and even confrontation with, the ethos of the surrounding culture and social institutions. Nazi totalitarianism was an obvious case in point. In the United States today, however, it can be plausibly argued that the situation is almost a mirror image of that which prevailed under Nazism. Our problem is cultural fragmentation not political absolutism, value diffusion not totalization, loss of a sense of the good of the whole not threats to the autonomy or freedom of the individual. Without irony, the question can be raised for those who advocate a countercultural stance in Catholic education whether there is anything like a unified culture in the United States to which one might stand in resistance. In such circumstances, fidelity to the Catholic tradition of the common good calls not for countercultural opposition but creative participation in the effort to reweave the fabric of society into something that more closely resembles a unified whole. This is a task for Catholic schools themselves as participants in the broader society. It is also a task the Catholic community needs to address in public education at much greater depth than it has yet done.

The suggestion that the Catholic community can make an important contribution to the common good in the United States through education also continues to face the thicket of issues connected with Church–State separation and the meaning of the First Amendment of the United States Constitution. It might be observed here by way of conclusion that the public life of a society ought not be identified with the social domain directly under governmental supervision or political control. The idea that society can be divided into a public sphere identified with government and a private sphere identified with the autonomous and frequently isolated individual is counter to the deepest traditions of American democracy. Democracy depends on the existence of strong bonds of association in civil society, including the bonds of religious community. As Tocqueville observed in the early days of the American republic, the development of civic virtue was one of the prime contributions of the Churches to the American democratic experiment. Murray knew that this was true in the twentieth century as well. The power of law and politics is limited.

David Hollenbach S.J.

Government can curb the most egregious forms of unsocial behaviour and vice. But it cannot make good citizens in a more positive sense. The fact that a school or educational model is state-run does not guarantee this outcome either. The issue is what goes on in the classroom, in the curriculum, and in the entire social context of the education that takes place. It is possible to argue, as Bryk *et al.* have done, that Catholic education is more public (in the sense of civic) than are state-sponsored schools in the United States today. To the extent this is the case, the entire jurisprudence of First Amendment case law since the 1940s needs to be rethought. The development of a good society and the achievement of its common good is dependent on the quality of the society's education. The recognition that the Catholic community has something crucial to contribute in efforts to address this issue in our pluralist society is a challenge that remains to be met in American public opinion, in First amendment law, and in the Church itself.

Notes

1 See the *Report of the National Advisory Commission on Civil Disorders* 1968, New York, EP Dutton, p. 1.
2 These statements are based on data and documentation provided in National Conference of Catholic Bishops, *Economic Justice for All*, Ch. 3. The bishops' numbers are for 1986, but the situation is very similar today.

References

BELLAH, R., MADSEN, R., SULLIVAN, W.M., SWIDLER, A., STEVEN, M. and TIPTON, S.M. (1985) *Habits of the Heart: Individualism and Commitment in American Life*, Berkeley, CA, University of California Press.
BERGER, P.L., BERGER, B. and KELLNER, H. (1973) *The Homeless Mind: Modernization and Consciousness*, New York, Random House.
BRYK, A.S., LEE, V.E. and HOLLAND, P.B. (1993) *Catholic Schools and the Common Good*, Cambridge, Harvard University Press.
COLEMAN, J.A. (1982) 'Religious liberty in American and mediating structures,' in *An American Strategic Theology*, New York, Paulist Press.
DIONNE, E.J. JR. (1991) *Why Americans Hate Politics*, New York, Simon and Schuster.
DOUGLASS, R.B. (1986) 'First things first: The letter and the common good tradition,' in DOUGLASS, R.B. (Ed) *The Deeper Meaning of Economic Life*, Washington, DC, Georgetown University Press.
DOWNS, A. (1981) *Neighborhoods and Urban Development*, Washington, DC, Brookings Institution.
DOWNS, A. (1991) 'Cities, suburbs, and the common good,' A Woodstock occasional paper, Washington, DC, Woodstock Theological Center.
GANNON, T. (1987) (Ed) *The Catholic Challenge to the American Economy*, New York, Macmillan.
GREEN, R., BIRNBAUM, N. and KATZ, M. (1989) *The Undeserving Poor*, New York, Pantheon.
HUNTINGTON, S.P. (1991) 'Religion and the Third Wave,' *National Interest*, **24**, Summer.
JOHN PAUL II (1984) *Apostolic Exhortation on Reconciliation and Penance*, in *Origins*, **14**, 2.

JOHN PAUL II (1992) *Sollicitudo Rei Socialis*, in O'BRIEN, D.J. and SHANNON, T.A. (Eds) *Catholic Social Thought: The Documentary Heritage*, **38**, Maryknoll, NY, Orbis Books.

LUTZ, C. (1986) (Ed) *God, Goods, and the Common Good*, Minneapolis, MN, Augsburg.

MILLER, W.L. (1986) *The First Liberty: Religion and the American Republic*, New York, Alfred A. Knopf.

MURRAY, J.C. (1960) *We Hold These Truths: Catholic Reflections on the American Proposition*, New York, Sheed and Ward.

NATIONAL CONFERENCE OF CATHOLIC BISHOPS (1986) *Economic Justice for All: Pastoral Letter on Catholic Social Teaching and the US Economy*, **22**, Washington, DC, United States Catholic Conference.

PRANGER, R.J. (1968) *The Eclipse of Citizenship: Power and Participation in Contemporary Politics*, New York, Holt, Rinehart and Winston.

RAWLS, J. (1987) 'The idea of an overlapping consensus,' *Oxford Journal of Legal Studies*, **7**.

STRAIN, C.R. (1989) (Ed) *Prophetic Visions and Economic Realities: Protestants, Jews, and Catholics Confront the Bishops' Letter on the Economy*, Grand Rapids, MI, Eerdmans.

WALZER, M. (1970) 'The problem of citizenship,' in *Obligations: Essays on Disobedience, War, and Citizenship*, Cambridge, MA, Harvard University Press.

WALZER, M. (1983) *Spheres of Justice: A Defense of Pluralism and Equality*, New York, Basic Books.

WILSON, W.J. (1987) *The Truly Disadvantaged: The Inner City, The Underclass, and Public Policy*, Chicago, University of Chicago Press.

Part 2

The Identity of the Catholic School

Chapter 7

What Makes a School Catholic?

Thomas H. Groome

To educate, to teach, to help keep a school! These activities reflect one of the noblest vocations in life; there is none worthier than to be an educator. So why designate some education, or schools, or teachers — 'Catholic', and how might the term qualify what goes on as educating or schooling, or who one is as a teacher. Why the qualifier 'Catholic' at all?

An occasional attitude is that 'it doesn't really matter, except for the religion teachers . . . but not for us math, or literature, or social science, or . . . teachers.' But this reductionism reflects some of the most debilitating myths of western education: that what people know should be divorced from who they are and how they live; that the disciplines of learning are not simply distinct but separate; that the environment and life of the school is not an aspect of its curriculum; that the 'personhood' of teachers does not impinge on how and what they teach; that all education, except what is clearly value laden (e.g., teaching religion), is value free. Beyond being untrue, such myths impede good education.

The qualifier 'Catholic' does mean something for 'education' so designated, but I first recognize some hazards in even inquiring about it. There are dangers of élitism, or worse still sectarianism. It could encourage a 'witch hunt' or turn the qualifier into a 'chapel call'. Though a Catholic educator is most likely someone whose 'being' is nurtured by the tradition of meaning and ethic that is Catholicism, there can be educators of other or even no religious persuasion who make fine 'Catholic' educators because they share the appropriate perspectives and commitments. And being Catholic can vary across many cultural expressions, theological positions, and with different degrees and styles of participation in the institutional expression of Catholicism.

Though we must proceed with caution, it seems imperative, however, for the integrity of Catholic education that we have some conceptual clarity about its qualifier. My proposal is a rather self evident one:

> that the distinctiveness of Catholic education is prompted by the distinctive characteristics of Catholicism itself, and these characteristics should be reflected in the whole curriculum of Catholic schools.

By 'curriculum' I intend the *content* taught, the *process* of teaching, and the *environment* of the school.

It is difficult to specify what gives Catholicism its distinctive character. Richard P. McBrien, writes, 'There is no one characteristic, apart from the Petrine doctrine, which sets the Catholic Church apart from *all other* churches' (McBrien, 1980, p. 1172). Beyond its Petrine office, however, McBrien adds that there are 'various characteristics of Catholicism, each of which . . . Catholicism shares with one or another Christian Church or tradition' but that 'a case can be made that nowhere else except in the Catholic Church are *all* of Catholicism's characteristics present in the precise *configuration* in which they are found within Catholicism' (ibid.). In other words, though Catholicism may share particular features to varying degrees with other Christian traditions, yet their combination and configuration within Catholicism constitutes its uniqueness — its 'Catholicity'.

'To see ourselves as others see us' is always advisable with questions of identity. This makes the work of Langdon Gilkey particularly helpful here; a world renowned senior theologian, Gilkey is an American Baptist. From his Protestant perspective, he poses four distinguishing features in the unique 'configuration' of Catholicism:

- Catholicism's commitment to *tradition*; its 'sense of the reality, importance, and "weight" of tradition and history in the formation of this people and so of her religious truths, religious experience, and human wisdom.'
- Catholicism's positive *anthropology*; its realistic but optimistic understanding of people as capable of sin but essentially good, and its emphasis on the relational nature and communal grace of human existence.
- Catholicism's sense of *sacramentality*; the conviction that God's life and love — grace — comes to us and that we go to God through the created order and the everyday things of life.
- Catholicism's commitment to *rationality*, to the place of reason in life and in faith. Gilkey notes 'throughout Catholic history a drive toward rationality, the insistence that the divine mystery manifest in tradition and sacramental presence be insofar as possible penetrated, defended, and explicated by the most acute rational reflection.' (Gilkey, 1975, pp. 17–22)

Building on Gilkey, and dividing his anthropological aspect into two, I propose five particular and distinguishing characteristics of Catholicism. These characteristics, overlapping but distinct, are:

1 its *positive anthropology* of the person;
2 its *sacramentality* of life;
3 its *communal emphasis* regarding human and Christian existence;
4 its *commitment to tradition* as source of its Story and Vision; and
5 its appreciation of *rationality* and learning, epitomized in its commitment to education.

These five might be called *theological characteristics* in that they are grounded in Catholic understanding of God and of human existence; there is theological warrant for them.

But beyond and permeating these theological characteristics, Catholicism has three other pervading commitments that are particularly relevant for Catholic education. Echoing the old distinction of the virtues into theological and cardinal, we can call these 'cardinal' characteristics in that they are the 'hinges' (latin, *cardo*) that permeate and bind the other five together. These three cardinal characteristics are:

- Catholicism's commitment to people's 'personhood', to who they become and their ethic of life — an *ontological* concern;
- Catholicism's commitment to 'basic justice' — a *sociological* concern; and
- Catholicism's commitment to 'catholicity' — a *universal* concern.

I will review the five theological characteristics with regard to their import for Catholic education, and then, more briefly, the three cardinal characteristics and how these lynchpins in the configuration of Catholicism are to permeate Catholic education. The collage of these eight characteristics constitutes education that is 'Catholic'.[1]

Anthropology: In God's Own Image and Likeness

The core of Catholic anthropology — its theological understanding of the human condition — is often described as a 'realistic optimism' about us. It recognizes our capacity and 'proneness' for sin, but insists that we are essentially more good than evil. Though 'fallen', our divine image and likeness was never totally lost through original sin. Rather we retain our innate capacity for good and for God. Practically this means that people are always in need of God's grace *and* have the capacity, with God's help, to make a positive contribution to our personal and common welfare. Further, we are held responsible for the choices we make, and our graced efforts for goodness and truth have historical significance.

This Catholic anthropology has been forged over history as a mediating stance between two other classic but extreme positions: the *total self-sufficiency* of Pelagius (circa 400), and the *total depravity* of Calvin and the radical Reformers. For example, at the great counter-Reformation Council of Trent (1545–63) Catholicism took a middle position between Pelagius' claim that we can 'save ourselves' and Calvin's that we are a *massa peccati*, a mass of sin, incapable of contributing anything to 'the work of our salvation' (Phil. 2, 12). Trent articulated the classic Catholic position that the human condition is not self sufficient but a 'fallen' one, and yet we are not totally depraved but remain 'inherently good'; we are responsible, by God's grace, for our own well-being and for that of others.

This anthropology originates in the Biblical story of our creation in God's own image and likeness (Gn. 1, 27), and undergirds all the covenants, including the new covenant in Jesus, that God makes with God's people thereafter. The biblical notion of covenant is that God bonds humankind with each other and with Godself in partnership to live by God's intentions for all creation. Both parties promise to fulfil their side of this partnership, implying that humankind, with God's help, is so capable. In the Christian dispensation, the goodness of the human condition is assured unequivocally by the Incarnation, the faith that God in Jesus Christ became human, was 'made flesh, to dwell among us' (Jn. 1, 14) and to forge a 'new covenant' of irreversible union between divinity and humanity. Likewise a Catholic theology of grace impinges here. Our conviction is that Jesus is the definitive catalyst of God's life and love irrevocably turned toward us; in Jesus 'grace abounded all the more' (Rom. 5, 20). The grace of God to us in Jesus builds upon our 'original grace', transforming our inner selves and empowering our human efforts to do God's will; and all this without violating our freedom or alleviating our responsibilities. In the pithy summary of Aquinas 'grace works through nature'.

This 'graced nature' anthropology gives us both rights and responsibilities. Our dignity in God's own image gives all of us inalienable human rights, but correspondingly our capacity to be partners and historical agents gives us responsibility to defend and promote similar rights for all humankind. Pope John XXIII, described our essential human rights and responsibilities as: to life and to a worthy manner of living; to respect as persons without discrimination on any basis; to pursue and express the truth; to be informed and educated; to worship God freely and to choose a state in life; to gainful employment, decent conditions, and just compensation for work; to organize, meet and associate; to participate in public affairs and to contribute to the common good (John XXIII, 1976, pp. 203–6).

Catholic anthropology of our innate capacity for good and for God, coupled with its theology of God's grace in Jesus as renewing and working through this 'nature', has prompted a rich Catholic tradition of spirituality. This tradition has many 'schools' of approach, (Benedictine, Dominican, Franciscan, Ignatian, etc.) but all reflect and serve the conviction that every Christian is capable of and called by baptism to a life of holiness as 'right relationship' with God, self, others, and creation. A Catholic sense of holiness also entails a life-long deepening of one's personal relationship with God in the context of a faith community, living with consciousness of God's presence in the midst of the world.

Overall, it can be said that a Catholic anthropology has encouraged its adherents to embrace life with enthusiasm, to approach it is a gift of God to be enjoyed, to defend it, celebrate it, affirm it, and to relish its essential goodness. Gilkey writes that Catholicism has 'a remarkable sense of humanity'; 'consequently, the love of life, the appreciation of the body and the senses, the joy and celebration, the tolerance of the sinner, these natural, worldly and "human" virtues are far more clearly and universally embodied in Catholics and Catholic life than in Protestants and Protestantism' (Gilkey, op. cit., p. 19).

For Catholic Education: This understanding of our human condition before God calls the whole curriculum of Catholic education to reflect and promote at least three commitments:

- to affirm students' basic goodness, to promote their dignity, to honor their fundamental rights, and to develop their gifts to the fullest — as *God's reflections*;
- to educate people to live responsibly, with God's help, for the fullness of life that God wills for self and others — as *responsible partners*;
- to convince and mold people to live as if their lives are worthwhile and have historical significance, that their every good effort advances the well-being of all — as *history makers*.

As *God's Reflections*: The content, process, and environment of Catholic education should reflect to its students that they are made in the image and likeness of God. They have a right to a curriculum that convinces them of their inherent goodness, that nurtures their sense of dignity and self-worth, that treats them with respect, that helps to develop their every good gift and talent — mental, emotional and physical, intellectual, interpersonal and aesthetic, and ultimately their spiritual appetite for personal relationship with God.

As *Responsible Partners*: Catholic anthropology demands an education that informs and forms its students in their responsibility to initiate and work with others for their own and human well-being. To Cain's age-old question 'am I my brothers (and sisters) keeper?' (Genesis 4, 9), Catholic education must dispose people to respond a resounding 'yes' and prepare them to respect and promote the human rights of all.

As *History-Makers*: The whole curriculum of Catholic education should help convince people of the deep worth-whileness and ultimate significance of their lives; that they *can* make a difference. It is to help them to take on, with historical agency, the stated purpose of Jesus, 'I have come that you may have life, and have it to the full' (Jn. 10, 10). They must be educated to cherish, value, and defend their own and all life, from womb to tomb. Counter-cultural to all forms of social fatalism, Catholic education prepares people to be 'history makers', creators and recreators of their context, confident that the seeds of every good effort will never be lost. Essentially it must prepare them to embrace and celebrate, to defend and promote the gift of God that is human life.

For Catholic education, the commitments demanded by its anthropology may be more pertinent for how people are taught and for the politics of the school environment than for the content of teaching, though the latter must clearly reflect such values as well. Affirming their goodness and dignity, promoting their rights and gifts, forming them in responsibility and with a sense of historical agency, all this is less likely with a pedagogy that treats students as passive receptacles for what Dewey called 'predigested knowledge' that teachers 'ladle out in doses' (Dewey, 1938, p. 46, p. 82). Called for, instead, is a pedagogy that engages students as active and creative participants in the teaching/learning dynamic, that draws upon their experiences and learning from life, that gives them direct access to enriching disciplines of learning and traditions of wisdom, and that encourages them to reach their own judgments and decisions. Likewise, the politics of the school environment should be permeated with a 'life-affirming' anthropology. In short, the whole curriculum should promote the ancient conviction of Irenaeus, that 'the glory of God is the human person fully alive'.

Sacramentality: 'To See God in All Things'

Catholicism has a cosmology — perspective on life and creation — very reson-ant with its anthropology. It takes the position that all of God's creation is essentially good; though we can misuse or abuse it, what God has made and makes is never inherently evil. This cosmology, in turn, encourages the Catholic principle of sacramentality.

For Catholics, mention of 'sacramentality' usually has an association with church and the seven sacraments. The liturgical sacraments, however, are climatic expressions of what Karl Rahner calls 'the liturgy of life' also described as 'the principle of sacramentality'. McBrien writes, 'No theological principle or focus is more characteristic of Catholicism or more central to its identity than the principle of *sacramentality*' (op. cit., p. 1180). This principle reflects the central Catholic conviction that God mediates Godself to us and we encounter God's presence and grace coming to meet us through the ordinary of life — through our minds and bodies, through our works and efforts, in the depth of our own being and through our relationships with others, through the events and experiences that come our way, through all forms of human art and creativity, through nature and the whole created order, through everything and anything of life.

A 'sacramental consciousness' means being aware of the presence of God as the backdrop and foreground of life. It is able to 'look through' reality to 'see' for oneself 'the beyond in the midst', the Ultimate in the immediate, the Transcendent in the ordinary, the Creator in the created, the Divine in what is very human. It experiences the ever present Spirit of God taking initiative and reaching out to us in the everyday. In the classic 'catholic' phrase of Ignatius of Loyola, a sacramental consciousness is able 'to see God in all things'. It is the epitome of a truly 'religious' consciousness in that it is perennially aware that everything is 'tied-back-into' (*re-ligare*) or anchored in an ultimate 'Ground of Being'.

The seven sacraments, then, are climatic instances of this principle of sacramentality. These liturgical rituals, through which the Risen Christ is essen-tially present by the Holy Spirit, intensify participants' everyday experiences of the outreach of God's life and love; but the mediating symbols between the people and God are still of the ordinary — bread, wine, water, oil, human love, and so on, and they are all celebrated as and through community.

Clearly a sacramental consciousness engages imagination, which is to say peoples' 'selves' as historical agents. In this it has an ethical impulse that enables us to imagine what might and ought to be, what we can and should do, and disposes our wills to choose accordingly (Kearney, 1988). A sacramental consciousness not only 'sees' God's presence in all but can 'see' what God wills for humankind. Here Christian faith nurtures people's imaginations with the Vision of God's reign, God's 'imaginings' for all creation, the realization of peace and justice, of love and freedom, wholeness and fullness of life for all, and the integrity of God's creation. In Jesus' description of the Last Judgment (Mt. 25, pp. 31–45), the 'goats' claim that they 'never saw' — the hungry, the homeless, the oppressed, — but it will not be a sufficient defense. Christian sacramental consciousness has the disposition 'to see' who should be seen, especially people overlooked or made invisible by society, and to respond as agents of God's reign; it encourages a faith that does justice.

For Catholic Education, the intention of forming students in a sacramental consciousness should permeate the whole curriculum of a Catholic school. This does not mean 'dragging in religion' in a contrived kind of way; there were instances of this at one time in Catholic curricula (e.g., in math class: 'if the rosary has five decades of ten Hail Marys each, how many Hail Marys in the rosary?'). Instead, education for a sacramental consciousness means encouraging students, regardless of what they are studying, to employ the critical and creative powers of their minds (reason, memory, and imagination) to look '*at*' life so intensely and rigorously that they begin to look '*through*' it. More perhaps by the questions they ask than by the statements they make, teachers can prompt students to realize that every life-question is eventually a religious one, that all truth is grounded in Divine truth (even math depends on the notion of infinity), that every answer leads on to a question, and eventually to Ultimate and Gracious Mystery.

Teachers themselves need to bring a sacramental consciousness to their teaching. Contrary to what some might expect, this is marked first by a commitment to academic rigour, in other words to study carefully and thoroughly, honoring the academic canons of the particular discipline. And then it is marked by the constant sense that 'there is always more here than meets the eye' — a critical (in the questioning sense) and creative posture that urges students on to see 'the more' that always awaits them.

For example, instead of studying literature with a technical rationality that dissects and 'masters' texts, it can be approached as a 'mirror of life' to surface life's perennial questions and to glean wisdom from how others have grappled with living humanly. With this attitude good literature can reflect a 'word' of God to students, not as revealed in scripture but as discovered from life. Most assuredly, all the arts can be approached as 'teachable moments' for a sacramental consciousness; nothing more stimulates the imagination — the primary mode of a sacramental consciousness. The Arts can turn participants toward the transcendent because they are 'a reflection of the divine beauty in tangible form', and by engaging their own creativity and aesthetic ability they enliven people's sense of identity with their Creator (The Congregation for Catholic Education, 1988, par. 61). Students can study the social sciences in a way that they come to 'see' the deep relationality of humankind, and to discover that we are 'made for each other'. The natural sciences too can be taught with a style that prompts students to look 'through' reality to plumb the pattern, design, mystery, beauty, awe, and wonder of God's creation. They can discover that 'the whole of creation, from the distant celestial bodies and the immeasurable cosmic forces down to the infinitesimal particles and waves of matter and energy, all bear the imprint of the Creator's wisdom and power' (ibid., par. 54). And so on for every discipline of learning; all can be taught with and to encourage a sacramental consciousness in students.

Community: 'Made for Each Other'

Catholicism has a strong emphasis on the 'communal' nature of human existence: that we find our identity and true selves in relationship with others. This characteristic combines aspects of its anthropology and cosmology; the first suggests that we have a natural affinity for relationship and are capable of 'right relationship' with others, and its cosmology that the social structures and cultural expressions of our 'public' world, instead of being a 'city of sin' as the Reformers might have it, can be an instrument of Gods saving grace. This communal characteristic has been reflected in Catholicism's social and ecclesial emphases throughout its history, its accent on the social responsibility of Christian faith to contribute to the 'common good', and the necessity for Christians to actively participate in a Christian community — the Church. In fact, theologically, Catholicism's communal emphasis arises from its conviction that we need to be 'church' — a community that welcomes all — for the sake of our salvation.

The Hebrew scriptures are the story of a people called to become a 'people of God' by entering into covenant with God and each other. Since the call of Abraham and Sarah, they are to live as 'the people of God'. Throughout their history, the Israelites are always aware that their well-being — their salvation — depends on this covenant and community. Their sins and their graces, their faithfulness to God and their wandering away, are as a 'people'. Recent New Testament scholarship has deepened awareness that Jesus called his followers together into 'an inclusive community of disciples' (Fiorenza, 1983). The inclusiveness of his table fellowship alone, welcoming the socially marginalized and public sinners, is a powerful parable of the kind of community he intended among his people. Paul posed the image of the Church as 'the body of Christ' (see 1 Cor. 12, 12–31, etc.), a compelling analogy for communal solidarity and 'catholicity'.

When the Reformers rejected this ecclesial emphasis of Catholicism (and for some good reasons — corruption, exaggerated power of Church authorities, etc.), Catholicism clung to its emphasis that we encounter God as a community of faith, that the primary mode (not the only one) of God coming to us and our going to God is as 'Church' — now the sacrament of Christ to the world. So deep was this Catholic conviction about the communality of Christian faith that it insisted on the solidarity of the whole Church of saints and sinners, living and dead. Over the Reformers' objections, it reiterated that the baptismal bond of the Body of Christ is never broken, not even by death, that the living and dead can intercede for each other before God.

The Second Vatican Council deepened and amplified this characteristic of Catholicism by returning to a more clearly communal understanding of the nature and mission of the Church. Likewise, recent Church teaching has clarified the kind of community that the Church should be within itself and in its mission to the world. Within itself, the Church is to be a community of deep love, of total inclusion, and of 'right relationship' — the biblical description of justice. 'While the Church is bound to give witness to justice, it recognizes that anyone who ventures to speak to people about justice must first be just in their eyes. Hence we must undertake an examination of the modes of acting and of the possessions and lifestyle found within the Church itself.'[2] For its mission to the world, the 'mind of the Church' seems clearer than ever that it is to be a community of effective action and witness — a sacrament — of God's reign of peace and justice to the world, a catalyst for the 'common good'. And, as throughout its tradition, Catholicism sees its schools as crucial agents in this communal mission to be Church and sacrament to the world. 'The Catholic school finds its true justification in the mission of the Church' (The Congregation for Catholic Education, 1988, par. 34).

For Catholic Education: Though this communal characteristic of Catholicism should permeate the content and process of the school's pedagogy, it is clearly most significant for the life of the school itself. A school influences people's identity, perspectives, and values — socializes them — primarily through the 'implicit curriculum' (Eisner, 1979, ch. 5) of its ethos, structure, and style, by its whole way of being together as school. The environment of a Catholic school needs to reflect community, not simply as an ideal taught but as a value realized. (It is heartening to note the empirical evidence that community is, in fact, a notable value of Catholic schools) (Covey, 1992, p. 33, p. 108). In the words of Vatican II, Catholic education 'aims to create for the school community an atmosphere enlivened by the gospel spirit of *freedom* and *love*' (Abbott, 1966, par. 8, p. 646).

Its spirit of freedom should be reflected in an atmosphere of openness, intellectual and social, where students and faculty feel free to become their own best selves and to pursue knowledge and truth wherever they can be found, where the school strives to be a community of welcome and hospitality for all. The love commitment of the school should be realized as a profound care and 'right relationship' among and between teachers, administrators, and students, and toward the school's extended community of parents, former students and the parish(es) of its local context. For analysis, we can think of this communal characteristic of Catholicism requiring a school to be both *a public community* and an *ecclesial community*.

The Catholic school is to be a *public community* that educates its students in social responsibility, informing and forming them to contribute to the 'common good'. In this, Catholic education is often counter-cultural to the mores of rugged individualism, self-sufficiency, and social indifference that permeate western society. It will socialize its students to care about and contribute to the common good through its own ethos of 'right relationship' and social consciousness, through its operative values of peace and justice, and by credible concern for the marginalized and suffering of society. Its explicit curriculum will teach for such 'right relationship' and 'common good' by allowing this ethic to permeate its formal content, and more effectively, perhaps, by its very style of teaching.

Commitment to community advises a pedagogy grounded in relationship, and marked by participation, by conversation, and by cooperation. Teaching styles that reflect domination, passivity, monologue, and competition would seem antithetical to this communal commitment. And formation in a social consciousness calls for teaching styles that encourage critical reflection and questioning of the social/political context, that nurture creative imagination about what can and should be done in the public arena. Stated negatively, if a school does not challenge and encourage its students to oppose racism, sexism, militarism, ageism, and all other such 'isms' that bedevil our society and world, its education is not Catholic.

We can note two emphases in the Catholic school as an *ecclesial community*: its close association and partnership with the local church, and through this affiliation its bond with the universal Church; and second its efforts to be a Christian faith community within itself. The Catholic school should always think of the Church, local and universal, as its primary sponsor, as the parent community to which it belongs. Always its mission finds its warrant and ideology, and is realized within the broader mission of the Church. Even for its own well-being, it needs a partnership with the faith community(ies) of its context, and to develop networks of support. This is the 'functional community' of Catholic schools that provides their 'social capital,' and which Coleman credits as a significant factor in the schools' effectiveness (Coleman and Hoffer, 1987, p. 378, note 6).

A Catholic school is not a parish. Yet its very nature and purpose calls it to be a community of Christian faith. As such, it is to share in the traditional tasks of a Christian community, albeit in an educational way. Since the earliest days, the Church has recognized that the mission of God's reign in Jesus entails at least four historical tasks: to teach, preach, and evangelize the *word* of God in scripture and tradition (*kerygma*); to *witness* as a community of faith, hope and love in the world (*koinonia*); to *worship* God in prayer and communal liturgy (*leitourgia*); and to care for human *welfare* (*diakonia*).

In a school community, these functions of *word, witness, worship,* and *welfare* cannot be relegated to the chaplaincy or the religion department, but should permeate and engage its whole shared life and curriculum. Clearly students should have access to the scriptures and traditions of Christian faith (elaborated under Tradition below). But beyond that, the school is to offer opportunities for prayer, communal *worship*, and intensified spiritual experiences (retreats, etc.); it should be an effective *witness* — a sacrament — of Christian faith through every aspect of its communal life (style of administration, discipline procedures, hiring and promotion policy, means of evaluation, school governance, projects and group activities, school assemblies, outreach, relationships, etc.); and it should be a communities of *welfare* or service to its own students, and give them opportunities to care for the welfare of others. John Dewey claimed that the schools of a democratic society should be democratic societies themselves in 'embryonic form' (Dewey, 1971). Likewise, a Catholic school should be a Christian faith community in 'embryonic form'.

Tradition: To Share 'Story and Vision'

The Second Vatican Council states that Catholic education 'strives to relate all human culture eventually to the news of salvation, so that the light of faith will illumine the knowledge which students gradually gain of the world, of life, and of (human) kind' (Abbott, op. cit., p. 646). The core of this 'news of salvation' is the person of Jesus Christ. Everything else about Christian faith must be permeated by the Incarnation, the conviction that God became human in Jesus of Nazareth. Christianity is now the historical movement of God's word continuing to 'become flesh' by being realized and lived in every time and place. Because it is essentially an enterprise of Catholic Christian faith, Jesus and this incarnational principle is the heart of Catholic education. Encounter with the person of Jesus Christ and his 'good news of salvation' is mediated now through Christian Story and Vision — the meaning and ethic of Christian faith; they should be at the core of the curriculum of a Catholic school.

Christian 'Story' refers the whole scripture and tradition that grew up before Jesus in the ancient people of Israel, around him from his person and preaching, and after him down through the ages as his community of disciples, the Church, continued to develop in their understanding, living, and articulation of Christian faith. As Vatican II stated, 'The *tradition* which comes from the apostles *develops* in the Church with the help of the Holy Spirit . . . there is growth in the understanding of the realities and the words handed down . . .' (Abbott, op. cit., p. 116). As a metaphor for the whole reality of Christian faith, 'Story' helps to avoid Reformation polemics (scripture and/or tradition), gives a sense of something that continues to unfold, and it captures what Gilkey intends by Catholicism's characteristic emphasis on Tradition. He means to highlight the Catholic resistance to the Reformer's cry of *scripture sola* — scripture alone, and its insistence on carrying the whole 'Story' of Christian faith as it unfolds over history as symbol of revelation now. The 'Story' of Christian faith, then, includes: its scriptures and liturgies; its creeds, dogmas, doctrines and theologies; its sacraments and rituals, symbols, myths, gestures and religious language patterns; its spiritualities, values, laws, and expected lifestyles; and so on. Any symbol that reflects and carries the historical reality of Catholic Christian faith is an aspect of Christian Story.

The metaphor 'Vision' emphasizes that the Christian Story always has historical import; it is not simply to be remembered but realized again, not simply to be known about but lived (see Groome, 1991, Ch. 4). What the Story means for us, how we are to live it on all levels of existence (personal, interpersonal, and social/political), and who we are to become in response to it, this is the Vision of Christian faith. Ultimately this Christian Vision is the reign of God — the ongoing coming to fulfilment of God's intentions of shalom and fullness of life for humanity, history, and all creation. More immediately, Vision refers to the meaning and ethic, the hopes and responsibilities, the promises and demands that every aspect of Christian Story symbolizes for adherents.

For Catholic Education: Catholic education should intentionally catechize its students in Christian Story and Vision. Catholic catechesis has never settled for a 'religious studies' type of programme, a learning about the Catholic or other religious traditions. Beyond 'learning about', Catholic education intends students to 'learn from', and even, with ecumenical sensitivity and respecting students' backgrounds, to be personally influenced and enriched by Catholic faith. The Catholic school is to educate the very 'being' of its students, to inform, form, and transform their identity and agency — who they are and how they live — with the meaning and ethic of Christian faith. Beyond knowing about Jesus, it intends that they become disciples of his 'way'. Beyond knowing about justice and compassion, it intends its students to become just and compassionate, and so on for every symbol of Christian Story.

Such catechesis, however, cannot be some form of indoctrination nor settle for uncritical socialization.[3] Catholic catechesis must be marked by good education, education that brings people to know the data of the tradition, to understand it, to personally and critically appropriate it, and to come to life decisions in response to it. Precisely because the intent is to move beyond knowledge to wisdom, beyond information to the 'being' of participants, such pedagogy must personally engage students, all of their capacities and dispositions. My own proposal is for a catechesis that actively engages students to name and reflect on their lives in the world, brings them to personally encounter the Story/Vision of Christian faith, and enables them to place these two sources of God's ongoing revelation in dialogue with each other, to critically appropriate the 'faith handed on' to their lives, and to make historical decisions in response to it (See Groome, op. cit.).

Clearly this commitment to Tradition calls for a specific catechetical curriculum in Catholic schools. But, like all these characteristics, it should also permeate the whole curriculum. Every teacher in a Catholic school, regardless of what discipline of learning he/she teaches, has umpteen teachable moments for mediating between the lives of students and Christian Story/Vision. When the sophomore talks to the math teacher as a friend about the recent death of a grandmother, this is likely to be a more teachable moment about Christian faith in resurrection and eternal life than might be available in the formal religion class. The first grader who wonders 'where babies come from' in reading class is likely to be most teachable then about the mystery, sacredness, and God-giftedness of life. And beyond such explicit catechesis and teachable moments, Catholic Christian Story and Vision should be the pervasive ideology that undergirds the Catholic School, lending its distinct identity and *raison d'être*, shaping its style and commitments, bonding its members into a cohesive community.[4]

Rationality: 'Faith Seeking Understanding'

Though it may surprise some Catholics, Gilkey is correct in crediting Catholicism with an abiding commitment to rationality. The clearest historical expression of this characteristic is its commitment to education, and to a 'humanities' curriculum centred upon the liberal arts, classic texts, and critical rationality.

The Jewish context of Christianity gave deep roots to its commitment to education. And Catholicism came to at least three theological warrants of its own for commitment to scholarship, rationality, and thus to education:

- its optimistic but realistic anthropology that affirms both the need and potential of education;
- a *this* as well as an *other* worldly understanding of salvation, for both here and hereafter, thus recommending humanizing education as an aspect of 'the work of our salvation' (Phil. 2, 12); and
- the conviction that reason and revelation are essential partners in the life of Christian faith.

Striking a path between fideism (blind faith) and rationalism (sufficiency of reason), Catholicism has been convinced that understanding and faith, reason and revelation, need and enhance each other. Though there has always been support for Tertullian's defiant stance that 'Jerusalem has no need of Athens', Catholicism has favoured a more balanced view, well summarized in a classic statement of Aquinas: 'just as grace does not destroy nature but perfects it, so sacred doctrine presupposes, uses, and perfects natural knowledge' (Thomas Aquinas, *Summa Theologica*, Ia, I 8 ad 2).

The early Apologists (c.120–220) used their classic education to present Christian faith in a compelling way to the learned. At Alexandria, a group of scholars began to forge a 'Christian paideia', a synthesis of the gospel and secular learning into a Christian humanism. Under the leadership of Clement (c.150–215) and Origen (c.185–254), this 'school' educated people in Christian faith and the best of classic culture, convinced that the latter could be 'stirrups to reach the sky' of spiritual wisdom (Origen). It became the model for other Christian schools throughout the Empire. St Augustine (354–430) reiterated this appreciation of secular scholarship, arguing that as the Israelites had taken booty from Egypt, so Christians should make their own the best of pagan learning. Throughout the 'dark ages' (c.450–950), the Church's monastic schools were beacons of learning. Monks like Alcuin and Rabanus Maurus led the Carolingian renaissance (c.800), and the monastery and cathedral schools of that era became the founding roots of the great universities of the West (Paris, Oxford, Salamanca, etc.).

At the dawn of the second millennium, the great scholastics — Anselm, Abelard, Peter Lombard, and then the greatest of them, Aquinas, forged a new Christian paideia. They married faith and reason into the science of theology and enabled it to hold its own in the universities; in fact it became the 'queen of the sciences'. The Reformers found good cause to eschew 'the whore reason' (Luther) because of the undue rationality that had overtaken Christian theology (the proverbial 'how many angels can fit on the head of a pin?'). They insisted that 'faith alone' is enough for salvation. Though rightly chastened, Catholicism insisted at the Council of Trent (1545–1563) that while 'faith alone saves', people's faith is strengthened by reason and understanding. This complementarity was reiterated at the First Vatican Council (1869–70): 'Faith and reason can never disagree; . . . they are even mutually advantageous. For right reason demonstrates the foundations of faith and, . . . faith . . . sets reason free . . .'[5] The Catholic Church, at its best and when faithful to its own long tradition, champions the right of people to think critically for themselves, and encourages the dynamic interplay of faith and reason.

Catholicism places particular emphasis on the historical responsibility of reason to serve human well-being. In this it rejects the disembodied rationality of Cartesianism, and avoids the dichotomous schema of Kant that separates theoretical from practical reasoning, and thus science from ethics. It rejects the now common assumption that reasoning is 'objective' (non-perspectival) and 'value free' (above ethic). Instead, Catholicism sees reason as a gift of God that is to bring us to both understanding and moral responsibility.

Bernard Lonergan is a fine contemporary instance of a Catholic rationality. Lonergan, acknowledging his indebtedness to Aquinas, delineates the dynamics of cognition (the acts we perform when we come to 'know' something) as four-fold: *attending* to the data of experience and tradition, *understanding* this data through reasoning, *judging* the truth or accuracy of our understanding, and *deciding* responsibly what to do with what one 'knows' (Lonergan, 1972, Ch. 1). Note that the outcome of this schema moves beyond understanding to judgment and responsibility.

For Catholic Education: Catholic education should not tell people what to think but prepare and practice its students to think for themselves. It should form them in the habit of critical reflection, a kind of questioning that engages people's reason, memory, and imagination, and is critical in the sense of becoming aware of the historical source and responsibility of all knowledge. Building on Lonergan's schema, this means that Catholic education should encourage students: to attend to their own historical reality and to actively engage the knowledge and wisdom of the ages in all the sciences of learning; to try to personally understand their lives and the disciplines of scholarship; to make their own informed judgments in dialogue with others; and to reach responsible decisions that are conceptually and morally adequate, i.e., make sense, and are life-giving for self and others.

Such rationality coupled with Catholic anthropology means encouraging people to think for themselves, to trust their own discernment and decision making. Its sacramentality suggests helping people to think with imagination and perception, to discern the ultimate in the immediate, and to be critically conscious about society. Rationality coupled with community encourages students to think in dialogue and conversation, to test their reasoning in discourse with others and with communities of wisdom and faith. Catholicism's commitment to tradition coupled with rationality means enabling students to critically appropriate the tradition to their lives rather than passively inheriting it, to make it their own rather than accepting it blindly, and to think about tradition in ways likely to encourage personal and social responsibility.

'Personhood': An Ontological Concern

Catholic education intends to inform and form the very 'being' of its students, to mold their identity and agency — who they are and how they live. In traditional philosophical terms, its intended learning outcome moves beyond the epistemological (*episteme*, knowledge) to the ontological (*ontos*, being), without leaving the former behind. Catholic education 'aims not only to influence what students know and can do but also the kind of people they will become' (Bryk *et al.*, op. cit., p. 10).

This characteristic is not to be taken for granted; in fact it is countercultural to much of modern education. So much education has fallen prey to the diminution of epistemology that severs people's 'knowing' from their 'being' and reduces knowledge to a technical rationality, a 'know how' for productivity. I say diminution because for Plato to know the good is to become good, for Aristotle knowing arises from and shapes one's 'being' in the world. Likewise in the Hebrew and Christian traditions, 'to know' means a wisdom that brings one's very 'being' into right relationship with God, self, others, and creation; ultimately to know is to love, and 'the one without love knows nothing of God' (1 Jn. 4, 8).

Western philosophy, however, failed to maintain this ancient unity and severed knowing from being (Descartes being a leading culprit). Now the pervasive assumption is that knowledge is 'objective' and 'value-free', as if it is not to engage persons as 'persons' or influence their ethic. Catholic education has consistently refused this dichotomy, and insists on engaging and educating the 'being' of its students.

This ontological commitment permeates the *anthropology* of Catholic education as it engages the whole 'being' of people to empower them to become 'the glory of God fully alive'. The *sacramentality* of Catholic education is ontological as it shapes people's outlook on life and forms the perspective that, as Gerard Manley Hopkins insists, 'the world is charged with the grandeur of God'. Its *community* emphasis is ontological as it nurtures people in social responsibility and ecclesial identity. Catholic catechesis is ontological as it teaches *tradition* in a way that molds people's very 'being'. And the *rationality* of Catholic education is ontological as it encourages people to think for themselves — forms them as thinkers, with intent of both conceptual and moral adequacy.

Justice: A Sociological Concern

Catholicism has always had an accent on 'practical charity'; witness its tradition that the corporal and spiritual works of mercy are integral to Catholic life. However, for a variety of reasons, Catholic consciousness has shifted 'beyond charity' to justice, to see that Christian faith has serious social responsibilities (Groome, op. cit., pp. 389–93). Justice is a central mandate of our faith. In fact, 'action on behalf of justice and participation in the transformation of the world fully appear to us *a constitutive dimension of the preaching of the Gospel*, or, in other words, of the Church's mission for the redemption of the human race and its liberation from every oppressive situation' (See Gremillion, 1971, p. 514) (my emphasis).

Justice is clearly a Biblical mandate. In the Hebrew scriptures, God's covenant with humankind calls people to live in 'right relationship' with God, self, others, and creation. This summarizes the biblical sense of both justice and holiness of life; God's people are to be holy like their God in their relationships with each other (see Lev. 19, pp. 2–35), and especially by imitating God's special favour for those to whom life is most denied — the poor, widows, orphans, and aliens in the land — people of other races (see Jer. 7, 6, etc.). In Luke's Gospel, Jesus announces his life and mission as fulfilment of the most radical social innovation of his Jewish tradition — the Jubilee Year of Isaiah 61, pp. 1–2, a promise of 'good news to the poor', 'release to the captives', 'sight to the blind', and 'to let the oppressed go free' (see Lk. 4, pp. 18–19). The first Christians, following Jesus' preaching and praxis of agapaic love, added an emphasis to justice as 'doing the truth with love' (See Eph. 4, 15; 1 Pt. 1, 22; 1 Jn. 3, 18, etc.), and reiterated the 'favor for the poor'. Catholicism appropriates this Biblical mandate of justice with a distinctive accent, namely, a dual commitment to the *dignity of the person* and to the *common good* of all. This is reflected in its description of 'basic justice' as *commutative* (one on one), *distributive* (group to person), and *social* (person to group) (see Hollenbach, 1979, p. 155).

Justice permeates the *anthropology* of Catholic education as it treats students with dignity, and prepares them to respect and promote the human rights of all. Justice is reflected in its *sacramentality* as it enables people to 'see' and respond to the poor and oppressed of society, and to imagine how to change unjust social structures and oppressive cultural mores. Justice is taught as the school *community* embodies 'right relationship', and educates students in their responsibility to the 'common good'. The *Tradition* fosters justice when teachers highlight God's liberating actions in the Hebrew Scriptures and in Jesus, and propose the Vision of God's reign as shalom and fullness of life for all. And justice permeates its *rationality* as it encourages students in a critical social consciousness with the practical interest of living the truth, doing the good.

Catholicity: An Inclusive Concern

In *Finnegans Wake* James Joyce writes: 'Catholic means here comes everybody.' Etymologically, 'catholic' has its roots in *kata holou*, meaning 'embracing the whole', or better still 'including everything and everyone'. This suggests that the best synonym for 'catholic' is 'inclusive' rather than the often used 'universal'. The latter can mean one aspect dominating everything else and excluding or destroying all that is 'other'. Both Nazism and Communism had ambitions of universality, but in a dominating way. 'Catholic', on the other hand, means to include and welcome all, to embrace diverse 'others', in a participative and bonded community. In this, Joyce was right.

To claim to be *the* Catholic tradition of Christianity is rather pretentious. Some Christian communities settle for naming themselves by a central doctrine (Baptists), or after their first mentor (Lutherans), or by their form of governance (Presbyterians), and so on. Our claim to be 'Catholic' should confront us with our sins of exclusion and sectarianism, and ever challenge us to become an inclusive community with hospitality and openness to all. Clearly this commitment must permeate Catholic education.

Catholicity is reflected in its *anthropology* as the curriculum affirms each person's worth and engages all their gifts in a holistic way. Its *sacramentality* is catholic as it encourages people to appreciate both the unity and diversity of life, to experience God's Spirit as the love energy of all creation. Its *community* emphasis is catholic when the school is truly a place of welcome and inclusion, and educates its students that 'neighbour' has no limits. Teaching the *Tradition* is catholic as it convinces students of the universality of God's saving presence and love for all peoples, and grounds them in this particular tradition without prejudice or sectarian bias. And its *rationality* is catholic as it opens people to the truth, wherever it can be found.

What I have laid out here is surely more the Vision than the Story of Catholic education, more what we are called to than what we ever fully realize. Some participants in the conference on *The Contemporary Catholic School and the Common Good* at St Edmund's College, Cambridge in July 1993, found my proposal unduly positive and optimistic, giving insufficient attention to the 'underside' of Catholicism. They pointed out persuasively that it has often preached and taught a negative anthropology, tried to control and limit the sacramentality of life, practised its communality as a system of domination and exclusion, failed to institutionally represent the richness and depth of its own tradition, discouraged critical rationality especially in matters of 'faith', often neglected its priority for persons and concern for justice, and failed in its own 'catholicity'. I readily admit that the pages of history are strewn with such 'evidence to the contrary'. Certainly the Vision I propose above needs to be empirically realized. But that it has been much sinned against does not lessen the authenticity of such a Vision. It is, I am convinced, warranted by the whole broad sweep of Catholicism, albeit at its best. To propose it, with so much evidence to the contrary, may sound as 'foolishness' (1 Cor. 1, 21). I insist, however, that we must reclaim and renew this Vision to inspire and sustain our efforts. Without it 'the people perish' (Prov. 29, 18), and to concede a lesser Vision will be to settle for less than Catholic education.

Notes

1   It is interesting to note that these characteristics are echoed in empirical research on the characteristics of Catholic schools. For example, Bryk *et al.* found 'three major characteristics that are widely shared by Catholic secondary schools: an unwavering commitment to an academic programme for all students, . . . ; a pervasive sense . . . of the school as a caring environment . . . ; and an inspirational ideology that directs institutional action toward social justice . . .' (p. 10).
2   From the statement of the Second General Synod of Catholic Bishops (1971). See Gremillion, J. op. cit., p. 522.
3   Bryk, Lee and Holland are correct in saying that Vatican II's insistence on freedom in matters of faith implied a profound change in the style of Catholic catechesis. 'The concept of faith as a free choice made over time by an informed, educated conscience replaced the spirit of indoctrination into the mind of the Church, which had been enacted through such instruments as the Baltimore Catechism.' (Bryk *et al.*, op. cit., p. 49).
4   Here again research indicates that such a shared ideology does, in fact, contribute to the effectiveness of the school. See Bryk *et al.*, op. cit., esp. pp. 301–4.
5   See *The Church Teaches: Documents of the Church in English Translation*, 1973, Rockford, IL, Tan Books, p. 34.

References

BRYK, A.S., LEE, V.E. and HOLLAND, P.B. (1993) *Catholic Schools and the Common Good*, Cambridge, MA, Harvard University Press.
COLEMAN, J.S. and HOFFER, T. (1987) *Public and Private High Schools: The Impact of Communities*, New York, Basic Books.
COVEY, J.J. (1992) *Catholic Schools Make a Difference: Twenty Five Years of Research*, Washington, DC, NCEA.
DEWEY, J. (1938) *Experience and Education*, New York, Collier Books.
DEWEY, J. (1971) 'My pedagogic creed', in DWORKIN, M.S. (Ed) *Dewey on Education*, New York, Teachers College Press.
EISNER, E. (1979) *The Educational Imagination*, New York, Macmillan.
FIORENZA, E.S. (1983) *In Memory of Her*, New York, Crossroad.
GILKEY, L. (1975) *Catholicism Confronts Modernity: A Protestant View*, New York, Seabury Press.

GROOME, T.H. (1991) *Sharing Faith: A Comprehensive Approach to Religious Education and Pastoral Ministry*, San Francisco, HarperCollins.

HOLLENBACH, D. (1979) *Claims in Conflict*, New York, Paulist Press.

KEARNEY, R. (1988) *The Wake of Imagination*, London, Hutchinson.

LONERGAN, B. (1972) *Method in Theology*, New York, Seabury Press.

McBRIEN, R.P. (1980) *Catholicism*, Vol. 2, San Francisco, Harper and Row.

POPE JOHN XXIII 'Pacem in terris', in GREMILLION, J. (Ed) (1976) *The Gospel of Peace and Justice*, Maryknoll, Orbis Books.

THE CONGREGATION FOR CATHOLIC EDUCATION (1988) *The Religious Dimension of Education in a Catholic School*, United States Catholic Conference, Washington, DC.

Chapter 8

Catholic Education and Catholic Identity

John Haldane

Introduction

Let me begin with two short passages from writings by G.K. Chesterton. The effect of bringing them together is to suggest the need for a philosophy of education.

> Philosophy is merely thought that has been thought out. It is often a great bore. But man has no alternative, except being influenced by thought that has been thought out and being influenced by thought that has not been thought out. The latter is what we commonly call culture and enlightenment today. (Chesterton, 1950, p. 176)

> Every education teaches a philosophy; if not by dogma then by suggestion, by implication, by atmosphere. Every part of that education has a connection with every other part. If it does not all combine to convey some general view of life it is not education at all. (op. cit., p. 167)

Whenever I read Chesterton I am left wondering why his non-fiction writings are not more widely discussed. Certainly there are circles of loyal devotees, but the Chestertonic is most effective when not consumed so liberally as to induce intoxication and nostalgic melancholy. One gains most, I think, from taking small portions of his work, such as an individual essay or book chapter, and letting them refresh one's mind. Chesterton is not best read for reassurance but for stimulation; and the stimulation he provides enables one to start thinking again about matters which previously seemed closed or intractable.

A few years ago, inspired by a chapter of his 1908 book *What's Wrong with the World*, I wrote an essay on Chesterton as a philosopher of education in which I linked aspects of his thought to elements in the writings of Thomas Aquinas (Haldane, 1990). It seemed to me then that there was need for a contemporary study of Catholic educational philosophy, and in the meantime I have become convinced that any such work ought to include an account of how concerns with education connect with more general issues in social and political philosophy and with the question of Catholic identity (On this see Carr *et al.*, 1995). Elsewhere I have explored the former issues, arguing that a Roman Catholic cannot accept certain liberal doctrines such as the moral neutrality of the State, (Haldane, 1992) and on an earlier occasion I defended the traditional idea that general orthodoxy is non-optional for the Catholic (Haldane, 1989). Here I want to reflect briefly on such matters as they relate to the question: what is the proper function of Catholic schools? I shall be making five points as follows:

- It is important to distinguish issues of experience from those of identity.
- The question of Catholic identity is inescapable.
- There is a distinctive Catholic identity.
- Catholic identity is partly constituted by authority and dogma.
- The primary function of Catholic schools is to transmit Catholic truths and values.

Questions of Experience and of Identity

What does it mean to be a Roman Catholic? The question is ambiguous. Understood in one way it enquires about personal and social attitudes and is the sort of thing that an interviewer might ask expecting a personal biography or cultural description. When interpreted in this way let us call it 'the question of Catholic experience'. This contrasts with a second interpretation according to which what is being sought for is some sort of objective essence, or at least a broad definition identifying central features of Roman Catholicism. When taken in this latter sense let us call it 'the question of Catholic identity'.

My first point then is this: when thinking about Roman Catholicism many of those raised in that tradition now tend to confuse the two questions and assimilate the issue of identity to that of experience. At the conference on 'The Contemporary Catholic school and the Common Good' at St Edmund's College, Cambridge from which some of the chapters in this volume derive, Thomas Groome addressed the issue: what makes a school Catholic? and asked those present to consider what they took to be distinctive of Catholicism. (See chapter 7). I found myself immediately thinking about such ideas as the duality of Holy Scripture and Holy Church, the special mediating functions of the priesthood, the Mass, transubstantiation, the extraordinary magisterium, the Papacy, the communion of saints, the Marian dogmas, prayers of intercession and so on. When the time came to report our thoughts, however, I was struck by the fact that those who spoke all recalled personal memories of childhood and youth, memories of priests and nuns, of authority and discipline, of particular rituals and pieties, and the such like. Many, in fact most, spoke in terms that suggested that they thought the old ways had gone and that things in the Church were now better for this. At least two things are significant in these responses: first, the preference for the present over the past; and second, the fact that no-one else seemed to have taken the speaker to be posing the question of *identity* rather than that of *experience*.

The programme included a couple of 'retrospectives' for one of which I had been detailed to reflect on some of the main issues discussed throughout the conference. These fell under several heads including the different legal and institutional circumstances of schools in the US and in the UK, questions of social justice, the role of Catholic schools and the issue of Catholic identity. Commenting on the latter, I began by noting that my own perspective was partly determined by the fact that I live and work in St Andrews, a town and university strongly associated with the Scottish Reformation. The legacy of the sixteenth century in Scotland continues to give greater prominence to questions of religious identity than they generally have in England, and Roman Catholicism has only recently begun to enjoy 'non-alien status'. Additionally, something of the reformed heritage was in my own Scottish childhood, since although my mother was a cradle Catholic and I spent ten years at a Jesuit school, my father had a Presbyterian upbringing and only converted to Catholicism in middle-life.

Such circumstances, together with the fact that as a philosopher I am concerned with trying to understand the 'essences' of things, contribute to my interest in the question of identity. However, and this is my second point, this issue is anyhow inescapable if one begins to think seriously about the nature and purpose of Catholic schools. In recognition of this necessity and in the hope of getting clearer about differences in attitudes to the distinguishing features of Catholicism, I produced the following diagram and considered various possible differentiae:

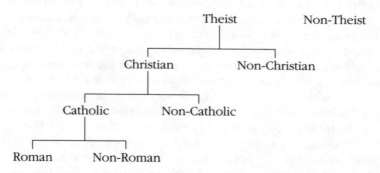

My third point arises from this exercise. However difficult it may be to produce a definition of the essence of Roman Catholicism there are relevant and important differences between theists and non-theists, Christians and non-Christians, Catholics and non-Catholics, and Romans and non-Romans. This may seem too obvious for comment. However, I have been struck by the fact that as well as conflating questions of personal experience and of ecclesial identity, many people in Catholic circles are concerned to deny that there are differences of genuine significance between Catholics and certain other religious groupings — at least at any level that really matters. One illustration of this point would be to say that the issues between Anglicans and Romans over the matter of authority are not theologically deep but reduce to variety in the cultural realization of certain ideas. Or again it is sometimes said that the religious practices of non-Christians are equally significant and deserving of religious respect to those of Catholicism — as when, for example, members of a Catholic Commission suggested that Rastafarianism is a 'valid religious experience' and that its followers should be allowed the use of Catholic premises for worship. Similar claims are made by many Anglicans and other Christians.

One way of bringing out disagreements over such matters of purported identity and difference, and I believe it is important for Catholics to recognize and explore these disagreements, is by considering the diagram and asking oneself the following questions: Where am I located? Why should I be there? Do I want to bring others there also? For those in the Victorian and Edwardian periods confronted with challenges to religion from science and politics, as for those in the inter-war years struggling with the competing claims of Catholicism and Communism, or like George Orwell trying to find a humanist philosophy different from each, the resolution of issues of theological and philosophical doctrine and the implementation of their practical corollaries were not viewed as unwelcome intrusions in the effort to live well, or to establish respectful relations with others, but as preconditions of the possibility of doing so (Norman, 1985, Ch. 4 and 5; Haldane, 1989). What has changed? One possible answer is 'the Roman Catholic Church'.

Authoritative and Dogmatic: Vices or Virtues?

There is a widely held view that sometime during or after the Second Vatican Council the Church underwent a radical and irreversible change in its self-conception. To the extent that such distinctions are drawn, proponents of this view, whom I shall call the 'revisionists', would say that the transformation in question is not just, or even primarily, a sociological one but is theological and cognitive. In other words the Church has not merely undergone certain stylistic changes. Rather, the initiatives of the Council and the resulting post-conciliar reorientation mark a progression towards a truth previously unseen, lost sight of, or even deliberately obscured. For instead of regarding itself as an autocratic structure primarily concerned with preserving Tridentine orthodoxy through authoritative teaching and priest-administered sacraments, the Church now knows itself to be a community of equals moving uncertainly as a pilgrim body towards a more just social order.

Of course this way of speaking raises the question: who or what is the Church? And one problem in maintaining the revisionist view is that it seems to be at odds with that presented by Pope John Paul II and by Cardinal Ratzinger, the Prefect of the Sacred Congregation for the Doctrine of the Faith, both of whom have been concerned to combat what they regard as serious lapses from authentic Catholic teaching. Given some perspectives, to find oneself in disagreement with the occupants of these offices is to have reason to presume that one is in error. But of course from the revisionist perspective the authority of these Papal and Congregational offices is precisely a matter on which traditionalist occupants are likely to be mistaken. In other words assertions of, and demands for, orthodoxy are regarded as question-begging, reactionary measures against revisionist advances.

Clearly there is no quick or single way to resolve this dispute. But it is worth considering the plausibility of the competing interpretations of Catholic teaching during what both parties can agree has been a period of social change and religious questioning. Consider, for example, the important area of social issues as these have been addressed in Papal documents during the last century. According to the traditionalist the Church is committed to a core of unchanging norms and values which it has long propagated and which it continues to affirm with authority. On this account the passage from Leo XIII's *Rerum Novarum* (1891), via Pius XI's *Quadragesimo Anno* (1931) and John XXIII's *Pacem in Terris* (1963), to John Paul II's *Veritatis Splendor* (1993) is one of unbroken commitment to the same essential doctrines. In the revisionist view, however, Vatican II marked an important shift in the Church's understanding of morality and politics as it belatedly came to terms with liberalism and contextualism. Thus while it will be conceded that the present Pope's thinking is similar to that of pre-Conciliar Pontiff, that very fact is taken to show that he is a reactionary, drawing back from enlightenment and retreating into the darkness of anti-modernism.

This latter impression is widely shared but it is doubtful whether it stands up to much scrutiny. Consider for example the claim that in his social teaching John XXIII inaugurated a new liberalism in Catholic thought. In *Pacem in Terris* he writes:

> Every human being has the right to respect for his person; to his good reputation, the right to freedom in searching for truth and in expressing and communicating his opinions within the limits laid down by the moral order and the common good.
>
> Every human being has the right to honour God according to the dictates of an upright conscience and therefore the right to worship God privately and publicly . . .
>
> Human beings have the right to choose freely the state of life which they prefer and therefore the right to establish a family with equal rights and duties for man and woman and also the right to follow a vocation to the priesthood or religious life. (John XXIII, *Pacem in Terris*, 16, 25)

Initially this may seem to be at odds with the anti-liberal claims of previous Popes and the purported 'illiberalism' of the present incumbent, but while it is certainly true that John XXIII sought to avoid the authoritarian tones of his predecessors and recognized the fact that many societies had become pluralist democracies, the teaching retains its original and essential orientation towards an objective moral order and preserves its Papal authority. Notice, for example, the way in which the liberties are qualified by reference to permissible or required ends. The right to intellectual freedom is specified in terms of the pursuit of truth and is constrained by the demands of morality; religious liberty is described as the right to worship God; the right to choose freely one's state of life does not extend to pre- or extra-marital affairs or homosexual relationships. In other words the heralded freedoms are tied to prescribed ends.

In addition to the *matter* of Papal and Conciliar teaching there is the critical question of its *form*, more precisely that of its authority. Traditionally the Church claims to be the repository of Divine revelation and to possess an Apostolic magisterium, in respect of the essentials of the Faith. Within this it defines an extraordinary magisterium the agents of which may be Councils or the Pontiff pronouncing *ex cathedra*. This 'magisterial' aspect of Catholicism has been the subject of much revisionist criticism. It is sometimes said to be a relatively late accretion at odds with the understanding of the early Church. At other times it is rejected as triumphalist and offensive to non-Catholic and non-Christian believers. Furthermore it is held to be philosophically untenable in a post-Cartesian age.

Once again I can do little more than suggest considerations to the contrary. First, the idea that the Church is possessed of a special teaching authority is as old as systematic reflection upon the nature of Christ's mission and of that of the Apostles. Famously in Matthew we have the commissioning of Peter (*Matthew*, 16, 17–19), and prominent in John's Gospel are Christ's repeated promises of the coming of an Advocate, the Holy Spirit, who will be with the Church forever as a source of truth (*John*, Chs, 14–16 *passim*). Writing in the fourth quarter of the second century and building upon such scriptural foundations Irenaeus advises:

> It is not necessary still to seek amongst others for the truth which it is easy to receive from the Church. Since the Apostles most fully committed unto the Church as into a rich repository all things pertaining to the truth, that whosoever wills may draw out of it the drink of life. (St Irenaeus, 1868 Ed, p. 264)

And elsewhere he writes:

> This, beloved, is the preaching of the truth, and this is the manner of our salvation, and this is the way of life, announced by the prophets and ratified by Christ and handed over to the Apostles and handed down by the Church in the whole world [i.e., the ecumenical or 'Catholic' Church] to her children. This must be kept in all security, with good

will and by being well-pleasing to God through good works and sound moral character. (St Iranaeus, 1952 Ed, p. 108)

Of course such claims can be rejected but that is not to the point. I have no ambition here to argue the truth of Catholic teaching, only to maintain that it has a distinctive content of the sort I have indicated and to urge that reference to this is central in answering any question about Catholic identity.

As regards the notion of doctrinal authority as such, and of its correlative, *viz. dogma*, it is a long standing claim of the Church of Rome that it shows its truth in part precisely through its making authoritative pronouncements. This idea needs to be properly understood. The assumption is not the obvious absurdity that claiming an inerrant teaching authority is *sufficient* for possessing it; but rather that a *necessary* condition of having such authority is that one presumes oneself to be in possession of it. As a matter of philosophy, but independent of Cartesian or any other theory of epistemological warrant, no person or institution that does not claim to teach with authority, either explicitly or by implication, can coherently be regarded as authoritative. While this fact does not guarantee the truth of doctrine it undermines the claim of revisionists to be advancing legitimate developments of Catholic teaching. My fourth point, therefore, is that whatever the nature of a Church that has only the most limited, if any, defined doctrines, that claims no special authority and regards itself as on a par with other faiths in respect of its grasp of truth, it is *not* that of Roman Catholicism.

The Catholic Church has a distinctive nature, part of which unites its members with other non-Christian theists and with the faithful of other Christian denominations, and parts of which distinguish them as separate. At the level of essences this is a matter of theology not of sociology or of psychology. While Catholic identity, therefore, is not a question of experience, nevertheless membership of the Catholic Church or extended encounters with its members should make a difference to one's experience. Sadly of course the difference is not always found to be beneficial, as was testified to by some of the reminiscences prompted by Thomas Groome. While that must be a matter for regret, the Catholic can only regard it as providing reason for improving the quality of lived Catholicism and not as grounds for shifting to some other religious foundation.

Catholic Education and Catholic Schools

At this point, then, let me return to the question of Catholic education and again quote from Chesterton.

The fashionable fallacy is that by education we can give people something that we have not got ... These pages have, of course, no other general purpose than to point out that we cannot create anything good until we have conceived it . . . Education is only truth in a state of transmission; and how can we pass on truth if it has never come into our hand? (Chesterton, 1910, pp. 198–200)

In the context of schooling, education is a deliberate process whereby the cognitive, affective and practical potentialities of the pupil are realized and given determinate content (Haldane, 1995). The primary function of Catholic schools, therefore, is to provide forms of education through which the essential doctrines and devotions of Catholicism are transmitted. In the present day that is not an easy task either to plan or to implement; but nor was it unproblematic throughout most of Christian history, and I believe it follows from what has been said that the task is a non-negotiable one. It is a duty.

Against this, however, may be brought such objections as that the vocation of the Church is primarily to promote social justice, and that in multi-culture, multi-faith societies the religious function I describe is 'exclusivist' and as such both undesirable and impractical. In their recent book *Catholic Schools and the Common Good*, Anthony Bryk, Valerie Lee and Peter Holland attribute part of the success of Catholic secondary schools in the USA to what they describe as 'an inspirational ideology that directs institutional action toward social justice in an ecumenical and multicultural world' (Bryk *et al.*, 1993, p. 11). However, since others who do not share Catholic, Christian or any religious beliefs are also moved by considerations of social morality the question arises: What is this 'inspirational ideology' and how is it related to other aspects of Catholic faith?

In tracing the origins of this ideology the authors refer to the Neoscholastic revival initiated by Leo XIII's encouragement to Catholic scholars to study the work of Aquinas, and they go on to describe something of Maritain's Christian philosophy of education, one of the foundations of which is a social ethic involving the idea of the common good. In brief, this builds upon the natural law tradition giving special emphasis to the Thomistic-Aristotelian claim that human beings are social creatures constituted as persons through their relationships with others (Maritain, 1943). This is all to the good; however it hardly seems to point to an 'inspirational ideology' that is necessarily religious, never mind distinctively Catholic. Indeed, in what they say subsequently Bryk and his co-authors appear to widen the gap between the social philosophy of the common good and traditional Catholic theology.

Although selected Neoscholastic scholars such as Maritain . . . offered Catholics a way to engage with modernity, the more conventional and doctrinaire interpreters of Thomas wreaked much havoc. Their scholarship reinforced a hierarchical conception of the institutional Church, in which the magisterium would think and the flock would follow . . .

Further, Neoscholasticism's very strengths were also its weaknesses. Its aggressive resort to intellectualising faith diminished the common appeal of the Christian message . . . Neoscholasticism distracted

John Haldane

many Catholics from the more concrete imperatives of the gospel message to advance human goodness through hope in the vision of the 'final Kingdom'. (Bryk *et al.*, op. cit., pp. 40–1)

What follows this is an account of the adaptation of Catholicism to the facts of 'modernity' and 'postmodernity', the upshot of which is said to have been the shattering of 'the monolith of Neoscholastic thought as the authoritative synthesis of the "Catholic position"', leading to the employment of 'multiple rationales to ground social action'. However something of the earlier Neoscholastic tradition is said to remain and to constitute the Catholic contribution to social thought:

Postmodern thinkers increasingly speak of the need to rekindle a sense of social responsibility and public participation in a diverse and pluralistic American life. In the search for a grounding for this renewed social commitment, these two residuals of Neoscholasticism — the capacity of reason to arrive at truth and the need for moral norms and principles in social life — represent an active, vital, coherent Catholic voice in this extended dialogue. (op. cit.)

Admiring as I am of the authors' sociological study, I think that this assessment bears the marks of the revisionist tendency with which I was concerned earlier. It is undeniable that as a matter of historical fact moral theologians have drawn back from the claims of their predecessors. More to the point I am happy to admit that some of the assertions and arguments of the scholastic manuals do not bear close (or even middle-distance) scrutiny. The critical issue, however, is approached when one asks the question: Is Catholic social teaching coincident with an objectivist ethic of the common good? There is scope for much philosophy here. Certainly it asserts the objectivity of values and claims that certain goods attach to society as a whole. But the interesting and troublesome issues arise when it is asked if such a view is tenable on other than theological grounds, and whether a theological foundation supports, and even necessitates, more extensive claims.

In place of lengthy argumentation permit me to conclude by merely sketching a line of thought. Just as in Catholic metaphysical theology Grace perfects nature, so in its moral and social teaching a theological ethic transforms what would otherwise be a mundane natural law structure. From this perspective no account of values can begin to be adequate unless it has at its heart the recognition that mankind has an eternal destiny. The primary purpose for which we were created is certainly *not* that of loving ourselves, as the ethical egoist might have it; but nor is it that of loving one another. Rather it is that of loving *God*. Of course this last is not incompatible with an ethic of brotherly concern — we are not to love God *as opposed to* loving one another — but such brotherly concern is made sense of, as more than a romantic metaphor, by the claim that we are fellow creatures brought into existence by the one and only Divine creator.

A Catholic philosophy of education cannot limit itself to the claim that there are objective social goods. It must build an extensive structure around the simple yet unlimited claim that we exist for the sake of God's glory. It has to be acknowledged that this is nowadays an extraordinary and divisive claim. It is certainly 'exclusivist' in the sense of being incompatible with certain other secular and religious philosophies. But it is surely not open to the Catholic to believe that the design and implementation of an educational philosophy based on this assumption is 'undesirable' and 'impractical'. On the contrary, it is the thought that in pursuing it we are doing God's will that assures us that it can, and ought, to be achieved. My fifth and final point, then, is that the primary function of Catholic schools is to transmit Catholic truths and Catholic values. Everything else, no matter how important, is secondary to this.

References

BRYK, A.S., LEE, V.E. and HOLLAND, P.B. (1993) *Catholic Schools and the Common Good*, Cambridge, MA, Harvard University Press.

CARR, D., HALDANE, J., McLAUGHLIN, T. and PRING, R. (1995) 'Return to the Crossroads: Maritain fifty years on', *British Journal of Educational Studies*, XXXXIII, pp. 162–178.

CHESTERTON, G.K. (1910) *What's Wrong with the World*, London, Cassell.

CHESTERTON, G.K. (1950) 'The revival of philosophy: Why?', in *The Common Man*, London, Sheed and Ward.

HALDANE, J. (1989) 'Critical orthodoxy', *Louvain Studies*, **14**.

HALDANE, J. (1990) 'Chesterton's philosophy of education', *Philosophy*, **65**.

HALDANE, J. (1992) 'Can a Catholic be a liberal?: Catholic social teaching and communitarianism', *Melita Theologica*, XLIII, pp. 44–57.

HALDANE, J. (1995) 'Education: Conserving tradition', in ALMOND, B. (Ed) *Introduction to Applied Ethics*, Oxford, Basil Blackwell.

JOHNSTONE, R. (1982) *The Will to Believe*, Oxford, OUP.

MARITAIN, J. (1943) *Education at the Crossroads*, New Haven, Yale University Press.

NORMAN, E. (1985) *Roman Catholicism in England: From the Elizabethan Settlement to the Second Vatican Council*, Oxford, OUP.

ST IRENAEUS (1868 Ed) *Adversus Haereses*, III, 4, 1; in ROBERTS and RAMBANT, *Anti-Nicene Christian Library*, Edinburgh, T and T Clark, **1**.

ST IRENAEUS (1952 Ed) *Proof of the Apostolic Preaching*, in SMITH, J.P. (Ed and trans), London, Longmans, Green and Co.

Chapter 9

The Distinctiveness of Catholic Education

Terence H. McLaughlin

In the thirty years since the end of the Second Vatican Council, Catholic education has faced a continual demand for the clarification of the precise respects in which it is, or should be, *distinctive*. At the level of fundamental principle, there has been much discussion of the distinctiveness of the aims, purposes and values of Catholic education, whilst at the level of educational policy and practice, attention has been focused on the distinctiveness of the various pedagogic, curricular and institutional processes through which these aims, purposes and values may be implemented and realized.

This concern with the analysis of the distinctiveness of Catholic education is apparent on both sides of the Atlantic. In England and Wales, for example, the question of distinctiveness has featured prominently in reports and debates (see, for example, Study Group on Catholic Education, 1981, Ch. 2; Ch. 5 especially sec. 3) and much attention has recently been given by the Catholic Education Service to encouraging both primary and secondary Catholic schools to address questions of distinctiveness in a sustained and practically significant way (Catholic Education Service, 1994a). Such a concern with distinctiveness is mirrored in the United States, where the nature of the distinctiveness of the Catholic school is central to the important recently published study 'Catholic Schools and the Common Good' (Bryk *et al.*, 1993).

It would be unwise to claim that this preoccupation with the distinctiveness of Catholic education is a phenomenon of the post Vatican II period. Throughout its history, the Church has been concerned to clarify and to emphasize the distinctiveness of its educational vision. Underlying the modern preoccupation with distinctiveness, however, are a number of factors. One is a trend for Catholic schools to become, for a range of reasons, less straightforwardly distinguishable from schools of other kinds. The spirit and tone of Catholic schools have changed. Evennett's famous observation (quoted in Hornsby-Smith, 1987, p. 30) that the quintessential left by a Catholic education is a lasting consciousness of the fact and meaning of death, seems difficult to apply to present-day Catholic schools. This is true also of Anthony Flew's criticisms, developed nearly thirty years ago, of the 'wholehearted' and 'successful' religious indoctrination effected in Catholic schools, which were, in his view '. . . determinedly founded, and are stubbornly maintained, precisely and only in order to produce indoctrinated Roman Catholics' (Flew, 1968, p. 88). Fears about the anti-democratic influence of Catholic schools is an important ingredient in the history of these schools in the United States (see, for example, Bryk *et al.*, 1993, Ch. 1). Yet today, far from being seen as anti-democratic, Catholic schools are now viewed in many quarters as making not only a valuable contribution to the development of citizens and to the common good in a pluralist democratic society, but also to be in certain respects succeeding in achieving these aims more effectively than their public school counterparts (Bryk *et al.*, 1993).

Underlying this trend for Catholic schools to be less readily distinguishable from schools of other kinds are complex factors of many sorts, in which wide ranging theological, philosophical, sociological and cultural considerations are prominent.[1] Catholic belief in general, and the personal beliefs and behaviour of individual Catholics, have become less sharply distinguished from other beliefs and lifestyles, and it is no surprise that this is true also of Catholic educational principles and policies.

This does not mean, of course, that Catholic education, any more than Catholic belief in general, does not have, as a matter of both logic and fact, distinctive — and indeed unique — characteristics. However it may suggest that, in virtue of their complexity and elusiveness, these characteristics may be more difficult than in the past to specify and elaborate.

In this chapter I shall explore some questions relating to the distinctiveness of Catholic education, and shall adopt a broadly philosophical approach. I shall focus upon the Catholic school system for pupils up to the age of 18. In the United States, there is an extensive discussion of the distinctiveness of Catholic higher education (see, for example, Hauerwas and Westerhoff (Eds), 1992; Hesburgh (Ed), 1994), but I shall not pursue issues relating to higher education here.

The Clarification of Distinctiveness and the Role of Philosophy

The need for the distinctiveness of Catholic education to be clarified is in many respects a straightforward one. Without such clarity, Catholic education will lack direction and focus. Catholic educational leaders and policy makers, and Catholic teachers themselves, need a clear sense of what it is that they are striving to achieve. Shared clarity of educational vision is a well known general requirement for educational effectiveness. Clarity is particularly needed by Catholic schools, however, as a central element in the complex exercise of judgment and discernment which they must bring to bear upon their educational mission in the contemporary world. On the one hand, such schools need to avoid a merely *de facto* or pragmatic acceptance of, or conformity to, educational norms and circumstances in the world as a whole, where there is a danger of acquiescence in the face of pressures which may not support, and in some cases may undermine, the properly Catholic aims and values of the school. Catholic education, after all, is an enterprise which is in significant respects conducted 'against the grain of the world'. On the other hand, however, the school must gain a clear and appropriately sophisticated grasp of what the nature and implications of Catholic educational aims and values actually are. Part of this process requires discernment about which features of the general educational landscape need to be resisted and rejected and which are to be seen as compatible with, or maybe even expressions of, Catholic values. Other parts of the same process require attempts to move beyond the rhetoric in which the distinctiveness of the Catholic school is often discussed and to bring an appropriate understanding of Catholic educational aims and values to bear upon the range of familiar policy questions which confront the contemporary Catholic school. For example, is the major purpose of such a school the formation of Catholic believers, or can wider purposes be discerned consistent with, and perhaps required by, Catholic principles, which can articulate a role for the school in relation to pupils who are not Catholics? Is there a case for keeping open Catholic schools in areas of urban deprivation, where the number of Catholic pupils on roll may have declined, but where the school may be seen as witnessing to Catholic educational values in a new way? What is the proper form which Catholic religious education should take? Clarity alone cannot resolve such questions, although it is an indispensable ally in relation to them.

But what sort of clarity is needed? An important enemy to be identified in general educational debate is 'edu-babble' — imprecise and platitudinous rhetoric — which offers to educators a kind of spurious clarity in the form of slogans. Slogans such as 'education is of the whole child', 'we should teach children and not subjects' and 'process is more important than content' sound intuitively plausible and appealing. Such slogans are often brandished in educational discussion and debate, where the important truths they seem to embody can make a seemingly decisive contribution to an argument. However, whilst such slogans are not wholly uninformative, their meaning, let alone their truth, is unclear. They are therefore better seen as contributing suggestively rather than decisively to educational argument, and to opening up educational discussion rather than closing it down. They cannot be a substitute for sustained thought. There is a distinctively Catholic variant of 'edu-babble', which is typically forged out of phrases drawn from the various educational documents of the Church. Often these documents are 'mined' for such phrases in a rather eclectic way. Phrases such as 'The school should be based on the values of the Gospel' and 'The Spirit of Christ should permeate everything that is done in the school' can sometimes bring discussion of the Catholic distinctiveness of the school to an end and give the impression that the matters at stake have been satisfactorily dealt with. But like 'edu-babble' in general, such phrases are primarily useful as spurs to deeper discussion, not as a substitute for it. For example, in relation to a phrase of the sort 'The school should

be based on the values of the Gospel', a deeper discussion should inter-
rogate in some detail how the 'values of the Gospel' are to be understood,
together with the respects in which they are properly seen to be distinctive to
the Catholic school.

The sort of clarity which is needed in relation to the distinctiveness of
Catholic education needs therefore to go 'beyond the edu-babble'. More specifically, sustained attention to questions of the meaning and justification of
central concepts and claims are needed, together with an attempt to delin-
eate an overall substantial framework of Catholic educational thought. This
leads naturally to the need for a 'Catholic philosophy of education'. It has been
observed that, within contemporary philosophy of education, no distinctively
Catholic systematic account of the nature and role of education has yet emerged,
to sit alongside those derived from other sources, including analytical philosophy
(Carr, D. *et al.*, 1995, pp. 162–3). There is therefore a need for a distinctively
Catholic philosophy of education to be developed (see Haldane, 1995), which
can draw not only upon the philosophical resources of notable Catholic thinkers
such as Aquinas, Newman, Maritain, Chesterton and Lonergan but which will
also address directly matters of current educational concern. The lack of a
coherent modern statement of a Catholic philosophy of education deprives the
Catholic educational community of important resources with which to confront
questions of distinctiveness. Topics of great relevance to Catholic education
and to its distinctiveness, such as the aims of education, the personal autonomy
of the individual, moral education and education in religion have tended to be
addressed in the literature of philosophy of education and in educational literature more broadly, independently of Catholic concepts and arguments. Nor has
this been an impoverishment simply for Catholic education, since a Catholic
philosophy of education seeks to illuminate the nature not merely of Catholic
education, but of education as such (Carr, D. *et al.*, 1995, p. 163). Part of this
discussion can be seen as an indication of some of the work which lies open
for the future development of such a Catholic philosophy of education.

The Distinctiveness of Catholic Education

In this section I shall attempt to outline a number of distinctive features of
Catholic education with reference to some of the central educational documents of the Church. This way of proceeding has its drawbacks. One such
drawback is that Church documents of this kind require interpretation and
elaboration. They are not fully self-sufficient, but need to be understood by
reference to the wider belief, tradition and practice of the Church (on this see,
for example, McBrien, 1994; Catechism of the Catholic Church, 1994), and in
the light of *inter alia* sustained philosophical analysis. As indicated earlier,
there are dangers in basing discussion of Catholic educational principles on
phrases drawn from documents of this kind. An adequate account of these principles cannot be derived from such documents alone. However, the documents

can provide a guide to central features and elements of Catholic educational principles, and it is for this purpose that I make reference to them here.

The educational documents to which I shall refer are as follows: The Second Vatican Council's Declaration on Christian Education 'Gravissimum educationis' (in Flannery, 1988, Vol. I, Section 55; hereinafter GE), the *General Catechetical Directory* (Sacred Congregation for the Clergy, 1971; hereinafter GCD), the Apostolic Exhortation 'Catechesi tradendae' (Pope John Paul II, 1979; hereinafter CT) and three documents from the Congregation for Catholic Education 'The Catholic School' (Sacred Congregation for Catholic Education, 1977; hereinafter CS), 'Lay Catholics in Schools: Witnesses to Faith' (Sacred Congregation for Catholic Education, 1982; hereinafter LCWF) and 'The Religious Dimension of Education in a Catholic School: Guidelines for Reflection and Renewal' (Sacred Congregation for Catholic Education, 1988; hereinafter RDCS). Also of interest is a document on a specific aspect of education 'Educational Guidance in Human Love: Outlines for sex education' (Sacred Congregation for Catholic Education, 1983; hereinafter EGL). The documents chosen for attention are relatively recent, and I am unable to explore the development in the educational thinking of the Church revealed by its earlier statements on education. In addition, attention is confined to Church documents with a directly educational focus. As implied earlier, attention to the full range of the thinking of the Church is needed in an adequate account.

The documents are a rich source of Catholic educational principles. A number of these relate to matters which cannot be explored here. These include claims about the rights of all people to education in general and to a Christian education in particular (GE paras 1, 2), the right and duty of the Church to engage in education (GE para. 3) and to establish its own schools (GE para. 8; CS paras 14–15), the paramount rights of parents in relation to education, particularly concerning choice of school (e.g., GE paras 3, 6), the duty of parents to send their children to Catholic schools wherever this is possible (GE para. 8), and the corresponding duty of states to ensure the true freedom of parents with respect to choice of school which may require the provision of public subsidies (GE paras 6, 7). Clearly, there is an important distinction between Catholic education and Catholic schooling. The former does not require the latter, although it may welcome it as a 'privileged means' of achieving its aims (CS para. 8). Here I shall often refer to 'Catholic education' and 'Catholic schools' somewhat interchangeably, conscious of important distinctions which need to be drawn in a more detailed treatment.

Three related general features emerge as distinctive of Catholic education.

1 *The embodiment of a view about the meaning of human persons and of human life*

Catholic education is based on, and seeks to promote, a particular view of the nature of human beings and of human life in general. Catholic education is therefore based on a 'substantial', 'thick' or 'comprehensive' theory of the good in contrast to the 'procedural', 'thin' or 'restricted' theories of the good which are typically invoked as underpinnings of public education and the 'common school' in pluralistic liberal democratic societies (McLaughlin, 1995). Thus, in the Catholic school '. . . a specific concept of the world, of man, and of history is developed and conveyed' (CS para. 8). The educational task of the Catholic school is based upon a specific theological and philosophical perspective about the nature of reality and of human beings and their flourishing and destiny, at the heart of which is the person of Jesus Christ as understood by, and mediated through, the Church (cf. Dunne, 1991, pp. 23–4; Lane, 1991, pp. 81–5). There is therefore a direct connection between the Catholic faith and Catholic education, which gives Catholic education a distinctive aim and character (cf. Pring, 1968) in which all its aspects are related to Christ (CS paras 34–7) and an attempt is made to assist pupils to achieve a synthesis of faith, culture and life (CS para. 37; RDCS para. 34).

Relevant to this general feature of Catholic education are two points. First, as Archbishop Beck puts it '. . . the question of what man is — or what we mean by human nature — is . . . ultimately the basis of every system of education . . . Only when we know what man is can we say how he should be educated' (Beck, 1964, p. 109). Whilst it is true that to have a coherent account of education one needs at least some kind of an account of the sort of thing a human being is (Haldane, 1989, p. 174), the Catholic perspective insists that only a full account of the sort it offers can generate an adequate understanding of education (RDCS para. 63). A second point is the claim that every form of education teaches implicitly or explicitly a philosophy of man (for Chesterton's remarks on this see Haldane, 1990, p. 65; cf. CS para. 29).

In contrast to typical forms of public education in the 'common school' in pluralistic liberal democratic societies, Catholic education is therefore based on a particular and detailed 'philosophy of life'.

2   An aspiration to holistic influence

The distinctiveness of Catholic education is not something which is merely added on to a pre-existing and independently determined education. As Walsh insists, it does not involve '. . . a Christian icing on the cake of a pre-baked education . . . (but) . . . a secret ingredient *in* that cake, the special yeast of the Gospel parable' (Walsh, 1983, p. 4). At the heart of what is involved here is the claim that the Catholic school '. . . so orients the whole of human culture to the message of salvation that the knowledge which the pupils acquire of the world, of life and of men is illumined by faith' (GE para. 8). The Catholic school therefore offers a kind of 'integral formation' in which there is a synthesis of 'culture and faith': an integration of '. . . all the different aspects of human knowledge through the subjects taught, in the light of the Gospel' (CS para. 37; cf. CS para. 49). Indeed, if this were not so, it would be difficult to see the force of the claim that Catholic education is particularly favourably conducted in its own, separate, Catholic schools, as distinct from in (say) classes supplementary to public education.

Quite what it involved in this second distinctive feature of Catholic education requires sustained attention. It includes the identification by pupils of those elements of culture which are opposed to the Gospel, an attempt to enrich the perception of subjects such as science, history, the humanities and the arts with a religious perspective, the study of philosophy and its relationship to divine wisdom and the unification of the programme of the school as a whole with a distinctive understanding of the human person (RDCS paras 51–65). Also involved in this is a distinctively Catholic approach to personal and social education (see Catholic Education Service, 1995).

With regard to the enrichment of the understanding of subjects, part of what is intended is illuminated by the claim that 'A teacher who is full of Christian wisdom, well prepared in his own subject, does more than convey the sense of what he is teaching to his pupils. Over and above what he says, he guides his pupils beyond his mere words to the heart of total Truth' (CS para 41). Since all genuine knowledge is a reflection of, and an insight into, the mind of God, lying behind all subjects are '. . . eternal realities' (CS para. 42). Another aspect of this question is the search for a form of 'unity' across the disparate elements of the curriculum. Christopher Dawson, in his book *The Crisis of Western Education* (Dawson, 1961) claims that, under the influence of utilitarianism and secularism, modern education has become 'a disintegrated mass of specialisms and vocational courses' (Dawson, 1961, p. 99). The mind needs to be given '. . . a unifying vision of the spiritual sources from which Western civilization flowed' (Dawson, 1961, p. 99). Dawson therefore favours the integrated and systematic study of Christian culture as an entry into the study of western civilization and as a way of achieving the 'unifying vision' he refers to (Dawson, 1961, especially Ch. 8–12). Although Dawson acknowledged that, because of the overall view of life which they embody, Catholic schools are particularly favoured in being able to engage in a project of this kind, he insisted that the educational responsibility of Catholics should not be confined to Catholic schools. Society as a whole has deep seated spiritual needs, and Christianity must exert a transformative influence through culture (Dawson, 1961, Ch. 13).

The claim that 'a distinctive understanding of the human person' should act as a unifying element in the programme of the school is further illuminated by the findings of the study 'Catholic Schools and the Common Good' (Bryk *et al.*, 1993). Underpinning all the elements identified as distinctive of Catholic schools is an 'inspirational ideology' derived from the intellectual and social tradition from which the schools spring, central features of which emphasize a 'Christian personalism' involving a moral conception of social behaviour in a just community, a concern for social justice and the common good in an ecumenical and multicultural world and the development of personal responsibility and social engagement (Bryk *et al.*, 1993, especially Ch. 1). The Catholic school extends '. . . an invitation to students both to reflect on a systematic body of thought and to immerse themselves in a communal life that seeks to live out its basic principles' (Bryk *et al.*, 1993, p. 335). The reference to the 'communal life of the school' emphasizes the point that the Catholic school exerts its holistic influence through its distinctive communal and organizational ethos and structure (cf. RCDS para. 111).

There are therefore a number of dimensions to the claim that Catholic education has implications for the entire educational experience of the child. It is important to note that emphasis is laid in these dimensions upon the need to respect the independence of the disciplines. It is insisted, for example, that subjects should not be seen as mere 'adjuncts to faith' or as useful for the purpose of apologetics (CS para. 39) and that they must be seen as properly autonomous (RCDS para. 53) and be taught with 'scientific objectivity' (RCDS para. 51).[2]

3 Religious and moral formation

Catholic education seeks to bring about a distinctive and moral formation of its students. This formation is seen as extending beyond the transmission of beliefs to the shaping of religious and moral personhood and character. Thus, students are to be helped to '. . . know and love God more perfectly' (GE para. 1; cf. para. 2), as part of the educational duty of the Church '. . . of proclaiming the way of salvation to all men, of revealing the life of Christ to those who believe, and of assisting them with unremitting care so that they may be able to attain to the fulness of that life' (GE para. 3).

In the Catholic school, therefore, catechesis involves not the teaching of an abstract body of truths, but rather '. . . the communication of the living mystery of God' (CT para. 7), an '. . . education of the believing conscience' (CT para. 16) in which Christian Doctrine is imparted in an organic and systematic way with a view to initiating the hearers into the fullness of Christian life (CT para. 18). In this the school seeks on the part of pupils not merely intellectual assent to religious truths but a total commitment to the Person of Christ (CS para. 50) in which prayer has an important role (GCD para. 25). The pupils are therefore encouraged to achieve '. . . a personal integration of faith and life' (CS para. 44).

In this, Catholic faith must be presented in its entirety under the guidance of the Magisterium (GCD para. 38; cf. para. 134; CT para. 6), respecting the hierarchy of truths (GCD para. 43) and ensuring integrity of content (CT paras 30–1; cf. paras 49, 52–3). There is therefore a persistent need to discern the essential features of the Christian message which is to be transmitted to pupils (GCD Pt 3, Ch. 2).

A marked feature of more recent treatments of the aspiration of Catholic education to form religious faith is the respect for freedom of conscience which is involved. Thus, frequently applied to catechesis is the well known statement of the Second Vatican Council on Religious Liberty '. . . every human being has the right to seek religious truth and adhere to it freely . . . "without coercion on the part of individuals or of social groups and any human power" in such a way that in this matter of religion, "no one is to be forced to act against his or her conscience or prevented from acting in conformity to it"' (CT para. 14). To proclaim or to offer faith is not to engage in the 'moral violence' of imposition, forbidden by both the Gospel and Church law (RDCS para. 6). Catechesis aims at faith which is 'fully responsible' (GCD para. 20), mature and enlightened (GCD para. 21). Human beings are 'fundamentally free' (RCDS para. 63) and the aim of catechesis is spiritual, liturgical, sacramental and apostolic maturity (RDCS para. 69). Adherence to the Faith on the part of those to be taught is seen as the fruit of grace and freedom (GCD para. 71). Other elements in modern accounts of catechesis include an emphasis upon the living character of the tradition (GCD para. 13) and upon the rational basis of faith and the need to acknowledge the scope of its intellectual demands (GCD paras 88; 97 (d)). Further, great respect is called for those pupils in the school who are not Catholics (LCWF para. 42, cf. para. 50).[3]

It is important to discern the precise relationship between 'freedom' as understood within the Catholic framework of thought and as understood in wider contemporary educational traditions. For example, 'genuine freedom' is interpreted in a way which stresses its relationship to the moral law in the order of nature and of grace (GCD para. 61), the greatest obstacle to which is sin (GCD para. 62). Further, personal autonomy, for example, is distinguished both from subjectivism and from the belief that human beings can seek their salvation by their own powers alone (GCD para. 86; cf. RDCS para. 53). In addition, whilst God's call does not apply constraint, it does not follow from this that the call is not binding in conscience (CT para. 69).

Included in the task of catechesis, though in some respects distinct from it, is the task of moral formation. The Church is a repository of moral as well as spiritual wisdom. This moral formation, which is also seen as under the guidance of the Magisterium, has as some of its distinctive features the insistence that there are absolute moral norms which bind everyone everywhere (GCD para. 63), which alone give meaning and value to human life (CS para. 30). Again, the role of the Catholic school here is seen as going beyond mere intellectual transformation. It has a particular concern for character formation (CS para. 12).

One of the most distinctive areas for Catholic moral formation is that of sex education. Unsurprisingly there is an emphasis here upon the centrality of values and moral norms (EGL para. 19) and of a general Christian vision of sexuality (EGL paras 21–47). The distinctive features of this vision include the importance of the holistic formation of the person in the context of Christian faith as a whole, with its emphasis upon the spiritual life, virtues such as modesty and friendship and the significance and reality of sin. As well as an understanding of Christian marriage, there is an emphasis upon education for chastity, (EGL para. 18; cf. para. 60), part of which is education in the value and significance of virginity and celibacy (EGL para. 18; cf. para. 31). Other issues emphasized include attitudes to family planning (EGL para. 62), pre- and extra-marital sex (EGL paras 95–7), autoeroticism (EGL paras 98–100) and homo-sexuality (EGL paras 101–3) (compare Catholic Education Service, undated b).

It is important to note that the moral influence of the Catholic school should not be seen as confined to such specific areas. As indicated in the last section, it embraces the wider social and political attitudes which are part of the 'inspira-tional ideology' to which Bryk and his associates have drawn attention.

Catholic education, and the Catholic school, is therefore distinctive in virtue of its embodiment of a particular view about the meaning of human persons and of human life, its aspiration to engage in a certain kind of holistic influence, and its concern with the formation of its students in its own religious and moral tradition.

Catholic Education and Public Education: Contrasts and Affinities

The distinctive general features of Catholic education which have been identified mark it out in significant respects from the concept of public education typically found in the common schools of pluralistic liberal democratic societies.

It is important to note that the concept of 'public education' is itself com-plex and many faceted. For our purposes, however, it is possible to outline a number of central features of a recognizable conception. The task of 'public education' in a pluralistic liberal democratic society confronts two important realities. First, education of whatever form is inherently value-laden, the values involved being of many different kinds. No form of education can be value-free or value-neutral (on these points see, for example, McLaughlin, 1994). The question which arises for education is therefore not *whether* it should be based on, and should transmit, values but *which* values should be invoked. The second reality is the well-grounded, deep-seated and perhaps ineradicable differences of view about many questions of value which are characteristic of plural-istic liberal democratic societies. This is not to suggest that such societies are entirely bereft of value agreement and consensus. If this were so it would be hard to see how these societies could achieve stability and coherence, much less satisfy the value demands implicit in democracy, such as justice, freedom and democracy. There are, however, large areas of disagreement about many questions, most notably about overall views of life as a whole, or 'compre-hensive' theories of the good.

In the light of these two realities, public education in pluralistic liberal democratic societies seeks to base its value influence on principles broadly acceptable to the citizens of society as a whole. This requires that public edu-cation cannot assume the truth of, or promote, any particular vision of the good life. Rather, it aims at a complex two-fold influence. On matters which are widely agreed and which can be regarded as part of the common or basic values of the society, public education seeks to achieve a strong, substantial influence on the beliefs of pupils and their wider development as persons. It is unhesitating, for example, in promoting the values of basic 'social morality' and democratic 'civic virtue' more generally. On matters of significant disagreement, where scope for a legitimate diversity of view is acknowledged, public education seeks to achieve a principled forebearance of influence: it seeks not to shape either the beliefs or the personal qualities of pupils in the light of any substantial or 'comprehensive' conception of the good which is significantly controversial. Instead, public education is either silent about such matters or it encourages pupils to come to their own reflective decisions about them. One way of expressing in an overall way the nature of educational influence on this view is that it exerts a complex combination of centripetal (unifying) and centrifugal (diversifying) forces on pupils and on society itself.

Although much more needs to be said in the articulation of this general view and its presumptive relationship with the notion of the common school (on these matters see, for example, McLaughlin, 1995), it is hopefully clear enough for our purposes. Public education does not in principle lack a value basis. It must, however, be constantly alert to the need to articulate and to handle in a fair way differing perspectives on matters of significant controversy, and this gives rise to a number of complexities in the work of the common school (McLaughlin, 1995, pp. 244–52).

The contrasts between public education and the distinctive features of Catholic education outlined in the last section can be readily brought into focus. With regard to (1), the respects in which public education cannot presuppose a particular 'philosophy of life' is clear. Any aspiration of public education to exert a holistic influence of the sort indicated in (2) gives rise to difficulties arising from its lack of ability to invoke an overall view of human good or perfection. There is no easily available 'overall point of view' from which 'integration of perspective' can be achieved. With regard to (3), public education has a clear role in the development of moral character, although it can assume the truth or acceptability of only the 'common' or 'public' values of the pluralist society. It lacks, however, the mandate to exert wide ranging influence across the moral domain as a whole. On matters of religion, public education is either silent, or sees its role as one of illuminating the religious domain in general for reflective consideration and judgment.[4]

Bryk and his associates note that, in the contemporary United States, 'moral inspiration' is largely lacking from public education and questions of the good are largely relegated to the private domain. Therefore the *de facto* vision of human life which is conveyed is that of *homo economicus* (Bryk *et al.*, 1993, p. 319) in which matters are judged by '. . . a utilitarian calculus of individual self-interest . . .' (*ibid.*, p. 320). Public education, in the view of Bryk and his colleagues, mirrors the spiritual vacuum and emptiness at the heart of contemporary US society and inculturates this in children (*ibid.*, p. 322). One of the major lessons which they consider can be learnt by public schools from their Catholic counterparts is the need to engage in debate and to renew public discourse about what it means to be an educated person in a postmodern democratic society (*ibid.*, p. 327).

An interesting question raised by this critique is whether the failings ascribed to public education are merely contingent ones, or arise from the philosophical basis of public education itself. Defenders of public education have argued that, at least in principle, an aim such as the development of democratic citizenship can constitute a sufficiently 'thick' overall aim to provide the educational process with substance and direction: it need not be bereft of a 'guiding vision'. Evaluation of this matter requires consideration of the wide ranging critiques of the philosophical theory of liberalism which have emerged in recent years from a broadly 'communitarian' perspective. Such critiques assert that liberal values, and the political community they generate, lack the substantiality needed to enable persons to achieve defensible and necessary forms of affiliation and commitment to a 'larger moral ecology' beyond their own individual, and indeed individualistic concerns. Such a 'moral ecology' embodies a social ethos, a consensus of the common good and notions of loyalty and responsibility to the community as a whole as well as a framework of wider beliefs and values providing (at least to some extent) a culture of 'narrative coherence' as well as of 'freedom' for lives. The liberal view, it is claimed, does of its very nature lead inevitably to individualism in its various forms, and a tendency for individual choice and self-definition to be based on arbitrary preference or self-interest, rather than a view of life which is more coherent and other regarding. In addition, attention is drawn to the corrosive effects of private economic pursuits and consumerism on the notion of a caring public ethos, the negative effects of an undue separation of public and private realms and so on (on this critique and its educational implications see, for example, McLaughlin, 1992a; see also Walsh, 1993; Carr, W., 1995; Hogan, 1995; Jonathan, 1995).

Without pursuing this critique at this point, it seems clear that, in general, a case can be made for the acceptability, and indeed desirability, of at least certain forms of religious schooling as an alternative within the overall educational system (see McLaughlin, 1992b; cf. Scheffler, 1995). Such schooling can be seen as compatible with liberal democratic educational principles, not least by providing a particular substantial starting point for the child's eventual development into autonomous agency and democratic citizenship, and by making a distinctive contribution to democratic life (cf. Dunne, 1991, pp. 31–4). The 'openness with roots' (Bryk *et al.*, 1993, p. 334) which Bryk and his associates discern as characteristic of Catholic schools in the United States is a good example of this. Far from being narrow, divisive or sectarian, 'The Catholic school argues that schooling demands an impassioned rationality shaped by a vision of the common good, a vision that itself is always open to challenge and clarification. Such an education is accomplished through inspiration, not coercion; through dialogue, not dogma' (*ibid.*, p. 320). This general thesis about the role of Catholic schools in a liberal democratic society resonates with the debate about the reinvigorated role that contemporary Catholicism may have with respect to common culture and also with continuing discussions of the relationship between Catholicism and Liberalism[5] (on this see, for example, Bruce Douglass and Hollenbach (Eds), 1994; Haldane, 1992; Hannon, 1992; Langan, 1990).

Since the possibility of an 'overlapping consensus' between contrasting comprehensive views of the good is an important feature of, and requirement for, a liberal democratic society (Rawls, 1993, Pt 2 Lecture 4), it should not surprise us that important affinities between Catholic education and some of the aims and principles of public education can be discerned.

Church documents contain a number of elements which indicate the 'openness' of Catholic education. A number of these, such as the stress upon the need to respect the autonomy of academic subjects and freedom of conscience with regard to religious formation have already been mentioned. In addition, there is an acknowledgment of the significance of Catholic schools containing non-Catholic pupils (GE para. 9; cf. RDCS para. 6), and a special emphasis upon those pupils who are poor, without the help and affection of family and those who do not have the faith (GE para. 9). Further, the Catholic school is explicitly encouraged to be open to civic demands and to wider concerns (RDCS paras 45–6), including the needs of others and the demands of justice (CS paras 56–8; 62). Further, there is much in current emphases in Catholic education which are generally attractive, including the claim that, in a Catholic school, the pupils should experience their dignity as persons before they know its definition (CS para. 55).

The Clarification of Distinctiveness: Issues and Difficulties

Catholics who work in Catholic schools are strongly urged to achieve '. . . a clear realisation of the identity of a Catholic school and the courage to follow all the consequences of its uniqueness' (CS para. 66). It is not enough for Catholic education to be motivated by a vaguely Christian spirit, rather than by the reasoned faith of the Church (Haldane, 1995, p. 30). Any attempt to pursue these matters of distinctiveness in a sustained way confronts a range of issues and difficulties. Some of these relate to the social and cultural context in which the work of Catholic schools must be conducted (see, for example, GCD Pt 1). Others relate to the need for more research evidence, particularly in England and Wales, on which Catholic educational policy can be based. One of the problems relating to research on the outcomes of Catholic education is the dimension of hiddenness and time that is related to many Catholic educational aims (cf. Dunne, 1991, p. 29; Nichols, 1978, p. 43; CS para. 84). Needless to say, the full range of issues involved cannot be addressed here (cf. O'Keeffe, 1992).

In what follows, I shall indicate a number of central issues which all arise from an attempt to address the distinctiveness of Catholic education in a sustained way, and which generate difficult questions which are often not pursued with sufficient rigour.

The first issue arises from the point made earlier that each of the elements of Catholic education which have been identified require interpretation and judgment. Often these matters of judgment require the determination of the proper balance to be struck between different emphases or aspects of the Catholic tradition. For example, Bryk and his associates note how the religious education programmes in the Catholic schools they studied had changed over recent years. Among these changes include a move away from dogma and a conception of faith as received truth to an emphasis upon the importance of human relationships and human justice and the formation and use of conscience (Bryk *et al.*, 1993, pp. 110–13), within a form of religious education '. . . broadly defined for life in society' (*ibid.*, p. 335). Associated with changes of this kind are a number of well known disputes about the appropriate form which Catholic religious formation should take and about what is required in a balanced and authoritative presentation of the faith, an issue to which the publication of the Universal Catechism is relevant (Catechism of the Catholic Church, 1994; see also Bishops Conference of England and Wales, 1994; The National Board of Religious Inspectors and Advisers, 1994). Another aspect of this general point concerns the extent to which the Catholic schools in the Bryk *et al.* study placed sufficient emphasis upon specifically religious distinctiveness. Although the schools did not lack religious activities and roles in addition to their formal religious curriculum (Bryk *et al.*, 1993, pp. 136–9; 140–1), the Catholic teachers reported that they valued traditional academic goals and the development in students of qualities of compassion, tolerance and a commitment to justice more highly than the 'more traditional' elements of religious formation such as a knowledge of, and a commitment to, Church doctrine and moral teaching — although there was a difference between lay and religious teachers in this respect (*ibid.*, pp. 134–5). In addition, religious controversy rarely surfaced within the schools (*ibid.*, p. 135), which suggests perhaps that robust debate on religious topics, and on the detail of Catholic doctrine, was lacking. Further careful analysis is needed of *inter alia* claims that the beliefs which articulate the Catholic high school are expansive, liberating and humanizing rather than narrow, restricted and closed (*ibid.*, p. 144). Bryk *et al.* note that a tension exists between different emphases of the role of the Catholic school (*ibid.*, pp. 334–5) with the danger that any return to the more traditional concept of this role may undermine the public functions which such schools now perform. The major point here is that the interpretative task which is required in relation to such matters can uncover deep seated differences of emphasis and view.

The second issue concerns precisely the general phenomenon of dispute and disagreement within the Church. The increasing heterogeneity of belief and practice among Catholics has been widely noted by sociologists (see, for example, Hornsby-Smith, 1987, Ch. 3, 1991, especially Parts II, III). This leads to a number of well recognized and significant tensions within the Catholic community as a whole and in relation to its educational work (on some of the contemporary tensions felt by Catholic teachers of Religious Education see, for example, Richards, 1994). One strategy for approaching such disagreements and conflicts is through a 'culture of silence' about certain matters. This seems to be, at least to some extent, a strategy used in the Catholic schools studied by Bryk *et al.* In such circumstances rhetoric, ambiguity and obfuscation can have a lubricative role in relation to the management of the school and elsewhere (cf. McLaughlin, 1994, p. 459). Such a strategy does, however, significantly undermine the aim of achieving clarity about Catholic educational distinctiveness.

A third issue concerns the centrality to its educational mission of the example of the teacher in the Catholic school. It is widely acknowledged that teachers are a crucial factor in whether the Catholic school achieves its purposes (GE para. 8) '. . . inspired by an apostolic spirit, they should bear testimony by their lives and their teaching to the one Teacher, who is Christ' (GE para. 8). Thus the teacher is one who not only transmits knowledge but is seen as forming human persons by communicating Christ (LCWF para. 16). He or she must provide a 'concrete example' of the Catholic concept of the human person (LCWF paras 18, 32), provide an example of Church membership (LCWF para. 22), be a source of spiritual inspiration (*ibid.*, para. 23), extend horizons through their personal faith (*ibid.*, para. 28), have a 'mature spiritual personality' (LCWF para. 60) and provide a wide ranging example of faith witness (*ibid.*, paras 32–3, 40–1, 59). For reasons such as these the life of Catholic teachers involves not merely the exercise of professionalism but also of a personal vocation (*ibid.*, para. 37) in which '. . . they reveal the Christian message not only by word but also by every gesture of their behaviour' (CS para. 43; cf. para. 53). In addition, teachers must have '. . . a keen social awareness and a profound sense of civic and political responsibility' (LCWF para. 19).

It might be thought that these requirements of teacher example in the Catholic school are appropriate only for certain teachers in the school, such as those concerned with the teaching of religion (cf. RDCS para. 96) and with the exercise of key leadership roles. However, at least at the level of principal, this cannot be so. This is because of the aspiration of Catholic education to provide a holistic educational experience. As was noted earlier, this 'aspiration to holistic influence' is one of the major reasons why the Church considers that separate Catholic *schools* are such an important part of its educational mission. Therefore all teachers in the school must share a view of life and of the educational task of the school — a common purpose and commitment — so that 'unity in teaching' and the development of community and ethos can be achieved (CS paras 29, 59–61; RDCS para. 26).

One of the central difficulties here is that of ensuring a sufficient supply of Catholic teachers with these qualities. What is needed here are not only Catholic teachers who are practising their faith but who are also willing to give an appropriate form of witness to it as part of their professionalism. At least in England and Wales, there is strong evidence of a significant supply problem concerning Catholic teachers in certain sectors of the Catholic school system (see Catholic Education Service, 1994b). Relevant to this general question is the urgent need to give serious attention to the distinctive character of Catholic teacher training.

The clarification of the distinctiveness of Catholic education is an important task. Undertaken with the appropriate degree of rigour, however, it can be a demanding and painful one. As indicated earlier, there is an urgent need to bring sustained philosophical reflection to bear upon Catholic education, which can illuminate all the distinctive elements of Catholic education which have been outlined, and, at least to some extent, the particular problems which have been identified.

Notes

1 On the transformation in the nature, aims, composition and ethos of Catholic schools during the post-war period, the essential elements of which are well known, see, for example, Bryk *et al.*, 1993, Prologue, Ch. 1; see also Hornsby-Smith, 1987; Chadwick, Ch. 2.
2 For a summary of criteria relevant to the overall religious perspective that should govern the Catholic school see RDCS para. 57; cf. LCWF paras 28–31. For further discussion of the specific respects in which education as a whole might be viewed from a Catholic perspective see Catholic Education Service (undated a); Lonergan, 1993, especially Ch. 5, 6, 9, 10; Walsh, 1983; Walsh, 1991, especially Ch. 8, 11, 12. On an attitude to philosophy which might be compatible with a Catholic attitude see Hadot, 1995.
3 On the relationship between catechesis and rational criticism and judgment see, for example, Nichols, 1978, especially Ch. 1–5, 1979, especially Ch. 1, 3, 4, 6, 1980, 1992a, 1992b. On the relationship between religious education and catechesis and related matters see Gallagher, 1988; Groome, 1980, 1991; Purnell, 1985; Rossiter, 1990. On contrasting views of Anglicans and Catholics on catechesis see, for example, Chadwick, 1994, Ch. 2.
4 On these matters see, for example, Astley, 1994; Astley and Day (Eds), 1992; Astley and Francis (Eds), 1994; Cooling, 1994; Francis and Thatcher (Eds), 1990; Francis and Lankshear (Eds), 1993; Noddings, 1993; Office for Standards in Education, 1994; Thiessen, 1993; White, 1994. On the complexities of the Anglican attitude to the common school in England and Wales see, for example, Chadwick, 1994, Ch. 2.
5 For discussions of the notion of a 'Catholic moment' see a series of articles published by *The Tablet* in 1994 by Neuhaus (24 September), Weakland (1 October), Chittister (8 October), Langan (15 October), Dulles (22 October) and Cromartie (29 October).

References

Astley, J. (1994) *The Philosophy of Christian Religious Education*, Birmingham, AL, Religious Education Press.
Astley, J. and Day, D. (Eds) (1992) *The Contours of Christian Education*, Great Wakering, McCrimmons.
Astley, J. and Francis, L.J. (Eds) (1994) *Critical Perspectives on Christian Education: A Reader on the Aims, Principles and Philosophy of Christian Education*, Leominster, Gracewing.
Beck, G.A. (1964) 'Aims in education: Neo-thomism', in Hollins, T.H.B. (Ed) *Aims in Education: The Philosophic Approach*, Manchester, Manchester University Press.

Terence H. McLaughlin

BISHOPS' CONFERENCE OF ENGLAND and WALES (1994) *What Are We to Teach?: Foundations for Religious Teaching in the Light of the Catechism of the Catholic Church*, London, Bishops' Conference of England and Wales.

BRUCE DOUGLASS, R. and HOLLENBACH, D. (Eds) (1994) *Catholicism and Liberalism: Contributions to American Public Philosophy*, Cambridge, Cambridge University Press.

BRYK A.S., LEE, V.E. and HOLLAND, P.B. (1993) *Catholic Schools and the Common Good*, Cambridge, MA, Harvard University Press.

CARR, D., HALDANE, J., McLAUGHLIN, T. and PRING, R. (1995) 'Return to the crossroads: Maritain fifty years on', *British Journal of Educational Studies*, **43**, 2, pp. 162–78.

CARR, W. (1995) 'Education and democracy: Confronting the postmodernist challenge', *Journal of Philosophy of Education*, **29**, 1, pp. 75–91.

CATECHISM OF THE CATHOLIC CHURCH (1994) London, Geoffrey Chapman.

CATHOLIC EDUCATION SERVICE (1994a) *Evaluating the Distinctive Nature of a Catholic School*, 3rd ed, London, Catholic Education Service.

CATHOLIC EDUCATION SERVICE (1994b) *The Supply of Catholic Teachers to Catholic Schools: A Research Paper*, London, Catholic Education Service.

CATHOLIC EDUCATION SERVICE (1995) *Spiritual and Moral Development Across the Curriculum: A Discussion Paper for the Professional Development of Teachers in Catholic Schools*, London, Catholic Education Service.

CATHOLIC EDUCATION SERVICE (undated a) *Curriculum Guidance*, London, Catholic Education Service.

CATHOLIC EDUCATION SERVICE (undated b) *Education in Sexuality: Some Guidelines for Teachers and Governors in Catholic Schools*, London, Catholic Education Service.

CHADWICK, P. (1994) *Schools of Reconciliation: Issues in Joint Roman Catholic-Anglican Education*, London, Cassell.

COOLING, T. (1994) *A Christian Vision for State Education: Reflections on the Theology of Education*, London, SPCK.

DAWSON, C. (1961) *The Crisis of Western Education*, London, Sheed and Ward.

DUNNE, J. (1991) 'The Catholic school and civil society: Exploring the tensions, in CONFERENCE OF MAJOR RELIGIOUS SUPERIORS (IRELAND)', *The Catholic School in Contemporary Society*, Dublin, Conference of Major Religious Superiors.

FLANNERY, A. (1988) *Vatican Council II: The Conciliar and Post Conciliar Documents Vols I and II*, Northport, NY, Costello Publishing Co.

FLEW, A. (1968) 'Against indoctrination', in AYER, A.J. (Ed) *The Humanist Outlook*, London, Pemberton.

FRANCIS, L.J. and LANKSHEAR, D.W. (Eds) (1993) *Christian Perspectives on Church Schools: A Reader*, Leominster, Gracewing.

FRANCIS, L.J. and THATCHER, A. (Eds) (1990) *Christian Perspectives for Education: A Reader in the Theology of Education*, Leominster, Gracewing.

GALLAGHER, J. (1988) *Our Schools and Our Faith: A Pastoral Concern and Challenge*, London, Harper Collins.

GROOME, T.H. (1980) *Christian Religious Education: Sharing Our Story and Vision*, San Francisco, Harper and Row.

GROOME, T.H. (1991) *Sharing Faith: A Comprehensive Approach to Religious Education and Pastoral Ministry: The Way of Shared Praxis*, San Francisco, Harper.

HADOT, P. (1995) *Philosophy as a Way of Life: Spiritual Exercises from Socrates to Foucault*, DAVIDSON, A.I. (Ed), Oxford, Basil Blackwell.

HALDANE, J. (1989) 'Metaphysics in the philosophy of education', *Journal of Philosophy of Education*, **23**, 2, pp. 171–83.

HALDANE, J. (1990) 'Chesterton's philosophy of education', *Philosophy*, **65**, pp. 65–80.

HALDANE, J. (1992) 'Can a Catholic be a Liberal?: Catholic social teaching and communitarianism', *Melita Theologica*, **XLIII**, 2, pp. 44–57.

HALDANE, J. (1995) 'Philosophy and Catholic education', *The Sower*, **16**, 3, pp. 30–1.

HANNON, P. (1992) *Church, State, Morality and Law*, Dublin, Gill and Macmillan.

HAUERWAS, S. and WESTERHOFF, J.H. (Eds) (1992) *Schooling Christians: 'Holy Experiments' in American Education*, Grand Rapids, MI, William B. Eerdmans Publishing Company.

HESBURGH, T.M. (Ed) (1994) *The Challenge and Promise of a Catholic University*, Notre Dame, University of Notre Dame Press.

HOGAN, P. (1995) *The Custody and Courtship of Experience: Western Education in Philosophical Perspective*, Blackrock, The Columba Press.

HORNSBY-SMITH, M.P. (1978) *Catholic Education: The Unobtrusive Partner*, London, Sheed and Ward.

HORNSBY-SMITH, M.P. (1987) *Roman Catholics in England: Studies in Social Structure Since the Second World War*, Cambridge, Cambridge University Press.

HORNSBY-SMITH, M.P. (1991) *Roman Catholic Beliefs in England: Customary Catholicism and Transformations of Religious Authority*, Cambridge, Cambridge University Press.

JONATHAN, R. (1995) 'Liberal philosophy of education: A paradigm under strain', *Journal of Philosophy of Education*, **29**, 1, pp. 93–107.

LANE, D.A. (1991) 'Catholic education and the school: Some theological reflections, in CONFERENCE OF MAJOR RELIGIOUS SUPERIORS (IRELAND)', *The Catholic School in Contemporary Society*, Dublin, Conference of Major Religious Superiors.

LANGAN, J. (1990) 'Catholicism and liberalism: 200 years of contest and consensus', in BRUCE DOUGLASS, R., MARA, G.R. and RICHARDSON, H.S. (Eds) *Liberalism and the Good*, London, Routledge.

LONERGAN, B. (1993) *Collected Works of Bernard Lonergan, Volume 10: Topics in Education, The Cincinnati Lectures of 1959 on the Philosophy of Education*, DORAN, R.M. and CROWE, F.E. (Eds), Toronto, University of Toronto Press.

LUNDY, D. (1995) 'A vision for catechesis in the 1990s', in GREY, M., HEATON, A. and SULLIVAN, D. (Eds) *The Candles Are Still Burning: Directions in Sacrament and Spirituality*, London, Geoffrey Chapman.

McBRIEN, R.P. (1994) *Catholicism*, 3rd ed, London, Geoffrey Chapman.

McLAUGHLIN, T.H. (1992a) 'Citizenship, diversity and education: A philosophical perspective', *Journal of Moral Education*, **21**, 3, pp. 235–50.

McLAUGHLIN, T.H. (1992b) 'The ethics of separate schools', in LEICESTER, M. and TAYLOR, M.J. (Eds) *Ethics, Ethnicity and Education*, London, Kogan Page.

McLAUGHLIN, T.H. (1994) 'Values, coherence and the school', *Cambridge Journal of Education*, **24**, 3, pp. 453–70.

McLAUGHLIN, T.H. (1995) 'Liberalism, education and the common school', *Journal of Philosophy of Education*, **29**, 2, pp. 239–55.

NICHOLS, K. (1978) *Cornerstone: Guidelines for Religious Education 1*, Slough, St Paul Publications.

NICHOLS, K. (1979) *Orientations: Six Essays on Theology and Education*, Slough, St Paul Publications.

NICHOLS, K. (1980) 'Commitment, search and dialogue', in NICHOLS, K. (Ed) *Voice of the Hidden Waterfall*, Slough, St Paul Publications.

NICHOLS, K. (1992a) 'Roots in religious education', in WATSON, B. (Ed) *Priorities in Religious Education: A Model for the 1990s and Beyond*, London, Falmer Press.

NICHOLS, K. (1992b) 'The logical geography of catechesis', in ASTLEY, J. and DAY, D. (Eds) *The Contours of Christian Education*, Great Wakering, McCrimmons.

NODDINGS, N. (1993) *Educating for Intelligent Belief or Unbelief*, New York, Teachers College Press.

OFFICE FOR STANDARDS IN EDUCATION (1994) *Spiritual, Moral, Social and Cultural Development: An OFSTED discussion paper*, London, Office for Standards in Education.

O'KEEFFE, B. (1992) 'Catholic schools in an open society: The English challenge', *Aspects of Education: Journal of the Institute of Education*, The University of Hull, **46**, pp. 34–51.

Terence H. McLaughlin

Pope John Paul II (1979) 'Apostolic exhortation: Catechesi tradendae', in Flannery, A. (1988) *Vatican Council II: The Conciliar and Post Conciliar Documents Vol. II*, Section 121, Northport, NY, Costello Publishing Co.

Pring, R. (1968) 'Has education an aim?', in Tucker, B. (Ed) *Catholic Education in a Secular Society*, London, Sheed and Ward.

Purnell, A.P. (1985) *Our Faith Story, Its Telling and Its Sharing: An Education in Faith*, London, Collins.

Rawls, J. (1993) *Political Liberalism*, New York, Columbia University Press.

Richards, C. (1994) *Who Would a Teacher Be?: Wrestling with Religious Education*, London, Darton Longman and Todd.

Rossiter, G.M. (1990) 'The need for a "creative divorce" between catechesis and religious education in Catholic schools', in Francis, L.J. and Thatcher, A. (Eds) *Christian Perspectives for Education: A Reader in the Theology of Education*, Leominster, Gracewing.

Rummery, G. (1980) '1970–1980: The decade of the directories', in Nichols, K. (Ed) *Voice of the Hidden Waterfall*, Slough, St Paul Publications.

Sacred Congregation for the Clergy (1971) 'General catechetical directory', in Flannery, A. (1988) *Vatican Council II: The Conciliar and Post Conciliar Documents Vol. II*, Section 114, Northport, NY, Costello Publishing Co.

Sacred Congregation for Catholic Education (1977) 'The Catholic school', in Flannery, A. (1988) *Vatican Council II: The Conciliar and Post Conciliar Documents Vol. II*, Section 115, Northport, NY, Costello Publishing Co.

Sacred Congregation for Catholic Education (1982) 'Lay Catholics in schools: Witnesses to Faith', in Flannery, A. (1988) *Vatican Council II: The Conciliar and Post Conciliar Documents Vol. II*, Section 116, Northport, NY, Costello Publishing Co.

Sacred Congregation for Catholic Education (1983) *Educational Guidance in Human Love: Outlines for Sex Education*, London, Catholic Truth Society.

Sacred Congregation for Catholic Education (1988) *The Religious Dimension of Education in a Catholic School: Guidelines for Reflection and Renewal*, London, Catholic Truth Society.

Scheffler, I. (1995) *Teachers of My Youth: An American Jewish Experience*, Dordecht, Kluwer Academic Publishers.

Study Group on Catholic Education (1981) *Signposts and Homecomings, The Educative Task of the Catholic Community: A Report to the Bishops of England and Wales*, Slough, St Paul Publications.

The National Board of Religious Inspectors and Advisers (1994) *Broad Areas of Attainment in Religious Education: A Statement about Catholic Religious Teaching at the Key Stages*, London, Rejoice Publications for The National Board of Religious Inspectors and Advisers.

Thiessen, E.J. (1993) *Teaching for Commitment: Liberal Education, Indoctrination and Christian Nurture*, Montreal and Kingston, McGill-Queen's University Press.

Walsh, P. (1983) 'The Church secondary school and its curriculum', in O'Leary, D. (Ed) *Religious Education and Young Adults*, Slough, St Paul Publications.

Walsh, P. (1993) *Education and Meaning: Philosophy in Practice*, London, Cassell.

White, J. (1994) 'Instead of OFSTED: A critical discussion of OFSTED on "spiritual, moral, social and cultural development"', *Cambridge Journal of Education*, **24**, 3, pp. 369–77.

Chapter 10

Wholeness, Faith and the Distinctiveness of the Catholic School

V. Alan McClelland

The major principles influencing the theoretical bases of Catholic education are clearly delineated in the key document of the Second Vatican Council on the subject, *Gravissimum Educationis*, although, not surprisingly, it encapsulated little not already manifest in Pius XI's encyclical letter of some thirty-five years earlier, *Divini Illius Magistri.*[1] Essentially it is argued that the Church's commitment to education is an exemplification of the Divine mandate 'to announce the mystery of salvation and to renew all things in Christ' (Flannery, 1975, p. 726). Within this theological principle lies the essence of the meaning and purpose of Catholic schooling — the conservation and the transmission of Divine Teaching and transcendental values, the commitment to the missionary imperative of the propagation of the good news of the gospel in and through transformation of human lives in daily service.

At the heart of this single and single-minded educational philosophy lie two fundamental issues: what is understood by 'the unity' of education and what constitutes an acceptable immediate aim for the educative process. They are inter-connected issues. If education is to be a self-consistent and cohesive process, educational theory and practice must converge within a purposeful and integrated approach to the living of the Christian life in the world. The process has been effectively described by the nineteenth-century Italian philosopher, Antonio Rosmini-Serbati, when he declared 'by education . . . I mean that which leads a man to the highest moral perfection possible to him,' achieved 'by means of a well-ordered development and harmonious cultivation of all his faculties'.[2] This, in turn, means that the Catholic school must witness to a living community of faith and love and must generate a sense of active apostolate within the wider society in fulfilment of those virtues. As *Gravissimum Educationis* puts it, Christians should be trained to live their lives 'in the new self, justified and sanctified through the truth' (Flannery, op. cit., p. 728). In this discovery of the self, an authentic missionary apostolate is born.

In a message marking World Mission Day, in July of 1993, Pope John Paul II emphasized anew the apostolate of the 'missionary formation of children' in families, schools and parishes (*The Universe*, 1993, 18 July, p. 6). He thus re-emphasized that from this theology of education emerges the Christian commitment to an integrated, personal and social education, one faithful to the teaching of the *magisterium*, one which places sound judgment and the acquisition of Christian beliefs and values at the heart of the process of social-ization in a Catholic school. Indeed, the Second Vatican Council solemnly urged pastors to be aware of the grave obligation 'to do all in their power to ensure that this Christian education is enjoyed by all the faithful and especially by the young who are the hope of the Church' (Flannery, op. cit., p. 728). Personal commitment in faith and personal morality arising out of and in conformity with that commitment constitute the twin features of Christian harmony at the essence of the concept of Catholic education. Edward Hulmes, in treating of the problems engendered in teachers by the apparent polarities of 'commitment' and 'neutrality' in religious education teaching in schools, embodied the Catholic ideal in a postulate that 'religion lays claim to the *whole* person and at the same time refuses to be classified as just one of many possible ways of apprehend-ing reality' (Hulmes, 1979, p. 17). Contributors to that *wholeness* have been subsequently defined by him as:

affirmation, authority, autonomy, beauty, belief, choice, community, conscience, detachment, discernment, discretion, enjoyment, esteem, failure, faith, freedom, integrity, justice, love, order, peace, persever-ance, pluralism, quietness, reconciliation, relativism, reparation, re-sponsibility, self-control, success, suffering, tolerance, tradition, truth, uncertainty, unity. (Hulmes, 1994, p. 4)

Cultivation of such values, however, in the process of the formation of 'wholeness' is for the Christian but 'the privilege of sharing in the holiness of God'. Its corollary is that 'the one who is taught by Christ is under an obliga-tion to teach others', a belief that inspires and is inspired by doctrinal sub-scription to the Community of Saints. Hulmes argues that 'coherence is provided only by reference to a moral centre' and insists that Education corrupts 'if that moral centre is lacking' (ibidem.). On such a crucial issue, however, the Catholic Church in England and Wales seems to have lost its way. It certainly cannot be maintained that either unity of purpose or commitment to the missionary intent of Catholic education are sustained by the approval given by the epis-copal conference to the inadequate philosophical underpinnings of its own National Catechetical Project for the 1990s. *Weaving the Web*, constituting resource material provided for secondary schools (although often treated in practice as if it were a *syllabus* for religious education) and *Here I Am*, a corresponding scheme for primary schools — to write nothing about recent subscriptions to unmitigated pluralism in the approach to sex education — fall far short in their commitment to what one bishop has recently called the rooting of Catholic schools in 'a shared vision' and the provision of an education which is, therefore, 'integrated and wholesome'.[3] The project, in its anxiety to cope with increasing numbers of non-Catholic children seeking entry to Catholic schools, has lost sight of the schools' theological *raison d'être*. The Bishop of Salford, addressing his clergy in 1987, pointed out the dangers in a policy of open enrolment: 'To open our schools to those who are not Roman Catholics, besides being deeply incompatible without massive resourcing to our claimed philosophy of education, runs the risk of undermining their character' (Kelly, op. cit., p. 18). While this 'might secure in existence a school on a certain site, it does not secure determination to offer a Roman Catholic school'. He argued;

> We are a community which takes seriously the accomplishment of salvation, which is accurately described as wholeness in and through wholeness of body, mind and spirit. We do not accept that we can include RE in any curriculum and be content that our duties are fulfilled. Nor can we be satisfied with a situation where each teacher is competent in a particular discipline but does not share in an agreed vision of the whole task . . . (ibid., p. 10)

It is clear, then, that education structured upon a definition of 'wholeness' implies that physical, spiritual, moral and intellectual advances take place within an understanding of harmony and relationship, a totality of human development resting upon the support provided by outside agencies, home, Church and environment. Parents, pastors and professional pedagogues are indispensable cooperative and interactive forces in ensuring concepts of 'wholeness' and 'inner harmony' are sustained. It is the peculiar concern of the Catholic school, therefore, to create in its daily life, its curricular approaches, its social structures and its moral and religious conditions, an appropriate *métier* within which the Spirit can function. Holley has commented that 'it is personal transcendence which is holiness' and it is life within a loving community that will provide the conditions necessary for it to germinate (Holley, 1978, p. 56). Holley maintains 'education has to do with persons who are in depth spiritual beings whose objective self-integration is a matter of spiritual fulfilment if it is anything' (op. cit., p. 168). To Hulmes, this posits a dynamic 'associated with growth, vulnerability, decision and change' (Hulmes, 1979, p. 87). Rosemary Haughton has argued for the spark of commitment to be ignited which may set fire to the whole person — 'there must be fuel that is inflammable, there must be a person formed for loving' (Haughton, 1968, p. 225). This is not far distant from the view of Islam, carefully presented by Syed Ali Ashraf in July 1994:

> True humanism lies not in playing with some intellectual counters but in purifying the self of all forms of narrowness and greed and this is possible when the love of God is generated within the soul. The sense of eternal values which are already there in that soul has to be nurtured and refined and given free play in the context of the society and humanity as a whole. (Ashraf, 1994, p. 37)

The tessellations of this formidable mosaic have been elucidated by Cardinal Basil Hume in his positing in a recent book, *Towards a Civilization of Love*, of a threefold mission for the Catholic school. He writes: 'The Church . . . does not see education simply as a means to an end but as an integral part of her mission to evangelise, reconcile and renew' (Hume, 1988, p. 104). In this process 'the power of the spirit comes through influence, persuasion and the values of the Gospel' and her educative mission is fundamentally one of pastoral care — 'of the timeless truths of faith, hope and love, and of support for all those who strive to serve tirelessly for the betterment of the lives of all peoples' (McGettrick, 1991, p. 7).

But a note of caution is to be sounded. There must be more in all this than merely a social dimension. Archbishop Desmond Connell of Dublin has cautioned against such a temptation in a recent radio broadcast in which he reminded his hearers that while Christianity is concerned with 'constantly transcending the idols we all have', and about the overcoming of 'fragmentation, conflict, sectarianism, ideologies and all kinds of divisions' in the world around us, it is also about the spiritual formation needed for such things to become part of our own salvation history. This timely reminder returns us to the person-centred emphasis of the Council document on education for, as Dermot Lane has expressed it, 'the person is only truly person in relation to others (but) ultimately in relation to the Supreme Other we call God' (Lane, 1991, p. 8).

Tradition, too, has a particular role to play in the philosophical under-pinning of the Catholic school. It has been argued elsewhere that when the Church uses the concept of the 'family', it has before it the great theological truth of the communion of saints (McClelland, 1992a, pp. 5–6). It is within that particular extended family that tradition is rightly located, an organic relationship with the whole human family of God's creation *in Christo*. Where the communion of saints lies at the very heart of concepts of family, community, wholeness and integration, a serious challenge is presented to a society whose world is bounded by time and space. Within the context of the communion of saints, 'tradition', 'continuity', 'development' and 'change' assume a significance that is integrative and harmonious (McClelland, 1988, pp. 20–2).

In recent years, Catholic schools in England and Wales have been confronted by sharply focused philosophical and theological questions in the aftermath of the passing of the Education Reform Act of 1988. The two key concepts informing the legislative change are the desire to ensure maximum *devolution* of power and responsibility for the day-to-day management of schools from local government agencies to schools themselves and their 'clients' and, secondly, the desire to introduce greater *accountability* into the education service. The twin shibboleths of devolution and accountability constitute the new touchstones for measuring quality within a national system of education.

Catholics are apprehensive that the current political orthodoxy constitutes a threat to humanistic and transcendental values, emphasizing a selfish individualism at the expense of social concern and collective responsibility. Consumerism and competitiveness are seen as presenting a challenge to Christian precepts of compassion and cooperation (McClelland, 1992b, pp. 31–6). Accountability and the devolution to schools of responsibility for their own affairs, however, place a premium upon need-fulfilment, quality of service, recognition of parental rights and duties and the provision of academic opportunity. Such consequences of the educational reform lie also at the heart of the belief in the effectiveness of the Catholic school and, indeed, can be welcomed as the legitimate extension of a Christian philosophy of education. The main criticism of recent Government policy remains, however, that it treats parents mainly as consumers with legal rights rather than participants in a 'joint commitment to a common purpose' as the 1993 report of The National Commission on Education describes it (National Commission on Education, 1993, p. 168). Well over a decade ago, the British Council of Churches argued there could be no value for Church schools in being merely a bland alternative to the State system of schooling (British Council of Churches, 1981, p. 5). Unless the Christian ethos is preserved in Church schools, a condition 'in which the individual is valued and differences are seen as an opportunity for tolerance and understanding', there can be no reason for their continued existence (Culham Institute, 1991).

Speaking at the North of England Education Conference in 1988, the then Secretary of State for Education described forthcoming educational legislation as being concerned with 'competition, choice and freedom', a search for excellence in education. Ultimately it concerned the 'health and wealth' of the country. A Catholic philosophy of education must relate ill to an enterprise culture that stresses economic development at the expense of giving priority of place to transcendental and caring values. Cardinal Hume castigated the new philosophy as one of loss, 'a curious collective amnesia, a loss of any sense of history, and a cynicism about the future which leads to an emphasis on short-term objectives and immediate quantifiable results' (Hume, op. cit., p. 105). Nevertheless, the Church's philosophy of education, with its dual function of 'nurturing the intellectual faculties' (a task shared with non-Christian schools) and the induction of children into the religious heritage bequeathed to them has withstood the test of time. At the core of its belief is its subscription to the centrality of community, the binding together of children, parents and guardians, Church and school to constitute a culture for growth 'animated by a spirit of liberty and charity' based upon the gospel. This concept of community 'orients the whole of human culture to the message of salvation' in such a way that 'the knowledge which the pupils acquire of the world of life and of men is illumined by faith'.[4] Children educated in such a *métier* have an opportunity of becoming 'a saving leaven' within the wider societal community and of bringing to bear upon the world the full richness of the faith.

It is in the process just described that the missionary arm of the Church becomes most evident in the corrective contribution it makes to the competitiveness and consumerism of the market place economy. As the Sacred Congregation for Catholic Education put it in 1977: 'it is precisely in the Gospel of Christ, taking root in the minds and lives of the faithful, that the Catholic school finds its definition as it comes to terms with the cultural conditions of the times' (Flannery, op. cit., p. 608). That such a view is in fundamental continuity with those of earlier years can be exemplified when it is compared, for instance, with Archbishop Richard Downey's speech, delivered at a meeting commemorating the centenary of Catholic Emancipation in 1929. 'The Catholic Faith', he declared 'is to the Catholic schools what the soul is to the body, the vital animating principle . . . Religion is not simply a subject to be imparted at stated hours: it is something to be lived out every moment, something to engage every faculty of soul and body, something which is inseparable from the well-being of the soul as the air we breathe is from the physical welfare of the body.'[5] Despite the years which have elapsed since these words were first uttered, the teaching that religious education in Catholic schools is not, and cannot be, confined to set periods of formal instruction, remains a central core of the Catholic philosophy of education and is ultimately associated with the concepts of 'wholeness', 'community' and 'sense of identity' which permeate the educational thinking of Vatican II, encapsulated in Bishop Patrick Kelly's recent statement: 'we . . . do not see the various elements which are part of a young person's formation as fragmented and unrelated' (Kelly, op. cit., pp. 5–6). What this means in practice has been spelled out by a Catholic headteacher: the Catholic school 'will function professionally in respect of all the educational disciplines, but the enterprise will be informed throughout by the values of the Christian ethic, and the centrality of Jesus Christ' (McCann, 1992, p. 112). Such a holistic nature of the Catholic educational ideal has been seen as embracing a concept of schooling exemplifying caring, community, reconciliation, forgiveness, prayer and witness, which is definitive of the kind of society as a whole that Christians should be seeking.

Pope John Paul II, in *Catechesi Tradendae*, issued early in his pontificate (1979), saw the special character of the Catholic school as perceived *only* in the integration of religious teaching with the general education of pupils. He reminded Catholic teachers that any distinction that may exist between religious instruction and catechesis does not change the fact that 'a school can and must play its specific rôle in the work of catechesis too' (Congregation for Catholic Education, 1988, para. 69). This internal ethos of the Catholic school merges with an external position that is open, welcoming and cooperative, helping to break down what Christopher Dawson once described as 'the closed, self centred world of secularist culture', with which it has to have a meaningful encounter (Dawson, 1967, p. 150). In so doing, Catholic education is capable of giving human society that new spiritual purpose 'which transcends the conflicting interests of individual class and race', because it is, as Edward Hulmes puts it, an invitation 'into a vision of the love of God' (Hulmes, op. cit., p. 102).

Notes

1   The point is expounded more fully in my chapter on *Education* in Hastings, A. (1991) *Modern Catholicism: Vatican II and After*, pp. 72 seq.

2 See *Epistolario Completo di Antonio Rosmini-Serbati, 1887–94*, 13 vols, Vol. X, p. 739.
3 See Bp. Patrick Kelly of Salford Diocese in *Catholic Schools*, a briefing for priests, especially those who are governors of schools, 9 December 1987, pp. 5–6. For further debate on this issue see McClelland, 1992a.
4 See *Gravissimum Educationis*, op. cit., pp. 732–3.
5 Printed in *Pulpit and Platform Addresses*, 1953, pp. 46–7.

References

ASHRAF, S.A. (1994) 'Responding to the Challenge of Secularism', in *Aspects of Education*, volume 51.
BRITISH COUNCIL OF CHURCHES (1981) *Understanding Christian Nurture*.
CONGREGATION FOR CATHOLIC EDUCATION (1988) *The Religious Dimension of Education in a Catholic School*.
CULHAM INSTITUTE (1991) *A Rôle for the Future: Anglican Primary Schools in the London Diocese*.
DAWSON, C. (1967) *The Crisis of Western Education*, London, Sheed and Ward.
FLANNERY, A. (1975) *Vatican Council II, 1*, Northport, NY, Costello Publishing Company.
HOLLEY, R. (1978) *Religious Education and Religious Understanding*, London, Routledge and Kegan Paul.
HOUGHTON, R. (1968) 'The Foundation of Religious Teaching', in JEBB, P. (Ed) Religious Education: Drift or Decision London, Darton, Longman and Todd.
HULMES, E. (1979) *Commitment and Neutrality in Religious Education*, London, Geoffrey Chapman.
HULMES, E. (1994) 'Society in Conflict: The Value of Education', in *Aspects of Education*, volume 51.
HUME, B. (1988) *Towards a Civilization of Love: Being Church in Today's World*, London, Hodder and Stoughton.
LANE, D.A. (1991) 'Catholic Education and the School: Some Theological Reflections', in CONFERENCE OF MAJOR SUPERIORS (IRELAND), *The Catholic School in Contemporary Society*, Dublin, Conference of Major Religious Superiors.
McCANN, J. (1992) *A Theological Critique of Christian Education*, Unpublished PhD thesis, Durham University.
McCLELLAND, V.A. (1988) 'Christian education and the denominational school', in McCLELLAND, V.A. (Ed) *Christian Education in a Pluralist Society*, London, Routledge.
McCLELLAND, V.A. (1992a) 'The concept of Catholic education', in *Aspects of Education*, **46**.
McCLELLAND, V.A. (1992b) 'A changing ethos in Irish education', in SWAN, D. (Ed) *The Moment of Truth in Irish Education*, Dublin Education Department U.C.D.
McGETTRICK, B. (1991) 'Why we need and why we must value Catholic schools in a state education system,' Paper read at the Association of Management of Catholic Secondary Schools' Fourth Annual Conference, Dublin 9–10 May.
NATIONAL COMMISSION ON EDUCATION (1993) *Learning to Succeed*, Report of the Paul Hamlyn Foundation.

Chapter 11

Recognition and Responsivity: Unlearning the Pedagogy of Estrangement for a Catholic Moral Education

James M. Day

In this chapter I argue that despite some accounts to the contrary, there exists a serious breach between public and private moralities in Catholic schools and in practices of Catholic moral education.[1] In so doing, I endeavour to give voice to some of the hundreds of teachers and students with whom I have worked as professor, counselling psychologist, and consultant in the field of moral education. Using their accounts as my points of departure, I consider some consequences of the breach to which they speak for their psychologies, and suggest that such consequences are dire not only for them but for the Catholic community. Finally, I propose that elements of the Catholic tradition both hinder, and may help to mend, the split between private and public moralities in Catholic education.

Catholic Moral Education and Tradition

Every effort at Catholic education, and Catholic moral education in particular, automatically involves the public morality of the Catholic Church, and its associated traditions of moral theology, philosophy, and training for virtue, and the private moralities of those persons who do the educating — students, teachers, administrators, and parents. Every person in the process brings to it his or her own efforts to work out the pressing moral questions of life: how to define good and practice it, how to distinguish right from wrong, what balance to strike between the needs of self and others given demands for both, what story to bring or fashion in a world of multiple narratives about what it means to be a moral person.

Within the tradition of the Church there is of course a rich supply of foundational and procedural argumentation as to what morality ought to be, how it is related to the nature of persons, and in what ways it might best be nurtured and cared for in individuals and groups. To name the thinkers that this tradition has produced and elaborated would be unforgivably tedious. My point here is simply to acknowledge that they are there in abundance, and that much may be learned from them. Despite the claims of Bryk, Lee, and Holland (1993) that most of today's Catholic schools are, since Vatican II, given to a democratic vision of who shapes what in moral education and beyond, my sense of things is that 'the tradition' is a phrase most students and teachers use to refer to something fixed, received, and little subject to the personal concerns of those involved.

Indeed they point to a kind of heaviness in the same tradition that has produced so much of what they readily acknowledge to be of value. In the Catholic tradition, they note, the divine authorization of institutional hierarchy adds to the weight, and what has been humanly constructed or divinely initiated is, by definition, sometimes hard to separate. As one teacher put it 'The longer something has been around, the more likely it is to be thought of as divinely issued and certified. The human complexities involved in its shaping, whether we're talking about theory or practice, get lost, to the detriment of all of us who are struggling to work out a Christian moral life today.' The oft-demonstrated and very real power of the Church to exclude from its midst those who appear to be in conflict with authority, adds to the conflict that the subjects of Catholic education sometimes feel. As another teacher observed 'I express my reservations privately, because it has been made clear to me that I am not to introduce questions or personal material into the curriculum, even if those are the things which reach my students, or come from the students themselves.' I have received an official letter saying that my closeness to students is appreciated, but that any effort to open Catholic morality to their questions will mean the end of my career. After I got the letter and asked for guidance from the director of my school, he sat down with me and said:

Look, it's very simple: The answers are here in the teachings of the Church, and in the book we ordered for you last year; they cover everything that is important. Go over those, make sure the students get the point, and test their knowledge at the end. A multiple choice test will do nicely for that. They'll either get the right answer or they won't. If they have problems on the test you can help them then. Show them where they are in error, send them back to the text or the syllabus, and tell them what they need to do to get it right. If they fail at that point, you've done your job, and the rest, quite frankly, is not really your business anyway.

A Pedagogy of Estrangement

On practical grounds, the public morality of the Church and those who represent it in schools is well defined. The public stance of the Church on what constitutes good and bad, right and wrong, justice and injustice, human dignity and responsibility, and the practice of virtue in matters of individual conduct, is, regardless of the enthusiasm with which it is met, a coherent and clearly articulated outline as to what the moral life involves. What is at issue here is whose tradition the teachings are thought to be, on what grounds they have been and may be shaped, and how appropriation is to be practised. The voices I encounter in the students and colleagues with whom I have worked in university, elementary, and secondary school settings say for the most part that this tradition is one to which they are outsiders. At their most alarming — and I take this crisis to be commonplace — these voices speak to the very personal cost of dissociation, a cost that has very real consequences for cherished notions I assume most of us to hold; respect, community, concern for those who are our neighbours. They are saying to us clearly that dispossession breeds disrespect, disavowal, and depreciation of self and other. There is for many a pronounced splitting between being a 'good Catholic' for public consumption while guarding a secret moral life for which there is no language or support. Catholic education for those most closed out of its content and processes, can be an experience of dislocation and fragmentation injurious to all the parties concerned. It is, as one bright student in a Catholic university called it 'an education for amnesia, in which what you do or feel is not admissable. You just give the right answers and around the people in authority try to act right and be polite. The rest you hope you can forget, or that you don't get into too much trouble. But if you unavoidably run into the truth of yourself, if you start to think for yourself, whatever they say about conscience and freedom, your Catholic days are really over.'

For too many of our students, Catholic education, and morality, are inscribed in a tradition perceived to be inaccessible to their experience, instructed through materials and methods and persons who make for a pedagogy of estrangement. Many of their teachers, like the ones I have quoted here, feel torn in what they cannot say or speak to, in the yearning of their students to participate and be heard. For them too the strains are major. Yet another teacher observed 'You just wince and hurt every day. Everything's officially fine and in order, but you can see the students' disrespect. What they need to say can't be considered, what they yearn to discover is not allowed, the issues they're already living are taught as though they happen, if at all, years from now. And we teachers go through the motions knowing we're making fools of ourselves.' Such observations are at odds with the holism and solidarity suggested by many Catholic writers and apologists for Catholic education, and they are ironic in the light of the efforts educators make to cast Catholic education in a particularly moral light.

Bryk, Lee, and Holland (1993) sound the theme that to Catholics and non-Catholics alike, educational institutions related to the Church are associated with a claim to the centrality of moral education for their mission, which is sometimes said to distinguish their orientations from those of competing schools. One sees this frequently in the literatures of attraction that such schools employ; a concerted effort is made to portray the Catholic school as a caring community devoted to the development of the whole person, and parents are told that they can fully expect their children to receive a training in virtuous thought and conduct that has all but disappeared from the curricula of state supported schools.

Recently a parent explained in some detail how it was that she selected a school for her child, and this language played a major role in her attraction to the school and her decision to enrol her daughter there. She said 'For me it was really important that Janet goes to a school that would teach values. I feel that's so important today, when it seems that kids are left to themselves so much of the time. They need guidance, don't you think? And the caring and concern for the whole child, for every person in the school, the idea the school's a community; that's why we decided to send her there.'

When I asked Janet what she thought of her school in light of the school's brochure and its language of this kind, she said, checking to see whether her mother was safely distant from the room,

> Well, it doesn't work that way at all in practice, but at least its consistent with the tradition.

She went on to describe a picture vastly different from what her mother's description entailed, and offered her own description of moral education in her school.

> They tell you all the problems you'll face, and what to do about them. They tell you why, which is because some guy who was Catholic said so, some Church father or big deal saint or some such, and you just learn to give the answers they did. But the kids laugh about it because, you know, get real! I guess most of them didn't have sex or anything because their answers are completely out in left field compared to what's going on now. Like so many girls I know are doing it, but they've learned to not tell anyone. You'd never have any idea that they would know about that in school. We would never talk to them about it, never, because, for one, they wouldn't believe it's true. And, for another thing, they'd already know it was completely wrong, and how can you talk to someone who you know already has your answer for you? They don't really care about us but about doing what they have to do. I know girls who have sex all the time, and with different guys, girls who like eat and then throw up in the school bathroom, a girl who like thought she was lesbian and tried to kill herself and stuff and nobody knows that on the staff. All these parents are kidding themselves if they think it's a moral school. Unless by moral you mean they just tell you what to think and then tell you what to do even if it has nothing to do with who you really are.

At 14, Janet is at once matter-of-fact and distraught over the situation in her school, and a discernible shakiness enters her voice as she speaks of the 'real-life' behaviour of her peers. One gets the impression that they are very much indeed young people in need of guidance, but that their understanding of what such aid would mean runs counter to what they find in the school.

The moral curriculum there is a formality which functions to remind students and those who would teach them, of the gap that exists between their communities of concern.

In its most extreme form, the public–private split, and the inadmissability of experience which characterize so many schools and their efforts at moral education, results in sufferings as difficult to hear as they are to speak. In a world where to speak about the real is to be disqualified, where to question is to be forbidden, and where the need to be known is denied and thus demeaned, emergencies of the worst kind become routine. The following sample of such a condition speaks both to the system of separation to which I point, and describes the multiple and corrupting dissociations that are possible in the moral realm when such distinctions order the day.

A Case of Estrangement: Lisa

Lisa was an honours student at the Catholic university where for some time I worked in the counselling service. Active in student life organizations, the elected representative of her hall in the government of her student house, and, according to her, 'the perfect product of Catholic education', Lisa was articulate in describing a terribly painful personal situation that, on her account, was directly related to the Catholic education she, and the others who were party to her suffering, had received.

She had come to talk about an abortion she'd had. She told the receptionist that she had a pressing problem that she needed for someone to understand, and that her need for an appointment with a counselling professional was fairly desperate. She inquired about confidentiality, was obviously worried and distracted in her appeal, but began her counselling contact with the following description of her difficulties. 'I've done something wrong, but it's happened and it's over. I need to move on but I don't know how. I don't know whom to tell but I have to tell someone. I don't know what to say but I feel I need to talk. I guess there are lots of people with problems, probably more important than mine, but I hope you have the time for me.' She thought a lot about killing herself, and she had stopped eating and going to class. She had fights with her room-mate and others of her friends, and she had been reported to the campus police for disturbing the peace at an off-campus party.

In the beginning of our counselling relationship Lisa moved markedly between two kinds of stories and descriptions, two ways of talking to herself, two sets of parties when she was addressing me. On the one hand were expressions of anguish, and intimate pain. On the other were commentaries aimed at the Church and at those whom she had known in it. I was at once counsellor to her emotional life and a stand-in for authorities she had otherwise learned to distrust. In making her assessments, she was testing who I could be, and trying to find a place for both herself and me in my role as a representative of the Catholic world. The following excerpts from transcripts of our meetings, provide some sense of the way she moved between these voices, and show how she tried to connect the two.

Lisa repeated several times that she was the perfect product of Catholic education. Asked what she meant by this testimonial, she said

> I have learned how to have a life that is perfectly split, on the one hand made for public view and for the appearance of virtue and being sociable, on the other hand angry, frightened, and horribly alone. I have learned along the way that reason and faith are good, that feelings don't count, and that the latter are a danger to the first. When I've tried to think about what to do, what I should do, I've only heard this chatter of voices, confused, detached from myself and my feelings, because I don't have a real voice of my own, no one who's me that I can turn to in trying to figure out what should come next. It's weird, you'd think that natural, to have a way to talk to yourself, but I've just learned to not be a person, in the sense of this, you know what I mean? I mean, when I've needed, needed someone in myself to turn to, I've had no way, I mean no words, no real possibility of finding that. Maybe that's really what I'm here for, to find a self who can help me morally. [She continued . . .] I'm the good girl, the one of whom my teachers and parents have always been proud. But this is only because they know neither me, nor themselves, nor the truth about how we relate to one another. As far as I'm concerned, the whole Catholic world is a conspiracy of silence, punctuated by occasional bouts of warmth that don't really go anywhere.

Lisa went on to describe her moral challenge as that of learning to care for herself, and for the process of staying close to, and documenting, her own moral experience, a process which she said she had never been given the tools for in her Catholic education.

The main ingredients of Lisa's story were these. Her father had sexually abused Lisa from the time she was 11 to her eighteenth birthday. She had begged him to stop but he didn't do so. Her efforts to speak with her mother were in vain, as her mother disbelieved her and insisted she was lying. She had told a priest in high school and again at university, and in both cases was told to pray and to try to forgive her father's 'mistakes'. 'Focus on yourself' one of the priests had said 'What is it in your own sinfulness that draws your father to you and which makes him do these things?' The same priest later made a pass at her in the course of a spiritual retreat. They were in a darkened hallway after the last prayers of the day had been said. He had tried to kiss her, had grasped at her breasts, had suggested they have sex. Her father was a member of the parish council and of a prominent organization of Catholic businessmen. Her parents were involved in Catholic 'Marriage Encounter' where they were highly esteemed by the other members, and as a child Lisa had constantly been told what a perfect and admirable family she came from. One of her brothers, meanwhile, had tried to kill himself. And she had a sexually promiscuous sister, at another school, who was in constant trouble with their parents. The father was a major contributor to the university, of which he was a graduate. Her mother was active in church activities, did volunteer work for a Catholic organization, and occasionally drank too much at parties. Lisa became pregnant at the university when, during a party, she got drunk, stayed up talking in the room of a male friend, and was forced to have intercourse with him and one of his friends. When she learned of the pregnancy, it wasn't clear who was the father. She had been told by her father that if she ever told about him or got pregnant before marriage he would kill her. She told a priest who told her to have the baby, and focused on her fault in in getting drunk and staying up late 'when you surely would have known how boys sometimes behave'. It was after that she had an abortion, downtown, on a weekday afternoon. She scheduled it to follow her moral theology class.

On Lisa's view the situation was decidedly Catholic. There was the truth that consisted in what was supposed to be; a kind of seamless continuity of virtuous thought and action, well regulated, documented, and transmitted, and a whole undercurrent of reality about human life, a reality of emotions and desire, of the body and the need to be known, that didn't fit. Her experiences of abuse, pregnancy and abortion, 'were not about me — I mean, these things couldn't happen in the Catholic world I knew. Here I was the good Catholic girl in the perfect Catholic family, and these things were happening to me?'. They were what assured her aloneness and lack of 'person within' which she spoke of as her 'real self' or 'voice'. Her experience led her to wonder whether the whole manufacture of Catholic morality, sustained in the training that the Church had given her, wasn't in some way flawed, and it was only then, when she decided to connect what she called her 'miseducation' and the suffering that resulted from the 'split' within her, that she showed any signs of improvement with regard to her suicidality and functional difficulties at school. She was insistent on this point, that there had been no place in her Catholic world in which to be real, known, understood as an embodied, feeling, trustworthy informant of her own experience, moral or otherwise, and she hypothesized that there was a split of similar kind in her father, mother, and priests, that was a function of their Catholic experience.

Lisa also invoked Catholic standards and values to describe the insufficiencies of her experience within the Catholic world. Her father, mother, teachers and priests had failed in large part because of the differences between what they had done and what they had espoused, and she called upon Biblical stories to describe what a more acceptable moral experience would be like.

> I kept looking within the Church for someone who would listen instead of tell, who would care instead of instruct, who would let me say my own story. I kept thinking of Jesus with the woman at the well, about how even if you were bad you needed, you were someone maybe worth listening to, and how everyone I met in the Church knew that

story. Yet there was no one who could know me or see me for the person that I was, no one who could look beyond the appearances, no one who wanted to know the truth.

There are some, I suppose, who would like to think of Lisa's story as exceptional, who would like to evade the point she has made by looking to some individual defect on the part of herself or of her father, or of a priest, or who perhaps don't see the problem she is speaking to. Perhaps there are some who do not understand how this could have happened, at all, for whom the platitudes she describes are self-sufficient and in their seamlessness not vulnerable to the details of her account. Such tales, however, were legion in the university where I worked, and rife in other Catholic universities where psychologists I know worked in the counselling services. What typifies these narratives, across their diversity, is their repetition of three related themes. The first has to do with a loss of voice, the lack of sense of personal authority for charting the moral landscape; the second consists in disillusionment with the Catholic world and a systematic effort to describe and come to terms with the public–private split experienced as part of growing up in it; the third factor involves an effort to find something positive, even redemptive, in the Catholic tradition and its moral values. Often, as in Lisa's case, this is located in a Biblical story of Jesus' encounters with persons who were morally marginal, stories which contain an image of reception and acceptance which comes to serve as a point of reference for judging the speaker's experience of life in Church communities. Lisa's account is representative, then, as a tale of personal dissociation implicated in a world of contradictions between the taught and the lived, the ordained and the perceived, between the permitted and the known. Finally, it speaks, with its reference to Jesus' encounter with the woman at the well, to her location within her tradition of some point of reference; to a kind of barometer of moral conduct which says how she ought to be, how she might deserve to be treated, and how those with power ought to manage it. To focus on the particulars of Lisa's case, and to miss the systematics of it, is to reproduce our failure, and her suffering, and to learn nothing.

Unlearning the Pedagogy of Estrangement

Up to this point I have suggested that the public–private split in Catholic moral education has a corollary for many in the lived experience of Catholic moral life; there is a personal experience of dissociation which accompanies the disenfranchisement that occurs in many of our schools. Teachers and students alike speak of the pain that results from their efforts to live with, or to resist, the pedagogy of estrangement in which they find themselves.

I don't claim that such estrangement is unique to Catholic institutions, and I know students and teachers who have found something better in Catholic schools. It seems to me pertinent, however, both to document the voices of the kind presented here, and to engage fellow educationists in a discussion of how the particulars of a lamentable predicament operate within the Catholic world. This, inevitably, suggests broader discussion of moral psychology and education, and of what Catholic resources there might be for improving our understanding and effort in educational research and practice.

It is generally agreed by psychologists of moral behaviour that generosity and responsiveness develop only when a sense of security, recognition, and ongoing care are present to the moral agent in question. When and if these elements remain constant features of the moral atmosphere, people can be invited to participate in the formulation of the rules and regulations in the groups where they live and work, and they are likely to comply and to support the maintenance and sensitive adjustment of these rules if they are given role-definition by those authorities who are charged with leadership of the group. Those authorities must act consistently with what they espouse, and there must be opportunities for members of the group to call those authorities to account. Persons must be given opportunities to make their moral experience known, to discuss and shape the contexts in which rules and roles are developed and played out, and must be invited to participate in the maintenance and adjudication of consequences when the rules they have made are violated. The qualities upon which these skills depend — the ability to take the role of another, to make rules that take the rights and responsibilities of all parties into account, to make decisions fairly, and with care, are dependent upon a foundation of secure and reliable attachment, recognition and reception. Strategies for empirically assessing 'moral atmosphere' in light of such conditions, and for training teachers and administrators in the development of adequate pedagogies and communication skills, are available and might be employed by diocesan authorities and other officials to critically examine the processes at work in the schools for which they are responsible.

Some researchers have observed significant differences between girls and boys, women and men, in the way such development occurs or is jeopardized in social processes. There is ample evidence to suggest that experiences of dispossession, loss of voice, a tendency to depression and a loss of self-esteem, are particularly characteristic of girls becoming women at adolescence. Girls are at risk in western post-industrial societies of a dangerous compromise that injures their development of self-awareness and their capacity to build relationships of respect for themselves as well as others, because it impairs their capacity to track their own needs while reading and responding to the needs of others (Brown and Gilligan, 1992; Demitrack, Putnam, Brewerton, Brandt, and Gold, 1990; Elder and Caspi, 1990; Hetherington, 1981; Peterson, 1988; Peterson and Ebata, 1987; Rutter, 1986; Simmons and Blyth, 1987; Werner and Smith, 1982). In Lisa's account the variables of gender, power, and identity are intertwined with themes of loss of voice and Catholicity. It would seem imperative that Catholic schools which purport to concern themselves with issues of justice and care would more explicitly engage in educational efforts designed to empower girls, to disrupt sexist cultural messages (in the media, in textbooks, etc.) and subject their own practices to critical examination. How do girls and women in Catholic institutions fare in terms of self-esteem, depression, and the like, relative to their peers in the broader culture where they are clearly at risk? The possibilities for research in this area are numerous.

Meanwhile, there is abundant evidence that educational environments in which students have opportunities to be heard, known, and received in the fullness of their moral experience may lead to different outcomes. In order for this to happen, there must be a trustworthy teacher who is prepared to enter into a dialogical relationship with his/her students, who listens as well as tells, who receives and consecrates as well as directs and admonishes, who is prepared to hear and hallow the reality of the person before offering advice. There must be ongoing opportunities for students to name, describe, and assess their own experiences; to authorize what it is they know, to be trusted as knowledgeable informants as to what the moral life involves, and to make clear what it means for their life to be moral in the fullness of its lived context, about which they must be assumed to be most expert (Brown and Gilligan, 1992; Day, in press 1994a, 1994b, 1994c, 1993a, 1993b, 1991a, b; Day and Tappan, 1994a, 1994b; Tappan, 1991; Tappan and Brown, 1989). The challenge here would be to find within the Catholic tradition those elements of theological, philosophical, and theoretical support for an enterprise of education in which attentive discourse, genuine dialogue, and the authorization of its students and faculty is present. Without these ingredients, the real moral experience of many Catholic students will be missed, the damage will continue, and debates over the formalities of moral-educational curricula will be beside the point.

Without ongoing opportunity for students to make themselves heard, for their stories to be known, for their real-life conflicts and contexts to be explicated and reviewed, all the nostalgics of 'character education' (Ryan, 1986; Vitz, 1990) individual provocation of 'values clarification' (Hall, 1973), and the rationalist bantering of constructivist efforts to promote the development of moral reasoning (Jennings, Kilkenny and Kohlberg, 1983; Selman, 1976) will sound and in effect be empty. The moral audience of one, who gives credence to the lived and the known, who enters into dialogue and the narrative of the other, who grants authority to what the other speaks through her attention to what is said; this is a starting point in the renewal of Catholic moral education. The Catholic context, beyond that, is deeply in need of co-conspirators in a responsive reading of the text our students bring to us; one already richly alive with moral thought, adventure, and intrigue, already ripe for intervention, but only after we have discovered it to be there. Where such a will is lacking, where such individuals and responsive communities cannot be found, the breach is reproduced. Where it is present the words of tradition may be heard and spoken anew, for they will be seen as part of a common quest that belongs to the parties involved. If the voices I have tried to let speak in this chapter are correct — and as you can see, I believe them — there has to be responsivity if there is to be responsibility. One's own story including its sub-plots of moral characters, quests and conflicts, has to be received before one can be provoked to renarratize one's self or the world. Our faith that we love because we have first been loved mirrors the psychological evidence to this effect and the data from educational research give us practical tools with which to practise what we preach. It remains to us to translate faith into action, and to make lively the love that we have for both the students and others with whom we work. Together, I think, we can unlearn our miseducation, and overcome the split that otherwise renders us both pained and ineffectual.

Note

1 Conversations cited in this chapter occurred in the course of my work as a counselling psychologist and as a psychologist of moral development in Catholic primary, secondary, and higher education environments, in Belgium, England, Germany, Scotland, and the USA. Some of the details of what the subjects in question said have been deleted to ensure confidentiality.

References

Brown, L. and Gilligan, C. (1992) *Meeting at the Crossroads: Women's Psychology and Girls' Development*, Cambridge, MA, Harvard University Press.

Bryk, A.S., Lee, V.E. and Holland, P.B. (1993) *Catholic Schools and the Common Good*, Cambridge, MA, Harvard University Press.

Day, J. (in press) 'Exemplary sierrans: Stories of the moral,' in Mosher, R., Connor, O., Day, J., Kaliel, K. and Whiteley, J. *Character in Young Adulthood*, Columbia, SC, University of South Carolina Press.

Day, J. (1991a) 'The moral audience: On the narrative mediation of moral "judgment" and moral "action",' in Tappan, M. and Packer, M. (Eds) *Narrative and Storytelling: Implications for Understanding Moral Development: New Directions for Child Development*, **54**.

Day, J. (1991b) 'Role-taking revisited: Narrative and cognitive-developmental interpretations of moral growth,' *Journal of Moral Education*, **20**, 3. pp. 305–15.

Day, J. (1993a) 'Moral development and small group processes: Learning from research,' *The Journal for Specialists in Group Work*, June.

Day, J. (1993b) 'Speaking of belief: Language, performative, and narrative in the psychology of religion,' *The International Journal for the Psychology of Religion*, **3**, 4, pp. 213–31.

Day, J. (1994a) 'The primacy of relationship: A meditation on education, faith, and the dialogical self,' *Occasional Papers in Education*, **2**, pp. 1–20.

Day, J. (1994b) 'Moral education, moral development, and the moral self,' Paper presented at the 1994 Congress of the Association of Catholic Institutions of Educational Sciences (To appear, in French, in *Pédagogie*, and, in Italian, in *Pedagogia et Vita*).

Day, J. (1994c) 'Moral development, belief, and unbelief: Young adult accounts of religion in processes of moral decision-making,' in Hutsebaut, D. and Corveleyn, J. (Eds) *Belief and Unbelief: Psychological Perspectives*, Amsterdam, Rodopi, pp. 155–75.

Day, J. and Tappan, M. (1994b) 'The narrative approach to moral development: From the epistemic subject to dialogical selves,' Under review at *Human Development* (forthcoming).

DAY, J. and TAPPAN, M. (1994a) 'Identity, voice, and the psycho/dialogical: Perspectives from moral psychology,' *American Psychologist*, **50**, 1, pp. 47–8.

DEMITRACK, M., PUTNAM, F., BREWERTON, T., BRANDT, H. and GOLD, P. (1990) 'Relation of clinical variables to dissociative phenomena in eating disorders,' *The American Journal of Psychiatry*, 1479, pp. 1184–8.

ELDER, G. and CASPI, A. (1990) 'Studying lives in a changing society: Sociological and personological explorations,' in RABIN, A., ZUCKER, R., EMMONS, R. and FRANK, S. (Eds) *Studying Persons and Lives*, New York, Springer.

HALL, B. (1973) *Values Clarification*, New York, MacMillan.

HETHERINGTON, E. (1981) 'Children of divorce,' in HENDERSON, R. (Ed) *Parent–Child Interaction*, New York, Academic Press.

JENNINGS, W., KILKENNY, R. and KOHLBERG, L. (1983) 'Moral development theory for youthful and adult offenders,' in LAUFER, W. and DAY, J. (Eds) *Personality Theory, Moral Development, and Criminal Behavior*, Lexington, MA, DC Heath-Lexington Books.

PETERSON, A. (1988) 'Adolescent development,' *Annual Review of Psychology*, **39**, pp. 583–607.

PETERSON, A. and EBATA, A. (1987) 'Developmental transitions and adolescent problem behavior: Implications for prevention and intervention,' in HURRELMAN, K. (Ed) *Social Prevention and Intervention*, New York, Aldine De Gruyter.

RYAN, K. (1986) 'The new moral education,' *Phi Delta Kappan*, **68**, pp. 228–33.

RUTTER, M. (1986) 'The developmental psychopathology of depression: Issues and perspectives,' in RUTTER, M., IZZARD, C. and READ, P. (Eds) *Depression in Young People: Developmental and Clinical Perspectives*, New York, Guilford Press.

SELMAN, R. (1976) 'Social-cognitive understanding: A guide to educational and clinical practice,' in LICKONA, T. (Ed) *Moral Development and Behavior: Theory, Research, and Social Issues*, New York, Holt, Rinehart and Winston.

SIMMONS, R. and BLYTH, D. (1987) *Moving into Adolescence: The Impact of Pubertal Change and School Context*, New York, Aldine De Gruyter.

TAPPAN, M. (1991) 'Narrative, authorship, and the development of moral authority,' in TAPPAN, M. and PACKER, M. (Eds) *Narrative and Storytelling: Implications for Understanding Moral Development, New Directions for Child Development*, **54**.

TAPPAN, M. and BROWN, L. (1989) 'Stories told and lessons learned: Toward a narrative approach to moral development and moral education,' *Harvard Educational Review*, **59**, pp. 182–204.

VITZ, P. (1990) 'The use of stories in moral development: New psychological reasons for an old educational method,' *American Psychologist*, **45**, pp. 709–20.

WERNER, E. and SMITH, R. (1982) *Vulnerable but Invincible: A Study of Resilient Children*, New York, McGraw Hill.

WHITELEY, J. and YAKOTA, N. (1988) *Character Development in the Freshman Year and Over Four Years of Undergraduate Study*, Columbia, SC, Center for the Study of the Freshman Year, University of South Carolina Press.

Part 3

Social Justice, Diversity and the Catholic School

Chapter 12

No Margin, No Mission

Joseph O'Keefe S.J.

In the United States today, schools for the poor present a powerful challenge to the Catholic community. In the midst of a culture in which margin determines mission, it is important to identify new opportunities and reasons for hope. The first opportunity involves increasing skepticism about the ethos of individual autonomy in favour of a new belief in the common good. Everywhere in the US — in religion, education, and even in Clintonian political rhetoric — people discuss the yearning for community, what Amatai Etzioni calls 'the search for a new *Gemeinschaft*' (Etzioni, 1993, p. 167). Given its tradition of solidarity and the preferential option for the poor, along with its potential to operationalize its profoundly multi-cultural membership, the Catholic Church can raise the debate to new levels. The Church can also benefit from this new interest as it seeks to define its institutional initiatives as a post-immigrant church in a post-modern society. Second, members of the academic community, especially Catholic universities, can engage in further critical inquiry about inner-city Catholic schools. Moreover, in contrast to the current practice of minimizing the impact of school closings, educational and ecclesiastical leaders should make available to the public dimensions of the crisis and be resolute in demanding an appropriate response from the Catholic community. Third, in the face of declining low-income schools, Catholic institutions that enjoy fiscal stability must redouble efforts to create welcoming communities for low-income students of colour. Though there have been some initiatives to understand the culture of Catholic schools (Lesko, 1988; O'Keefe, 1991), much more needs to be done. Finally, Catholics must explore together the complex and controversial ecclesiological issues of identity and diversity. Unless the Catholic community discovers anew the model of 'church as servant' (Dulles, 1987), Preston Williams' prediction about the demise of Catholic schools will come true. He wrote:

> The silence of the Church in the face of the conservative undercutting of the option for the poor leads many to believe that the Church itself is politically conservative or racist and lacking in a commitment to its moral formal teaching on racial equality and its option for obligation in a just society. In the minds of many the Church is seen as willing

to ignore or to expend very little energy upon the poor in order to embrace a conservative social program that includes other aspects of its special interest. (Williams, 1990, p. 318)

Facing the Future: Threats and Opportunities

If the contemporary rationale for Catholic schools is grounded in the values of the affluent, ethnically assimilated, suburban, secularized and generally content Catholic majority, the data on school closings are not problematic. On the other hand, if the rationale is the one I outline below — a clear and compelling vocation to provide for the needs of the poor and to foster appreciation of the human family in its rich diversity — the closing of even one school in an inner-city area is intolerable. While the financial threat to schools for the poor is well established, new opportunities must be explored.

The need is great for 'broad experimentation in the administration and financing of Catholic schools instead of studies that end up always in the closing of more schools' (Greeley, 1992). New efforts to finance urban schools (Cardinal's Big Shoulders in Chicago, Inner City Scholarship Committee in Boston, the Student-sponsor Program in New York, to name a few) must be redoubled. Educational leaders must experiment with cost-effective ways of staffing schools: the Alliance for Catholic Education at Notre Dame, the Inner-City Teaching Corps in Chicago, the Teacher Service Corps of the Archdiocese of Washington provide interesting new models. Given the enhanced role of the people of God in the post-Vatican II Church and the decline of clergy in numbers and credibility, Catholic education should be reconfigured as a ministry of the laity; new models of leadership are necessary.

The 1990s will see the continued assimilation of large segments of the Catholic population into mainstream American life and values, the ethos of individualism and secularism that typifies post-modern culture (Bellah *et al.*, 1985, 1991; Galbraith, 1992). Moreover, findings of a recent study of young Catholics in the United States do not bode well for the future: In 1963, 71 per cent of the Catholics surveyed attended church weekly or more often, but only 55 per cent did so in 1972, or a loss of sixteen percentage points. Since then, attendance has dropped again by about as much: from 55 per cent to 40.5 per cent in 1990. Much more ominous is the fact that church attendance among the young is dropping much faster (Hegy, 1993). The problems that afflict the Catholic church generally seriously impair efforts to revitalize schools for the poor.

The most immediate ramification of declining church membership is a decrease in philanthropic success. A recent national survey indicates a drop in charitable giving in Catholic households. In an address to the National Catholic Stewardship Council, Lilly Foundation's Fred Hofheinz reported that the reserve funds of the New York archdiocese were virtually exhausted and claimed that Detroit, Chicago, St Louis, Philadelphia and many smaller dioceses are in similar straits (Hofheinz, 1992). In fact, while giving increased among religiously affiliated people generally, it has decreased among Catholics during the 1990s both in the percentage of those who contribute and the amount of their contribution. Many factors contribute to the decline of Catholic philanthropy. First, scandals in organizations like the United Way, a nationwide consortium of charities, have made people skeptical of non-profit bureaucracies and, as a result, there has been an increase in restricted giving. Can centralized diocesan fund-raising efforts succeed in this environment? Second, in the wake of revelations of sexual abuse, of church cover-ups, clerics are not seen as credible stewards of funds. Greeley reports: Most of the decline in financial contributions can be explained by lay anger, particularly on matters of sexuality, authority and the treatment of women in the Church. Moreover, the correlation between anger and contributions disappears completely whenever the laity rate the performance of their pastor as excellent (Greeley, 1992). Finally, the decrease in spending power among middle-class Americans cannot be overlooked in this discussion (Newman, 1988, 1993; Phillips, 1990, 1993). Tuition payments at Catholic schools are beyond the range of many; free-will contributions are impossible. Catholic schools for the poor are threatened most significantly by the reluctance of white middle-class suburban Catholics to see themselves in communion with poor, urban minorities. Henry Cisneros, Secretary of Housing and Urban Development, posited that the refusal of taxpayers without children to fund public schools at adequate levels is intensified when those children are black, brown, foreign and poor (in Cose, 1992). As middle-class Americans become inured to the plight of urban citizens (DeMott, 1990), financial pragmatism and market efficiency cloud religious conviction. Even with Republican control of the legislative branch of the federal government, it is unlikely that Catholic schools will receive significant government funding because constitutional and fiscal barriers would cause lawmakers to spend too much political capital on a minor plank of their 'Contract with America'. It seems that 'No margin, no mission' could well become the motto of the 1990s.

Pressing Need and Proven Effectiveness

The demographic profile of the United States is changing dramatically. In every state of the union the percentage of non-Hispanic Whites continues to decrease (Population Reference Bureau, 1992). Immigration rates in the 1980s came close to the levels known at the beginning of the century (Portes and Rambaut, 1990; Cose, 1992). Despite this change in minority status for people of colour, disparities in educational attainment, health, mortality and income increase (National Council of la Raza, 1991; Jencks and Peterson, 1991; Orfield and Ashkinaze, 1991; Massey and Denton, 1993) and geographic segregation continues — 86 per cent of minorities live in urban areas (O'Hare, 1992, p. 23). Twenty-five years ago the Kerner Commission warned that unless drastic steps were taken the United States would become 'two nations, separate and unequal; one black, one white; one rich, one poor; one urban, one suburban'. Andrew

Joseph O'Keefe

Hacker (1992) posits that the prophecy of the late 1960s has been realized. Statistics that reveal vast disparities in income, housing options, health care and educational opportunities have shattered our image of a large and growing middle class where volition determines opportunity (Phillips, 1990, 1993). Marian Wright Edelmen and many others paint a bleak picture of this bifurcated society in which the young, especially those in the cities, suffer most (Children's Defense Fund, 1991; Hewlett, 1991). Since 1980 poverty rates have increased significantly for children under 6, while remaining more or less stable for other people (National Center for Children in Poverty, 1992). Today, one-fourth of America's children live in poverty, 100,000 of them are homeless; inadequate housing and health care for so many places us low on the list of industrialized nations. And in the future, a growing percentage of those in poverty will be children of colour. In a recent demographic analysis one reads, 'By the year 2000, one in three children will be from a minority population, compared with about one in four today. Child poverty rates, however, are two to three times higher for minority children than for non-Hispanic Whites' (Ahlburg and DeVita, 1992). The authors of a recently published review of the literature on students at risk surmise:

> Economic and demographic trends give a new urgency to education reform efforts, yet the personal and social costs of school failure have been apparent for decades. Huge disparities between the educated 'haves' and the poorly skilled 'have nots' intensify social divisions and contribute to urban decay and violence . . . Most poorly educated young people do not become lifelong criminals or career criminals. Too many of them labor long hours at dead-end jobs for wages that fail to raise their families out of poverty; they enroll in store-front vocational 'colleges' that immerse them in debt and fail to prepare them for promised career opportunities; they struggle to read the employment application or the letter from their child's teacher that demands more literacy skills than they possess; they die at early ages from illnesses and diseases related to poverty. (Montgomery and Rossi, 1994, p. iii)

Most schools contribute to these inequalities. In his characteristically homiletic style, Jonathan Kozol vividly illustrates the ongoing segregation of the wealthy and the poor in US schools (Kozol, 1991). Numerous court cases across the country challenge the inequitable funding of public education. And while compensatory education schemes of the past suffer from a '. . . consistent paucity of well-designed evaluations', several strategic areas for reform emerge: academic success, relevance, positive relationships within the school and supportive conditions beyond the school (Montgomery and Rossi, 1994, p. 86, p. 111). Because of a strong emphasis on academic achievement without tracking, high levels of student engagement and teacher commitment, decentralized governance based on the principle of subsidiarity, explicit moral norms based on the principle of personalism, and recognition of the power of symbol as an integrative force Catholic schools tend to fulfil the reform mandate (Bryk *et al.*, 1993).

In a recent review of research about Catholic schools (Convey, 1992, pp. 16–22), the author acknowledges that the most significant Catholic-school studies in this past decade were done by James Coleman and his associates (Coleman, Hoffer and Kilgore, 1981; Coleman, Hoffer and Kilgore, 1982; Coleman and Hoffer, 1987). Based on statistical data from the High School and Beyond Study [HS&B] they found that Catholic schools were more effective than other schools in fostering the academic achievement of students with less well-educated parents, Blacks and Hispanics. Coleman conjectured that students do well in school cultures where they feel a sense of belonging, cohesiveness and connection, what he calls 'social capital'. In response, Greeley (1982) and Hoffer, Greeley and Coleman (1985) used HS&B data to corroborate findings about the effectiveness of Catholic schools with minorities while other studies refuted Coleman's claims (Elford, 1981; Erickson, 1981; Keith and Page, 1985). Bryk, Lee and Holland (1993) used findings from two other databases, the National Assessment of Educational Progress [NAEP] and the National Educational Longitudinal Study [NELS], to confirm and extend HS&B.

Though large-scale quantitative studies are encouraging for Catholic school leaders, statistical analyses tell only part of the story. Aaron Pallas, commenting on Coleman's findings, wrote that while there is strong evidence that Catholic schools have more desirable climates than public schools, 'these data do not tell us why this is so' (1988, p. 551). Bryk, Lee and Holland (1993) complemented their statistical analyses with qualitative field studies at seven sites. Other particularistic studies corroborate statistical findings (Schneider, 1989; Hunt and Gendler, 1991). Anecdotal evidence affords further insight. For example, a recent review of stories in the secular press since 1990 reveals a popular belief that inner-city Catholic schools fare better than their public counterparts in destitute communities. Clearly, many important questions about the effectiveness of inner-city schools remain unanswered. However, an antecedent question looms: How many inner-city Catholic schools have closed in the face of enormous fiscal limitations?

Urban Schools for the Poor: Requiescant in Pace?

Patterns of Closings in the 1990s

Andrew Greeley wrote that while the Church has insisted vigorously on its obligation to the poor '. . . at the same time it has phased out as quickly as it could much of the most effective service it has ever done for the inner-city poor in Catholic schools' (Greeley, 1990, pp. 2–5). Though many would disagree with Greeley's assertion of bad faith, many concur that Catholic schools for the poor are disappearing rapidly. Some data expose a gulf between the espoused vocation of Catholic schools and their lived reality. For example, though there are some effective schools with a large number of students from low-income families, Catholic high schools tend to have middle-class constituents; few students come from families with an annual income below $15,000 or above $50,000 (Bryk *et al.*, 1984). And though Catholic schools have made concrete efforts to have a large representation of low-income people of colour in the student body, these students are highly represented in parochial or diocesan schools that are in the greatest, financial peril (Vitullo-Martin, 1981; Bryk *et al.*, 1993; Cibulka, 1988). Do Catholic schools for the poor face extinction in the United States? Using variables of race, wealth and educational attainment, I take a panoramic and then a telescopic look at the neighbourhoods in which schools are closing.

Several methodological issues warrant attention. First, given the unavailability of detailed data on the socio-economic status of students, I chose to look at the demographics of the neighbourhood ('zip code') in which the school is located cognizant that students in Catholic schools may come from distant communities. Moreover, there exists often within an urban zip-code area bipolar distribution of wealth and educational attainment, as well as discrete racial communities. This study does not account for those differences. In addition, the very presence of vibrant institutions in disadvantaged areas has a salutary effect (Etzioni, 1993). Second, because of the way 1990 census statistics are tabulated in the *Sourcebook of Zip-code Demographics* I was not able to break down the percentage of Hispanics in the ethnicity variable. Using racial categories, the US census provides information for each zip code on the percentage of the population that is white, black, Asian or Native American. For the sake of simplicity, I report the percentage of the population identifying itself as white. A subsequent study will focus on the closure of Catholic schools in Hispanic neighbourhoods. Third, data collected by the National Catholic Educational Association and Market Data Retrieval, Inc. do not distinguish closings from mergers in a consistent manner. Since 'merger' can be a euphemism for 'closure' it is likely that my sample underestimates the extent of the problem. Mergers are not a solution to the financial crisis because social capital, the element that makes Catholic education so successful, grows out of familial relationships that thrive in smaller, non-bureaucratic, community-based schools (Bryk and Driscoll, 1988; Greeley, 1992).

A Panoramic Perspective

Between September 1990 and June 1994, 435 Catholic schools closed in the United States. In the first three tables, I show general patterns of closing by year and geography. Table 12.1 indicates that no trend emerges in year-by-year

Table 12.1: Number of Catholic-school closings by year

Year	1990–1991	1991–1992	1992–1993	1993–1994
# of closings	123	81	154	77

Table 12.2: Number of Catholic-school closings by region

US Geographical Region	# of closings	% of total US
New England (MA, RJ, NH, ME, CT)	55	12.6%
Mideast (NJ, NY, PA, DC, MD)	168	38.6%
Great Lakes (IL, IN, MI, OH, WI)	95	21.8%
Great Plains (IA, KS, MN, MO, NE, ND, SD)	30	7.0%
Southeast (AL, AR, FL, GA, KY, LA, MS, NC, SC, TN, VA, WV)	55	12.6%
West/Far West (AK, AZ, CA, CO, HI, IO, MT, NV, NV, NM, OK, OR, TX, UT, WA, WY)	32	7.4%
Total US	435	100%

Table 12.3: Number of Catholic-school closings by state

Rank	State	# of closings
1	New York	92
2	Pennsylvania	47
3	Illinois	38
4	New Jersey	23
5	Connecticut	21
6	Wisconsin	20
7	Massachusetts	18
8	Minnesota	17
8	Ohio	17
9	Louisiana	15

analysis. Many commentators suggest that the decrease in the number of closings last year marks the beginning of a trend. To date, there are no data to confirm such a hope. Parenthetically, while the number of schools has continued to decrease, the number of students in Catholic schools has increased in the recent past, from 2,550,863 in 1992 to 2,567,630 in 1993 to 2,576,845 in 1994. Much of the increase in numbers is due to a 400 per cent increase in preschool enrolment over the last decade. While the 435 schools closed in all regions of the country, Table 12.2 shows that most of them closed in the northeast. Table 12.3 shows that, in reflection of more general trends of decreasing population, higher median age and a large Catholic population, 308 out of the 435 schools closed in ten states. Table 12.4 shows the national average for the three variables: 75.2 per cent of the population graduated from high school; 13.1 per cent of households live below the poverty line; and 80.3 per cent of the nation's people describe themselves as white.

In Table 12.5, by measures of educational attainment, social class and race, I analyse the social composition of the neighbourhoods in which school

Table 12.4: National percentages by zip-code area for high school graduates, households living below the poverty line; and race

	% High School Graduates	% of Households Below Poverty	'% White
National Average	75.2%	13.1%	80.3%

Table 12.5: Description of zip-code areas in which Catholic schools closed during the 1990s (by educational attainment, socio-economic status and race)

% Intervals	Number of School Closings Where '% of Population in School Community who Graduated from High School' Falls in Given % Interval	Number of School Closings Where '% of Households in School Community Living Below the Poverty Line' Falls in Given % Interval	Number of School Closings Where '% of Population in School Community who are White' Falls in Given % Interval
0 to 10%	2	172	17
10 to 20%	0	140	19
20 to 30%	1	60	28
30 to 40%	7	42	28
40 to 50%	20	14	29
50 to 60%	61	4	16
60 to 70%	97	0	20
70 to 80%	128	1	31
80 to 90%	97	1	50
90 to 100%	22	1	197

closings have taken place. Operationally, I use census data to explore three variables pertaining to each of the neighbourhoods, determined by zip-code area: first, the percentage of the population that graduated from high school; second, the percentage of households that live below the poverty line; third, the percentage of the population who are white.

Zip-code areas in which Catholic schools closed between 1990 and 1994 tend to reflect national averages for educational attainment and percentage of households below the poverty line. With respect to the percentage of high-school graduates, 383 of the school closings took place in areas where this percentage was between 50 and 90 (national average is 75.2); 225 of the school closings took place where the percentage of high-school graduates was between 60 and 80. Regarding the percentage of households in a given zip-code area below the poverty line, 414 schools closed in areas where this percentage is less that 40; 312 in communities where this percentage is less than 20; and 172 in areas where the percentage is less than 10 (national average is 13.1 per cent).

Zip-code areas in which Catholic schools closed tended to be significantly less white than the national average. While 80.3 per cent of the US population identify themselves as white, 188 schools closed in areas where the percentage of Whites is less than 80 per cent; 137 where the percentage is less than 60 per cent; and ninety-two in areas less then 40 per cent; and thirty-six in areas less than 20 per cent white.

While gross averages indicate that Catholic schools have closed in many white affluent areas, a significant number have closed precisely in those areas where educational needs are greatest. Slightly over sixty (15 per cent) of the schools that closed during the 1990s were in areas with large numbers of poor (over 30 per cent below the poverty line), non-Whites (over 70 per cent black, Asian or Native-American), and poorly educated (over 55 per cent without a high-school education). Approximately twenty schools (4.5 per cent) closed in areas with over 40 per cent below the poverty line, over 50 per cent without a high-school education and over 85 per cent non-White. If in fact 'no sacrifice can be so great, no price can be so high, no short-range goals can be so important as to warrant the lessening of our commitment to Catholic education in minority neighborhoods' (National Catholic Conference of Bishops, 1979, p. 11) these closings are unacceptable.

A Telescopic Perspective

Broad acontextual statistics are best complemented by particularistic inquiry. Therefore I offer a telescopic glance at four major archdioceses: Boston, New York, Philadelphia and Chicago.

Boston

Between 1985 and 1990 thirty schools closed in the archdiocese. In 1991 a planning committee announced that more schools would probably close or merge because of fiscal and enrolment crises. The committee also mandated that within a five-year period each school would operate with 70 per cent of its revenue from tuition, as opposed to the average 56 per cent. At the end of the school year 1992, five high schools and seven elementary schools closed. Ironically, two years earlier at a national meeting of the National Catholic Conference of Bishops Cardinal Law went on record opposing the tendency of some large urban dioceses to close Catholic schools that must be subsidized because of declining parish membership in neighbourhoods going through racial change. Following the meeting he stated that

> . . . bishops should think twice before closing schools even on what may seem reasonable fiscal grounds. Catholic education is important not only in terms of evangelization but also in terms of empowerment. Many of the black leaders of the civil rights movement in the south obtained part of their early education in Catholic institutions, whether or not they were Catholic. (Franklin, 1989)

Joseph O'Keefe

Financial constraints forced the Cardinal to make unfortunate choices. The school closings prompted public protest at the Cardinal's residence and there were numerous media accounts of the sad decision. The following front-page article is typical of the genre:

> Amid tears of sadness and anger at the Boston Archdiocese that their school is being closed, students and faculty members of St Gregory's High School in Dorchester spent the last day of school yesterday saying goodbyes to each other and also, they said, to a tradition that will be lost forever. 'It's a very sad day,' said Sister Mary Jude, CSJ, principal of the girls' school. 'St Gregory's has always been very important to the children of the inner city, with a school population that is 80 to 85 per cent minority and virtually a League of Nations.' (Negri, 1992)

Two years later, the Salesians planned to close Dom Savio, a high school in a blue-collar neighbourhood. In response, parents formed an independent board of trustees to continue the school's operation. For the moment, the school is in existence. Given financial problems in the archdiocese and what many priests of the diocese describe as a 'lack of enthusiasm' on the part of pastors, it is likely that more schools like St Gregory's and Dom Savio will cease to exist. In the 1992–3 academic year, six schools closed in the archdiocese, all of them in neighbourhoods that are poorer, have lower educational attainment and more non-Whites than the national average. In 1993–4 two schools closed, one of which was in an ethnically diverse inner-city neighbourhood.

New York

In 1990 the archdiocese reduced by one-half ($20 million) its subsidy to 160 of the 243 schools. Schools scrambled to cut their meagre budgets and to seek volunteer staff (Goldman, 1990). Four years ago it was announced that forty-one schools were being considered for closure because of the lack of middle-class support for the system. A funding initiative to save the 140 schools in the city, the Partnership for Quality Education, raised only $23 million of the $100 million necessary to offset the archdiocese's $19 million operating deficit. The campaign focused on the effectiveness of Catholic schools: 87 per cent of the 51,428 students were members of minority groups and 25 per cent were non-Catholic; the system's dropout rate of 1 per cent stood in stark contrast to the public system's rate of 30 per cent; 80 per cent of the students went to college (Putka, 1991). Fifteen schools eventually closed (Goldman, 1991). In the 1992–3 academic year, seven schools closed, all of them in neighbourhoods with fewer high-school graduates than the average, smaller than average percentages of Whites [58.4 per cent, 56.2 per cent, 29.4 per cent, 26.4 per cent, 26.4 per cent, 25.6 per cent and 23.8 per cent — national average 80.3 per cent]. Six of the schools were in neighbourhoods with an above-average percentage of families below the poverty line (15 per cent, 15 per cent, 18 per cent, 31.9

per cent, 31.9 per cent, 51.2 per cent — national average 13.1 per cent). All of the schools were in areas with low educational attainment (three in the 60th percentile, two in the 50th and one in the 30th — national average 75.2 per cent). Last year it was announced that four schools would close. While only one is in a neighbourhood with an above average household poverty rate (14.8 per cent), all are in ethnicly diverse areas (71.9 per cent, 68.4 per cent, 32 per cent, 32 per cent).

Philadelphia

In 1992 a commission recommended that schools must close in significant numbers because the projected $10.4 million deficit for the 1992–3 school year unabated would soar to $86.4 million by the end of the century (Woodall, 1992). The archdiocese closed thirteen schools in neighbourhoods marred by racial minority status, extreme poverty and low educational attainment. In an editorial commentary, a leading columnist saw in the decision evidence that Catholicism is becoming a suburban religion in Philadelphia and that Catholic education may in the future be the province of the white middle class. He saw in the closings 'victory for anti-city folks', a breaking down of the archdiocese 'along racial lines' (DeLeon, 1992). The 1993–4 academic year showed a marked reversal. Only one school closed, and it was in a zip-code area where 99.3 per cent of the population is white and only 6.9 per cent of the households live below the poverty line.

Chicago

In Spring of 1992 archdiocesan officials announced that four suburban and two city schools would be closed because of antiquated facilities, shrinking enrolment and debt (Fogelman, 1992). In September, schools reopened for 147,000 students of whom 64 per cent are white, 17 per cent black, 16 per cent Hispanic, 4 per cent Asian and 16 per cent non-Catholic. In the city of Chicago itself, 49 per cent are black; 31 per cent Hispanic; 15 per cent white; 4 per cent Asian; 37 per cent non-Catholic (Hirsley, 1992). At the end of the year, more schools closed and the reaction was vociferous. The following is typical of the newspaper reports:

> About 20 demonstrators endured brutal cold Friday to picket the Arch-diocese of Chicago's downtown offices, protesting plans to close an elementary school in the Pilsen neighborhood. Accompanying them was Alderman Ambrosio Medran (25th) who represents the Near West Side Neighborhood. 'In the last eight years they've closed five schools there. Ours is one of the hardest-hit communities by the closing of Catholic schools, and 90 per cent of Hispanics are Catholic. It seems like the Catholic Church is abandoning the Hispanic community.' 'It's like a death in the family' said Salvador Esparza, 28, a Chicago police

officer. Esparza attended Providence as did six of his brothers and
sisters. Now his son, Salvador, is a third grader there. 'I want my son
to get a Catholic education,' Esparza said. 'I don't want to send him
to a public school, but now I may have no choice.' (James, 1992)

Mr Espaza probably does not have a choice; twenty-four more schools have
closed since 1992.

In the 1992–3 academic year, eighteen Chicago Catholic schools closed,
the majority in extremely poor ethnically diverse communities with low educational attainment. Five closed in a zip-code area where only 29.7 per cent
of the population is white, 43.4 per cent of the households live below the
poverty line and only 45.8 per cent of the population are high-school graduates;
three closed in an area where the percentages are respectively 17.8 per cent,
31.6 per cent and 37.5 per cent; three others 22 per cent, 17 per cent, 63.9 per
cent; one 28.4 per cent, 17 per cent and 63.9 per cent; and another 0.05 per
cent white, 43.3 per cent below the poverty line and 53.2 per cent high-school
graduates.

Such statistics should serve as a wake-up call to US Catholics. Increasingly, however, the dynamics of the market — competition among self-interested
consumers for scarce resources — dominates. The motto of an unnamed financial official of the archdiocese of Chicago illustrates the point. When asked to
comment on the closing of schools, he responded, 'No margin, no mission.
That's just the way the world is today' (Hirsley, 1992).

A Renewed Purpose for Catholic Schools

Historical Considerations

The Catholic sensibility is marked by a keen sense of history, a desire for
continuity and tradition, what sociologist of religion Robert Bellah calls 'a
community of memory' (Bellah *et al.*, 1985). The collective memory of the Catholic community in the United States can be a source of insight into the experience of marginalized peoples today. Intolerance of the Catholic minority in the
United States took many forms — from outright violence to subtle measures of
exclusion to forced assimilation. The public school, known in the nineteenth
century as the common school, was the primary instrument of assimilation.
With the exception of several bishops, most notably John Ireland of St Paul,
the hierarchy responded defensively to public educators' reform efforts. By the
time of the Third Council of Baltimore in 1884, Catholic parents were obliged
to educate their children under the auspices of the Church. Religious congregations of women and men, many of them founded explicitly to serve the poor,
opened schools which served as a wall, a strong fortress to defend this religious, social-class and multi-ethnic minority from a hostile majority. Catholic
schools provided more than safety from persecution and a grounding in the

traditions of their constituents however; they also offered a means of upward
mobility for an emerging Catholic meritocracy (Fass, 1989). As ties to European
homelands faded, inter-marriage among various ethnic groups, Catholic and
non-Catholic, increased. Moreover, almost all Catholics moved out of culturally
homogeneous urban neighbourhoods into religiously and ethnically diverse
suburbs. Anglo Protestant values and style provided a common cultural grounding in these new contexts (Alba, 1990; Waters, 1990). The movement out of
ethnic ghettos accompanied a movement up in social status (Greeley, 1990;
Neuhaus, 1987). For example, Gallup and Castelli (1987) report that by the mid-
1980s, only Episcopalians and Presbyterians outranked Catholics in the percentage of members in the $40,000 per year plus income bracket. Given the
relative size of the populations — Catholics make up 28 per cent of the population and Episcopalians and Presbyterians 2 per cent each — Catholic affluence
has had a greater impact.

Since the mid-1960s the Second Vatican Council has shaped the spiritual
momentum of American Catholics. For example, the Constitution of the Church
in the Modern World opened up a new rationale for the Church and its institutions; the entities that once protected and preserved a tradition now serve
the world. In the wake of Vatican II, Catholic bishops from around the world
met in order to 'scrutinize the signs of the times'. Out of their scrutiny came
the 'preferential option for the poor' (Vatican Council II, vol. 11, p. 695). In
the United States, the preferential option for the poor was matched by a growing commitment to combat racism in all its forms. With the collapse of the
fortress walls, Church leaders have been invited to discover a new vocation with
echoes of past experience, a renewal of the spirit of a Jean Baptiste de la Salle,
a Don Bosco or a Mother MacAuley. A community of immigrants, once poor
and marginal, who had tasted discrimination and prejudice and had become
wealthy and influential, are now able to provide educational opportunities for
low-income minorities in the United States. In its history of alienation and
exclusion, the American Catholic community has a singular opportunity to
respond to William McCready's claim that there is no model for post-immigrant
Catholic institutions. African-American Protestant theologian Preston Williams
has articulated this new vocation:

Roman Catholic schools, which have already demonstrated their ability to teach the high culture of the west and to educate the poor in that
culture, will have the challenge of educating African-Americans and
other people of color in their own cultures. The Church will have an
opportunity to demonstrate its global and not simply Western character. This will mean the retention of inner-city schools and evangelization
in the inner city and among people who are not white. White children
and adults need to be involved in these schools as learners as well as
teachers. In the schools they must come to know people and cultures
that are not their own and the manner in which these people and
cultures illuminate the Christian and democratic understandings of life.

My remarks entail the alteration of the curriculum and extra-curricular
activities of these schools in a manner that enables them to become the
vehicles for multicultural and multiracial learning. A school with such
a redefined curriculum and ethos would enable the Church to become
a greater embodier of the Christian Gospel. It would also serve as the
beacon light for demonstrating how African-Americans and white Americans might come together to form a more perfect union. (Williams,
1990, p. 21)

Theological Considerations

The historical rationale for maintaining Catholic schools for the poor is enhanced
by a contemporary articulation of the Church's teaching on social justice. In the
United States, the commitment to the poor is linked to Catholic teaching about
racism since ethnic minorities suffer the effects of poverty disproportionately,
both those who have historically endured caste status (Ogbu, 1992) as well as
recent immigrants.

A Preference for the Poor

There has been of late considerable debate over the notion of the preferential
option for the poor, especially if it implies a materialistic reading of the gospel
or resentment toward the wealthy (Byrne, 1993). Steven Pope claims that 'the
special priority given to the poor is not a priority of one class over another,
but a commitment that incorporates *all* of its members of the community and
its good' (1993, p. 270). In other words, social arrangements and institutional
choices emanate from and must enhance solidarity among diverse groups. In
the *Universal Catechism* one reads that 'Socio-economic problems can be solved
only with the help of all forms of solidarity: solidarity of the poor among themselves, between rich and poor, of workers among themselves, between employers and employees in a business, solidarity among nations and peoples'
(1994, #1941, p. 424). Solidarity is not simply a pragmatic response to social
crisis, however; it is an imperative that flows from the Catholic understanding
of the nature of God:

> Beyond human and natural bonds, already so close and strong, there is
> discerned in the light of faith a new model of the unity of the human
> race, which must ultimately inspire solidarity. This supreme model
> of unity, which is a reflection of the intimate life of God, one God in
> three Persons, is what we Christians mean by the word 'communion'.
> (John Paul II, 1987, 40, p. 75)

The implication for Catholic schools is obvious. If segments of the population
are marginalized, the Church is obliged to make extraordinary efforts to rectify

social fragmentation. The pastoral letter on the US economy set an important precedent. The bishops did not restrict their critique to the secular world; they challenged Catholic institutional leaders to be exemplary in labour relations, to guarantee that the poor had access to all services, and to insure that this Gospel-based critique become the *raison d'être* of any Catholic organization (National Catholic Conference of Bishops, 1986).

Affirming the New Creation: Combating Racism

In the United States, issues of class are inextricably linked to issues of race (Zweigenhaft and Domhoff, 1991). Though the US bishops' pastoral letter on racism *Brothers and Sisters to Us* is 17 years old, the analysis of subtle and covert racism that permeates capitalist culture, is more salient today than it was when it was written. The bishops wrote:

> Crude and blatant expressions of racist sentiment, though they occasionally exist, are today considered bad form. Yet racism itself persists in covert ways. Under the guise of other motives, it is manifest in the tendency to stereotype and marginalize whole segments of the population whose presence is perceived as a threat. It is manifest also in the indifference that replaces open hatred. The minority poor are seen as the dross of post-industrial society — without skills, without motivation, without incentive. They are expendable. Many times the new face of racism is the computer print-out, the graph of profits and losses, the pink slip, the nameless statistic. Today's racism flourishes in the triumph of private concern over public commitment and personal fulfillment over authentic compassion. It is Christ's face that is the composite of all persons, but in a most significant way of today's poor, today's marginal people, today's minorities.

The bishops found that scarcity of spending-power among the middle class further fragments society and

> . . . reveals an unresolved racism that permeates our society's structures and resides in the hearts of many among the majority. Because it is less blatant, this subtle form of racism is in some respects even more dangerous — harder to combat and easier to ignore. Major segments of the population are being pushed to the margins of society in our nation. As economic pressures tighten, those people who are often Black, Hispanic, Native American and Asian — and always poor — slip further into the unending cycle of poverty, deprivation, ignorance, disease and crime. Racial identity is for them an iron curtain barring the way to a decent life and livelihood. (National Catholic Conference of Bishops, 1979, p. 13)

Joseph O'Keefe

It is particularly nefarious that unjust economic conditions make racial identity an iron curtain instead of a reflection of God. In *The Church and Racism: Towards a More Fraternal Society*, the Vatican has articulated the moral consequences of the Church's teaching on race: respect for differences, fraternity, and solidarity built on the dignity of every human being (Pontifical Commission for Justice and Peace, 1988, p. 33). Here the Church eschews a model of assimilation to European cultural patterns and adopts a philosophy of cultural pluralism. Solidarity and communion do not demand uniformity, but a positive appreciation of the complementary diversity of peoples. Catholic institutions must enhance a 'well-understood pluralism' that can resolve 'the problem of closed racism' (Pontifical Commission for Justice and Peace, 1988, p. 45). In a similar vein, *Brothers and Sisters to Us* called for a new look at the past, one freed from the cultural lens that 'obscures the evil of the past and denies the burdens that history has placed on the shoulders of our Black, Hispanic, Native American and Asian brothers and sisters' (National Catholic Conference of Bishops, 1979, p. 5). The bishops saw clearly that racism is a fundamental sin, a primary pathology in human society, 'a radical evil dividing the human family and denying the new creation of a redeemed world. To struggle against it demands an equally radical transformation in our own minds and hearts as well as the structure of society' (p. 10). The bishops made explicit recommendations to their own flock. The pastoral letter calls for the conversion of Catholics from this social sin, recruitment of people of colour to ministry within the Church, social programmes for migrant workers and undocumented aliens, fair employment practices in Catholic institutions and responsible investment of the assets of those institutions, financial support of groups advancing the cause of racial minorities, and the continuation and expansion of Catholic schools in the inner cities and other disadvantaged areas because '. . . no sacrifice can be so great, no price can be so high, no short-range goals can be so important as to warrant the lessening of our commitment to Catholic education in minority neighborhoods' (p. 13).

In 1983, the bishops wrote another letter on racism, this time focused on Latinos. In *The Hispanic Presence: Challenge and Commitment* the bishops made an argument from history in its advocacy of positive steps to enhance the welfare of this rapidly growing ethnic minority:

Historically, the Church in the United States has been an 'immigrant Church' whose outstanding record of care for countless European immigrants remains unmatched. Today that same tradition must inspire in the Church's approach to recent Hispanic immigrants a similar authority, compassion and decisiveness. (National Catholic Conference of Bishops, 1983, p. 4)

Authority, compassion and decisiveness are realized most effectively in education. Once again, the bishops publicly committed the Catholic Church to combating racism, not only on a theoretical level, but through the commitment of limited resources. Likewise, the National Catholic Education Association called for redoubled efforts among Catholic educators in favour of Spanish-speaking peoples in the document *Integral Education: A Response to the Hispanic Presence* (1987).

In 1990, the National Catholic Educational Association published a book on the Asian presence in the United States. Research indicates that immigrant parents look to Catholic schools for education in faith, discipline, moral training, a counter-cultural value system, and security. In addition, they want their children to retain some native traditions and hope that the Church will assist them in accomplishing this goal. Like their African-American and Latino counterparts (Barnds, 1988) many Asians indicated that they would like to send their children to Catholic schools here but expensive tuitions are beyond their ability to pay (National Catholic Educational Association, 1990).

Welcoming the Stranger

As indicated above, there is an unequivocal historical precedent for serving immigrants in US Catholic schools. Recent theological articulation of the social mission of the Church gives a new rationale to this long-standing practice. Today it is incumbent upon affluent communities to have a preferential concern for those who flee political or economic conditions that threaten their lives and physical safety (Pontifical Council for the Pastoral Care of Migrants and Itinerant People, 1992, p. 10). What the Vatican teaches about refugees applies to other ethnic minorities and the poor, namely that '. . . solidarity helps to reverse the tendency to see the world solely from one's own point of view'. There are weighty implications for Catholic schools because '. . . indifference constitutes a sin of omission' (p. 15). In an era of referenda and legislation aimed against illegal and legal immigrants, the theological commitment to welcome the stranger makes new personal and institutional demands on US Catholics.

Conclusion

Inner-city Catholic schools serve some of the most underprivileged children in the United States. In keeping alive a legacy of educating those outside the ethnic and socio-economic mainstream, context and identity meet; the needs of the world coincide with the strengths of the organization. At the outset of the 1990s many schools closed precisely in those areas where they were needed most. The good news about fewer closings in 1994 is tempered by the decline in church attendance, a stumbling block for fundraisers. The future may be uncertain, but one truth remains: the strength of Catholic schools is in mission, not margin.

Joseph O'Keefe

References

AHLBURG, D. and DEVITA, C.J. (1992) 'New realities of the American family', *Population Bulletin*, **47**, 2, Washington, Population Reference Bureau.
ALBA, R. (1990) *Ethnic Identity: The Transformation of White America*, New Haven, Yale University Press.
BARNDS, M.L. (1988) 'Blacks in low income serving Catholic high schools: An overview of findings from the 1986 National Catholic Education Association study', in SLAUGHTER, D.T. and JOHNSON, D.J. (Eds) *Visible Now: Blacks in Private Schools*, New York, Greenwood Press.
BELLAH, R.N., MADSEN, R., SULLIVAN, W., SWIDLER, A. and TIPTON, S. (1985) *Habits of the Heart*, New York, Harper and Row.
BELLAH, R.N., MADSEN, R., SULLIVAN, W., SWIDLER, A. and TIPTON, S. (1991) *The Good Society*, New York, Knopf.
BRYK, A.S. and DRISCOLL, M.W. (1988) *The High School as Community: Contextual Influences and Consequences for Students and Teachers*, Madison, WI, National Center for Effective Secondary Schools, University of Wisconsin.
BRYK, A.S., HOLLAND, P.B., LEE, V.E. and CARRIEDO, R.A. (1984) *Effective Catholic High Schools: An Exploration*, Washington, National Catholic Educational Association.
BRYK, A.S., LEE, V.E. and HOLLAND, P.B. (1993) *Catholic Schools and the Common Good*, Cambridge, Harvard University Press.
BYRNE, P.H. (1993) '*Ressentiment* and the preferential option for the poor,' *Theological Studies*, **54**, 2, pp. 213–42.
CATECHISM OF THE CATHOLIC CHURCH (1994), London, Geoffrey Chapman.
CHILDREN'S DEFENSE FUND (1991) *The State of America's Children*, Washington, Children's Defense Fund.
CIBULKA, J.G. (1988) 'Catholic school closings: Efficiency, responsiveness and equality of access for Blacks', in SLAUGHTER, D.T. and JOHNSON, D.J. (Eds), *Visible Now: Blacks in Private Schools*, New York, Greenwood Press.
COLEMAN, J.S. (1989) 'Schools and communities,' *Chicago Studies*, **28**, 3, pp. 232–44.
COLEMAN, J.S. and HOFFER, T. (1987) *Public and Private High Schools: The Impact of Communities*, New York, Basic Books.
COLEMAN, J.S., HOFFER, T. and KILGORE, S. (1981) *Public and Private High Schools*, Washington, National Center for Educational Statistics.
COLEMAN, J.S., HOFFER, T. and KILGORE, S. (1982) *High School Achievement: Public, Catholic and Private Compared*, New York, Basic Books.
CONVEY, J. (1992) *Catholic Schools Make a Difference: Twenty-five Years of Research*, Washington, DC, National Catholic Educational Association.
COSE, E. (1992) *A Nation of Strangers: Prejudice, Politics and the Populating of America*, New York, Morrow.
DAVIS, W. and MCCALL, E. (1991) *The Emerging Crisis: Current and Projected Status of Children in the United States*, Portland, ME, University of Maine, Institute for the Study of At-Risk Children.
DAVIS, M. and WEINSTEIN, A. (1992) Racial divisions split youth. Lake Forest: Who's Who Among American High School Students.
DELEON, C. (1992) 'The scene in Philadelphia', *The Philadelphia Inquirer*, 11 November.
DEMOTT, B. (1990) *The Imperial Middle: Why Americans Can't Think Straight about Class*, New Haven, Yale University.
DORR, D. (1983) *Option for the Poor: One Hundred Years of Vatican Social Teaching*, Dublin, Gill and MacMillan.
DULLES, A. (1987) *Models of the Church* (Expanded edition), New York, Image.
ELFORD, G. (1981) 'Self-selection: First a flaw, then a finding', *Momentum*, **12**, 3, pp. 8–10.

ERIKSON, D.A. (1981) 'The Superior Climate of Private Schools', *Momentum*, **12**, 3, pp. 4–8.

ETZIONI, A. (1993) *Community in America*, New York, Crown.

FASS, P.S. (1989) *Outside In: Minorities and the Transformation of American Education*, New York, Oxford University Press.

FOGELMAN, J. (1992) 'School closings nothing new to some Catholics', *Chicago Tribune*, 24 January.

FRANKLIN, J. (1989) 'Cardinal law warns against school closings', *The Boston Globe*, 18 June.

GALBRAITH, J.K. (1992) *The Culture of Contentment*, Boston, Houghton-Mifflin.

GALLUP, G. and CASTELLI, J. (1987) *The American Catholic People*, New York, Doubleday.

GLENN, C.L. (1988) *The Myth of the Common School*, Amherst, MA, University of Massachusetts Press.

GOBER, P. (1993) 'Americans on the move', *Population Bulletin*, **47**, 2, Washington, Population Reference Bureau.

GOLDMAN, A. (1990) 'On a shoestring, a Catholic school braces for cuts', *New York Times*, 17 December.

GOLDMAN, A. (1991) 'Catholic schools worry as closings draw near', *New York Times*, 8 March.

GOLDMAN, A. (1992) 'Catholic schools in danger of closing', *New York Times*, 16 February.

GREELEY, A.M. (1982) *Catholic High Schools and Minority Students*, New Brunswick, New Jersey, Transaction Books.

GREELEY, A.M. (1990) *The Catholic Myth: The Behavior and Beliefs of American Catholics*, New York, Charles Scribner's Sons.

GREELEY, A.M. (1992) 'A modest proposal for the reform of Catholic schools', *America*, **166**, 10, pp. 234–8.

HACKER, A. (1992) *Two Nations: Black and White, Separate, Hostile, Unequal*, New York, Scribner's.

HEGY, P. (1993) 'The End of American Catholicism?: Another look,' *America*, **168**, 15, pp. 4–9.

HEWLETT, S.A. (1991) *When the Bough Breaks: The Cost of Neglecting Our Children*, New York, Basic Books.

HILL, P.T., FOSTER, G. and GENDLER, T. (1990) *High Schools with Character*, Santa Monica, The Rand Corporation.

HIRSLEY, M. (1992) 'Archdiocesan school rolls hold steady', *Chicago Tribune*, 28 August.

HODGKINSON, V. and WEITZMAN, M. (Eds) (1994) *Giving and Volunteering in the United States: Findings from a National Survey*, Washington, DC, Independent Sector.

HOFFER, T., GREELEY, A. and COLEMAN, J. (1985) 'Achievement growth in public and Catholic Schools', *Sociology of Education*, **58**, pp. 74–97.

HOFHEINZ, F. (1992) 'Catholic giving and the signs of the times', Address delivered to the National Catholic Stewardship Council, 26 October.

JAMES, F. (1992) 'Pilsen parents vie to keep school open,' *Chicago Tribune*, 28 January.

JENCKS, C. and PETERSON, P. (1991) *The Urban Underclass*, Washington, DC, The Brookings Institute.

JOHN PAUL II (1987) *On Social Concern (Solicitudo Rei Socialis)*, Boston, St Paul Books.

KEITH, T.Z. and PAGE, E.B. (1985) 'Do Catholic Schools Improve Minority Student Achievement?', *American Educational Research Journal*, **22**, 3, pp. 337–49.

KOZOL, J. (1991) *Savage Inequalities: Children in America's Schools*, New York, Crown.

LESKO, N. (1988) *Symbolizing Society: Stories, Rites and Structure in a Catholic High School*, New York, Falmer Press.

MASSEY, D.S. and DENTON, N.A. (1993) *American Apartheid: Segregation and the Making of the Underclass*, Cambridge, Harvard University Press.

McCready, W. (1989) 'Catholic schools and Catholic identity: Stretching the vital connection', *Chicago Studies*, **28**, 3, pp. 217–31.

Montgomery, A. and Rossi, R. (1994) *Educational Reforms for Students at Risk: A Review of the Current State of the Art*, Washington, DC, Office of Educational Research and Improvement, United States Department of Education.

Murnion, P. and Wenzel, A. (1990) *The Crisis of the Church in the Inner City*, New York, National Pastoral Life Center.

Murnion, P. (1992) 'A peaceful reflection on a modest proposal,' *America*, **166**, 6, pp. 528–9.

National Catholic Conference of Bishops (1979) *Brothers and Sisters to Us: US Bishops' Pastoral Letter on Racism in Our Day*, Washington, United States Catholic Conference.

National Catholic Conference of Bishops (1983) *The Hispanic Presence: Challenge and Commitment*, Washington, United States Catholic Conference.

National Catholic Conference of Bishops (1986) 'Economic justice for all: Catholic social teaching and the US economy', in *Origins*, **16**, 24, pp. 410–55.

National Catholic Conference of Bishops (1990) 'Here I am, send me: A conference response to the evangelization of African Americans and the National Black Catholic pastoral plan', Washington, DC, United States Catholic Conference.

National Catholic Educational Association (1985) *The Catholic High School: A National Portrait*, Washington, National Catholic Education Association.

National Catholic Educational Association (1986) *Catholic High Schools: Their Impact on Low-income Students*, Washington, National Catholic Education Association.

National Catholic Educational Association (1987) *Integral Education: A Response to the Hispanic Presence*, Washington, DC, National Catholic Education Association.

National Catholic Educational Association (1990) *A Catholic Response to the Asian Presence*, Washington, DC, National Catholic Education Association.

National Center for Children in Poverty (1992) *Five Million Children*, New York, Columbia University School of Public Health.

National Council of La Raza (1990) *Hispanic Education: A Statistical Portrait*, Washington, DC, National Council of La Raza.

Negri, G. (1992) 'Tears, regrets mark closing of St Gregory's High School,' *The Boston Globe*, 13 June.

Neuhaus, R.J. (1987) *The Catholic Moment: The Paradox of the Church in the Postmodern World*, San Francisco, Harper and Row.

Newman, K.S. (1988) *Falling from Grace: The Experience of Downward Mobility in the American Middle Class*, New York, Vintage.

Newman, K.S. (1993) *Declining Fortunes: The Withering of the American Dream*, New York, Basic Books.

Ogbu, J. (1992) 'Understanding cultural diversity and learning', *Educational Researcher*, **21**, 8, pp. 5–24, November.

O'Gorman, R.T. (1987) 'The Church that was a school: Catholic identity and Catholic education in the United States since 1790', A monograph on the history of Catholic education in the United States written for the Catholic Education Futures Project.

O'Hare, W.P. (1992) *America's Minorities: The Demographics of Diversity*, Washington, DC, Population Reference Bureau.

O'Keefe, J.M. (1991) 'Higher achievement scholars: A study of the experience of low-income minority students', Unpublished doctoral dissertation, Harvard University.

Orfield, G. and Ashkinaze, C. (1991) *The Closing Door: Conservative Policy and Black Opportunity*, Chicago, University of Chicago Press.

Phillips, K.P. (1990) *The Politics of Rich and Poor: Wealth and the American Electorate in the Reagan Aftermath*, New York, Random House.

Phillips, K.P. (1993) *Boiling Point: Republicans, Democrats, and the Decline of Middle Class Prosperity*, New York, Random House.

PONTIFICAL COMMISSION FOR JUSTICE and PEACE (1988) *The Church and Racism: Towards a More Fraternal Society*, Washington, DC, United States Catholic Conference.

PONTIFICAL COUNCIL FOR THE PASTORAL CARE OF MIGRANTS and ITINERANT PEOPLE (Corunum) (1992) *Refugees: A Challenge to Solidarity*, Vatican City, Libreria editrice Vaticana.

POPE, S.J. (1993) 'Proper and improper partiality and the preferential option for the poor', *Theological Studies*, **54**, 2, pp. 24–71.

POPULATION REFERENCE BUREAU (1992) *The Challenge of Change: What the 1990 Census Tells Us about Children*, Washington, Center for the Study of Social Policy.

PORTES, A. and RAMBAUT, R. (1990) *Immigrant America: A Portrait*, Berkeley, University of California Press.

PUTKA, G. (1991) 'New York archdiocese begins campaign to save schools', *Wall Street Journal*, 30 January.

QUALITY EDUCATION FOR MINORITIES PROJECT (1990) *Education That Works: An Action Plan for the Education of Minorities*, Cambridge, MA, Massachusetts Institute of Technology.

SCHNEIDER, B.L. (1989) 'Schooling for poor and minority children: An equity perspective', in BOYD, W.L. and CIBULKA, J.G. (Eds) *Private Schools and Public Policy: International Perspectives*, New York, Falmer Press.

SEBRING, P.A. and CAMBURN, E.M. (1992) *A Profile of Eighth Graders in Catholic Schools Based on the National Educational Longitudinal Study*, Washington, DC, National Catholic Educational Association.

TYACK, D.B. (1974) *The One Best System: A History of American Urban Education*, Cambridge, MA, Harvard University Press.

VATICAN COUNCIL 11 (1988) *The Conciliar and Post-Conciliar Documents* (2 vols.) in FLANNERY, A. (Ed) Northport, NY, Costello Publishing.

VITULLO-MARTIN, T. (1981) 'How federal policies discourage the racial and economic integration of private schools', in GAFNEY, E.M. (Ed) *Private Schools and the Public Good*, South Bend, Notre Dame Press.

WATERS, M.C. (1990) *Ethnic Options: Choosing Identities in America*, Berkeley, University of California Press.

WILLIAMS, P.N. (1990) 'A more perfect union: The silence of the Church,' *America*, **162**, 12, pp. 315–18.

WOODALL, M. (1992) 'Did the Archdiocese wait too long?', *The Philadelphia Inquirer*, 1 November.

ZWEIGENHEFT, R.L. and DOMHOFF, W.G. (1991) *Blacks in the White Establishment*, New Haven, Yale University Press.

Chapter 13

Equality, Race and Catholic Schools

Leela Ramdeen

'God help Britain! How can we build a nation when someone can win a local council election on a racist ticket!' This was the cry of distress uttered by a Catholic Asian woman living in the east end of London on hearing the news that the British National Party had won its first seat on a local council in the vicinity — of the Isle of Dogs — on 16 September 1993. Truly this result is a sad reflection of the sign of the times in the UK.[1]

As each political party denounced the result I wondered what action each would take to ensure that there would never be a repeat of this disgraceful situation. I wondered also how many of the 1,480 people who voted for the BNP were Catholics? We know from Fr Hynes, parish priest in the area, that 'some stalwart Catholic parishioners are also very racist'.

It is interesting to note that the leader of the Ku Klux Klan in the 1980s was a Catholic. Indeed, the night after Quaddus Ali was beaten brutally by a group of racist thugs in the east end of London in September 1993 and lay in hospital attached to a life-support machine, Channel 4 screened *Birth of a Nation*, a poisonous and inflammatory three-hour programme which glorifies the Ku Klux Klan. What irresponsible journalism, at a time when we are still reeling from the racist killings of Stephen Lawrence, Ruhallah Aramesh, Rolan Adams, Rohib Dugal, Ashiq Hussain and others and from the countless attacks on black people who are still seen as 'other' in this country.

The Current Context

There are approximately 15 million people from minority ethnic communities residing in the twelve member states of the European Union, out of a total of 325 million people. In the UK there are about 3 million out of a total of about 55 million. Although, unlike many other European countries, the UK has race legislation, it needs strengthening. Racial harassment is still not a criminal offence. Between 1992/3 the British Crime Survey indicated that there were over 140,000 racist attacks and fourteen racially motivated murders in the UK (Aye-Maugh and Mirlees-Black, 1993). Across Europe we are experiencing an unprecedented rise in racism. Marie Macey paints a disturbing picture of an upsurge in hostility towards migrants and black people in Europe (Macey, 1992). In Britain every aspect of black people's lives is affected by racism e.g., education, employment, the criminal justice system, immigration, housing, social services, the media. In the foreword of the Home Office document *The Response to Racial Attacks: Sustaining the Momentum* (1991), the second report of the Inter-Departmental Racial Attacks Group, the ex-Home Secretary, Kenneth Baker recognizes that 'challenge . . . to overcome what is unquestionably the most obnoxious and destructive aspect of the racial discrimination that still festers in our country' i.e., racial attacks and harassment. Police figures show that a racist attack occurs every twenty-eight minutes in Britain. This is the context in which we are considering issues concerning equality, race and Catholic schools.

Defining Racism

Racism is not only related to physical violence, it is 'a many sided phenomenon, made up of racial myths and ideologies, prejudice, discriminatory behaviour of various kinds and, in the extreme, racial violence. It is especially damaging when it permeates the institutions of society and becomes indistinguishable from the ordinary practices and policies of those institutions' (Catholic Association for Racial Justice, 1994).

Minority ethnic families have been trying for many years now to bring their agenda of concerns into the education system and still there seems to be a mismatch in perception about the rights, hopes, aspirations and potential of pupils from these communities. Part of the problem is an unwillingness to listen to what people from these communities are saying. For example, in November 1994 I contributed to a London-wide Conference on issues relating to young people in our society. This was a Catholic gathering which included many teachers from schools.

After sharing information, based on research and on my own case work with minority communities, it transpired that reports from one or two discussion groups sought to deny that the information that I had shared was true. These groups were denying the reality of the experience of young people from minority ethnic groups.

At the end of the day there was a liturgical session during which each person was allowed to pray for his/her own intentions. My heart sank as I heard someone behind me say: 'Let us pray for those who see themselves as victims and blame others for it.' I prayed in return: 'Let us pray for those who have eyes but will not see.' I left full of sadness knowing that unless people are prepared to listen and to develop their awareness of the harmful effects of racism, there will be little hope of eliminating it.

What kind of Christian values are we fostering in our Catholic schools and how are these schools playing their part in eliminating racism? The kind of resources — human and material — that we present to our children is important as they can either help to dismantle or perpetuate stereotypes. For example, the picture on the cover of a Bible used in many of our schools portraying Cain as a black man about to kill Abel, a white man, does not promote love of neighbour. Nowhere in the Bible do we read that Cain and Abel were of different colour from each other.

At a time when racial harassment is on the increase in schools and the Far Right is targeting vulnerable young people as part of a recruitment campaign and distributing racist leaflets at school gates, it is important that, in the formation of 'persons', Catholic schools ensure that their pupils do not grow up with a distorted view of their place in this world. Some time ago I invited one of the Caribbean bishops to address primary-aged pupils at a Catholic school assembly. He dressed in his full regalia for the visit. The pupils enjoyed his humorous contribution but he admitted that he left feeling saddened by the fact the he could not convince some of the white pupils that he was a bishop. They 'innocently' stated that he could not be a bishop because bishops are not black. The hidden curriculum is a very powerful influence on the formation of pupils. A member of church documents denounce racism as a sin that affects the entire community because it prevents us from recognizing our common humanity and from building a community of love. Racism divides God's family.

The Role of Catholic Schools

Catholic schools have a major role to play in promoting racial justice. In 1988 the bishops of the diocese of Westminster issued useful guiding principles entitled: *Equality of Race and Opportunity in Catholic Schools* for all Catholic schools in the diocese. These principles, based on the gospel, highlighted the fact that 'the gospel itself leaves us in no doubt, that our belief in its values should place us in the forefront of the movement for racial justice and harmony, not in the rear'.[2]

Much has been written about the distinctive nature of a Catholic school. *Gravissimum Educations* (1965) tells us that the role of a Catholic school is 'to develop within the school community an atmosphere animated by the spirit of liberty and charity and based on the Gospel so that the knowledge pupils acquire of the world, of life, and of men is illumined by faith' (Catholic Truth Society, 1965). As schools focus on the spiritual life, knowledge of the truths of the faith, the principles of Catholic morality, and the social teaching of the Church, uppermost in the minds of all should be the commitment to apply gospel principles to the teaching and learning process by addressing issues of racial injustice.

A Catholic school, as part of a local community, must help to build community. Recently, I was pleased to be able to work with others to assist the headteacher of a Catholic school in the east end of London. She was concerned about the racist attitudes being expressed by a significant number of pupils at the school in relation to the local Bangladeshi community. As we worked each day with a different year group, I could not help noticing the Easter friezes on the walls. The wording read: 'Down from the cross, out of the grave, and into our lives.' The sad thing was that Christ was not truly in the lives of some of these young people because they did not recognize Him in the neighbour.

Bullying, harassment and violence linked to the ethnic origin of individuals in schools and in the local community remains an area of concern in the UK. There are a number of national reports, for example, *Learning in Terror* which deal with this issue and are of use to educationalists in formulating effective plans to eliminate such behaviour (Commission for Racial Equality, 1988). Many Local Authorities, for example, Haringey, and schools have developed *Anti-racist Guidelines and Code of Practice for the Elimination of Racial Harassment* and they have put in place monitoring processes to support the implementation of the guidelines.

Successful Schools Criteria

It is necessary for Catholic schools to reflect on what needs to be done to make a good school — for *all* their pupils. While accepting that successful educational outcomes may be dependent upon a variety of factors, schools do matter. Many local authorities have developed 'successful schools criteria' which highlight a number of characteristics which in the context of the school are likely to contribute to successful learning. These relate to (for example) effective school management emphasizing shared values and mission, consultation, teamwork and participation, together with accountability and a concern for quality. Effective partnership with parents is also an essential component of an effective school.

The quality of pupils' learning is at the heart of effective management. It is important that we attend to the aims and ethos of the school, curriculum management and organization, curriculum 'delivery' and implementation. The introduction of headteacher and teacher appraisal in UK schools, linked to an effective staff development programme, should enhance the skills of educators and benefit pupils.

The Hidden Curriculum

Each school is required to develop and maintain a comprehensive policy statement and a school development plan which outlines how policy will be translated into practice and what monitoring procedures and performance indicators will be used to chart progress and to indicate areas for development. Whole school planning/policies must take into account aspects of the hidden curriculum such as attitudes, expectations, school and classroom organization and interaction, pastoral system, rewards and sanction, e.g., who benefits?

The existence of an effective homework policy is also important. A head-teacher in a Church school, was sharing her concern with me recently that some teachers in her school refuse to allow certain pupils to take books home because they will smell of curry when they are returned. This is a good example of the sort of attitudes which disadvantage pupils.

Displays around the school also need to be reviewed to ensure that they reflect cultural diversity. I recall going into a classroom in a Catholic school where the topic work display was on babies. Every picture on the wall was of a white baby while over 70 per cent of the pupils in the class were from minority ethnic communities. Recently I participated in an event at the Barbican, a major exhibition and conference centre in London. While I was there I observed that the Barbican had an exhibition on 'Families in Europe' to mark the UN International Year of the family. All the families displayed were white. I looked on as scores of school children filed past sapping up this eurocentric view of Europe. As I watched I recalled how as a teacher I had to work hard whenever I took pupils to visit art galleries to undermine the stereotypes that assailed their senses as they observed countless paintings depicting black people in subservient positions either as servants or, particularly in those paintings that portray Britain's colonial past, young black 'playthings' at the feet of the colonial masters and mistresses. These images do nothing to promote the dignity of the human individual (Greater London Council, 1986).

Schools should review their Assessment procedures including testing, work sampling, Records of Achievement, recording, reporting and marking to ensure that each pupil is treated fairly. Schemes of work that are developed should provide breadth, balance, relevance differentiation, coherence, continuity and progression as an entitlement for *each* pupil and in accordance with his/her educational needs.

The Commission for Racial Equality has produced some useful documents on issues such as ethnic monitoring in the careers service which highlight the fact that unless care is taken, discrimination could affect the career prospects of pupils from minority ethnic communities (Commission for Racial Equality, 1991). Many schools include work experience as part of the curriculum they offer and this is included in each pupil's Record of Achievement which employers are supposed to refer to when school leavers are seeking employment. The destination routes of all pupils should be analysed also by schools as an aid to reviewing action that may be needed in relation to the achievement of pupils from minority ethnic communities.

The Curriculum

In relation to the Curriculum itself, it is important that it refers to all the learning opportunities offered by a school i.e., both formal and informal programmes — the quality of relationships, the values that are promoted, extra curricular activities, teaching and learning styles, and the learning processes which seek to 'deliver' the aims and purposes of education. Schools must try to minimize the differences between the curriculum as planned, the curriculum as 'delivered' and the curriculum as received by pupils.

Access to the Curriculum is crucial if a pupil is to have any significant chance of educational success. Unfortunately, since across the UK there is evidence that a disproportionate number of black pupils, particularly black boys, are excluded from school, and in some cases they are not reinstated in a mainstream school or may remain out of school for long periods of time, their life chances are affected adversely.[3] This was an issue of particular concern to those who attended the first Congress of Black Catholics in London in 1990. (Catholic Association for Racial Justice, 1990). Schools should evaluate their rewards and sanctions policy to determine whether it is fair and just.

Clearly if a school is excluding large numbers of pupils it should review it behaviour policy and consider whether there are factors within the school itself that are contributing to unacceptable behaviour. There are many instances where whole school policies on behaviour remain simply papers which are not implemented. The issue of behaviour needs to be placed within a wider context encompassing school policy and organization, whole school policies on discipline, governor training and support, community involvement and clear decision-making frameworks. It is essential that schools include as part of their exclusion procedures, structures such as 'early warning systems' based on closer collaboration with parents to ensure that attempts are made to be fair to each pupil.

Resources

The content of the curriculum needs to reflect cultural diversity and the contribution made to human development by people from minority ethnic communities. This links closely to the kind of resources available to support pupils' learning. For example, while many schools still use certain books that perpetuate stereotypes about black people, they fail to counteract such stereotypes by purchasing books that celebrate the contributions that black people have made to human achievement. It is not necessary to dispose of all books that contain negative stereotypes about black people. Indeed, providing teachers are aware of the issues, they can use some of these books to highlight pupils' awareness of the nature and effects of racism and include such critical analysis as part of a wider programme to foster in pupils a love of neighbour. All God's children *are* of worth. I have seen some excellent lessons where teachers have used Shakespeare's *Othello* and the *Merchant of Venice* to critically analyse stereotypes about black people and Jews.

I recall how much concern was expressed by those concerned to promote cultural diversity when a list of 'Golden resources' was published in the *Times Educational Supplement* in an article written by a prominent primary school educator (18 March 1988). The list did not include one book written by or about people from minority ethnic groups. Since the 1988 Education Reform Act was being introduced at that time, it would have been an ideal opportunity to encourage schools to remember that when responsibility for their own budgets was transferred to them from the local authority, they should ensure that their purchasing policy for materials were based, *inter alia*, on a concern to promote cultural and linguistic diversity.

It is sad to note that the National Curriculum Council's approved reading list of books that pupils at each key stage of their primary and secondary school lives were expected to read included only four books written by black authors (*Times Educational Supplement*, 24 December 1992).

The Role of Governors

Governors have an important role to play in promoting quality/equality in their schools. There is a need for representation from minority ethnic communities on governing bodies and genuine involvement of individuals from these communities who become governors. The demands on governors are great and adequate governor training is essential if they are to carry out their duties effectively. Governors have a key role to play in analysing their school's exam results, including an ethnic breakdown of the results. They need to ask challenging questions aimed at promoting higher standards, particularly if large groups from minority ethnic groups are failing.

Governors also need to consider whether their admission policy is discriminatory in any way. Members of minority ethnic communities continue to express concern that certain Catholic schools, particularly some of those that are viewed by the community as 'prestige schools', deny children access by operating racist admission policies. Indeed this concern was expressed by black parents during research conducted by Cardinal Hume's Committee (Cardinal Hume Advisory Group, 1986).

It is important that the composition of teaching and support staff in schools should reflect cultural diversity. This is still not the reality in most schools, including Catholic schools. The situation remains one in which people from minority ethnic communities are more likely to be employed as 'dinner ladies', playground supervisors and the like but not as teachers or senior managers.

High Expectations

There is some evidence to show that where schools are doing well by all their students, pupils from minority backgrounds are more likely to succeed. I organized a party for my niece and her friends recently. They had all passed their school examinations (GCSE) with very high grades. This particular Catholic school set high standards and parents gave substantial financial and expert support thus enhancing the quality of the resources available. There are high expectations of pupils from minority ethnic groups. There is no ceiling put on their potential. The girls made the following comment: 'We're not treated like second class citizens . . . I transferred to that school because in my first year at my local secondary school I felt the teachers were not stretching me. They did not think I was bright. They thought I was cheeky when I kept asking for more homework and when I brought my mum to ask for homework for me I got told off after by my form tutor. At this school they make you work hard and if you have problems they tell you where you are going wrong.'

Teacher Intervention

Positive and appropriate teacher intervention is crucial to pupils' success, for example, in giving practical guidance in helping pupils to develop study skills and strategies for approaching problems. I recall working on the production of a videotape on classroom interaction when I was an inspector in the Inner London Education Authority. In this context, although the class teacher knew we were videoing a particular maths lesson, he was obviously so used to treating certain pupils differently that he took no steps to alter his practice.

The tape showed that during the course of the lesson, a black boy of Afro-Caribbean origin constantly puts his hand up, eager to answer questions. He is constantly ignored and other pupils, some of whom do not know the answers, are given opportunities to respond to the teacher's questions. As a result of being constantly ignored, it appears that the black pupil eventually becomes despondent, demotivated and begins to misbehave. Expectation creates roles for both teacher and pupils. Such treatment of students soon lets them know where they stand and it also influences peer group perception of black pupils, thus giving them a distorted view of their place in the world.

Catholic schools should help to empower young people by standing alongside them, developing their knowledge and skills so that they can do things for themselves. It has been said that the power of compassion is the power of making connections, letting God's love for us flow through to each other and responding accordingly — truly being as Cardinal Newman said: 'A link in a chain, a bond of connection between persons.'

Equality in the Sight of God

Catholic schools can make a difference by working in fidelity and witness to Jesus Christ and the educational mission of the Church. They can confirm the Christian message of equality of all in the sight of God. As Pope John Paul II said in his Apostolic letter to young people a few years ago: 'Responsibility for this present reality and for its shape and many different forms lies first of all with adults.' (John Paul II, 1985).

Each of us must play our part to transform this reality so that the educational needs of our young people from minority ethnic communities are met and the school community achieves the aim set out in a mission statement like that of St Thomas More Catholic School in North London: 'Since we are part of a multicultural society, all children should be educated towards an understanding of, and commitment to, that society, and every effort should be made to secure the elimination of racism.'

The equality of pupils from minority ethnic communities rests essentially on their dignity as persons and the rights that flow from it. Catholic schools should be guided by the following: 'Every form of social or cultural discrimination in fundamental personal rights on the grounds of sex, race, colour, social conditions, language or religion, must be curbed and eradicated as incompatible with God's design.' (Walsh and Davies, 1984).

The contemporary Catholic school must stand in solidarity with all God's children. Bishop Howard Tripp, in his introduction to *The Christian in Public Life* rightly speaks of 'the obligation upon everyone always to play their part in the life of the community in which they live so as to build a society that is just and good for everyone. A Christian has an obligation to do this' (Tripp, 1993). I end with the words of Maritin Luther King as a reminder of the task that is ours:

> The ultimate measure of a man is not where he stands in moments of comfort and convenience, but where he stands at times of challenge and controversy. The true neighbour will risk his position, his prestige, and even his life for the welfare of others. In dangerous valleys and hazardous pathways, he will lift some bruised and beaten brother to a higher and more noble life. (Ansbro, 1992)

Notes

1 Parts of this chapter appeared in *Priests and People*, January, 1994 Vol. 8 No. 1 as 'Who is my neighbour?' This material is reproduced here with permission of the editor.
2 Statement from the bishops of the Diocese of Westminster to all governing bodies and teachers in Catholic Schools of the Diocese: *Equality of Race and Opportunity in Catholic Schools*, 28 September, 1988, Diocesan Education Office, London.
3 See Office for Standards in Education (Ofsted) (1993) *Exclusions*, also *Education for Disaffected Pupils*.

References

ANSBRO, J. (1992) *Martin Luther King, Jr. The Making of a Mind*, New York, Orbis Books.
AYE-MAUGN, N. and MIRLEES-BLACK, C. (1993) *British Crime Survey*, **81**, Home Office, Research and Planning Unit.
CARDINAL HUME'S ADVISORY GROUP (1986) *With You in Spirit*, London, The Print Business Ltd.

CATHOLIC ASSOCIATION FOR RACIAL JUSTICE (1990) *Congress of Black Catholics Report*, London, St Vincent's Centre.

CATHOLIC ASSOCIATION FOR RACIAL JUSTICE (1994) *Racism in British Society, Including a Selective Review of Research 1980–93*, London, St Vincent's Centre.

COMMISSION FOR RACIAL EQUALITY (1988) *Learning in Terror: A Survey of Racial Harassment in Schools and Colleges in England, Scotland and Wales, 1985–1987*, London, CRE.

COMMISSION FOR RACIAL EQUALITY (1991) *Ethnic Monitoring and Careers Services: A Good Practice Guide*, London, CRE.

GREATER LONDON COUNCIL (1986) *A History of the Black Presence in London*, London, GLC, Public Relations Branch.

JOHN PAUL II (1985) *Apostolic Letter of Pope John Paul II to the Youth of the World on the Occasion of International Youth Year*, London, Catholic Media Office.

MACDONALD, I., VHAUNONI, R., KOHN, L. and JOHN, G. (1989) *Murder in the Playground: The Report of the Macdonald Enquiry into Racism and Racist Violence in Manchester Schools*, London, Longsight Press.

MACEY, M. (1992) 'Greater Europe: Integration or ethnic exclusion?', in CROUCH and MARQUAND (Eds) *Towards Greater Europe?: A Continent Without an Iron Curtain*, Political Quarterly Special Issue, Basil Blackwell.

TRIPP, H. (1993) *The Christian in Public Life, Four Catholics on Their Own Experiences*, London, Catholic Truth Society.

WALSH, M. and DAVIES, B. (Eds) (1984) *Proclaiming Justice and Peace: Documents from John XXIII to John Paul II*, London, Collins Liturgical Publications.

Chapter 14

Who Do We Serve and What Do We Offer?: Race, Equality and Catholic Schools

Richard Zipfel

As an expatriate American I have a particular interest in the international dimension of the issues of race, equality and Catholic schools. Before settling in Britain twenty years ago, I taught at St Ignatius High School, a Jesuit secondary school on the near south side of Chicago. I also had a passing contact with St Francis mission school on the Rosebud, Sioux reservation in South Dakota.

Since coming here, in 1972, I have had extensive contact with Catholic schools in Britain. Among other things, I was secretary to a working group of the Bishops Conference on 'Catholic education in a multiracial, multicultural society'. The working group visited fifty Catholic schools as well as the seminaries and colleges of Education and in 1984 published a report entitled *Learning from Diversity: A Challenge for Catholic Education* (Department of Christian Doctrine and Formation of the Catholic Bishops Conference of England and Wales, 1984).

In this chapter, I will draw anecdotally on my experiences both here and in the United States and reflect on two questions which I see as fundamental to Catholic education

- Who do we wish to serve?
- What do we have to offer?

Who Do We Wish to Serve?

In asking the question 'Who do we wish to serve?' we could advance a number of possible answers:

- We wish to serve the Catholic community.
- We wish to serve the whole community.
- We wish to serve especially the poor and marginalized.

The search for answers, of course, leads us into a very complicated discussion. Each of the answers has validity and they are not necessarily mutually exclusive. Moreover, the question of who we serve cannot be simply identified with who we admit to our schools. One could argue, for instance, that by educating Catholics to be responsible citizens we are serving the wider community and by educating them to be committed to social justice we are serving the poor and marginalized. Nonetheless, there is clearly a tension between the three answers and it is not easy to find Catholic schools which give similar priority to serving the Catholic community, the wider community and the poor and marginalized.

It was clear who St Ignatius High School was serving — it was serving the intellectually gifted Catholics on the south and west sides of Chicago; and the most fundamental thing they wanted from St Ignatius was a good education leading on to university and financial security. This is certainly what most of the parents wanted. Some of those parents were middle and upper middle class and wanted their sons to have a similar life. Others were first and second generation immigrant families from a variety of European countries. In some cases, they could not speak English and often enough both parents would work long hours in menial jobs to send their boy to a very good school.

The school was situated just at the edge of Chicago's black south side. Yet, out of 1,100 boys my recollection is that we had only about a dozen black students. This was certainly not from any desire on the part of the school to exclude them. It was from a combination of factors that were 'beyond our control'. The situation has probably changed considerably in the more than twenty years since I left.

There is certainly some evidence that in those twenty years Catholic schools in the United States are increasingly serving poor, minority communities, and they appear to be doing especially well in providing minority students with a good education.

The first thing to be said about the situation in Britain is that we have no comparable statistics or research. We do not know what percentage of students in Catholic schools are from ethnic minority backgrounds. Nor do we know how well these pupils are doing in our schools.

We can say with some confidence that there are poor and ethnic minority communities that have been well served by Catholic schools in Britain — most notably the Irish, but also Poles, Italians, and others from European backgrounds.

The black community here has not been so well served by Catholic schools. The black population of Britain is made up of people from the Caribbean, Africa and the Indian Subcontinent and from a variety of cultural backgrounds and religious traditions. The black Catholic communities here have their origins in the 'Catholic' islands of the Caribbean, in Goa and in various parts of Africa; and there is overwhelming anecdotal evidence as to the struggle black Catholics have had getting into Catholic schools.

In the mid-1970s the then Catholic Commission for Racial Justice published a pamphlet entitled 'Where Creed and Colour Matter'. In his introduction, Bishop Cleary stated

> The fierce debate about integration and bussing in America hasn't yet touched our English schools. Yet a milder form of segregation does exist here in Catholic schools, which contain only a small proportion of coloured [sic] children . . . Catholic schools are still making little contribution to the education of coloured immigrants . . . A great tradition of commitment and concern has been built up in the Catholic school system. The Commission hopes that this can now be extended to benefit especially the children of racial minorities. (Commission for Racial Justice, 1975)

The pattern which Bishop Cleary pointed to has begun to change. In some areas, schools which ten or fifteen years ago had only a small number of black children now have 30 per cent or 40 per cent black Catholic pupils. In other places, a few schools have taken in significant numbers of children from other faith traditions. Nonetheless, there are still Catholic schools which are perceived as white islands, usually in geographical areas where the black population is predominantly Asian and from other faith traditions.

In such areas, Catholic schools may be faced with the choice between remaining a white island in a multi-racial neighbourhood or accepting children of other faiths. There have been different reactions to this dilemma. Some dioceses have settled on a notional 15 per cent as the number of non-Catholic children that a school might absorb without losing its distinctive Catholic ethos. In a few places, for a variety of reasons, Catholic schools have opened their doors to larger numbers of Muslim, Sikh and Hindu children.

At the moment, however, if there is a trend it seems to be moving back towards the tradition of Catholic schools for Catholics. Some of the most interesting and successful experiments are under threat. A Catholic primary school in the North of England which had become 70 per cent Muslim has been handed over to the local authority. Catholic schools in the east of London have resisted pressure to take in Bangladeshi children whom the local authority could not cope with. A pioneering Sixth Form College in the Midlands has a very uncertain future (see the chapter by Vince Murray in this volume). In another diocese, authorities seem to be reconsidering an earlier trend towards admitting Muslims into some of their schools.

The reasons for such decisions are complex and the pattern across the country remains fluid. Anomalies and ironies proliferate. The prevailing fear in this country that significant numbers of children of other faiths might undermine the Catholic ethos of our schools contrasts starkly with the mission experience which many Asians have seen at first hand.

One prominent Asian Catholic, who has been involved with schools in east London for some years, found it hard to understand the reluctance of Catholic schools in the area to make special provision for Bangladeshi children. He himself had attended a Catholic school in India where most of the children were Muslim and where he as a Catholic was in the minority. Such situations are not uncommon.

I heard the story not long ago of a Christian brother in India working with a local community worker to set up a school for 'untouchables' who were Catholic but couldn't get in the Catholic school in the area which was full of middle-class Muslims. Against the background of such experiences in other countries, the practice here can be perceived as narrow, inconsistent and even racist.

The question 'Who do we wish to serve?', therefore, addresses a very important and unresolved tension that runs through the Catholic educational community internationally. It is closely linked to the second question 'What do we have to offer?'

What Do We Have to Offer?

The most obvious thing which we have to offer in Catholic schools on both sides of the Atlantic is 'good education' in the traditional even old fashioned sense of the term. Our schools tend to be well run and disciplined, offering sound academic education, within a caring community, underpinned with a coherent ideology. The result is an effective path from primary school, to secondary school, and on through further or higher education to a decent job and a secure life.

This is the core of what I and most parents of any social class or ethnic background want when we send our children to a Catholic school. And the Catholic community's ability to provide good education in this sense is an immense international achievement. It is particularly useful to the sons and daughters of minority families who attend our schools. For them it can be a step up from a state of inequality and marginalization. If I go on to raise a few questions about what we are offering in our schools, it is only after recognizing and valuing this achievement.

The inspiration for our schools and the education we offer is the Gospel and Christian faith, and to some extent the Gospel is in tension with the world around us. It evokes questions concerning the values on which that world is based and concerning our natural desire to succeed in that world.

Such questioning, which can ultimately lead to our own transformation and to the transformation of society, is a fundamental part of genuine education of any quality. But is it a central priority in Catholic schools? A friend of mine, who taught at St Francis mission school on the Rosebud Sioux reservation in South Dakota tells the following story of his experience. He had noticed that many of the Sioux children seemed to go through a personal crisis around the age of 11. He felt intuitively that it had something to do with their sense of identity as native Americans. Naturally, he asked himself what he could do as a teacher for these children and what the mission school was offering them. This reflection led to an educational experiment.

The following year, on the first day of school, he went in to his classroom and told the students to take out their 'American history' textbooks. He asked them to bring their books and follow him; and he led them out of the room, down the corridor and outside into the nearby school parking lot. Here he had them all gather around and place their history books in a pile on the tarmac. He then took a match and burned the books while the students watched.

Back in the classroom, my friend gave each child a pencil and a notebook. He asked them to go home and talk to their parents and grandparents, their aunts and uncles and the old people in the tribe about 'the old days'. Out of this grew a native American history project that seemed to bring the youngsters to life and unearthed a story of the Rosebud of which the children and my friend had been only vaguely aware.

The incident gives rise to further questions. If those American history textbooks were reinforcing a crisis of identity among children on the Rosebud, what were similar textbooks doing to white middle class Catholic children in other parts of the United States?

Coincidentally, a few years later, having crossed the Atlantic and settled in Britain I formed another friendship and heard a similar story. This British friend, who is now one of Her Majesty's Inspectors of Schools, was at the time a young Catholic teacher in a county school in Brixton which is a well-known, racially mixed area of south London.

As my friend tells the story, it was his first year teaching and he had been asked to teach a class in European social and economic history although this was not his specialism. He was therefore attempting to stay a few weeks ahead of the class. One day after class a black youngster came up to him and asked whether he saw any connection between the French Revolution and what was happening in the Caribbean at the time. He was dumbfounded; and admitted that he had not. The youngster then pulled from his bag a copy of CLR James's *The Black Jacobins* which relates the history of the 1791–1803 successful slave revolt in France's most profitable colony of San Domingo, ending in the establishment of the black state of Haiti. My friend borrowed the book from the young man; and reading it he was led through a process of self-questioning that radically changed his outlook. He asked himself, for instance, why England and France who were supposedly enemies were nonetheless cooperating in putting down a revolution in the Caribbean. More importantly, however, he asked himself why such questions were never raised in his own training. He began thinking about the history of black people in this country and with his students became involved in research which culminated some years later in his authorship of a history textbook for secondary schools *The History of Black Settlers in Britain 1555–1958* (File and Power, 1981).

The process of questioning that these two teachers went through took them outside the ethnocentric limitations of the knowledge which their schools were imparting to students. Though it is not common, it is possible for schools to build such questioning into the education they offer.

One school tried to do this with its geography syllabus. While attempting to impart all the traditional skills appropriate to geography study, the 'key ideas' which guided the choice and treatment of content focused on the contrast between the 'developed' and the 'underdeveloped' world.

The syllabus was designed to challenge the common stereotype that assumes 'Third World' countries are poor because the people living there are inferior. In place of this stereotype, such a syllabus encourages the students to explore the political, social and economic causes of 'underdevelopment' and to understand the relationship between Third World poverty and western affluence. Secondly, by examining the various meanings of the word 'development' and by coming to understand that common notions of development may not be in the interest of 'Third World' countries the students were enabled to move beyond a western, ethnocentric notion of development to a more complex and intellectually challenging concept.

Similarly, students of English literature could be helped to understand that it contains contrary threads. On the one hand it embodies the myth that enshrined and justified British culture, colonialism and empire. On the other hand, it sees through hypocrisies and self-deception, criticizes culture, and satirizes the self-justifying myth. Defoe's *Robinson Crusoe* can be seen as an adventure story which also embodied the self-justifying myth of English imperialism. Crusoe is the hero of white, Anglo-Saxon, Protestant mercantilism. However, there are other strands in our literature. Swift, for instance, could be devastating in his satirical critique. Kipling's popular novels generally embody the myth, although his last novel *Kim* is more ambivalent. The novels that are critical of the colonial enterprise from various points of view could be the subject of a study in themselves. They include Conrad's *Heart of Darkness* and *Nostromo* and some of the novels of Joyce Cary and Graham Greene and certainly Forster's *Passage to India*.

I hope it is clear that I am not advancing a crude theory of ethnocentric bias. There are now and have been in the past both people and ideas which break beyond the limits of a prevailing mentality. Such critical thoughtfulness ought to have a central place in our schools. Does it have such a central place? My doubt arises from my lifetime's experience of Catholic schools, but more specifically from ten years of work in race relations in this country, including considerable contact with schools. The evidence that exists would seem to support my doubt.

In 1979, in response to growing concern over the 'underachievement' of West Indian children in schools, the Government established a Committee of Inquiry into the Education of Children from Ethnic Minority Groups under the chairmanship initially of Mr Anthony Rampton and then of Lord Swann. That Committee worked for five years, and its 800 page report *Education for All* was published in 1985 (Lord Swann, 1985).

The report included a specially commissioned piece of research into 'all white' schools. The research found racism 'widespread' in these white schools.

ranging from unintentional racism and patronising and stereotyped ideas about ethnic minority groups combined with an appalling ignorance of their cultural backgrounds and life-styles and of the facts of race and immigration, to extremes of overt racial hatred and 'National Front' style attitudes. (ibid., p. 234)

Even among teachers in these schools the research found

the whole gamut of racial misunderstandings and folk mythology was revealed, racial stereotypes were common and attitudes ranged from the unveiled hostility of a few to the apathy of many and the condescension of others, to total acceptance and respect by a minority. (ibid., p. 236)

We may assume that most or all of the schools considered in this research were county schools. We might ask whether predominantly white Catholic schools are significantly different. Interestingly, at the same time that the Swann report was published another report, *Learning from Diversity*, was published. This was the result of two years' effort by a working party of the Catholic Bishops' Conference of England and Wales, including visits to fifty Catholic schools. The following is one of the key conclusions from that report:

Perhaps the issue which concerned us most was the overwhelming perception on the part of most headteachers and their staffs that multi-cultural education is only relevant to black children, and an almost universal lack of awareness of the need to educate white children from this perspective. This was demonstrated forcibly by the fact that, by and large, we discovered very little multicultural activity in schools with a small number of black children and by the frequent comment of the staff in such schools that 'we have no problem here'. (op. cit., p. 44)

Nineteen of the schools visited were predominantly white, secondary schools. Only one of these had a school policy dealing explicitly with multi-cultural education. Some said that the visit was the first time they had considered the matter. More than half said that it was not an issue that concerned them.

One headteacher said 'Multi-cultural education is not relevant to this area.' Another said 'We do nothing about it. The children don't know anyone who is not part of their own culture.' One head of religious education put it bluntly 'You attend to Blacks when you've got them.' The head of an English department said

We have been satisfied with Jane Austen and Thomas Hardy and for good measure we have Shakespeare which includes Othello. English must prevail and we have not added to anything that has served us well up to now.

By contrast, some teachers said they felt a multi-cultural approach was badly needed. As one put it 'I really try hard although I know much of what I teach is influenced by my own very English upbringing and training.' The answer of one ordinary teacher summed up the plight of many 'I'm rooted in the routine of O and A levels and somehow it slips by the board.'

Many of these reactions are so genuine, so honest and so understandable that one hesitates to make a critical comment. However, they do raise the serious question about what we are offering students in Catholic schools.

Our schools are good at educating for intellectual competence. They also seek to provide an environment for well-rounded human development. However, neither of these is the same as the capacity for thoughtful and critical questioning which is capable of transforming individuals and society. Such a capacity for questioning, rooted in Christian faith, is directly related to the formation of social conscience and responsible world citizenship. Nonetheless, it tends to be a secondary priority in most of our Catholic schools. It is often considered to be the interest of individual teachers and departments and of a few schools which are looked upon as being outside the mainstream. We could offer this type of critical and questioning education if we wanted to. In some places we do; but it is not common in Catholic schools in Britain and I wonder how common it is in the United States.

The two questions I have used as the basis for reflection 'Who do we serve?' and 'What do we offer?' point to fundamental and unresolved polarities in the Catholic community. Grappling with such questions is particularly difficult in the context of current economic and political situations in Britain and the United States. In the United States, because of the growing financial pressures on a self-funding Catholic school system and in Britain because of the rigidity and time constraints inherent in recent educational reforms we are deprived of the psychological space in which to adequately address such questions. It is vitally important that Catholic schools on both sides of the Atlantic recapture that space.

References

COMMISSION FOR RACIAL JUSTICE OF THE CATHOLIC BISHOPS CONFERENCE OF ENGLAND and WALES (1975) *Where Creed and Colour Matter: A Survey on Black Children and Catholic Schools.*

DEPARTMENT OF CHRISTIAN DOCTRINE and FORMATION OF THE CATHOLIC BISHOPS CONFERENCE OF ENGLAND and WALES (1984) *Learning from Diversity: A Challenge for Catholic Education,* Report of the Working Party on Catholic Education in a Multiracial, Multicultural Society.

FILE, N. and POWER, C. (1981) *Black Settlers in Britain 1555–1958,* London, Heinemann Educational Books.

LORD SWANN (1985) *Education for All* (Report of the Committee of Inquiry into the Education of Children from Ethnic Minority Groups), Cmnd. 9453, London, HMSO.

Chapter 15

Catholic Schools and Other Faiths

Paul A. Hypher

In April 1991 the Catholic Bishops' Conference of England and Wales, follow-ing a report from their Committee for Other Faiths, commissioned a study on the issue of 'The Catholic School and Other Faiths'.[1] This report was pre-sented to the full Bishops' Conference at their meeting in November 1994 and warmly welcomed by them. The Conference decided that, with some minor modifications, the report should be made available to a wider audience of pro-fessionals with a view to initiating a nationwide study at every level of the issues that arise regarding the relationship that Catholic Schools have with other faiths.

The Committee for Other Faiths had originally raised the issue with the Bishops' Conference because they had become aware from their own work of serious tension and stress within Catholic schools, particularly in inner-urban areas.

Evidence suggested that the practices followed in Catholic schools relating to young people of other faiths were not always informed by the teachings arising from the Second Vatican Council. Some schools in inner-city areas were admitting pupils of other faiths merely in order to keep open, whilst having no clear policy as to how to relate to these pupils in matters of religion. Other schools were being closed down, regarded as no longer viable as Catholic schools for Catholic pupils, thereby preventing the Church from being an effect-ive presence in inner-city communities which were often in great need and suf-fering great deprivation. Yet other schools were successfully recruiting sufficient Catholic pupils, but were at the same time ignoring the question of other faiths and ignoring the circumstances in which many of their own Catholic pupils were living.

There had also in the past been reports of some Church schools being used as an 'acceptable' means for isolating white children from the impact of the multi-racial areas in which they were living, to the detriment of children who were from other races and religions.

What has become clear is that there is no course of action, or inaction, which a Catholic school might decide to pursue in regard to other faiths, which is not fraught with complex problems.

Church Teaching and Demographic Change

In fact all these phenomena are symptomatic of two significant developments which have taken place in England and Wales and in the Catholic Church over the last forty years.

The first, originating in the Second Vatican Council, is the development in Catholic teaching as it relates to the Catholic Church's understanding of other faiths and their adherents, and as it also relates to the inalienable rights of the religious and moral conscience. This is discussed in chapters 16 and 17 in this volume.

The second development is the fact that since the 1950s England and Wales have become multi-racial and multi-cultural societies which for the first time include as citizens significant numbers of people of faiths other than Christian. This is a fact which Catholic schools cannot ignore.

In 1985 the *Swann Report*, commissioned for the Government by the then Department of Education and Science, reflected a wider debate that had arisen nationally, in questioning seriously the appropriateness of publicly funded Christian denominational schools in an increasingly multi-faith and multi-racial society (Lord Swann, 1985).

Since the end of the Second World War many of our inner cities have become home for significant numbers of ethnic minority groups — from Poland, Lithuania, Latvia, the Ukraine, Italy, Greece, from the newer Commonwealth countries like Pakistan, India and the West Indies and from the Philippines and Vietnam. There was also considerable Irish immigration in the 1950s and early 1960s.

Within the inner cities in England and Wales there is considerable social deprivation and often some educational disadvantage. For instance recent research has shown that educationally the most underachieving group are Pakistani (predominantly Islamic) males.

In the inner cities economically deprived Catholics will often be living cheek by jowl with other ethnic groups.

Some of the ethnic minority groups are Christian — for instance those from the newer Commonwealth countries, e.g., Afro-Caribbeans, Africans and some people from the Indian subcontinent and south-east Asia. However many are adherents of other faiths.

Immigration over the period accounted for a considerable proportion of the increase of the estimated Catholic population by some 1,700,000 between 1945 and 1970. The Catholic community in England and Wales is, therefore, and will remain, multi-racial and multi-cultural.

These demographic developments directly affected a minority of Catholic schools in England and Wales, which are situated alongside communities, currently mainly in inner-cities, which are predominantly multi-faith. In such areas ordinary state schools themselves may have a pupil roll which is up to 90 per cent or more of a faith other than Christian, e.g., Islamic or Sikh. A Catholic school in the same area is inevitably confronted with demands arising from the day to day contact its own pupils have with people of other faiths.

Sometimes it is subject to the pressures that arise from the desire of parents of other faiths to send their children to the school because of its religious ethos and its moral approach based on the Bible. Sometimes the pressures are a response arising from the school's academic standards or its perceived sense of discipline. If a Catholic school decides to admit pupils of other faiths, it will necessarily come under pressure to respect the religious sensitivities and obligations affecting pupils of other faiths and possibly also at the same time come under pressure from Catholic parents anxious about a dilution of Catholic faith or of educational standards. Sometimes these Catholic parents even exhibit fundamentally racist anxieties.

If the Catholic school does not admit such pupils, especially if there are vacancies in the school, then other tensions arise — accusations of exclusivity, or racism, of a lack of commitment to the poor, or accusations of a refusal to take its obligations with regard to community relations and dialogue seriously. Sometimes the pressures on the Catholic school will come from its own conscientiously felt need to be in solidarity with deprived communities, which may also be the victims of racism.

The Need for a Coherent Educational Policy

Many Catholic schools placed in such situations need support and guidance from the Church regarding their relationship to other faiths and their adherents. They may be only a minority of Catholic schools, but they are a highly significant minority, subject to very considerable pressures. Up to now it has not been possible to provide much clear guidance from Church authorities in England and Wales.

One difficulty in formulating a coherent educational policy in the face of such developments is that there is no full or accurate information in this country about exactly where the different trends regarding the admission of pupils of other faiths in Catholic schools are occurring, nor the reasons for the admissions. Nor is there information about what is actually happening in Catholic schools with regard to pupils of other faiths and with regard to multi-faith education. There are not even any figures on how many pupils of other faiths are in Catholic schools. Although the statistics gathered by the Catholic Education Service make it plain how many pupils are Catholic and how many are not Catholic, there are no figures for the religious or even denominational adherence of those who are not Catholic. Neither do we have any accurate information regarding the reasons why parents who are not Christians seek to send their children to Catholic schools, nor the numbers of such parents.

Granted the need for the acquisition of statistical information, there are still a number of background considerations which are relevant to the development of an appropriate educational policy.

In fact as early as July 1984 the bishops' own Committee for Community Relations set up a special working party to look at issues of racism and multi-culturalism as they affect Catholic voluntary aided or publicly supported schools. The working party made the following recommendations in its final report:

> the Bishops' Conference . . . [should] . . . commission, through an appropriate agency, . . . a feasibility study with regard to the possibility of setting up and running one or more multi-faith schools; and (commission) a review of those schools which have taken in large numbers of pupils of other faiths, to see whether some restructuring of those schools would be appropriate and desirable. (Catholic Media Office, 1984, p. 65)

No action was taken on these recommendations.

The following year, however, in March 1985 the *Swann Report*, as already mentioned, took the opposite line and questioned seriously the validity of pub-licly supported Christian denominational schools in a multi-faith and multi-racial society. It recommended that the Department of Education and Science, in consultation with religious and educational bodies, should review the provi-sions of the 1944 Education Act in relation to voluntary schools 'to see whether or not alterations are required in a society that is now very different' (op. cit., p. 515). Prior to coming to its conclusion the Swann Report stated:

> We would thus regard a democratic pluralist society as seeking to achieve a balance between on the one hand, the maintenance and act-ive support of the essential elements of the cultures and the life-styles of all the ethnic groups within it, and, on the other, the acceptance by all groups of a set of shared values distinctive of society as a whole. This then is our view of a genuinely pluralist society, as both socially cohesive and culturally diverse. (op. cit., pp. 5–6)

In July 1990 the UK Commission for Racial Equality published their own report *Schools of Faith*. In it they offered the following interpretation of this part of the *Swann Report*:

> the wording of this recommendation is vague, but a reasonable infer-ence is that religious schools of any denomination may no longer be considered appropriate in a multi-racial society . . . The question which must now be set down on the national agenda is what, if any, struc-tural relationship should there be between religion and the state edu-cation system in order to assist the positive development of a thriving multi-faith society . . . Public debate on the future of religious schools should be encouraged and broadened, but it should be concerned with the role of all religious schools in a multi-racial society, not just with minority faith schools. (Commission for Racial Equality, 1990)

As the majority of Catholic schools are largely supported by public statutory funding these statements placed the issue not only of the existence of Catholic schools but also of their relationship to other faiths firmly at the heart of national debate. They also highlighted as a matter of considerable importance the legal or moral obligations falling on Catholic schools as a consequence of public funding.

To put the underlying issues raised by the *Swann Report* and by *Schools of Faith* perhaps rather crudely, the liberal agenda in a plural society would seem to assert the claims of openness and integration into society while at the same time undervaluing the need for the affirming of identity. The agenda of some religious sectarians, on the other hand, would seem to undervalue openness and societal integration while asserting the importance of the preservation and the integrity of the inherited identity. The Catholic agenda, which is both about tradition and incarnation, about fidelity and mission, believes that a genuine openness can only arise from a conscious awareness and acceptance of one's identity, while at the same time a true fidelity to one's identity must include openness to the reality of the other and responsibility for the whole of society. This position arises from respect for religious freedom and recognition of God's Spirit at work in the faith of others, from a commitment to the uniqueness of Christian revelation and from an abhorrence of racism and injustice. These are all attitudes and beliefs explicitly required of Catholics by the official teaching of the Church.

The Catholic School in England and Wales: An Historical Perspective

An important element in the formation of an appropriate educational policy response of the kind required is an awareness of the history of Catholic schools in England and Wales.

The Church has always been directly involved in education, especially of the young. Following the Reformation many of the Catholic recusant minority in England and Wales were concerned to preserve the Catholic faith of their families and of the nation in a time of persecution by sending their children to Catholic schools founded for the children of English Catholics on the continent, especially in the Low Countries. Some existing schools in England and Wales are directly descended from these exile schools founded in the late sixteenth century.

Following the Napoleonic Wars and also Catholic emancipation in 1829, Catholic schools were founded in England and Wales, sometimes as poor schools, often by *emigré* religious communities. In 1870 universal elementary education became compulsory in Great Britain and as a result many Catholic schools were founded, often seeking grants from local authorities and trusts. The Catholic Church at that time became committed to establishing its own educational service.

'A place in a Catholic school for every Catholic child.' This was the declared aim of the hierarchy, led by Cardinal Manning. It has remained the declared aim of the Catholic Church in England and Wales right up to the present.

Behind this statement lay a vision and indeed an implied model of the Catholic school and of the Catholic parish. This model saw the norm as one in which the Catholic parish community naturally strove to focus its catechetical, educational role and its caring apostolate to the family on the Catholic school in which all of the pupils were expected to be Catholic.

Parish communities, who often struggled and saved to build and support schools without public grant, prior even to building adequate churches for themselves, aimed to create school communities in which they could be sure their children would receive a grounding in the faith from Roman Catholic teachers, themselves educated in Catholic traditions. Quite explicitly they sought to establish school communities in which their children would be protected from the errors of other religions and from secular influences.

This model of Catholic school is defined quite clearly in some of the diocesan and school trust deeds. In the light of it some RC Diocesan Schools Commissions and some governing bodies hold firmly to a stated maximum figure for the proportion of children who are not Catholic who may be admitted to their schools. Usually it is somewhere between 10 and 15 per cent. There is an anxiety that if the proportion begins to rise above this, then the distinctive Catholic ethos of the school may be harmed.

It is to the credit of the Catholic community that, helped by the 1944 Education Act, it was to a considerable extent successful in its educational aims. In fact, though, the model of Catholic school in which Catholic children are taught the Catholic faith by Catholic teachers was never fully realized and it is a truism that there was ever such a thing as a 'typical' Catholic school.

Some 40 per cent of Catholic children and young people did not or could not attend Catholic schools. Throughout the history of Catholic schooling in this country there have always been Catholic schools which accepted, and were even obliged to accept, sometimes very significant numbers of children who were not Catholic.

Historically the old elementary school (or so-called 'all age' school i.e., 5 years of age to compulsory school leaving age) was often a parish school in the best sense of the word — except for parents who chose to send their children to private schools. Such schools were often situated near the church and were a living part of parish everyday life, serving the vast majority of the children of the parish. In fact they were not just educational establishments, but active instruments for the social concern and family care of the parish, offering advice and support and even food and clothing, especially in areas of considerable need.

The situation, however, became more complex as Catholics in greater numbers chose schools for their children on academic, social, class and economic grounds as well as for religious reasons. This in itself divided some Catholic parishes along social and economic lines. For example if Catholic secondary or even comprehensive schools were required to compete with local county or Church of England grammar schools, then their intake would often be skewed towards the lower ability range, unless the Catholic school enjoyed high educational esteem. Schooling for many Roman Catholics has been a primary instrument of social advancement and this has had implications for the grounds on which parents choose schools.

At secondary level schooling was more diverse. There were publicly funded grammar and secondary modern schools, but also direct grant and fee paying schools. These divided the community both socially and academically and Catholic secondary schools often had to take larger numbers of pupils who were not Roman Catholic in order to be viable. The advent of the comprehensive system in the 1960s and 1970s meant that for the first time the Catholic community were able to promote schools at secondary level (11+) (and more recently at Post-16), which could in effect bring together the entire Catholic community.

This bringing together of rich and poor and of differently abled pupils in itself gives a potentially different experience of 'Church' and therefore of 'Catholic'. However the demands of modern education and a declining birth-rate have meant that, because secondary schools need to be large, they are often less viable as exclusively Catholic schools, except in more urban areas with a larger and more concentrated Catholic population.

Some schools have been able to maintain policies which admit 100 per cent church-going Catholic pupils. Sometimes these were academically popular schools. Other Catholic schools have also maintained 100 per cent Roman Catholic admissions, but their pupils have been drawn from areas with a low church-going rate. Such schools may often be situated in inner-city areas. The perceptions of 'Church' among the parents of these children are often very different from that of parents actively involved in the regular worship of the Church. This in turn affects the way in which they might apply the term 'Catholic' to their school. In fact adherence to Catholic identity among these parents may often derive from childhood experiences, from a desire for 'discipline' and from a general sense of well-being in a religious environment.

As already mentioned, there have always been Catholic schools with a significant number of pupils who were not Catholic. The families of pupils who were not Catholic valued the schools as 'good schools' and valued the coherent aims and community life of the Catholic school, its spiritual values, caring ethos and discipline. Such schools have surely done much to break down some of the old fears and prejudices about Catholics.

The Catholic School in England and Wales: Recent Trends and Developments

The decline in the birthrate and baptismal rate combined with social mobility have affected Catholic schools and have in many areas led to falling rolls.

Between 1978 and 1993 389 maintained Catholic schools were closed, 14.5 per cent of a total of 2,678 schools. The number of Catholic pupils in maintained Catholic schools fell by 22.3 per cent that is by 181,997 pupils.

However the proportion of Catholic pupils entering Catholic schools at the age of 5 as a percentage of Catholic baptisms has been steadily increasing from 55 per cent in 1975 to 72 per cent in 1993.

The proportion of pupils in Catholic schools who are not Catholic has also been steadily increasing. In primary schools from 1.6 per cent in 1974 to 10.2 per cent in 1993 and at secondary level from 3.2 per cent in 1980 to 16.0 per cent in 1993. The number of Catholic teachers in Catholic schools is declining. In 1978 there had been 30,331 lay Catholic teachers in Catholic maintained schools, by 1993 the number was 24,802.

Between 1978 and 1993 the number of teachers in our maintained schools who were not Catholic increased from 22 per cent to 29 per cent — in the secondary sector rising from 34 per cent to 40.2 per cent and in the primary from 9 per cent to 12.5 per cent. The number of professed religious teaching in Catholic maintained schools has declined from 1,445 in primary schools in 1974 to 351 in 1993 (by 75.7 per cent) and at secondary level from 917 in 1980 to 219 in 1993 (by 76.1 per cent). There have always been schools with a fairly large proportion of staff who were not Catholic, particularly at secondary level. Schools have always tried to maintain a high percentage of Catholic staff. The contribution, even in large numbers, of staff who were not Catholic but who were prepared to uphold and not do anything detrimental to the Catholic nature of the school, has usually been greatly valued, especially where those staff were active members of other Christian denominations. Between 1973 and 1993 the number of independent schools run by and in principle staffed by professed religious declined from 367 schools to 206 schools.[2]

There are also significant trends relating to regular worship and the overall profile of the Catholic population. Between 1970 and 1991 the overall number of people regularly attending Sunday Mass declined by 33.2 per cent from 1,934,853 in 1970 to 1,292,312 in 1991. Some of this decline will be part of a general population decline. For instance between 1965 and 1989 the annual national figures for live births declined from 862,275 to 687,725. Over the same period Catholic baptisms declined not only absolutely but they also declined as a percentage of the live birthrate from 15.5 per cent to 11.4 per cent. In 1965 Catholic baptisms peaked at 134,055. Between 1975 and 1988 they averaged 73,300. Since 1988 they have risen to nearer 80,000 a year. Some of the decline in Mass attendance will also be due to an aging Catholic population and an increasing death rate among Roman Catholics. This has risen from 36,596 in 1970 to 44,947 in 1985; more importantly it has doubled as a proportion of the annual baptismal rate to nearly 60 per cent[3] (Hornsby-Smith, 1989, pp. 2–3). The worshipping RC community would appear to have a strongly aging profile and its numbers are declining although the total number of baptized Roman Catholics in England and Wales is now increasing. The infant baptism and church-going trends both, therefore, suggest that the number of Catholics available to be pupils in Catholic schools will continue to decline, although for the moment it appears to have levelled out. One of the consequences of the model of the Catholic school which sees it as exclusively for the Catholic community, has been that often where there have been insufficient Catholic pupils in the vicinity as a result (say) of a declining birthrate or of social mobility, schools have been closed and the Church has effectively withdrawn from the human and social agenda of whole, often deprived, areas of our country. This means that opportunities for inter-religious understanding and dialogue have been passed by.

Other consequences of the model of a Catholic school consisting of a wholly Catholic pupil population can be a somewhat stunted understanding of Catholicism leading to a loss of a true understanding of the need for evangelization, and also narrow-mindedness or even unconscious racism. These can arise from a lack of opportunities for pupils and staff to experience direct partnership with people of different social, racial and economic circumstances, and, in the case of a school with 100 per cent practising pupils, a lack of insight into different levels of faith understanding and commitment.

In contrast, the model of Catholic school which consists largely of pupils and staff who are not Catholic has in fact always been common in so called 'mission' countries, especially in countries which had no extensive state funded education systems of their own. Indeed such schools were and still are invariably understood as a positive asset to the Church in its work of Mission. They have never been regarded as anything other than 'Catholic', because their motivation and ethos grew out of the faith of the believing community. Until recently such a model of Catholic school was regarded as inappropriate for the situation in England and Wales, especially in view of our state system and of the considerable number of Church of England schools.

Some Catholic schools have had a very positive impact well beyond the Catholic community, have been highly esteemed and have done much to overcome religious prejudice or ignorance. Others have had no relationship to or impact on the community in which they were situated, especially if they did not draw pupils from the area. Catholic schools, however, which drew pupils from poorer areas have very readily seen themselves as serving the needs of the local community. This ancient tradition is continued in many inner-city schools.

In recent years a newer model of Catholic school has been developing in some multi-racial inner-city areas. In these cases, the school, rather than being a Catholic school for the Catholic community, has seen itself as a Catholic and Christian presence at the service of all members of the local community. This model sees the Catholic school as itself an effective sacramental sign of faith in Jesus Christ to the whole community. This makes quite explicit a model of school and of Church that has always been present, but which up to now has mainly existed in so-called 'missionary' countries. Such schools explicitly take on that aspect of the Church's agenda which concerns mission and dialogue and the evangelization of cultures, over and above the agenda relating to maintenance and catechesis.

Since the Second Vatican Council another new model of school which has quite deliberately come into being is that of the joint or interchurch school. These are currently joint Catholic/Church of England schools as the Catholic community is not currently in educational partnership with any other denomination. Underlying such schools is not only an educational vision, but also a belief in the centrality of ecumenical commitment and practice to Catholic identity. Such schools seek to affirm and strengthen the religious identity, traditions and backgrounds of all pupils, while at the same time enabling pupils to recognize, understand and value not only the differences in the beliefs of others, but also the commonalities. In religious educational terms therefore such schools in which Catholics are partners would still wish themselves to be viewed and understood as Catholic schools, although at the same time also schools of another denomination. They would resist suggestions that they are 'ecumenical' and no longer Catholic, or properly denominational schools.

Anxieties have been expressed about indifferentism and the undermining of faith in schools which have a high proportion of non-practising pupils or pupils of other faiths and denominations. Those who are anxious appear to feel that conscious acceptance of the values of other faiths in a positive way, or even a non-judgmental acceptance of the 'lapsed', can only lead to indifferentism. There is little evidence that this is or need be the case.

The Methodology of the Working Party and Its Conclusions

The Catholic Church in England and Wales tends to steer a middle course between the extremes of the left and right wing perceptions of the Church. However the issues raised in the debate about Catholic schools and other faiths are so sensitive and acute that it proved difficult for the consultative group established by the Bishops' Conference to achieve a consensus. The project was put into the joint care of the Bishops' Conference Committees for Other Faiths and for Community Relations and the Bishops' Conference Department for Catholic Education and Formation. The consultative group selected consisted of about thirty members drawn from as wide a range of disciplinary background and experience and from as wide a geographical area within England and Wales as possible. Representation included educationalists, clergy, school chaplains, schools officers, practising teachers, community relations workers and theologians. It also included two members from the Church of England. It did not however include among its membership people of other faiths as, after much discussion, once it became clear that a consensus would be difficult to achieve it was felt that it would be better to bring people of other faiths into partnership in dialogue once the Catholic community had achieved some level of clarification of its own principles.

The consultative group met over a period of three years, usually with an attendance record of 75 per cent, on nine occasions for plenary meetings lasting approximately four hours and also for one overnight plenary residential session with a meeting time of some seven to eight hours. There were also three regional meetings in London, Leeds and Birmingham and many meetings of small drafting groups and of the steering committee. Some sections of the report went through as many as eleven draftings.

Some in the group had been involved in closing Catholic schools in inner-city multi-racial areas because of a lack of Catholic admissions. Others had had their schools closed in these circumstances. Indeed two members were facing the closure of their college throughout the actual consultation, precisely because of a dispute about the definition of Catholic school in relation to people of other denominations and other faiths. Some members worked in close and continual partnership with people of other faiths, while others were respons-ible for meeting the existing aspirations of the Catholic faithful. Some were concerned with the theological and educational principles at issue, whilst others found that too 'theoretical' and wished to get down to discussing detailed class-room practice. Some members felt that inter-religious or even ecumenical dia-logue is not for children, whilst others felt that schools which admit pupils of other faiths really belonged in so-called 'mission' countries rather than in Europe. Yet others felt that the assertion of denominational identity and the missionary role of the Church are both fundamentally inimical to true dialogue.

The eventual achievement of a consensus was largely the result of the fact that the group were able to establish an agreed methodology for conducting its work. The methodology was not based on the drawing of conclusions from theological or pedagogical speculation, but rather on drawing them from the existing documentation of the Church.[4] There was therefore a considerable narrowing of the group's purpose in order to achieve agreement on essential principles.

To some people the conclusions of the group might seem like a not very original statement of the obvious. Yet perhaps it should rather been seen as the small seed from which a big tree grows. The diversity of the group rep-resented the diversity of the Church in England and Wales. The achievement of a unanimous consent about principles and indeed the unanimous support of the members of the Bishops' Conference must bode well for the further develop-ment of the process throughout our parishes and schools.

The main conclusions of the Report of the Consultative Group, entitled *Catholic Schools and Other Faiths* presented to the Bishops' Conference in November 1994 are: first that the Second Vatican Council inaugurated profound developments in the understanding of what it means to be Catholic when considering our relationship to other denominations and to other faiths; and secondly that, as a result of the teaching of that Council, the role of the Catholic school particularly in its relation to other faiths, and indeed other Christian denominations, must be seen in the broader light of openness and dialogue. The report then stressed the relevance of these teachings to the Catholic community in England and Wales which since the Second World War has developed in multi-cultural, multi-racial and multi-faith contexts. It also stressed how working to promote openness and dialogue in relation to the faith, values and culture of others is an aspect of a continuing faithfulness, albeit in changed circumstances, to the Catholic tradition which the schools had been serving so well for so long.

In the light of changes in the circumstances of the Church in England and Wales and of the principles enunciated in Church teaching, the report made recommendations to the following effect:

- It recognized the need for the relationship between Catholics and people of other faiths to be accepted as an area for ongoing formation and education for priests, teachers and catechists and indeed for the entire Catholic community. This work, important in its own right, is a prerequisite for any development within our schools. It sought the inauguration of a process for raising awareness of people at all levels in the Church, including parish level, of the issues relating to other faiths and in particular to Catholic schools and pupils of other faiths.
- It felt that it was important that this process should be supported by dialogue and partnership with national representative bodies of the major world faiths represented in Britain concerning the spiritual development and support of pupils of other faiths in Catholic schools and colleges.
- In view of the new developments in the understanding of Catholic schools these schools would need to review their mission statements and their policies regarding their relationship to people of other faiths, including pupils of other faiths.
- Plainly, as the report *Catholic Schools and other Faiths* was only able to be concerned with matters of fundamental principle it was important that further investigations should be initiated into the prac- tical consequences for our schools resulting from the developments in the teaching of the Church. Guidelines will need to be produced. The paucity of accurate information also means that research is important in order to ascertain the relevant statistics regarding pupils of other faiths and Catholic schools.

The recommendations of the report have implications for all Catholic schools, whether or not they have pupils who are members of other faiths, or are situated in a multi-faith area. All need to examine and redefine their Catholic nature in the light of the Second Vatican Council. To be Catholic now means not only proclaiming the Gospel by the witness of being a living Catholic com- munity and by catechesis for the baptised, but also proclaiming the Gospel by recognizing where the Holy Spirit is at work in people of other faiths and relating to them in a dialogue of life and of religious experience, of action and of theological exchange.

Currently the Bishops' Conference is broadening the consultation to include all of the dioceses in the country in order to develop agreed guidelines which themselves can be the subject of further consultation at school and parish level. The Report *Catholic Schools and Other Faiths*, constitutes therefore the inauguration of a process which is intended to enable Catholics to reformulate this aspect of the life and work of the Church throughout England and Wales.

Policies Regarding Other Faiths and the Catholic School

Given that British society generally and the Catholic school in particular are both in the throes of a considerable transition with regard to the growth of a multi-ethnic, multi-faith society, what are the policies that should be developed?

Whether or not young people live in a multi-ethnic or in a predominantly white 'Christian' area, they cannot avoid the tensions, attitudes and prejudices that arise. Young people will inevitably be influenced by street corner prejudice and racism but also by street-corner inter-religious and inter-racial dialogue. The schools they attend and indeed their families, will convey hidden, or not so hidden, messages about human dignity, respect, freedom and faith. It is important that Catholic schools do not unintentionally support prejudice and injustice, conveying messages which undermine Catholic values. It is important that the schools are able to be supportive of young people in developing skills and sensitivities of genuine dialogue and respect.

The outline of the history of Catholic schools in this country demonstrates how fundamental these developments and changes are for many Catholic schools in England and Wales and also how complex the practical consequences are likely to be for everyday school life. Does the school, in its day to day life, show and promote respect for the faith and spiritual needs of each pupil, especially for those who are not Christians? Do its admissions policies have the effect of excluding non-white or deprived children and building up among them a sense of exclusion from Christianity and from the opportunities being offered to white (sometimes better off) Catholic neighbours? Does the school bus children in from affluent suburbs in a way that prevents it from being challenged by the injustice and deprivation to be found at its very doorstep?

Schools must study the explicit challenge presented to them by the Church's teaching and re-evaluate their work in the light of it.

Catholic schools in addition to offering a high quality academic education, need to nurture the faith and promote the spiritual and moral development of every person attending the school. They must develop an educational community characterized by openness and dialogue and place themselves at the service of the local community, especially the poor and deprived. These are essential parts of their educational mission.

The Roman document *The Religious Dimension of Education in a Catholic School* (1988) expresses this clearly: schools have the twofold duty 'to proclaim the Gospel and to offer formation based on values to be found in Christian education' and also to recognize and respect 'the religious freedom and the personal conscience of individual students and their families' (Sacred Congregation for Catholic Education, 1988, no. 6). .

The Church also 'earnestly entreats' the Catholic community in every part of the Church to 'spare no sacrifice' and

> to show special concern for the needs of those who are poor in the goods of this world or who are deprived of the assistance and affection of a family or who are strangers to the gift of faith. (Abbott, 1965, nos 8, 9)

More recently Pope John Paul II speaks of the 'ecumenical dimension' of catechesis and states that

> catechesis will have an ecumenical dimension if it tries to prepare Catholic children and young people, as well as adults, for living in contact with non-Catholics, affirming their Catholic identity while respecting the faith of others. (John Paul II, 1979, no. 32)

Later documents take the issue even further by relating it specifically to Faiths that are not Christian:

> Special attention is to be given to young people living in a pluralistic environment, who meet the followers of other religions at school, at work, in youth movements and other associations and even within their own families.[5]

> Therefore, while Catholic educators will teach doctrine in conformity with their own religious convictions and in accord with the identity of the school, they must at the same time have the greatest respect for those students who are not Catholic. They should be open at all times to authentic dialogue, convinced that in these circumstances the best testimony they can give of their own faith is a warm and sincere appreciation of anyone who is honestly seeking God according to his or her own conscience. (Sacred Congregation for Catholic Education, 1982, no. 42)

This role is not merely one of tolerance, but a positive one of promoting genuine spiritual values for these too are the gift of the Spirit. The Catholic School

> offers itself to all, those who are not Christian included, with all its distinctive aims and means, acknowledging, preserving and promoting the spiritual and moral qualities, which characterise different civilisations. (Sacred Congregation for Catholic Education, 1977, no. 85)

The Church clearly accepts that as a consequence of its understanding, there will need to be differentiation in approaches to teaching, even for Catholics.

It accepts that among Catholic pupils there will be 'many different levels of faith response' and states that 'the Christian vision of existence must be presented in such ways that it meets all these levels' (Sacred Congregation for Catholic Education, 1982, no. 28). It is clear that such subtlety of approach must also be used especially where pupils of other faiths are concerned. Religious education must be 'suited to the often widely varying religious situations of pupils' (John Paul II, 1979, no. 69).

One necessary consequence of this differentiation of approach and context for Catholic schooling is that 'Catholic schools can take on forms which vary according to local circumstances' (Abbott, 1965, no. 10). This will be true even within a single ecclesiastical region as small as England and Wales because of the diversity and plurality of society and social conditions.

Placed in this way within the context of the broader agenda of the universal Church, local issues take on a new significance. It becomes clear that Catholic schools founded with one set of objectives are now being required to adapt to newer objectives relating to openness, dialogue, mission, other faiths, option for the poor, racism and religious freedom, while at the same time remaining true to the heart of their original purpose.

It is not surprising that schools are looking for clear leadership from the Church in what is after all a radical shift both in perception and in their circumstances.

As a result of the acceptance of the Report *Catholic Schools and Other Faiths* by the Bishops' Conference of England and Wales, a process is now being initiated which which will enable people at all levels of the Church, priests, professional and lay, at parish level, at diocesan level and beyond, to undergo formation so that they may become partners in the discernment which is essential if our Catholic schools are to meet the challenge presented by our present society. Within this context of a broader awareness and understanding of the issues, the schools themselves will then be able to evaluate the situation and develop new policies to match the new circumstances and the obligations that arise from them.

Notes

1 Scotland and Ireland both come under separate Bishops' Conferences.
2 Figures and statistics from Catholic Education Council/Catholic Education Services Annual Reports and other records.
3 See relevant editions of the *Catholic Directory for England and Wales.*
4 • *Declaration on Religious Liberty* (*Dignitatis humanae*, 1965).
  • *Attitude of the Church towards the Followers of Other Religions* Secretariat for non-Christians, 1984, Rome.
  • *Dialogue and Proclamation* Council for Inter-religious Dialogue and the Congregation for the Evangelisation of Peoples, 1991, Rome.
  • *Catechism of the Catholic Church Libreria Editrice Vaticana*, English Translation, Geoffrey Chapman, London.

- *The Code of Canon Law 1983*, Canon, 803 par. 1, English translation, London, Collins.
- *Declaration on Religious Liberty* (Dignitatis humanae 1965) p. 675 sq.
5 See *Dialogue and Proclamation*, op. cit., no. 88.

References

Abbott, W. (1965) *Declaration on Christian Education* (*Gravissimum Educationis*) London, Geoffrey Chapman.

Abbott, W. (1965) *Decree on the Relation of the Church to non-Christian Religions* (*Nostrae Aetate*) Chapman, G. (transl.), London.

Catholic Media Office (1984) *Learning from Diversity*, London.

Commission for Racial Equality (1990) *Schools of Faith: Religious Schools in a Multicultural Society*, London, CRE.

Hornsby-Smith, M. (1989) *The Changing Parish*, London, Routledge.

John Paul II (1979) *Catechism in our Time. Catechesi Tradendae*, London, CTS.

John Paul II (1991) *Redemptoris Missio*, London, CTS.

Lord Swann (1985) *Education for All: Report of the Committee of Inquiry into the Education of Children from Ethnic Minority Groups*, Cmnd. 9453, London, HMSO.

Sacred Congregation for Catholic Education (1977) *The Catholic School*, Rome.

Sacred Congregation for Catholic Education (1982) *Lay Catholics in School — Witnesses to Faith*, Rome.

Sacred Congregation for Catholic Education (1988) *The Religious Dimension of Education in a Catholic School*, Rome.

Chapter 16

Catholic Schools in a World of Many Faiths: Church Teaching and Theological Perspectives

Michael Barnes S.J.

The consultation on 'the Catholic School and Other Faiths' which Paul Hypher describes in Chapter 15 in this volume began its first meeting in December 1991 with a number of papers to 'set the scene'. Among these was a brief presentation of Church teaching on the relationship between the Church and people of other faiths as it has developed since Vatican II. This overview, though very limited in scope, was found to be useful, not just because it reminded members of the consultation of what the Popes and Vatican Congregations and Councils have actually said over the last twenty-five years but because it raised many crucial theological issues which affect all aspects of the Church's life — including religious education in general and Catholic schools in particular.

Members of the consultation agreed that an analysis of the 'distinctive character of the Catholic school and education for life in a multi-faith society' called for some theological background and analysis as a necessary first step. What theological principles should guide the Catholic school when seeking to find its way in a pluralist society?

'Theology of religions' is an increasingly familiar subject in the academic world, but there is as yet no fully developed tradition of Catholic thinking on this subject. It was therefore felt to be more appropriate, and more useful for the immediate purposes of the consultation, to limit the section to an outline of Catholic teaching and a discussion of the specific contribution which the Roman Catholic tradition would make to such a theology.

The section based on the tradition of Church teaching serves, therefore, as a theological introduction to the final report. The present chapter does not seek to reproduce that section so much as to comment on the theological issues which formed the basis of much of the discussion.

Shift of Perception

Prior to Vatican II issues connected with inter-faith dialogue were usually treated under missiology or soteriology, answering a particular problem for the

Church about the salvation of those outside her visible bounds. More recently there has been a shift of perception. The continuing existence of other faiths is no longer just a 'problem' to be overcome through the development of new missionary or theological strategies. The experience of inter-faith dialogue presents Christians with a different sort of challenge. Inter-faith dialogue takes a number of forms — from formal academic discussions to the sharing of experience and co-operation in common endeavours. But, in whatever form it takes, the experience of learning how to relate to people of other faiths as neighbours in a pluralist society asks for careful theological analysis of some difficult but exciting questions. These demand a new look at many traditional areas of Christian reflection — salvation, mission, the person of Christ. But, more fundamentally, Christians are asked: How is it possible to be faithful to the best traditions of the Church, while respecting the demand of other people of faith that they be accepted for what they themselves claim to be?

The tension implied here, between faithfulness and openness, is not easily maintained. Christians claim to speak of a universal truth. What, then, are the limits to Christian acceptance of the claims of the other? On the other hand, the great world religions all make their own claims to truth. What are the risks to inter-faith harmony of a refusal to consider such claims? This tension is at the heart of the theology which has emerged since Vatican II.

In Relationship with the Other

Vatican II, of course, marked a major advance in thinking. The council looked at what was held in common by Christians and non-Christians. The Church is not set over against but in relationship with what is 'other' — the world, other Christian communities, the great world religions. Thus in the words of *Gaudium et Spes*, the Church sees itself as sharing the 'hopes and joys, the griefs and anxieties of the people of this age' (*GS* 1). At the beginning of the declaration on the relationship of the Church to non-Christian religions, *Nostra Aetate*, the attention of the Church is drawn to 'our times when every day people are being drawn closer together and the ties between various peoples are being multiplied' (*NA* 1). Since 'all peoples comprise a single community, and have a single origin', the council says clearly that the Church 'rejects nothing which is true and holy in these religions' (*NA* 2).

Nostra Aetate is the first positive statement ever made by a council on the status and value of the beliefs of non-Christians. In one of its most powerful statements Christians are called upon to 'acknowledge, preserve and promote the spiritual and moral goods' found amongst people of other faiths (*NA* 2). And in the final paragraph the council rejects 'as contrary to the mind of Christ' any discrimination based on 'race, colour, condition of life or religion' (*NA* 5).

Dialogue is commended, and the truths to be found in the great world religions — Judaism, Islam, Buddhism and Hinduism — are affirmed, albeit in the case of the last two very briefly. But, alongside such positive statements about openness and respect for people of other faiths, are to be found those which speak of the Church's traditional missionary role in a multi-faith world. *Lumen Gentium*, the constitution on the Church, for instance, opens with the statement that Christ is the 'light of the nations'; the Church's role is to shed that light on all peoples by 'proclaiming the Gospel to every creature' (*LG* 1). *Ad Gentes*, the decree on missionary activity, deliberates at length on the missionary's vocation to 'announce the Gospel among the nations' (*AG* 1), while *Gravissimum Educationis*, the declaration on Christian education, speaks of education as preparing students to 'promote effectively the welfare of the earthly city and . . . serve the advancement of the reign of God' (*GE* 8). Finally, having said that the Church esteems other faiths because they 'often reflect a ray of that Truth which enlightens all people', *Nostra Aetate* juxtaposes this statement with another, reminding the Church of the duty to 'proclaim Christ, the way, the truth and the life' (*NA* 2).

In pondering on these and other key conciliar texts and the Catholic experience of other faiths in Britain members of the consultation recognised that the tension noted above — between faithfulness and openness — had to be held together in any theology of religions, and, therefore, in coming to any conclusions about principles for religious education in a multi-faith society. It also became clear that, so far from ignoring the call to mission, the council was calling for a renewal of understanding of the missionary context in which the Church has always sought to live out its relations with people of other faiths. This is of crucial importance in understanding changes in the self-perception of the Church in the years immediately before and since the Council.

The Church's Missionary Vocation in the Context of Dialogue

The council thus called for a renewal of the missionary vocation of the Church *in and through* a recognition of a new context — that of dialogue with the world. Again Church documents and papal teaching formed the basis of the work of the consultation. To be noted is Paul VI's first encyclical, *Ecclesiam Suam*, often regarded as the great charter of dialogue. And the apostolic exhortation, *Evangelii Nuntiandi*, which appeared ten years after the council. Here the practical, if not theological, agenda for the Church's relations with the other are spelled out in some detail. Proclamation and catechesis are only one aspect of evangelization, which is to be directed not just at individuals but also at cultures; evangelization includes the call to human liberation, even though it may not be reduced to it.

More recently Pope John Paul II's *Redemptoris Missio* has sought to develop the same familiar conciliar theme. The emphasis throughout is on the 'permanent validity' of the Christian mission to proclaim Christ as the source of all salvation. The fact that by his death and resurrection Christ has redeemed the whole of humankind does not make missionary activity unnecessary. Rather such a vision should make for a stronger and clearer motivation to mission. In seeking to understand the mentality of the modern world Christians are called to illuminate and purify it with the light of Christian revelation. Seeds of the Word must be sought and acknowledged in other faiths. Inter-faith dialogue is to be seen as a particular component of the total mission of the Church. Thus the Pope urges Catholics to respect and esteem 'the values, traditions and convictions of other believers' (*RM* 3). The meaning of dialogue is expanded. It entails more than the largely intellectual exchange of ideas. The 'dialogue of life' — learning from one another, cooperation and common awareness — comes first.

The consultation thought it important to include in its deliberations some reference to two further documents which reflect quite specifically upon the faithfulness-openness tension as well as upon the experience of living in relationship with people of other faiths. The first, entitled *The attitude of the Church towards the followers of other religions*, was issued by the (then) Secretariat for Non-Christians in 1984. The second document is *Dialogue and Proclamation*, issued in 1991 under the joint auspices of the Pontifical Council for Inter-religious Dialogue and the Congregation for the Evangelisation of Peoples. Together these statements reflect a wider understanding of the Church's missionary vocation as including all activities which are undertaken for the building of the Kingdom under the inspiration of the values of the Gospel. 'In fulfilment of his plan of salvation, God, in his Son, has reached out to the whole of humankind' (*DP* 25). Christians are called upon to make this reality of salvation explicit, to help the 'seeds of the Word' grow wherever the Spirit has planted them. The ministry of the Church is to develop the Mystery of Christ understood as already present in the world of the 'other'.

Towards a Catholic Theology of Religions

This new context for mission clearly has major implications for Christian education. It is, however, not just a matter of *how* Christians are to learn about the call of Christ — how they are to respond to that call, and how they are to pass on the truth and values of the Gospel. To discern the 'seeds of the Word' implies a christology. It is, therefore, also crucially important to learn *who* Christ is in a multi-faith world. So far from relativizing the Gospel message, the inter-faith context raises in more acute fashion the christological question. All the Council documents and those Church statements which have appeared more recently are thoroughly christocentric and trinitarian in nature. The human dialogue, especially that which brings people of different faiths to share that faith with each other, reflects something of the mystery of a God who seeks always to reveal himself. The Father speaks his Word; the Son and the Father are joined in the Spirit of love.[1]

It is this concern to discern the fullness of the mystery of God's self-giving which has been the major impetus behind the typically Catholic theology of religions. This has often attracted the title 'inclusivism' (D'Costa, 1986, pp. 80–116). While acknowledging that there is an element of jargon in any shorthand, the consultation found the term 'inclusivism' helpful as an expression of the way in which, at its best, Catholic Christianity has sought to speak of its relationship with the other.

Some brief explanation of the term is necessary. 'Inclusivism' is very often understood by a deliberate contrast with 'exclusivism'; thus the 'open' Catholic approach is set against the 'closed' Protestant. Whatever truth there may be in this distinction, it is more helpful to see the two terms as different versions of a single *universalist* christocentric vision — the one based on Reformation principles the other on a Natural Law tradition. It is important to understand the difference. Catholic Christianity has a more developed sense of the *sacramental* than Protestant. Both seek to maintain a particular insight into the way God reveals God. But, whereas Protestants base their theology on a kerygmatic model, Catholics prefer an integrative wisdom-based way of speaking of God's action.

For Catholic theology the primary framework within which the Mystery of Christ is to be understood is the doctrine of creation. Catholics will always want to stress the unity of God's salvific and creative action, and to take the *broadest view* of the scope or extent of God's self-revelation. 'Inclusivism', should not, therefore, be explained as if it refers to a system of thought but rather as an 'instinct', representing the Catholic conviction of the ever-continuing redemptive presence of God in the world as a whole. By focusing on the continuities rather than the discontinuities between religions this 'Catholic instinct' is to seek always to include the other within the gracious scope of God's creative and saving action.

For Catholic theology it is important to allow at least for the *possibility* that God is at work in ways and forms which the Church may not know about. This is what is stressed in the Council documents. 'Those also can attain to everlasting salvation who through no fault of their own do not know the Gospel of Christ or his Church, yet sincerely seek God and, moved by grace, strive by their deeds to do his will as it is known to them through the dictates of conscience' (*LG* 16). The word to note here is 'can'. All *can* — but not necessarily *will* — be saved. Thus this section of *LG* finishes with a cautionary note about another possibility — the corrupting effect of evil and, therefore, the need to preach the Gospel 'to promote the glory of God and the salvation of all'. This statement acknowledges that there are always going to be difficulties in discerning the nature and extent of God's revelation, both within and outside the Church. But a Catholic approach to 'the other' will want to be careful about appearing to limit the scope of God's action.

What the Church knows in faith to be true is the good news that in Christ the promise of salvation is made to all people. What the Church does not know is the extent to which the Spirit may already be at work within the hearts of people of other faiths. At the very least, therefore, the Church must acknowledge that whatever she discerns which is 'true and holy' (*NA* 2) in other religions is there in terms of what she knows of the mystery of God's love made manifest in Christ. The unfortunately patronizing tone of some forms of inclusivist language is well-known. But 'inclusivism' is not a claim that the Church in some way 'owns the space' inhabited by the other. Rather the term expresses the conviction that Church and 'other' are not mutually exclusive terms but exist *in relationship*, related by that offer of saving grace made to all people by the Holy Spirit.

Ways of Being Church

It is this vision which the Church seeks to understand and to which it is called to witness. The two dimensions go together. As the eschatological community, the Church is charged with witnessing to the Kingdom of which it understands itself to be the sign and first fruits. At the same time, the Church shares with other people of faith the need always to be open and to learn, searching for the fullness of that truth. Thus the Church's identity as the people of God is always looking to the world of which it is inescapably a part *and* beyond that world, to the Kingdom.

The two demands implied in the faithfulness-openness tension reflect the two ways of being Church: teaching yet learning. They can only be held together by a continual conversion, a turning back to the God who leads all people of faith. Dialogue, of course, always involves speaking and listening. But the actual encounter with the other will also lead to an interior dialogue in which the Church listens to the Spirit who may be speaking through the voice of the other. The Church too must be continually evangelized, its conversion of heart based in a prayerful experience of God. This is the God of Jesus Christ, but also a God who 'has no favourites', a God who may be heard through the Spirit which 'blows where it wills'. If the Church is to be formed as a community that both makes known, yet goes on searching for, the Truth that is Christ, it can only be through an ever-deepening commitment to the demands of the Gospel revealed to the Church and in the acknowledgement of the 'seeds of the Word' (*AG* 11, 15) or 'rays of the truth' (*NA* 2) found outside the visible structures of the Church.

The resolution of the faithfulness-openness tension takes us back to the spiritual practice and liturgical life of the Church where the Church celebrates its call to respond to the mystery of God's self-revelation in Christ. The nature of the Church is a worshipping community for mission. The community of the faithful is formed through the Eucharist where it becomes aware *both* of its most hallowed traditions, where the Church comes from, *and* of what the Spirit is now saying, where she is called to follow. It is in the liturgy that the covenant between God and human beings is continually renewed.

A Theology for Christian Education

In conclusion it may be said that a fully developed Catholic theology of religions will seek to do things. There are, on the one hand, many complex problems attending the relationship of Christianity and people of other faiths. Such a reflection prepares for dialogue with the other. On the other hand, there is the need to reflect on the implications for Christian identity of the relationship *itself*. How does the co-existence of religious traditions affect our understanding of the way in which God reveals himself through Christ in the Church? The tensions noted above — between faithfulness and openness, between the teaching and the learning Church — mean that Catholic Christians have to acknowledge two principles which should guide our answers to this question. There is firstly the principle of dialogue: an engagement with the other who is yet a neighbour. Secondly, there is the conscious conviction of bearing a message which challenges and enlightens all people, both inside and outside the Church.

The aim of Christian education today — at whatever level — remains what it has always been: to be formed in Christ with a mature and strong sense of the Christian missionary vocation. In a pluralist world, however, the Church explicitly acknowledges this vocation to include the capacity to respond positively to the reality of the other in our midst. In short, the Christian must learn *in relationship with the other* to reflect positively on the inter-faith relationship and to learn the correct and discerning use of the two principles discussed above. Clearly the emphasis will vary, depending on various circumstances. The tension between the two, however, must always be maintained. To attempt to teach the one without the other would be both theologically and pedagogically inadequate.

Note

1   For a perceptive and helpful summary of Church teaching on the trinitarian dimensions of dialogue see the outline in *The Attitude of the Church towards the Followers of Other Religions*, op. cit., pp. 22–4.

Reference

D'COSTA, G. (1986) *Theology and Religious Pluralism*, Oxford, Basil Blackwell.

Chapter 17

Other Faiths in Catholic Schools: General Implications of a Case Study

Vince Murray

Sometimes within processes of change, one particular event or situation comes both to represent symbolically the tensions inherent within the transition and to act concretely as a focus for the direction of future change. St Philip's Roman Catholic Sixth Form College in Birmingham has been such a symbol and focus. The document of the Catholic Bishops of England and Wales, *Catholic Schools and Other Faiths* records the developments at a national level which required the issue of other faiths in Catholic schools to be addressed and makes recommendations for the future (see Chapter 15 in this volume). However, the case of St Philip's Roman Catholic Sixth Form College in Birmingham has been, and at the time of writing still is, that concrete example of a crux situation regarding the presence of students of faiths other than Christian within Catholic schools. Whatever the 'objective' analysis of the general issues, the inspiration, conflict, pain and joy of that particular educational community cannot be ignored in the search for an appropriate Roman Catholic response to our changing Church and British Society. This chapter attempts to demonstrate that its issues are the issues of the Christian Church and a multi-cultural society and that much can be learned about other faiths in Catholic schools by reflection on this particular educational experience.

The Recent History of St Philip's RC Sixth Form College

In 1976 St Philip's Catholic Boy's Grammar School became the first Sixth Form College (i.e., a college for students between the ages of 16 and 18) in the city and until now the only one in the diocese of Birmingham, with the approval of and under the trusteeship of the Oratory Fathers, Birmingham. The college continued to operate on the site of the old grammar school on land held in trust by the Oratory Fathers next to the Oratory. From that date up until 1987 the college received students from the Catholic feeder schools in Birmingham and an increasing number of students from other Birmingham secondary schools. The student intake began to represent the cultural and faith diversity found within the inner city and suburbs of Birmingham.

In 1987 the Oratory Fathers as foundation governors of the college informed the staff of their desire to close the college giving their reason that the low percentage of Catholics in the college was insufficient to maintain its Catholic character. This move was resisted by parents and staff under the then principal, Dr John Guy. As a result the college remained open but the trustees handed responsibility for the appointment of governors over to the Diocesan Schools Commission who could act on their behalf. During this time the college expanded in numbers to an annual average of 900 students, developed a wide range of academic and vocational courses and piloted a large number of educational initiatives which culminated in 1992 with the awarding of the prestigious Schools Curriculum Award for links with the local community.

The Interfaith Experience

Thus in February 1992 St Philip's was a successful, over-subscribed college offering courses for academic A-level students as well as those who had experienced very little previous academic success. An approximate breakdown of the student intake at that time was 32 per cent Catholic; 15 per cent other Christian; 18 per cent Muslim; 9 per cent Sikh; 5 per cent Hindu; 3 per cent Buddhist; some Jewish students and 15 per cent with no religious affiliation. Every student in the college was required to take one period of general religious education or personal education programme per week. Also A-Level religious studies had developed into an extremely popular subject with over sixty students taking it at examination level with options in Islam and Sikhism as well as the traditional Christian courses in philosophy of religion and New Testament studies.

The Department of Theology and Religious Education had developed a mission statement and articulated aims, processes and objectives which they considered educationally appropriate for the particular context.[1] This mission statement reads,

> As the Theology and Religious Education Department within a Roman Catholic College, our aims are based on the Gospel concern for the entire human community and a recognition of our place within it. This universal concern is grounded in an awareness of the many faiths and worldviews represented within the college and aims to support each member of the college community in making sense of their human existence.

Among the aims are

- to help students and staff make sense of their human existence by examining their own beliefs and the beliefs of others;
- the encouragement of the college community to explore ultimate questions especially questions of truth and justice; and

- the promotion of unity, dialogue, understanding and a respect for people's beliefs in our multi-racial and secular society.

There was also a great emphasis on issues of process, group interaction and allowing students some negotiating power over their own learning and participation.

A balance was attempted between valuing the students sufficiently to allow them the freedom to express their own views and encouraging a process of critical reflection on those views and on the views of others. In other words, initial exercises in trust building among the group (which always included the teacher!) allowed the students to express ideas without the fear of being put down or ridiculed. However, once the group had developed a degree of trust and acceptance of the person, the dialogue enabled each person to comment on the views of others from his or her own perspective and, at its best, to reflect on their own standpoint from the perspective of the other.

Fatima (Muslim) I can't question my faith as if I did I would lose everything and I wouldn't know who I am.

Jane (Church of England) That seems to me to show very little faith in your religion.

Fatima I have enough faith in Islam to stop me from needing to question.

Jane Faith is only important if you have thought it through for yourself. I think God is in everything . . . at least, that's what I think.

[One week later]

Jane Fatima and I are different. She doesn't question her faith and I do. But I am more confused; she has more contentment and peace than I have.

[Two weeks later]

Jane I can't stand being preached at; I want to be free to decide for myself.

Fatima But how can you know anything unless you hear it preached?

[Later, Fatima recorded her own personal faith journey as a result of this and similar classroom dialogues.]

Fatima Personally, I felt angry not at my friend but at myself because I was faced with a question that I did not answer logically and did not truly *face*. I just couldn't come to terms with this and so pushed it into the background. I did not even realize at the time that this very lesson would haunt me for a very long time.

[Several months later]

Fatima The subject Philosophy of Religion has obviously thrown up some questions which are very difficult to give an overall answer to but which require personal opinion. It is here that I am finding the most difficulty and I am still searching. But one thing I was scared of [and now

I realize why I would never face the issue of questioning] was losing faith in not only Islam but in God. After the inner turmoil I am now beginning to see things more clearly. I now have reason to say *why* I believe in God and *why* I practice my religion.

When trust built up between the group, and students came to feel that their views and faith backgrounds were respected, many students actually came to look forward to their RE lessons as being different from the other classes, where you could be yourself, learn about others and often get into a good healthy argument which might spill over into the corridor or student common room at lunchtime. There was a strong feeling among most of the staff that the social interaction and resulting cohesiveness and cultural aware-ness fostered by the general religious education/personal education programme was at the centre of the college's success in creating a friendly atmosphere within which the wider problems of society could be safely addressed, if not solved, within the college (see Pontifical Council for Interreligious Dialogue and the Congregation for the Evangelization of Peoples, 1991). One student wrote about these lessons shortly before leaving college,

To appreciate other people and take them for what they are, not to enforce your ideas down their throats but to listen and to understand the root of their ideas and then to discuss why you disagree, is one very large step in making yourself a more tolerant person which is the most important quality in an individual today.

Another interesting development within the college in recent years was the growth of a chaplaincy team from among the staff and coordinated by the lay college counsellor. This team was made up of interested staff and sisters and Jesuit novices from outside the college. As each contributed according to their particular interests and talents a range of activities flourished; retreats, meditation workshops, inter-faith encounter, individual counselling and spir-itual guidance, 'development days', creative liturgies. Interestingly, although almost all of this team was Catholic, students from all the faiths within the college were drawn to participate in many of the activities, especially the meditation or 'Sadhana' week. One Hindu student commented, 'This is great. Normally I have to pay for meditation lessons!'

A further initiative which provides an insight into the nature of the col-lege came directly from the students themselves. Following an initial Christian/ Muslim student encounter, where some Christians displayed anti-Muslim and racist attitudes, a group of Muslim students invited Christian students to enter into regular dialogue so that they could overcome mutual misunderstanding and increase religious tolerance. These meetings attracted an average of twenty-five students but the first meetings were extremely tense and difficult as each group felt the need to project a positive image of their own religion while being extremely critical of the other. Although male and female students were almost equally represented, only the male students took part in these heated exchanges while the female participants could be seen building bridges and following up discussions after the meetings. Their concern was for a harmonious process within the meetings rather than the resolution of doctrinal issues. Eventually when the group was on the verge of disintegration this concern won the day and the group agreed to share and listened to each person's personal faith journeys where no-one represented the whole of any religious tradition but took responsibility for their own particular faith journey and allegiance. Now the group is attended by students of all faiths and none, sharing is at a personal level and most of the participants are female! Leaders from within this group have gone on to contribute to inter-faith conferences throughout the city and some have represented Birmingham as part of a youth team at a series of interfaith meetings in India in 1993.

The Consequences

In February 1992 the Oratory Fathers, as trustees of the college, did not renew the contracts of the foundation governors appointed by the diocese and selected a new set of foundation governors. These new governors expressed a preference to close the college rather than to bring it into the Further Education sector the following April. Their reason was that, given the low percentage of Catholic students in the college, just over 30 per cent, they could not fulfil the Trust Deeds of the institution which was 'for the education, both religious and secular, of children and other persons, in accordance with the principles of the Roman Catholic Faith.' (FEFC, 1994a).

This argument was further developed in, 'St Philip's Roman Catholic Sixth Form College: A Statement from the Provost of the Birmingham Oratory and from the Chairman of Governors'.[2] It argued that what was distinctive about a Catholic school was the handing on of the Catholic faith within a predominantly Catholic community centred on Catholic worship. Two quotations provide some insight into the authors' views on what was happening in the college.

> But it is pointless to teach young people about other faiths unless they already know their own faith well, or else confusion is the result.

> Yet in a college where young people of many different faith and cultural backgrounds mingle freely with each other, religion of any kind is more likely to be a casualty than a winner.

As a result they concluded,

> We want to take this opportunity to renew and revitalize a Catholic school which has all but lost its Catholic identity.

243

Following this announcement a massive public campaign to save the college was launched by the staff, parents, students and Catholic groups in solidarity with the spiritual and social aims of the college.[3] This campaign was conducted at local and national levels both within the Catholic Church and in the wider political arena. Michael Walsh's Article 'The Battle of St Philip's', gives a history of the development of the situation to that point and the issues involved (Walsh, 1992). Gerard W. Hughes' article 'Shades of the Ghetto' provides a theological critique of the statement from the Provost and Chair of Governors which challenges not only their concept of a Catholic school but also their theological assumptions which underpin it (Hughes, 1992). It is interesting to note the groups and individuals which entered into this public debate and those which refrained from doing so. The local and national Catholic Associations for Racial Justice, the headmasters of Birmingham's Catholic Partnership, several members of the religious orders and the Birmingham Interfaiths Council all supported the campaign to save the college.[4] Nothing was heard in public from the Diocesan Schools Commission, the Diocesan Catechetical Centre, the Archbishop of Birmingham or any member of the Bishops' Conference.

A very revealing incident took place during the period of the campaign to save the college. The Muslim students had been given permission by the senior management of St Philips to use the college chapel for prayers during Ramadan. On Ash Wednesday were seen by one of the governors the Muslim students assembling for prayer and the next day the principal informed the staff in writing that 'in accordance with the Trust Deeds of the college, no permission for non-Catholic acts of worship could be given within the college.' The Muslim students held an extremely disciplined meeting during which they decided that their need to pray was greater than their need to have permission to pray and that they would continue to fulfil their religious obligations. The turning point in this dignified discussion came when a student asked the group to consider what would be the reaction of Muslim parents if they received a letter saying that their child had been suspended from college for praying during Ramadan! Eventually it was officially decided that they could use rooms hired by the college but not on trustee land and the students agreed, their need to pray now taking precedence over their need for prayer to be conducted within the boundaries of the college. The staff were incensed at this decision as they considered it to be a restriction of religious freedom contrary to the ethos which they were trying to foster within the college (Swain, 1993).

At the time of writing, the campaign to save St Philip's as a Roman Catholic College providing a form of education appropriate for modern Birmingham is ongoing. The public Government enquiry has described the governance and management of the college as 'seriously defective' and the Further Education and Funding Council has recommended to the Secretary of State for Education that the entire Governing Body be removed and replaced (FEFC, 1994b). Most significantly, an additional recommendation of the report was for a change in the legislation covering all designated or voluntary-aided institutions to make them more accountable and the FEFC advised the Secretary of State as follows;

> In the light of this case, the Department for Education should review the governance of other designated or voluntary aided institutions in the school as well as the further education sector so as to avoid the situation where a small body, independent of wider religious or other interests and inexperienced in management or education, has sufficient power over the appointment of governors to allow effective domination of the activities of the institution without sufficient regard being paid to the separate interests of the institution itself. (op. cit., 16b)

The Implications

The 'Battle of St Philip's' has become a major issue both within the Catholic Church and on a wider national level. I believe that it has done so not only because the questions raised by this particular situation are those which are also fermenting within the Church and society in general. The consultation referred to in Chapter 15 makes that clear. Why St Philip's has become and remains a national issue is fundamentally due to the commitment of the staff to campaigning, in solidarity with like minded groups and individuals, for a vision of education in which they profoundly believe. The implications of the case of St Philip's are to do with power and accountability as much as with issues of proportionality, Catholic Education and a multi-faith society. I propose to address these issues in the form of three questions:

- How many Catholics does it take to make education Catholic?
- What is the relationship between Catholic education and the Church's broader mission in the inner city?
- Within the dual system, what are the responsibilities and boundaries of power and accountability within Catholic education?

How Many Catholics Does It Take to Make Education Catholic?

The foundation governors of St Philip's argued that due to the low percentage of Catholics in the college they could no longer provide an education in accordance with the principles of the Roman Catholic faith; secondly that this also made it impossible to provide appropriate religious education for the Catholic students and finally that this had led to the college all but losing its Catholic identity.

I will look at each of these in turn. First, let us consider the argument of low Catholic percentages and the inability to provide an education in accordance with the principles of the Roman Catholic faith. The statement from the Provost and Chair of Governors states,

> A Catholic School is set up to assist the Catholic community in the process of handing on the knowledge and practice of the Faith to the next generation.

This is a concern that the Catholic staff of St Philip's would share wholeheartedly but it is how these principles are to be interpreted in practice which is at the heart of the debate. Both governors and staff would acknowledge that the basic principles of the Catholic faith are adherence to the Gospel and the traditions of the Church. The Gospel and the tradition of the Church as most recently expressed in the Documents of the Second Vatican Council honour equally the twin values of building up the community of faith and having a mission in the world (see Chapter 16 in this volume). No Catholic community exists just for itself but to fulfil the Church's mission of love and justice in the world. What applies to the mission of the Church in general, applies in each particular dimension of its activity including education. Education is not only for belonging but also, and at the same time, for mission. The very purpose of being an educational community of faith is to become 'the salt of the earth' and 'the light of the world'. Both of these tasks have been attempted, however imperfectly, in St Philip's, the former by the many opportunities for retreats, prayer counselling and a pastoral system which puts the person at the centre of the problem and not the problem at the centre of the person. The outward mission is fulfilled by providing educational opportunities for those on the margins, treating every student as a child of God as a result of their creation (not baptism) and acknowledging the presence of God in all faiths and individuals (Congregation for Catholic Education, 1977; Abbott, 1966).

All of this was put more simply by 16-year old Helen Myers in a lesson where the group were asked to prioritize the aims of religious education from a given list. In order of importance they gave:

1 developing one's own ideas and values;
2 creating a harmonious multi-faith society;
3 learning about other people's faiths;
4 teaching Christian ideals and values; and
5 teaching people morals.

Playing devil's advocate the teacher asked how Catholic parents might feel about sending their child to a school with these priorities. Helen immediately became very excited and exclaimed, 'But the first three *are* the Christian ideals and values.'

The second strand of the governors' argument is that a proper religious education cannot be provided to Catholics in the presence of many students from other faiths. Given that the college admits students in late adolescence the works of James Fowler on faith development and Erik Erikson on identity formation can shed some light on the educational issues involved. The governors are concerned with 'handing on the knowledge and practice of the Faith to the next generation' but handing on has as much to do with how students receive as it has to do with how teachers give (Segundo, 1992, pp. 244–7). How students appropriate 'the Faith' that is being handed on can be analysed in terms of personal faith development. Fowler claims that there are six stages in faith development, the most relevant for late adolescence being Stage 3, 'Synthetic/Conventional Faith', and Stage 4, 'Individual/Reflective Faith' (Fowler, 1987, pp. 53–71). Stage 3 is a 'conformist stage' in the sense that it is acutely tuned to the expectations and judgments of significant others and as yet does not have a secure enough grasp of its own identity and autonomous judgment to construct and maintain an independent perspective. Religious authority is invested outside the individual in the congregation or religious authority figure. The person is totally inside the belief system and has not reflected on it from any distance. Stage 4, sometimes brought on by leaving home either physically or emotionally, begins to maintain a reflective distance from the belief system and to develop an inner source of authority which judges the external sources of authority in the light of the internally appropriated values of the belief system itself.

Fowler claims that the different faith communities and educational environments create their specific climate of developmental expectation which determines the average expectable stage of faith development of its members. Members are expected to reach but not go beyond the community's modal stage of development (op. cit., pp. 116–19). In stating that the aims of religious education at St Philip's are to help staff and students think critically and to make sense of their own existence, the educational community there explicitly encourages the students to reach the Individual/Reflective stage of faith development and provides the pastoral support necessary in making that transition. The fundamental educational issue here is not the simplistic one of retaining or abandoning allegiance to Catholicism, Islam, Sikhism etc. It rather touches on the more complex issue of the cognitive and emotional modes of belonging and believing, especially the relationship of the individual to the source of authority within the religious tradition. On a theological level it could be argued that all faith traditions require a free assent of the individual and that this educational process enhances the possibility of that free response (Hughes, 1986, pp. 14–37). Fatima ultimately came to see herself as a better Muslim by questioning her religion where that questioning involved both the possibility of doubting the tradition and also engaging with it in the search for meaning. She eventually came to an understanding of the truth of Gerry Hughes' profoundly spiritual claim that 'it is the nature of true faith to trust that God is at work in everything and that there is no question that falls outside the scope of religious enquiry' (Hughes, 1985, p. 17).

One extremely interesting outcome of this educational approach was observed when a class, who by this time had been in college for almost two years, came to discuss how women were treated within different religions. Each member of the group was simply asked to give a personal response to this in turn. Without exception and without any prompting from the teacher they each prefaced their comments by stating their own particular religious upbringing and how they stood in relation to it at that time, e.g., 'I was brought up as a Catholic, but I'm not sure now', 'I am a practising Sikh.' Each accepted personal responsibility for their views while acknowledging the influences and allegiances that had helped to form them.

A brief classroom discussion on Fowler's theory might provide some insight into the theme of faith development which has underpinned the conflict at St Philip's and which might benefit from being brought closer to the surface.

Student Our parents wouldn't agree with education for Stage 4. They would say that if you are doing that you are losing the faith.

Teacher And in a sense that would be right. You would be losing the faith as something outside yourself which you accept unquestioningly. However you would not see yourself as losing faith as you moved to Stage 4.

Student But for them you ARE losing the faith as they understand it.

This raises a question for the Catholic Church and the role of education within it. 'To what level of faith development do we want to bring our young people?' And perhaps we need to ask a further, more painful, question. 'If many young people are becoming disillusioned with Church life and worship, is it because they are losing faith or because they are growing in it?'

Erik Erikson talks of late adolescence as the period of identity formation when all that has been received from family and close groupings is tested against the range of ideologies and world views which are increasingly seen to be offered as a basis for forging a meaningful way of life (Erikson, 1971, pp. 128–35). James Marcia outlines four possible stages of identity development; foreclosure, where the total received identity is accepted unquestioningly; moratorium, where all forms of adult identity become available for choice at a later date; diffusion, an unresolved state of identity crisis; and identity achievement which can only follow a period of moratorium (Patterson, Sochting and Marcia, 1992, pp. 10–14). The issue for Catholic education is whether the Church prefers identity characterized by foreclosure in which case it would be desirable to prevent 'young people of different faith and cultural backgrounds mingling freely' or an identity which at least provides the opportunity for identity achievement subsequent to moratorium which is the actual stage of religious identity development of many young people in late adolescence in Britain (The Congregation of Catholic Education, 1977). In the context of a college where students from different faith backgrounds interact it is unlikely that many students will opt for a conversion to a totally different religious tradition. The author is only aware of one case in the last five years. However, exposure to the range of religious expression and commitment within this environment both within and beyond the Catholic faith community provides, for Catholic students, the possibility of choosing from within the range of Catholic identities available in today's Church. Reflection on external plurality aids the search for internal integrity while avoidance of its reality reinforces internal rigidity (Erikson, op. cit., pp. 74–90). One Catholic student wrote, 'My experience here has helped me realize why I am a Catholic. It's helped me understand my faith more, by listening and finding out about other people's faiths.'

The third argument of the governors' was that the small percentage of Catholic students makes it impossible to maintain the Catholic identity of the college. The question here might appear to be whether Catholic identity is formed in isolation from or in relation to other groups as discussed above. But when we observe that the staff and governors hold very different views on this, the focus shifts to two further issues. 'Who has the right to define Catholic identity for whom?' which I will address later and 'Which mode of identity formation is more in keeping with the role of the Church in the modern world?'

Pierre Buhler writes that Christian identity was traditionally defined by three criteria: which religious group one belonged to, what set of doctrinal beliefs this particular group professed and what moral codes it adhered to (Buhler, 1988, pp. 17–27). Identity was static and could be defined without reference to any outside markers. He argues that in a world of increasing religious interaction and understanding these criteria are being revised. Thus how one's group relates to another group becomes an essential element in that group's identity. Secondly the professed religious beliefs are, and need to be, tested for intelligibility beyond the internal parameters of the enclosed belief system. Thirdly, the moral codes as well as maintaining an internal coherence must be judged on how they actually improve the human condition. Identity places itself under the scrutiny of inter-subjectivity, doctrinal relevance and moral relevance. It becomes essentially relational in character.

An example of how the latter understanding of religious identity actually worked itself out in practice at St Philip's was given by Muslim, Christian and Sikh students from the interfaith group when they wanted to make it better known by means of a full college assembly. They decided to address directly the reality of religious intolerance within the college which had spurred the group into existence. Firstly they presented a sketch which re-enacted the previous meeting in which Christians had expressed racist and anti-Muslim comments. It was surprisingly difficult to get volunteers to act as the 'racists' as students feared they would be labelled as such following the assembly. Then a Christian read 1 Corinthians 13, 4–7 on the nature of Christian love. There followed another sketch based on a previous meeting between Christians and Muslims where the Muslims highlighted and the Christians reluctantly acknowledged the imbalance between the Muslims' knowledge of Christianity and the Christians' knowledge of Islam. Re-enacting the original exchange, one young Muslim woman calmly addressed the Christians, 'As long as you admit that you are ignorant, that is the first step; we can go from there.' Then a Muslim gave an anti-racist reading from the Qur'an 49, 13 and a Sikh read from the Sikh Japji on human equality. An open invitation to the weekly interfaith meetings was extended to all the staff and students. The assembly finished with a quotation from Jonathan Swift, 'Mankind has enough religion to make them hate each other but not enough to make them love each other.'

Reflecting on the issues arising out of the events at St Philip's, the Catholic Church in England and Wales is faced with a choice. Will it continue to retreat behind barriers, institutional and educational, which will indeed forge a strong sense of group identity for those who choose to remain behind them but at the cost of their relationships with other people of faith, or will they confidently and in trust allow young people to find God within their own tradition by seeing the face of God mirrored within the deep spirituality of others? One can only hope that the invitation implicit within the commissioning by the Bishops of the consultation described in Chapter 15 will encourage Catholics to follow the latter path.

Catholic Education and the Mission of the Church to the Inner City

Another important issue raised by this debate is the relationship between the aims of Catholic education and the role of the Church in the inner city. Many inner city Catholic schools are now admitting a dwindling number of Catholic students yet their rolls remain high due to the popularity of the schools among other faith communities. If one follows the argument of St Philip's governors, these schools should be closed as they can no longer fulfil their educative task properly. If, however, an active concern for social justice is not only something which the school prepares people for, but is at the very heart of the institution's actual mission and structures, then remaining in the inner city with its challenge of working for those most on the margins and the opportunity which often accompanies it of being enriched by the faiths often found there, then these schools will remain open and flourish (Congregation for Catholic Education, op. cit., no. 8 and no. 30; Pontifical Commission, 1989, no. 28). The emphasis shifts beyond the concept of providing 'an education for the Catholic community' to incorporate the Post Vatican II understanding of mission as also providing 'a Catholic education for the community'. While it is possible to make a logical distinction between education for justice and education for interfaith understanding, the reality is that commitment to the former will often incorporate the latter as a necessary form of 'acting justly' in Britain's bigger cities. One St Philip's teacher remarked that if the college was allowed to close, then the Catholic Church's urban policy should be entitled, 'Faith in the suburbs'.

Power and Accountability within Catholic Education

The crisis at St Philip's developed because of certain unresolved (and unresolvable?) tensions within its structural and educational context. The first tension resides within the very nature of the dual system in British Education (whereby Catholic schools are supported from public funds) and the second arose out of the changing nature of the Post Vatican II Roman Catholic Church in England and Wales. I would suggest that the partnership between the Roman Catholic Church and State in Britain needs to be seriously reviewed in the light of the St Philip's affair (White, 1994). At the moment the assumption which underpins the partnership seems to be that there is a common, neutral 'core' in the educational process, sometimes referred to as the academic curriculum, which Church and State schools tackle in roughly the same manner. In addition the Catholic schools can then nurture Catholic values within a more 'spiritual environment'. The proportion of state and Church funding at least for non grant maintained Catholic schools reflects the distinction between common, academic objectives and unique educational aims reflecting Catholic/Christian values.

From the Catholic perspective, this arrangement had resulted in most Catholics believing that, given their 15 per cent contribution to capital funding, they have the right to confine the educational activity of Catholic schools to the spiritual and moral developments of the Catholic community. However, it might be argued that this 15 per cent set against the contribution from the wider community only gives the right to make a specific Catholic contribution to the shared task of educating *all* our children and that this contribution must recognize and respond to the needs of the wider community. The demands of Christian mission and the needs of society meet at the point where Catholics receive their agenda of service from the world. Neither education in the state sector nor in the Catholic sector are value -free and in accord with the biblical insight 'By their fruits shalt thou know them' these values are discovered in action rather than in policy and mission statements. Ideology is a verb, not a noun. Not all the actions of the Catholic Church reflect the values of the Kingdom of God just because they are actions of a Church and not all actions of the State are outside the plan of God just because they claim to be secular. The criteria of evangelization are the degree to which actions are 'good news' in an actual, historical and social sense for those on whose behalf it is claimed that these actions are taken (Segundo, 1984, pp. 16–20). The implications of this are that when the Church claims the right to challenge the State when it perceives it to be acting unjustly or unfairly, e.g., in the case of 'opted-out' grant maintained schools, it might also accept being challenged when the State's educational values and policy more deeply reflect the Gospel commitment to justice and harmony than its own current practice. Due procedure in educational management and 'encouraging respect for those holding different beliefs' might be two issues where the signs of the Kingdom are more evident outside rather than within the boundaries of the Roman Catholic Church in England and Wales (DFE, 1994). Many Catholic educationalists might fear a loss of autonomy arising out of the proposed change in legislation following the Government enquiry into the governance and management of St Philip's. An emotional but perhaps justified response to the proposal came from a priest who had risked much in the campaign to save the college. 'If the Catholic Church can't keep its own house in order, then maybe the Government will have to do it for them.'

This last point leads on to the tensions within the Roman Catholic Church itself thirty years from the end of Vatican II. As always, these tensions are not only theological but involve power, authority and decision making. We might have equal right to hold our various theological perspectives but we do not have equal access to putting the implications of these views into practice (Boff, 1985, Ch. 4, p. 42). The consequences of Vatican II are now becoming all too apparent. Many highly professional, theologically aware lay educators are working, often in partnership with religious orders, to develop forms of education which value the whole person and the demands of social justice. The source of their authority is their training, experience of difficult educational situations and their professionalism; it is authoritative. On the other hand, it is the bishop within each diocese who is responsible for the provision of Catholic education and only rarely is education his specialist area of ministry or expertise. In the case of St Philip's College, the conflicting perceptions of the governors and staff in relation to the college arose out of vastly differing experiences of the reality of college life. The governors would certainly feel that the exercise of their power was both legitimate and necessary to preserve what is important to them but their public analysis of the college just did not correspond with the staff's own reality which informed their views on Catholic education. In the light of the different experiences and consequent perceptions by which the staff and governors arrived at their conclusions, perhaps the central themes of Liberation Theology are being revisited and reworked in a debate whose deepest issue is not competing models of Catholic education but who has the right to conceptualize and develop those models. 'The Battle of St Philip's' is not just about what form of education will emerge, it is about what form of Church (Segundo, 1988, Ch. 1, pp. 7–9). A lot can be learned from how the young people of the St Philip's interfaith group eventually dealt with the reality of conflict and the desire for unity.

Notes

1   See 'Mission Statement, Aims and Objectives of the Department of Theology and Religious Education at St Philip's RC Sixth Form College', Copies available from the College, Hagley Road, Birmingham, B16 8UF.
2   See *St Philip's Roman Catholic Sixth Form College: A Statement from the Provost of the Birmingham Oratory and from the Chairman of Governors*, 3 October 1992. Available from St Philip's College.
3   See *St Philip's is a Successful Roman Catholic College*: A response from the Staff of St Philip's Roman Catholic Sixth Form College to the Statement, dated 3 October, from the Provost of the Birmingham Oratory and from the Chairman of Governors of St Philip's Roman Catholic College, 15 October 1992. Available from the College.
4   See a letter from the Birmingham Branch of the Catholic Association for Racial Justice to the Governors of St Philip's, dated 29 September 1992, available from the College and comments by the National Director of the Catholic Association for Racial Justice as reported in M. White (1994).

'The Future of St Philip's Sixth Form College', a statement by Birmingham's Catholic Partnership, dated 8 October 1992 and signed by all the secondary heads within the Partnership. Available from the College.

A motion was passed unanimously at the AGM. of the Birmingham Interfaiths Council in October 1992 praising St Philip's for its contribution to interfaith relations within the city and calling on the Governors to reverse their closure decision.

References

ABBOTT, W. (1966) *Decree on the Relation of the Church to Non-Christian Religions (Nostrae Aetate)*, London.

BOFF, L. (1985) *Church, Charism and Power: Liberation Theology and the Institutional Church*, London, SCM Press.

BUHLER, P. (1988) 'Christian identity: Between objectivity and subjectivity', in DUQUOC, C. and FLORISTAN, C. (Eds), *Concilium*, Edinburgh, T and T Clark.

CONGREGATION FOR CATHOLIC EDUCATION, *The Catholic School*, 1977.

DEPARTMENT FOR EDUCATION (1994) Circular No. 1/94, *Religious Education and Collective Worship*, London, HMSO.

ERIKSON, E.H. (1971) *Identity, Youth and Crisis*, London, Faber and Faber.

FEFC (1994a) 'The trust deed of the oratory of St Philip Neri in Birmingham', in CAINES, J. (Ed) *St Philip's Roman Catholic Sixth Form College: Report of an Enquiry into the Governance and Management of the College*, Coventry, The Further Education Funding Council, Annex C, Section C, p. 79.

FEFC (1994b) *Advice to the Secretary of State on the Government and Management of St Philip's Sixth Form College*, Press Release, 17 November, **3**, **7**.

FOWLER, J.W. (1987) *Faith Development and Pastoral Practice*, Philadelphia, Fortress Press.

HUGHES, E.J. (1986) *Wilfred Cantwell Smith: A Theology for the World*, London, SCM Press.

HUGHES, G.W. (1985) *The God of Surprises*, London, Darton, Longman and Todd.

HUGHES, G.W. (1992) 'Shades of the ghetto', *The Tablet*, 7 November, pp. 1396–7.

PATTERSON, S.J., SOCHTING, I. and MARCIA, J. (1992) 'The inner space and beyond: Women and identity', in ADAMS, G.R., GULLOTTA, T.P. and MONTEMAYOR, R. (Eds) *Adolescent Identity Formation*, Newbury Park, CA, Sage.

PONTIFICAL COMMISSION 'IUSTITIA ET PAX' (1989) *The Church and Racism; Towards a More Fraternal Society*, **28**, Sherbrooke, QC, Australia, Editions Paulines.

PONTIFICAL COUNCIL FOR INTERRELIGIOUS DIALOGUE and THE CONGREGATION FOR THE EVANGELIZATION OF PEOPLES (1991) *Dialogue and Proclamation: Reflections and Orientations on Interreligious Dialogue and The Proclamation of the Gospel of Jesus Christ*, Vatican City.

SEGUNDO, J.L. (1984) *Faith and Ideologies*, London, Sheed and Ward.

SEGUNDO, J.L. (1988) *The Liberation of Theology*, New York, Orbis Books.

SEGUNDO, J.L. (1992) *The Liberation of Dogma*, New York, Orbis Books.

SWAIN, H. (1993) 'Priests ban prayers at city college', *The Birmingham Post*, March.

THE CONGREGATION FOR CATHOLIC EDUCATION (1990) *The Religious Dimension of Education in a Catholic School*, Homebush, Australia, St Paul's Publications, Part I.

WALSH, M. (1992) 'The battle of St Philip's', *The Tablet*, 10 October, pp. 1261–2.

WHITE, M. (1994) 'Who governs the governors', in the *Catholic Herald*, 25 November.

Part 4

Catholic Schools: The Way Forward

Chapter 18

Renewing Teaching: Building Professional Communities of Hope and Inquiry

Catherine A. Lacey R.S.C.J.

This chapter focuses upon the renewal of those central to the work of Catholic education — the teachers. It argues that to the extent that teachers within Catholic schools act out of the depth of their own tradition and develop communities powerful enough to sustain the ongoing critique and transformation of their personal and communal practice, they can construct and, in turn, make the public contribution of truly imaginative alternatives to the norms of educational practice.

In order to do a prophetic work, however, Catholic educators must cultivate habits of critical analysis and hope. By examining a case study of a group of teachers — the Faculty Development Committee (FDC) of the Network of Sacred Heart Schools — this chapter explores concrete ways of supporting teachers in the building of strong communities of inquiry. Specifically, I explore how this committee of teachers has utilized narrative language and narrative analysis in its processes and planning to bring teachers' experiences and knowledge into articulate form and to collaboratively 'read' the texts created to inform its work. I have been researching the growth and development of this committee as an 'insider' since its inception (1988) in collaboration with an 'outsider' researcher, Jean M. Bartunek, R.S.C.J., Department of Organizational Studies, Boston College.

This is sometimes messy and painful work, since narratives are about trouble and content is brought to the worktable which is generally excluded in US workplaces. The chapter explores how the group's intentional use of narrative language strengthens the resolve of this community committed to an alternate vision of educational practice. Utilizing some metaphors of scripture scholar Walter Brueggemann (Brueggemann, 1991) to organize the analysis, I examine how the use of 'exodus' stories of 'pain and rescue' makes the discomfort of the teaching profession that is normally repressed available for public processing, evokes in the community a 'sacred discontent' with the dominant social order, and engenders 'new social proposals' of alternative social practice within the community as well as for wider publics.

The Challenge

The renewal of teaching is critical to the reconstruction of education — Catholic or otherwise — for the teacher stands at the crucial juncture of theory and practice. Daily, a teacher exercises very real power in interpreting culture for the twenty or eighty or 120 students who spend hours in his or her classroom. For in constructing a course unit or syllabus, a teacher determines whose story gets told and what body of knowledge gets valued. In organizing a classroom and using language within it, the teacher establishes norms of relationship and of communication. In reading texts and interpreting ideas, the teacher fosters patterns of thinking and privileges certain modes of inquiry and decision making. And in evaluating students' work, the teacher lets students know the acceptable range of self-expression and behaviour (Lacey, 1991; Lacey, Wood and Bartunek, 1990).

Yet we know that even as teachers act powerfully to shape cultural norms within the privacy of their classrooms, teachers and their classroom are powerfully shaped by the dominant norms of the field of education and of the broader culture (Weiler, 1988). In fact, far from asking elementary and secondary teachers to be creators of culture, much of the literature in the field of education asks teachers to be replicators of effective behaviours as defined by outside experts. And many of the products of the field ask teachers to be technicians not designers — implementors of teacher-proof curricula as designed by outside experts (Grumet, 1988; Schön, 1983). The broader culture, too, devalues the work of teachers, affording it low status both remuneratively and professionally.

Common sense tells us that in order to have liberated students we need liberated teachers, teachers skilled in analysing the constrictive forms of their own socialization and that of their curricula. As Grumet (1988) points out, this is especially important for the women who teach, for, although they constitute the majority of the profession in the United States, women are often excluded as both subject and object in the body of knowledge which constitutes the profession (Martin, 1982, 1985).[1] Ironically, these women most often stand in the ambiguous middle ground of teaching an academic canon which excludes the perspectives of women (and other marginal groups) (Belenky, Clinchy, Goldberger and Tarule, 1986; Keller, 1987; Martin, 1982; McIntosh, 1984), utilizing a pedagogical style of exposition and argumentation which favours traits genderized in western culture in favour of males (Martin, 1985), and assuming psychologies of development which rest on male-derived norms (Gilligan, 1982; Miller, 1976). Further, the persistent maternal ethos of teaching still presses those who do this 'women's work' to be unadulterated vessels of transmission, exercising nineteenth century virtues of docility, domesticity, purity, and piety. They ought to labour quietly within fluid work boundaries, giving without measure and without thought of earthly recompense (Grumet, 1988). As teachers internalize these low status and gender-laden images, a group reporting low self-esteem and little professional confidence or critical perspective emerges (Herbst, 1989; Lightfoot, 1978; Lortie, 1975; Maeroff, 1988).

The reform rhetoric of the past decade, too, has its impact. Dominated by the language of market economics, much of contemporary public school reform rhetoric in the United States stresses higher standards, better quality control, and measurable outputs — all for the sake of national competitiveness in the global market (Bryk, Lee and Holland, 1993). Ignoring the moral and philosophical dimensions of education and trivializing its political and social purposes, this discourse urges minor ameliorative responses instead of the major reconceptualization of education needed to transform a culture in crisis (Purpel, 1989, 1991). Instead of capturing and mining the personal knowledge, moral vision and imagination of teachers in reconstructing education for a new social context, ameliorative reform efforts aimed at teachers in the United States often attempt to control them or, more generously, to raise their professional status through external prescriptions such as competency testing, more extensive evaluation, or merit pay. Even more recent reform efforts aimed at empowering teachers through more participation in local decision making often seem to result in a superficial involvement in administrative tasks rather than a deep critique and change of classroom practice (Bartunek *et al.*, 1991; Cuban, 1990; Johnson, 1990).

The Question

How will teachers be prophetic and artistic, offering open, fresh, critical perspectives on the artifacts of culture to their students (Bruner, 1986; Grumet, 1988)? I would like to argue with Madeleine Grumet (1988) and Donald Schön (1983), and in the epistemological tradition of Paulo Freire (1986) and Thomas Groome (1980), that teachers begin the process of creating rather than reproducing culture when they bring their own professional knowledge into articulate form and interpret its meaning with others in a community of inquiry. Through this kind of communal work from *within* the profession, teachers realize the power of what they know from experience, and gain the courage and the desire to challenge and change their practice (Lacey *et al.*, 1990; Rothman, 1993).

Finding forums for this type of teacher talk and analysis is difficult in a school organized bureaucratically (Hill, Foster and Gendler, 1990) and in a profession characterized by isolation and silence (Lieberman and Miller, 1990). Yet, without building such communities of interpretation, teachers and educators run the risk of uncritically accepting the canon of others and not questioning, indeed, forgetting their complicity in perpetuating the 'savage inequalities' (Kozol, 1991) which permeate schooling in the United States. As Walter Brueggemann (1991) puts it:

A hermeneutic there must be; and without intentionality, the dominant rationality will claim the field at high cost to our humanness. (ibid., p. 62)

Catholic schools stand at a distinct advantage in developing such a shared hermeneutic among teachers, for their faith-filled philosophies and their communal organizations provide both the impetus and the means for analysing and re-envisioning practice (Bryk, Lee and Holland, 1993; Hill *et al.*, 1990). In the past twenty years, many of these schools have radically transformed themselves, developing a communal hermeneutic to interpret the 'signs of the times' and to actualize within the limits of their resources the principles of Vatican II in school curricula, organization, and life. Bryk *et al.* (1993) argue that the creative products of this communal adventure in the United States have produced a system of schools which expose 'a broad, diverse cross section of students to a distinctive vision of active participation in a humane society' (p. 11).

However impressive this record, the work is far from done, for Bryk *et al.* (1993) point out that the 'domestic tranquility' (p. 162) of Catholic schools in the United States both enables and disables the mostly women who work within them.[2] On the positive side, teachers find both moral inspiration and an arena for dedicated teaching and ministry in the mission-driven ethos of the Catholic school. On the negative side, the very commitment that characterizes Catholic school teachers (Coleman and Hoffer, 1987) can be used to rationalize the low salaries offered and the extended responsibilities asked of them in many of these schools. The pain of some of these teachers at having to choose annually between leaving an environment which supports their best personal and professional ideals, on the one hand, and, on the other, accepting a contract which implicitly devalues their work by underpaying it can be keen. For women, this choice is further complicated by the ambiguity of assenting to a 'full' exercise of ministry in curricular and extracurricular activities within a community where they are not recognized as 'full' ministers because of gender. The silence that characterizes some of these paradoxes at the heart of Catholic school teaching does not bode well if Catholic educators are to meet the prophetic challenge of the next century.

In the rest of this essay, I would like to address directly the discomfort expressed by Bryk *et al.* (1993) at some of the ambiguities at the heart of the lives and work of Catholic school teachers in the United States and examine through a case study some of its implications. In order to frame the analysis, however, I would like to step back and explore some metaphors from scripture scholar Walter Brueggemann.

Scriptural Metaphors for Building Communities of Hope and Inquiry

Appealing to contemporary Christian communities to be truly distinctive in order to provide alternatives to the dominant social order, Brueggemann (1991) urges them to make intentional use of language to reclaim vision and imagination. Brueggemann speaks of two conversations: the conversation on the wall (the conversation of public negotiation in which the leaders of nations or parties count warheads, negotiate power, establish truth claims and terms of debate, and determine public policy); and, the conversation behind the wall (the conversation of the particular community in which a people remember their history, retell their stories, renegotiate the significance of past events for future activity, and renew hope and commitment in the moral vision of the community). Brueggemann asserts that, unless communities develop strong conversations behind the wall, they will not come to the wall as full conversational partners, leaving the disabling hegemonic assumptions of the conversation on the wall unquestioned.

Using the confrontation of the Assyrians with Judah recorded in 2 Kings 18, 1–27, Brueggemann explores the uses of these two kinds of language in a situation which I would posit is not very different from our own, at least in the United States. Jerusalem is under siege; there is a mismatch between an imperial power and a tiny kingdom without visible resources. On the wall of the city, the conversation concerns numbers of horses and men. Assyria sets the terms for surrender, claiming that given these realities, the God of the Israelites will never be able to save them this time. The king of Judah withdraws from the conversation on the wall to the temple. There, a different kind of talk reasserts Yahweh's care for the people. The people cry out to Yahweh with all of their stories of exodus, of pain and rescue, and room is made for the prophetic voice as Isaiah is called in to help the people interpret the situation. The king and his people find strength to return to the wall able to reclaim hope in Yahweh and meet the powerful Assyrians with 'unintimidated naiveté'. Indeed, Yahweh does wreak havoc among the Assyrians during the night, and Judah is saved from its enemy once again. The king, however, does not decimate the remaining Assyrians, but invites them to feast with the Israelites before wending their way home.

Brueggemann argues that an intentional language of community, i.e., narrative language, is needed to strengthen the conversation behind the wall if any group is to reclaim the moral vision so sorely needed for constructive conversation on the wall. By recounting and reinterpreting its personal and communal stories of pain and rescue, of oppression and emancipation, a community develops perceptions of reality that run counter to those of the dominant order. A healthy suspicion of existing social conditions emerges as the pain usually repressed in public forums is given voice. This cry of pain destabilizes and delegitimates the status quo — indeed, all is *not* well in our land. Once heard and publicly processed, which can only happen in a community which intentionally permits and validates the knowledge born of experience, the cry of the poor functions first to provide a basis for organizing the local community in an alternative way, and, in turn, to provide a basis for imaginative proposals of alternative social practice to the nations.

Catherine A. Lacey

The Network Faculty Development Committee as a Case Study

I find this threefold movement of cry/critique/alternative social practice both evocative and true to experience, and use it here to frame a brief discussion of the work of the Network Faculty Development Committee of the Sacred Heart Schools in the United States. The Network Faculty Development Committee (NFDC) is a committee of seven experienced teachers from across the United States concerned with the development of the 1,500 teachers (mostly women and mostly lay) of nineteen independent, mostly Catholic (one ecumenical), mostly single-sex schools for girls. These schools are bound together by a common philosophy of education articulated in *The Goals and Criteria for Sacred Heart Schools in the United States* and informed by the heritage and vision of the Society of the Sacred Heart.

The committee emerged from a Think Tank of experienced teachers who met in 1987 to consider how to 'pass the torch' of Sacred Heart education and how to renew a key resource in the network — the teachers with long-term commitment as Sacred Heart educators. Complaining that the Network seemed to be for administrators and for students but not for teachers, they wanted more than the occasional meeting for teachers. They wanted and submitted to the coordinator of the network a formal proposal for an organizational mechanism through which the teachers' perspectives and needs could find voice in the network.

Once constituted, the Network Faculty Development Committee (NFDC) took very seriously its mandate from the 'think tank' that had birthed it to stay close to teachers and to tap their knowledge and desires in developing any of its projects. Coming as they did out of several years of rich discourse in their local schools about actualizing a particular philosophy of education, the members of the NFDC brought a relatively sophisticated ear to the suggestions about process which I and a lay colleague, Diane Wood, brought to the group as co-chairs.[3] Two decisions agreed upon by the group after careful consideration are relevant:

1   to make intentional use of narrative in our committee work and in the design of any of our projects (e.g., designing teacher institutes, publishing a journal of teacher writing) as a way of ensuring that our work flowed from the experiential knowledge of teachers; and
2   to reflect on our practice as a group of teachers seeking to empower teachers by researching the growth and development of the committee through an insider/outsider collaboration.

(Wood and I would be the 'insider' researchers as founding leaders of the group; Jean Bartunek, Professor of Organization Studies of Boston College, would be the 'outsider' as a researcher of organizational change).[4]

The second point is relevant because the insider/outsider collaboration has 'institutionalized' reflection on practice in the group and produced a wealth of data for analysis for this essay and others. Wood and I kept extensive notes about our theories and subjective experience and understandings as leader/members of the committee. Bartunek attended committee meetings (four to five a year), observing and taking notes, taping and transcribing the reflection sessions at the end of each meeting, met with Wood and me and subsequent co-chairs before and after each meeting to elicit our implicit assumptions, and interviewed each other member of the committee before and after meetings to glean each one's experience and perspectives.

It is the first decision to make intentional use of narrative in group processes and decision making that I want to pursue here, arguing that its use in this case illustrates a powerful means of developing a professional community of hope and inquiry. The members of this group established a practice of beginning each of their meetings by sharing narratives of professional experience, and then using the personal knowledge that emerged from these stories to inform their work with other teachers. It is a conversation 'behind the wall' that has changed profoundly the way in which these teachers break through the isolation felt by teachers to find together the strength to name and interpret their experience of teaching; the way in which these teachers maintain solidarity with their peers and begin to examine critically and challenge the terms and definitions of the work of teaching; and the way in which they find the courage to act collaboratively in developing alternate forms of practice — in committee work, in designing institutes for teachers, in classroom teaching.

Use of Narrative to Ground Work in the Knowledge/ Concerns of Teachers

In the five years of its existence, the Network Faculty Development Committee has worked with an expanding circle of teachers and administrators to foster the development and implementation of teachers' proposals for their own professional development through a variety of forums: three national-level institutes bringing at least two teachers and, gradually, teams of teachers and administrators from each of the nineteen network schools together to consider pedagogy, methodology, and mentoring; annual issues of a journal of teacher writing privileging pieces with an integration of narrative and theoretical approaches; an electronic network for the nineteen schools; a guide for teachers new to the Network; and, the encouragement of faculty development committees and teacher research in local school settings.

Teachers comprise the NFDC, yet worry about keeping their work grounded in the knowledge and concerns of teachers. Since teachers often experience inservice and professional development activities as 'top–down' efforts to change them, they wanted to move in the opposite direction, continually returning to teachers to find out what they perceived to be helpful for their development. With others, I have written elsewhere (Lacey *et al.*, 1990;

Wood and Lacey, 1991) of the self-conscious efforts of members of the NFDC during their first year to keep in touch with the real world of teaching by narrating their own experience and making use of it in their planning with and for others. The sense that their own experience represents a microcosm of teacher experience in the Network has deepened over the years:

> it's almost as if for the first time I realized . . . that the narratives and the friendships and the relating and all that we do is a microcosm of what goes on in the schools. And the pain that we experience and share is an inscape . . . of the larger landscape, and that it's so important for us to know that that is our way of staying in touch with the teachers. And that that maybe works far better than a poll or a questionnaire. (Middle School Teacher, transcript of reflection on NFDC meeting of May 1993)

Verbalizing experience in narrative form effects a 'laboratory' in which the teachers can study their own practice:

> . . . the fact that we, almost like a laboratory group, have allowed ourselves to be open enough and almost conduits for the feelings of the teachers across the network, so that we experience them together and individually in a way that makes us very in touch with what's going on out there. (Middle School Teacher, transcript of reflection on NFDC meeting of May 1993)

Thus, teachers may use a story about a problem one of them had with an administrator to remind each other of the need to be sensitive to the perspectives of those who head the schools and to strategize for positive communication with them at all stages of their work with teachers. They might use a description of rupture in the faculty community of one of the schools to reassess the difference between collegiality which is 'true' and that which is 'contrived' (Mooney, 1992). Or they might recall and re-evaluate some of the darker moments of their own workings as a committee to remember the different expectations people bring to an innovation and the need to surface unexamined assumptions whenever possible (Bartunek, Lacey and Wood, 1992).

The use of narrative helps the NFDC build community as it attempts to widen the circle of its activity and influence. Each of the faculty institutes hosted by the NFDC for teachers from across the country is characterized by storytelling within the context of prayer and/or reflection on the practice of teaching. When a group of fifty strangers began a few days together in the summer of 1991 by talking about the 'one child' for whom they would have chosen a career in teaching in a network school all over again, powerful bonds of professional camaraderie were forged very quickly. Even the 'war stories' inevitably exchanged in groups of teachers lose their discouraging edge as teachers gradually realize that they are not alone in the uncertainty of their craft and begin to imagine what they might do together to renew their practice (Lacey *et al.*, 1990).

Use of Narrative to Build Community and Find Common Ground for Action

Not only does the articulation and examination of narrative material keep NFDC members in touch with issues of daily importance to teachers and to one another, it also helps them to build community and to theorize and formulate hypotheses for action in planning developmental opportunities for their peers:

> I was always thinking our bonding was important because a group that trusts one another, that was bonded, works better. But now I'm seeing it's even much more important than that . . . I think that's why this group works in a way that so many groups don't work, because other people don't allow themselves to be open and such conduits for all kinds of feelings and experiences, and understand them in the light of a larger context, and how it can influence the work that we do and the decisions we make and the way we design things, and so on. (Middle School Teacher, transcript of reflection on NFDC meeting of May 1993)

A specific example of how narration provides a background and frame for decision making might shed some light. At the beginning of the February meeting of the fourth year (1991–2) of the NFDC, one of the teachers told the story of what had happened at her school when she challenged a long-standing tradition that involved senior girls in a Maypole dance. The whole school became abuzz with people talking in very complex ways about what the ceremony meant or did not mean to them. Upon hearing this story, the NFDC members began to discuss practices in their own schools, analysing the ways in which some traditions (and their own implicit attitudes and 'teachings' about them) may be sending contradictory messages about femininity to the young women being educated within them.

The Maypole story receded to the background as the committee moved into the central task of their meeting, finalizing a five-year plan to implement proposals that had emerged from teachers in prior national institutes. As they built budgets for these proposals, NFDC members articulated some working principles, tentatively defined as 'feminist' by the group. For example:

- The NFDC wanted to communicate that teachers do valuable work; therefore, when teachers gathered to do work at an institute, they should receive a stipend.

- The NFDC wanted to make it possible for any teacher to attend an institute if he/she wished; therefore, money for care of dependents should be available.

The committee members knew that the practical implications of these principles were problematic; they broke the silence surrounding the budgeting norms of a network with limited funds. Unfortunately, the resources within the network which had supported projects like the NFDC's were shrinking, and efforts to raise funds for them from outside sources were proving difficult in light of the private, Catholic identity of the schools. If the NFDC, with its rising credibility within the network for affirming the work of teachers and increasing the ownership of their own development, argued 'on principle' that stipends and dependent care should be built into its (and others') budgets, difficult questions would be publicly aired. The NFDC had raised the issue before and knew the probable response of the oversight committee of administrators which received such proposals: 'If we give this type of funding to you, we would have to give it to everyone . . .' In a network characterized by communal rather than adversarial relations between teachers and administrators, the NFDC had to weigh the political advisability of placing the oversight committee in the awkward position of having to reject budget items so explicitly linked by the NFDC to the 'valuing' of teachers' work.

As the members of the NFDC considered this question, they referred back to the narrative told at the beginning of the meeting about the Maypole dance and the subsequent conversation about practices which have the potential to devalue women's lives and work. Their conviction grew as they linked the earlier discussion to the budget decision that they faced a small but critical opportunity to provoke broader discussion within the network about institutionalized norms which may well need critique. In the end, the NFDC did decide to raise the question once again by including the problematic items in the budget, but its application of the learning gained through the sharing of narratives seemed to lead it further. They took extensive time to develop a comprehensive, non-adversarial rationale for their action. In strategizing how to communicate their thinking more effectively, they looked for ways to underscore their awareness of the complexities of distributing scarce resources.

This instance can be viewed as an example of the way in which the sharing of stories provided the committee with knowledge that informed its work. The group's effort to interpret the significance of the Maypole narrative for everyday life in schools moved the committee beyond a therapeutic exercise in 'mutual consolation' (Grumet, 1988) to critical reflection and concrete action.

Although this budgetary incident in the life of a committee of teachers may seem of little consequence in the larger scheme of things, it touches upon one of the most sensitive issues facing Catholic schools in the United States: how to sustain moral vision in an era of diminishing commitment of financial resources to education. In the nineteenth century and early twentieth century, the Catholic school in the United States concentrated on protecting its immigrant students from the 'evils' of Protestantism and modernism with very limited resources indeed. By the mid-twentieth century, however, Catholic schools ascended to middle class status and sought to prepare students to exercise Catholic values as full members of America's democratic society. The next century presents a very different call — a prophetic one of witnessing to and, therefore, educating to alternative social practice. Can the Catholic school, now threatened with the loss of its secure place within a bourgeois context, maintain its sense of mission in the face of school reform talk which emphasizes a corporate rhetoric of efficiency and a political agenda of economic competitiveness? Can Catholic schools use limited resources in a way that balances mission and margin, negotiating the drive to make schools into 'good' businesses with the power of prophetic imagination and moral critique?

Use of Narrative to Critique and Change Practice

As the NFDC has grown in its experience in using narrative and the knowledge it produces in all of its processes, it has grown in its conviction that it has developed some truly alternate modes of collaboration and decision making. Knowing the power of these alternative practices in their own work, it wants to share the fruits of experience with others in the Network. Thus, when some of its members began to work with a group of administrators in the fall of 1992 to plan a third institute of teachers and administrators on mentoring in the network, they were at first excited by the promise of a new type of collaboration with administrators only to be subsequently dismayed with what they perceived to be the task-driven nature of the group. Judging that traditional rather than collaborative roles for teachers and administrators were being reinforced by the approach of the planning, they began to strategize about how they could constructively challenge the prevailing norms and influence a different practice. Consequently, when the whole NFDC and the corresponding committee of administrators met together in January of 1993 to address some of the questions and snags that had arisen in the planning group, the NFDC suggested beginning with narratives about positive mentoring experiences:

> I thought the meeting with the School Committee [representatives of network administrators] went really well even though we had all these apprehensions and were very nervous. You could tell that they were nervous, too. But I think everybody felt really at ease and as you heard each story you learned a lot about that person. And I really felt we are on the same track together. Why was I so worried about that? (Lower School Teacher, transcript of reflection on NFDC meeting of January 1993)

Not only did the sharing of stories help to re-establish common ground for action; it subsequently proved to transform the very design and processes of the very successful institute to follow.

Another area in which the NFDC has consistently revised practice during its five years of existence is that of leadership. Over the years, the group has built up a repertoire of 'stories of the group', and retells them in incorporating new members. This retelling leads to re-evaluation, and, in turn, to revision of *modus operandi*, particularly in the exercise of leadership in the group. Lacey *et al.* (1990), Bartunek *et al.* (1991), and Bartunek and Lacey (1993) describe the gradual change in the way members viewed the role and function of the chair(s) of the group. When the group began, the teachers in it viewed the first co-chairs as working 'magic', attributing to them the 'empowerment' they were experiencing as a participant in new processes (Lacey *et al.*, 1990). After reviewing the dynamics of the first leadership succession, the group breathed a sigh of relief that its new co-chairs had 'understood' the vision of the founding co-chairs (Lacey and Wood) and began to attribute the growing collaborative culture to the reflective processes of the group, the use of narrative among them (Bartunek *et al.*, 1991). However, the stories that emerged from rocky times in the group raised yet new questions about leaders and leadership, as the group wondered whether the designation of 'chair(s)', and the assignment of 'special' responsibilities to her (them) did not diminish true collaboration in the group (Bartunek and Lacey, 1993). Members suggested that roles, functions, and responsibilities rotate in the group so that each member would own each dimension of the successful functioning of the group and understand the necessity of truly common effort. The latter change in *modus operandi*, while not always the most efficient, continues to have profound effects on how the teachers see themselves as creating alternative modes of social practice and contributing them to the network in which they work.

Conclusion

This chapter has explored some ways in which the members of a faculty development committee makes intentional use of narrative to strengthen the conversation 'behind the wall' in order to change themselves and educational practices 'on the wall' at home and in broader spheres. I have tried to suggest that this kind of effort in and among communities of educators can be transformative, locality by locality.

Catholic schools in the United States face steep challenges in continuing to promote an empowered community of adults committed to social analysis and educational transformation for the common good. Given the decline in numbers of religious teachers, Catholic schools must be all the more intentional in seeking out ways to develop truly collaborative communities of hope and inquiry among lay and religious teachers of varied religious, philosophical, and cultural backgrounds. Given the pressures of market-driven educational reform and market-driven efforts at institutional survival in the United States, Catholic schools must be all the more intentional in witnessing to authentic alternative purposes and practices of schooling. And, given the ongoing struggle over the role of women in the ministry of the Catholic church, Catholic schools must be all the more intentional in promoting a community of critique and agency among women, with the ironic hope that they will disrupt and transform the very social conditions which marginalize them and others in the Catholic school, the Catholic church, and the field of education. This conversation 'behind the wall' does not promise to be comfortable, but it may well cultivate prophecy in a country hungry for meaning and in great need of modes of approaching moral cohesion.

Notes

1   In 1987–88, over 70 per cent of all secondary and elementary teachers in the United States and 78 per cent of private school teachers were female (US Department of Education, 1992).
2   The US Department of Education (1992) reports that in Catholic schools 1987–8, 91 per cent of parochial school teachers, 78 per cent of diocesan school teachers, and 68 per cent of private, religious order school teachers were women.
3   At the founding of the committee (1988), I was in the third year of doctoral study after 18 years of teaching and administration in various schools of the Network. Diane Wood had been working in the Network for five years as a teacher and director of studies; she has subsequently begun doctoral study.
4   Although Bartunek is a Religious of the Sacred Heart, she has not worked within the Network of Sacred Heart Schools or on the elementary/secondary level of schooling for over twenty years. She brings the outsider perspective of a university-based social science researcher.

References

BARTUNEK, J.M., GALOSY, J.A., LACEY, C.A., LIES, B.B. and WOOD, D.R. (1991) 'Leadership succession in a group formed to empower its members,' in *Proceedings of the Eastern Academy of Management*, Hartford, CT, Eastern Academy of Management, pp. 252–5.
BARTUNEK, J.M. and LACEY, C.A. (1993) 'The role of narrative in a workgroup intervention to confront alcoholism,' Paper presented at the conference on Inquiries in Social Construction, Durham, NH, June.
BARTUNEK, J.M., LACEY, C.A. and WOOD, D.R. (1992) 'Social cognition in organizational change: An insider–outsider approach,' *Journal of Applied Behavioral Science*, **28**, pp. 204–23.
BRUEGGEMANN, W. (1991) *Interpretation and Obedience: From Faithful Reading to Faithful Living*, Minneapolis, Fortress Press.
BELENKY, M.F., CLINCHY, B.V., GOLDBERGER, N.R. and TARULE, J.M. (1986) *Women's Ways of Knowing: The Development of Self, Voice, and Mind*, New York, Basic Books.
BRUNER, J. (1986) *Actual Minds, Possible Worlds*, Cambridge, Harvard University Press.
BRYK, A.S., LEE, V.E. and HOLLAND, P.B. (1993) *Catholic Schools and the Common Good*, Cambridge, Harvard University Press.
COLEMAN, J. and HOFFER, T. (1987) *Public and Private Schools: The Impact of Communities*, New York, Basic Books.

CUBAN, L. (1990) 'Reforming again, again, and again,' *Educational Researcher*, **19**, 1, pp. 3–13.

FREIRE, P. (1986) *Education for Critical Consciousness*, New York, Continuum.

GILLIGAN, C. (1982) *In a Different Voice: Psychological Theory and Women's Development*, Cambridge, Harvard University Press.

NETWORK OF SACRED HEART SCHOOLS (1990) *Goals and Criteria for Sacred Heart Schools in the United States*, Newton, MA.

GROOME, T.H. (1980) *Christian Religious Education: Sharing Our Story and Vision*, San Francisco, Harper and Row.

GRUMET, M.R. (1988) *Bitter Milk: Women and Teaching*, Amherst, The University of Massachusetts Press.

HERBST, J. (1989) *And Sadly Teach: Teacher Education and Professionalization in American Culture*, Madison, University of Wisconsin Press.

HILL, P.T., FOSTER, G.E. and GENDLER, T. (1990) *High Schools with Character*, Santa Monica, CA, Rand.

JOHNSON, S.M. (1990) *Teachers at Work: Achieving Success in Our Schools*, New York, Basic Books.

KELLER, E.F. (1987) 'Women scientists and feminist critics of science,' *Daedalus*, **116**, 4, pp. 77–91.

KOZOL, J. (1991) *Savage Inequalities: Children in America's Schools*, New York, Crown.

LACEY, C.A. (1991) 'Epiphanies of the ordinary: Narrative analysis and the study of teaching,' Unpublished doctoral dissertation, Harvard Graduate School of Education, Cambridge, MA.

LACEY, C.A., WOOD, D.R. and BARTUNEK, J.M. (1990, April) 'A committee of teachers for teachers: The first year,' Paper presented at the annual meeting of the American Educational Research Association, Boston, (ERIC Document Reproduction Service No. ED 322 129).

LIEBERMAN, A. and MILLER, L. (1990) 'The social realities of teaching,' in LIEBERMAN, A. (Ed) *Schools as Collaborative Cultures: Creating the Future Now*, New York, Falmer Press, pp. 153–63.

LIGHTFOOT, S.L. (1978) *Worlds Apart: Relationships Between Families and Schools*, New York, Basic Books.

LORTIE, D.C. (1975) *Schoolteacher: A Sociological Study*, Chicago, University of Chicago Press.

MAEROFF, G.I. (1988) *The Empowerment of Teachers: Overcoming the Crisis of Confidence*, New York, Teachers College Press.

MARTIN, J.R. (1982) 'Excluding women from the educational realm,' *Harvard Educational Review*, **52**, pp. 133–42.

MARTIN, J.R. (1985) *Reclaiming a Conversation: The Ideal of the Educated Woman*, New Haven, Yale University Press.

McINTOSH, P. (1984) 'Interactive phases of curricular re-vision,' in SPANIER, B., BLOOM, A. and BOROVIAK, D. (Eds) *Toward a Balanced Curriculum: A Sourcebook for Initiating Gender Integration Projects*, Cambridge, Schenkman Publishing, pp. 25–34.

MILLER, J.B. (1976) *Toward a New Psychology of Women*, Boston, Beacon Press.

MOONEY, B. (1992) 'Education as sacrament: Its implications for faculty development,' *Network Journal*, **3**, pp. 1–8, Newton, MA, Network of Sacred Heart Schools.

PURPEL, D.E. (1989) *The Moral and Spiritual Crisis in Education: A Curriculum for Justice and Compassion in Education*, Granby, MA, Bergin and Harvey Publishers.

PURPEL, D.E. (1991) 'Education as sacrament,' *Independent School*, pp. 45–60.

ROTHMAN, R. (1993) 'Study urges "learning communities" to address the isolation of teachers,' *Education Week*, **12**, 25, pp. 1, 25.

SCHÖN, D.A. (1983) *The Reflective Practitioner: How Professionals Think in Action*, New York, Basic Books.

US DEPARTMENT OF EDUCATION NATIONAL CENTER FOR EDUCATION STATISTICS (1992) *Schools and Staffing in the United States: A Statistical Profile, 1987–1988,* Schools and Staffing Survey and Teacher Follow up Survey (July), Washington, DC, US Government Printing Office.

WEILER, K. (1988) *Women Teaching for Change: Gender, Class and Power,* New York, Bergin and Garvey Publishers.

WOOD, D. and LACEY, C. (1991) 'A tale of teachers,' *NWSA Journal,* **3**, pp. 414–21.

Chapter 19

Openness and Intellectual Challenge in Catholic Schools

Peter Hastings

Before the Second Vatican Council Catholic schools, through compulsory worship and buildings decorated with Crucifixes and statues, appeared to be 'worshipping communities of faith' composed of believing, practising Catholic staff and pupils. Their task was the transmission of a package of beliefs, 'faith', a gift of God and rejected at peril, and of rules, 'morals', imprinted by God on each soul.

This was often transmitted by manipulation using fear of damnation, feelings of guilt and sentimentality. Teaching could be clarified but not disputed; one could not dispute with God nor with the Church which spoke for Him. The compulsion included, often, the heavy use of corporal punishment, justified by 'making them do what they ought to do'. The level of religious thinking produced by this was labelled by many university chaplains as 'moronic'.

Obedience was the foundation of moral judgment. One did not need to decide what was good or bad; one could just ask a priest and accept his ruling. To be obedient to the Church, even if disagreeing, was itself a virtue, uniting one with Christ, who obeyed his Father even to death.

This was not a basis for moral maturity. Bishop Butler addressed the problem:

> A Carmelite prioress said to me: 'One of the troubles about the old system in our convents is that we have produced a lot of immature persons.' I think that what she meant was that the doctrine of a sort of passive obedience had stunted the personalities of many of the nuns, so that they were incapable of responsible decisions. (Bishop Butler, 1964)

Thus was created, in the context of the *Index of Forbidden Books* and the autocracy of the Church's structure, the Closed School: closed to personal intellectual enquiry in the religious field, closed to responsible decision-making by individual persons, closed, in practice, to the rights of the person.

Vatican II: A Blueprint for the Transformation of Catholic Schools

The Second Vatican Council provided a blueprint for the transformation of Catholic Schools into schools in which students would be treated with the dignity of persons (see Declaration on Religious Freedom, 1965).

- **Aims**

  This Vatican Synod urges . . . those . . . educating others . . . to form persons . . . who will come to decisions on their own judgement and in the light of truth, govern their activities with a sense of responsibility, and strive after what is true and right, willing always to join with others in co-operative effort. [Responsible autonomy replaces obedience.]

- **Methods**

  Truth is to be sought after in a manner proper to the dignity of the human person and his social nature. The inquiry is to be free, carried on with the aid of teaching or instruction, communication and dialogue. In the course of these men explain to one another the truth they have discovered, or think they have discovered, in order to assist one another in the quest for truth. Moreover, as the truth is discovered, it is by a personal assent that men are to adhere to it. [An open shared intellectual search and recognition of human fallibility replaces the undisputed package.]

- **Worship**

  Of its very nature, the exercise of religion consists before all else in those internal, voluntary and free acts whereby man sets the course of his life directly towards God. No merely human power can either command or prohibit acts of this kind. [In all important acts a person must be free.]

- **Each person's rights**

  . . . in the search for truth . . . men cannot discharge their obligations in a manner in keeping with their own nature unless they enjoy immunity from external coercion as well as psychological freedom. Therefore the right to religious freedom has its foundation, not in the subjective disposition of the person, but in his very nature. In consequence the right to this immunity continues to exist even in those who do not live up to their obligation of seeking the truth and adhering to it.

In 1966 I opened as headteacher a new Catholic grammar school which, in 1974, I merged with a secondary modern school to form a comprehensive, the Trinity School. I set out to translate the Council's documents, particularly the *Declaration on Religious Freedom* into living action, a new type of Catholic school, an open school. There could be other models; this was mine.

Blueprint into Practice

Some fantasize that Catholic schools are filled with practising, believing Catholics and some would prefer them closed to all who are not. The reality is different. In 1988 the National Catechetical Project recognized the religious diversity of the families using Catholic schools: those with committed, nominal or tribal Catholic parents, parents of various Christian Churches, other faiths or no religious tradition:

> We cannot organise the religious life of the school and the religious education offered in the school on the assumption that all pupils can be treated as if they were part of a faith community characterised by practising Catholics. (Gallagher, 1988)

I recognized this in the 1960s.

Further, it is children for whom a school should be organized. Parents have rights and duties but it is for the children to make their own religious decisions. Parents have to learn the message of Kahlil Gibran in *The Prophet*

> You may give them your love but not your thoughts, for they have their own thoughts.

We needed to be, in religious matters as in all others, with the child at the point where each child actually was. This meant producing what was indeed the best educational approach for all but especially for Catholics; a Catholic school open to dialogue with all.

What Should a School Offer?

Relationships

First, relationships; those are what God is. Whether we know it or not, insofar as we are true human persons we are already sharing in the activity and relationships of knowing and loving, which are God's life.

By relationship with the Son, who is Truth and Word, we share in His life, which is His relation with the Father. That relation is intense creative intellectual activity. Many of the names of the Son are intellectual: the Word, the Wisdom, the Image of the Knowledge of the Father. Aquinas maintains that the relationship of Father and Son is the intellectual generation of the Word and that this intellectual generation is the Word. If we are to enter into the relationship with the Father of the Word made Flesh, then we, the Flesh, must be made Word.

Nevertheless, although it may excite some to say that a school should provide 'an encounter with Christ', a child will not be able consciously to enter into a relationship with God, who cannot be seen, without learning to be in relationship with persons visibly around. Since 'The relation with man is the real simile of the relation with God' (Buber, 1937), the first call is to provide an encounter with many human persons and for all to learn to be valued as persons and to value persons (Hume, 1988). 'What was true of the apostolic experience is true for both catechist and catechized, namely that a pre-predicative, experienced relationship is the indispensable foundation of Christian revelation' (Gallagher, op. cit.). St Augustine was unable to learn from St Ambrose until they had first built a relationship. The role of a school is not the catechist's but the forerunner's, making smooth the way of the Lord.

So from the start we had to treat each other as persons. Children could call me 'Peter' or 'Mr Hastings' but I, and all members of staff, had to be given names, 'Sir' or 'Miss' were not acceptable; everyone should be named and treated as a person, not as a thing. The staff accepted this and soon most relationships were on Christian name terms.

Search for Truth

Knowing and loving being the great activities of life, a school aiming at relationships must pursue intellectual and moral search, involving growth in personhood and relationship.

A Catholic school should not offer a packaged answer about God or the meaning of life, but a hunger for, and determination to find, truth and rightness. For that children need to be, like Kipling's Elephant's Child, full of 'satiable curiosity', questioning everything and enjoying doing so.

Fra Lippo Lippi exclaims:

This world's no blot for us, Nor blank; it means intensely, and means good: To find its meaning is my meat and drink.

An open school will encourage all to seek this meat and drink, not only in the colours, lights and shades, changes and surprises of aesthetics, but also in the intellectual beauties of mathematics and the sciences, and in the philosophical and theological consideration of the rhyme and reason of it all. Many find it easy enough to accept poetry, art or music as expressing the search for God but find the pursuit of science peripheral, important only as providing material for the judgments of moral theology. Mathematics some find totally irrelevant. In fact mathematics is deeply theological, being almost the language for the description and understanding of creation. It was by intellectual search through the language of mathematics that Einstein knew that light bends; there was no observation or experiment that could help him. Only decades later did an eclipse enable astronomers to confirm this mathematical knowledge by sighting a star behind the sun.

Anyone may feel its impact. When Harold Loukes was a boy, his maths master commanded the class to define zero and then questioned each definition into collapse. He walked to the door and turned: 'See if you can do better with infinity next week!' Loukes said that week's thinking was the start of his discovery of God.

One of our students, fascinated by mathematical physics, wanted to combine that at university with philosophy because he found that physics asked questions which could only be answered by philosophy, and that he needed to pursue those questions until the ultimate truth. That is not far from St Augustine's statement that reading Cicero's *Hortensius* at the age of 19 aroused in him a burning 'passion for the wisdom of Eternal Truth . . . The one thing that delighted me in Cicero's exhortation was that I should love, and seek, and win, and hold, and embrace, not this or that philosophical school but Wisdom itself, whatever it might be' (St Augustine, *Confessions*).

In this search all areas must be open to discussion, debate, dispute. It is not possible to give persons the tools for search in physics and law, 'testing all things', but stifle them in theological or moral matters.

Search for Rightness

Alongside the search for truth must be the search for rightness, if bedevilled by the notion that we have the knowledge of right and wrong stamped on our souls.

I saw moral development as growth, not as diestamping, through a series of yardsticks, testing each from what parents first say to toddlers, through ever widening and clashing authorities — school, peer group, State, Church — 'testing all things' until one has accepted with understanding a yardstick by which one can judge all these others and oneself, 'holding fast that which is good'.

Vatican II urged openness to research in psychology. I found help in Kohlberg's stages. Accepting that these are hypotheses, they gave a working basis for the policy of the school concerning discipline. These stages mark a growth in understanding justice, which is important if one is to share, as a mature human person, in God's life.

Curiously, Kohlberg parallels Scripture: in the myth, Adam and Eve in the garden were in Stage 1, the stimulus being the fear of death. The serpent convinced them that they would not die; so they moved into Stage 2 and the desire for pleasure.

Such stories seem stuck in that pre-conventional area for a long time. Abram stated his Stage 2 motivation, 'I want', clearly seen as he virtually pawned Sarai in Egypt.

Transition to Stage 3 arrived when Abram's herdsmen conflicted with Lot's, causing Abram to propose a friendly solution. The Patriarchs were firmly in Stage 2, with a lot of sharp practice and an eye to the main chance, and tentatively in Stage 3, being 'nice boys' in their own particular group — yuppies in fact.

Meanwhile they had covenants with enormous incentive sizes in flocks, land and innumerable descendants, but easily broken, rather like voluntary codes of behaviour in the City. Then the Exodus brought a conflict of roles. Suddenly there were the Commandments in stone with all the rules that were built upon them, and Stage 4 had arrived.

Christ forced challenge to the law, Stage 5: 'Is it permitted to cure people on the Sabbath or not?' etc. John Chapters 9 and 10 spell out the inadequacy of those in Stage 4 to cope with Christ's questions. Having opened the door into Stage 5, he gave the rule for Stage 6: 'Always treat others as you would like them to treat you.'

Christ made explicit the context without which Stage 6 is unattainable: 'Love the Lord your God with all your heart, with all your soul, with all your mind and your neighbour as yourself.' Thus Christ offered us a Stage 6 in which the golden rules of justice would be united with, and controlled by, the releasing golden rule of love.

Through the whole working of the school there were the constant touchstone questions: 'Is this a way to treat a person? Is this a way for a person to behave?'

In structuring a process to help moral development I used Kohlberg's stages as a working hypothesis. I had children arriving stuck in Stage 1, like Adam and Eve in the Garden, motivated by fear of punishment, so I abolished corporal punishment, which helped to move them, along with Adam and Eve, into Stage 2 or 'I want'. 'I want' then had to become 'I want to be here' with the understanding: 'If I want to be here I must be nice.' After that, with firmly held boundaries against violence to persons, buildings or classes, I used various stratagems to bring individuals to further transition points of choice: a balancing act with over 1,200 people, each one probably in several stages.

Growth towards Responsible Autonomy

To grow towards autonomy, persons must learn to accept moral accountability for their actions and responsibility for others to whom they are significantly related, as well as for situations and actions in which they are involved.

We learn by doing; so there was free entry to the buildings and movement round them. There were no prefects and no organized patrolling staff. There was access to art rooms, workshops, gyms, music rooms, recording rooms, computer rooms and to most of the equipment.

Clearly the school could not have functioned in this manner if individual responsibility had not been as a rule accepted. Judgments and decisions were constantly being made on the basis that a rule is not needed where common-sense and consideration for others are accepted.

Vatican II urged us to educate persons to make their own decisions; therefore children needed decisions to make. We had no uniform; children decided how to present themselves and what was appropriate, bearing in mind the type of work they would be doing, safety factors and the feelings of others.

As they controlled their dress so they controlled their curriculum and learning process. There was little choice for the entry year but, after that, a rapid increase in it until only English, maths and theology remained as core — and maths was negotiable. The choice was as genuinely free as the constrictions of a timetable would permit and the range considerable. I took to heart Schumacher's advice; 'Find out what they are doing and help them to do it better.'

My task was to make each consider and understand the implications of choices and that everyone must accept responsibility for the consequences. If, after we had thrashed the matter back and forth, the pupils stuck to their guns, they had what they wanted. I tried to implant the notion that one has never shut one's future doors; that one can always, even if not easily, restart.

The courses themselves provided further choice, of book, investigation, essay title, of writing poetry or prose, and therefore more control by the child. The result was commitment to study and to the needs of others. When that commitment did not show we would usually find that parental separation, illness or debt, or some such problem, was causing intolerable pain and worry and our task was to make it bearable.

Control of what they wore, where they went and what they studied, all promoted growth towards autonomy, but a Catholic school is concerned with the full growth of autonomy which requires expression also in religion and worship: 'Of its very nature, the exercise of religion consists before all else in those internal, voluntary and free acts whereby man sets the course of his life directly towards God' (Declaration of Religious Freedom). In my understanding, an act of religious observance carried out under compulsion is not a religious act. I had no religious assemblies and there was no compulsory act of worship in my twenty-two years.

Nor was there manipulation. Children could say what they thought without looking for the approved statement. There were no leads — no 'holy' pictures or statues to act as statements of approved belief. We had a community Mass perhaps twice a term, and some 40–70 per cent would attend in a school with little more than 50 per cent baptized as Catholics, more from the older end than the younger, which was interesting. Mass was, with assemblies, concerts, theatre productions and open days, one of the most influential creators and focal points of our community and its web of shared ownership and overlapping activities.

HMI told my governors that they had found everyone in the school autonomous, the children rather more than the staff.

Language

Search requires tools; in view of the nature of all search and of the basis of relationships, I saw language as permeating everything, the essential tool to pursue the end. We acquire language by using it and most of our use is in speech. Our teaching methods encouraged constant discussion. In maths, science, history, music, art, everywhere, there was the steady noise of talk. The teacher was there to set up discussion and activity, to move around taking part and throwing in questions, and to push accurate technical language and other appropriate language for the genuine and cooperative exploration of ideas.

Methods

My statement to all was that a school exists to ask questions, not to give answers, and that important questions simply produce more questions. I quoted Aquinas: that the first rule of learning is to doubt the teacher, that all truth comes from the Holy Spirit and that one should consider what is said not who is saying it. I constantly reminded all that we should 'test all things holding fast that which is good'. Only so can we be open to learning how to learn, how to think, form hypotheses, weigh evidence, set up experiments, observe, listen, speak, question, cooperate, make decisions and accept responsibility.

The new carefully piloted Schools' Council courses enabled me to select those that were consistent with these principles across the curriculum. In all fields, sciences, humanities and arts, we were Socratic, heuristic, exploratory, examining evidence, doubting, testing and requiring proof.

It would seem that, if humans do their thinking this way, then Christians must. Like Socrates, Christ taught men and women to think by asking them questions and posing problems.

Since there were no suitable courses produced for the religious field, I had to construct our own. I might describe our approach as that of forerunners, preparing for the coming of Truth, giving children the skills and language to enable them to be open to Revelation.

I began with word meanings: What do we mean by true?: a true story, false, fact, fiction? Could fiction be true or fact untrue in messages they conveyed? We distinguished writings — fiction, fairy tales, legend, myth, allegory, history, law, poetry, song, science. We read different pieces and classified them, recognizing that this is not always possible without other evidence. We considered Pinocchio, Jonah and *How the whale got his throat*, and what messages these might give.

I gave Aquinas' definition of man as 'a rational animal capable of laughter' and children made their own lists of qualities that distinguish man. That introduced them to a picture that changed as we watched: tool choosing animals, bird art and a chimpanzee shaking with laughter after making a pun. We studied primitive peoples, cave paintings, films of Australian aborigines, cannibals and others with fascinating religious ideas. We listed Swanscombe, Neanderthal, Peking, *Homo Habilis* etc. and had to research, date and classify as human, not human or not known. We discussed whether memory of what happened to the first man could possibly have survived to the coming of writing. We looked at geology and astronomy and Genesis 1 and puzzled out what kind of writing that might be. The implication was that religious texts and ideas are open to scrutiny, and can only be understood if truth in other fields is accepted, not ignored.

At the start I taught every class in the first two years and experienced a range of parent and child reactions. My periods were simply titled 'H'. One parent told how her daughter had commented week by week: 'I think he's teaching us extra English — No! He's teaching us history — It might be religion — Mummy, I've just realized; he isn't teaching us anything: he's just teaching us to think!' One father recounted how his son had come home all sunny saying: 'Dad, don't worry about Genesis, I can help you to understand it' and had.

My course was very much my personal creation; it served as a meeting between me and everyone coming into the school; it was never named as religious education; it enabled the children to lie fallow after the excessive catechetics of the primary schools. As the school grew I collected our team of theologians, who constructed our theology and philosophy courses. These included core units on various religious ideas, the idea of God and Christology, with a range of options enabling exploration. Through the sixth form the basic theology continued with a menu of options backed by tough A-level courses in theology and philosophy, both piloted in the school.

The Team

Searches should be shared activities — child and teacher sharing with child and teacher. Somewhere in these searching teams must be those who know what questions are currently being asked; frontiersmen and women who can open new vistas.

Principles guiding appointment of staff are seldom easy to fulfil; my list of requirements was long and tough and one head told me that I was not looking for teachers but for archangels. In brief, I hunted teachers with enquiring minds, initiative and creativity, unafraid of mistakes, continuing to practise and study their subject, appreciating that learning and life should be fun, deeply and caringly interested in children, who realize that every child has special needs and that schools should be run for children, not for teachers, parents, LEAs, governments, industry or institutional churches. It was worth the hunt.

Besides committed, thinking Catholics aware of the conversation within the Church — never thick on the ground — I wanted committed, thinking, caring teachers of other faiths or no faith, with the integrity to respect and protect the character and aims of the school. These would force the Catholic staff to test ideas and to give a reason for the faith that was in us; if we could not do this for adult colleagues, we should not be offering it to children. These teachers were not in the school on sufferance, because we could not get anyone more suitable, but precisely because they were suitable with a positive contribution to make to the task of human and Christian maturation.

We found skilled teachers to form a dedicated staff, dedicated professionally, academically and to children. By the 1980s they had produced a society which they did not like leaving because, as one said after declining a head of department post elsewhere: 'Here I am one of ten mathematicians, three with Firsts; we intermix with the university and I have real mathematical discussions every day — there I would be the only mathematician. Here I interface with a science department of ten, five of whom are Firsts, who are continually experimenting, and a theology department that has entangled me in philosophy; how can I replace them?' The linguists were in the same position. If this was the level of the rare teacher departments, the others were fairly bubbling over with thought and skills, and the rarest of all, the Catholic theology graduates influencing the outlook of all, were there only because their ability to think and talk openly was protected.

Over all, there was a conversation about everything: war poetry, abortion, contraception, unemployment, rape, feminism, racism, the Falklands war. This conversation was between me, my eight theology and philosophy graduates, my other sixty-five committed and dedicated staff with their varied knowledge and faith positions, my full-time Dominican chaplain and our hundreds of children. It was a good conversation and an open conversation producing the opportunities for a great variety of personal developments.

The Success of Openness

Was openness shown, through our fruits, to be a good tree? I believe my criteria to be both sound and reflecting Vatican II: relationships, search for truth and right behaviour, with the language, skills and control that these require, and loving, autonomous persons the result. Nevertheless if I testify to myself my testimony is nothing, but there were others who testified to us.

After a three year study, Professor Jenkins, of Warwick University, reported to the County Authority (Warwickshire LEA, 1988):

> Its students are unusually alert, bright and enthusiastic, enjoy close working relationships with their first-name-terms teachers and are encouraged to take full responsibility for their own learning. . . . The school is very much a Catholic school but a post-Vatican II Catholic school that has replaced the wooden conformity of a compulsory religious service with a deep searching exploration on religious matters led by an imaginative Theology Department.

In 1988 the media flooded round us: Press, TV and Radio. These were not gullible strangers to the context; they were the experienced and critical education staff of the national organs. They went everywhere and talked with the full range, parents, staff, children, inspectors and administrators: so there we were, warts and all, for any to see. Their opinions were as enthusiastic as HMI's. One TV director made a full length film, Catching Alight, on some of the ideas behind the school, shown nationwide; Peter Wilby wrote at length in *The Independent*:

The creation is extraordinary. Other schools, though not often Church schools, introduce new ideas here and there. Trinity seems to introduce them everywhere and years before anyone else.

Biotechnology, robotics and aeronautics are among the subjects taught. From the second year, pupils can opt for media studies and make their own films and television programmes. Pupil musicians have worked with the London Sinfonietta. There is a theatre, from which one production has been shown on ITV.

As well as Latin and classical Greek, five modern languages are taught and the school plans satellite facilities to catch foreign broadcasts. The satellite will also be used to pick up programmes from Australia, New Zealand and the USA to help with a new A-level English language course. The maths department uses, with apparent success, an individual learning scheme, which involves every pupil in the class working on different problems. Sixth-formers are sent on work placements far and wide — to BBC and ITV stations, to Sellafield in Cumbria, to the Royal Observatory in Edinburgh.

It is a noisy school — because it encourages children to talk and to discuss things — and it buzzes with excitement . . .

There are stories of withdrawn, violent, anti-social children transformed by Trinity . . .

The school is highly regarded by HMIs and by county subject advisers. Its contribution to the Technical and Vocational Education Initiative is regarded as a model by the Manpower Services Commission. (Wilby, 1988)

One might have added that we introduced the first theology A-level in the country, that every year our students entered higher education to read theology or philosophy, that a number went on to teach theology in schools and that two started training for the priesthood as I retired.

The Future

We received a good HMI report:

The aims of the school reflect its Catholic nature and find their written expression for both parents and applicants for teaching posts in quotations from the Conciliar Fathers of Vatican II. In one document these aims are expressed thus:

'The school aims to give children the welcome and respect which are every human's due, to help them towards responsible autonomy and the intellectual and loving activities and relationships which are the human participation in the Trinity.'

It is a notable feature of the school that the attempt to meet these aims suffuses all the policies adopted in the school and that the aims relate extensively to practice both within and without the classroom. (DES, 1988)

Some, however, longed for the return of the old 'closed' Catholic school. The Secretary of State received a formal protest from the Archdiocese of Birmingham. The diocese also removed six governors, including a priest of the highest integrity, objected to the proportion of children and staff of other faiths and to an advertisement for 'a thinking Catholic'. The parents rose as one person in the school's defence and the archdiocese backed down rather than lose in court.

Trinity's parents and staff had the stamina and expertise to win, although the school was damaged in the process. The choice is now between a growth of openness to intellectual challenge and dialogue with the human race, and a continued censored conversation between obedient neophytes. The tension between intellectual activity and fear of change, between the thinkers — Congar, Rahner, Balthasar, Kung — persecuted for openness, (yet the real teachers of the council) and the Ancien Regime, (who fear the council) and have learned little and forgotten nothing, has been apparent for years. This has now extended to a highly educated laity, which has replaced the deferential peasant community of the past, requiring change and being refused it. This is the San Andreas fault of the Catholic Church; the earthquakes centred on Trinity School and also in St Philip's Sixth Form College in Birmingham. It may be small in scale but indicates the future for openness and intellectual challenge for as long as the Church proclaims principles but acts against them.

References

Bishop Butler, (1964) *Address to Superiors of Religious Communities*, Spode House Review.
Buber, M. (1937) *I and Thou* (trans. Gregor Smith, R.), Edinburgh, T. and T. Clark.
Cardinal Basil Hume (1988) *Towards a Civilization of Love*, Hodder and Stoughton.
DES (1988) *Report by HM Inspectors on The Trinity School, Leamington Spa, LEA: Warwickshire*, Department of Education and Science.
Gallagher, J. (1988) *Our Schools and Our Faith*, London, Collins.
Wilby, P. (1988) *The Independent*, 11 February.

Chapter 20

The Catholic School and Religious Education: Meeting a Variety of Needs

Jim Gallagher S.D.B.

To entitle this chapter 'The Catholic School and Religious Education' may give the impression of an attempt at a definition of the Catholic school and/or the religious education which should properly take place in a Catholic school. Such is not my intention. To do so would be to speak in abstract about the Catholic school and the religious education which should be provided in such a school. Throughout the world and in our own particular countries Catholic schools exist in a great variety of situations and are called to serve a diversity of need in pupils, families and localities. While considering 'The Contemporary Catholic School: Context, Identity and Diversity' it seems right to reflect rather on some aspects of the mission of our schools and of the service which religious education may offer pupils within a variety of situations in our contemporary society.

A Broad Catechetical Perspective

Several chapters in this book address the question of 'What makes a school Catholic' from a variety of perspectives — theological, philosophical, and from the perspective of a practical case study. In a sense I consider the question from a broad catechetical perspective insofar as I shall touch on issues concerning the faith dimension of our schools. I speak of a 'broad' catechetical perspective because the reflections will not be confined to what is considered catechesis in a narrow or strict sense but will touch on points which are on the borderline of catechesis, evangelization and religious education. I recognize and acknowledge that the activities are distinct yet complementary. The borderline between them is a fine one: they are distinct yet not separate, they overlap (Gallagher, 1986, p. 12; 1988, p. 14). Within this broad catechetical perspective I shall consider our schools in relation to the faith needs and development of Catholic pupils who are at different levels of interest in, and commitment to, the Catholic faith tradition. The presence of pupils from other Christian traditions and other faiths in a number of our schools demands that we seek to clarify how, while upholding the Catholic character of our schools, we address the spiritual and religious needs and development of these pupils. In these circumstances we have to ask ourselves in what sense we can call a Catholic school 'a community of faith'.

Scope and Limitation of This Discussion

My main focus will be particularly on the pupils who are Catholic, even if only nominally so. The question about children of other faiths in our schools is, in my view, one of the most urgent questions which we have to face in the coming years. Yet concentration on that question can, to some extent, distract us from examining and evaluating with greater care the way we educate 'Catholic' pupils to and in faith. For some it is more a question of educating to rather than in faith.

I can only speak from within my own experience and study which is mainly concerned with contemporary Catholic schools in England and Wales. For a number of years I was head of religious education in a school in Bootle in the North of England. In a recent report Bootle was designated one of the most deprived areas of Britain. I then lectured for twelve years in theology and religious education at Christ's and Notre Dame College, Liverpool Institute of Higher Education. For the past eight years I have worked for the Bishops' Conference of England and Wales as coordinator of the National Project of Catechesis and Religious Education, 'Living and Sharing Our Faith' (Gallagher, 1991, pp. 297–300). It is out of this experience that I reflect. Much of what I have to say will be more relevant to the secondary school and older pupils.

Schools and Our Faith

In his essay 'Education, Catechesis and the Church School' Hirst declares that 'in education any faith the educator has is irrelevant to his goals' (Hirst, 1981). In the Catholic understanding, faith can hardly be considered 'irrelevant' to our goals as educators. At its most basic, faith is the way we understand the meaning of human life, its significance, its dignity and its purpose. As Christians we recognize God and the significance of our human existence in Jesus Christ. What we believe about life and people cannot be 'irrelevant' to how we view and carry out the task of education in our schools.

> The point is that what a person 'believes in' is what has some real purchase in terms of what he thinks and feels and does, how he judges and decides, what attitude he adopts, what course of action he considers worth pursuing. In these we show what we are committed to, what we really regard as important — which is to say, what we believe in. (Rodger, 1982, p. 14)

Most, if not all, of our schools can hardly be called communities of faith in so far as not all who are in them pupils or teachers profess or are committed to the Catholic faith tradition. Yet if the name Catholic is to mean anything, all must be inspired and challenged by the values enshrined in the Gospel and our Catholic beliefs.

Our Faith: Not an Added Extra

Our faith is not an added extra which we teach and offer pupils, an appendage to a general or secular education. Our faith vision should permeate the whole life of the school and all aspects of the curriculum. It is conveyed and lived in the values and attitudes which are incorporated into the way our schools are managed, into the relationships between members of staff, and between staff and pupils, into the aims and priorities we set, and into the procedures by which we evaluate our success. While all in the school may not profess the same faith, they can share and uphold the ideals and values of the school. In the context of collaboration and concern for these ideals and values, diversity of religious belief and conviction can provide a valuable resource.

In our schools we undertake to live, celebrate and present our faith without in any way imposing it on pupils, staff or families. The document 'The Religious Dimension of Education in a Catholic School' states that 'the religious freedom and personal conscience of individual students and their families must be respected', such freedom is 'explicitly recognised by the Church' (Congregation for Catholic Education, 1988). In the context this is applied particularly to pupils who are not members of the Catholic Church. It equally must apply to Catholic pupils at their different stages and levels of faith. The document goes on to stress that 'a Catholic school cannot relinquish its own freedom to proclaim the Gospel and offer formation based on the values to be found in a Christian education'. Yet 'to proclaim or to offer is not to impose' which 'suggests moral violence and is strictly forbidden both by the Gospel and by Church law'.

A Fundamental Principle: A Twofold Fidelity

We must hold in delicate balance respect for persons on the one hand and on the other the duty to offer sound education based on the values which flow from our Catholic faith and beliefs. This is related to a basic principle of all catechetical activity:

> The fundamental law of all catechetical method is that of fidelity to the Word of God and fidelity to the concrete needs of the faithful. This is the ultimate criterion by which catechists must appraise their work — fidelity to God and fidelity to people . . . Here we are not dealing with

two different concerns but with one spiritual attitude . . . It is the attitude of the charity of Christ, The Word made flesh. (Dwyer, 1970)

This theme is taken up in *The General Catechetical Directory* and other documents. We proclaim a Word which interprets life. Faith becomes possible when the two stories meet: the story of God's plan in Christ, and the story of each one's personal quest and contemporary experience. As educators we must be immersed in both. In Catholic theology we have for long made an important distinction in discussing faith: *'fides quae'* and *'fides qua'*. *'Fides quae'* refers to the faith of the Church, the faith which we believe. This is the faith we profess and wish to share with, hand on to the younger generation. *'Fides qua'* speaks of the personal search and journey to and in faith, how individuals come to make their own the faith of the Church. It is imperative that as educators we attend to both, that we be bridge builders between the two. It is on this aspect in particular that I wish to reflect and offer some thoughts.

At the Service of People

I no longer speak of the Catholic school because this runs the danger of imagining some abstract reality, a sort of Platonic idea. Unfortunately, there are those who hold such a conception of the Catholic school and who crudely judge existing schools against some abstract, universal norm. To do so can burden our schools with unrealistic expectations since it takes no account of the people in them and the particular situation in which they work. Schools do not exist without people: pupils, teachers, families who live and work in a specific locality. Recently I was somewhat taken aback when a priest who had attended one of my in-service sessions for teachers and governors expressed his delight that we had spent the time talking about pupils. When I asked him what he considered so special about that, he pointed out that, as chair of governors, he attended many meetings concerning the recent policy changes in education and found that the children were rarely mentioned.

Many teachers complain of the number of meetings and the amount of paper work which the changes involve and which, in their view, prevents them getting on with the job of teaching the children. While there is much that is good and necessary in all of this, there is the danger of being caught up in the mechanics of administration, in the system for its own sake. People are at the heart of all our educational endeavours. The document *Lay Catholics in Schools, Witnesses to Faith* stresses the fact that the teacher is not simply a professional person who systematically transmits a body of knowledge in the context of a school; the teacher is 'an educator, one who helps form human persons' (Congregation for Catholic Education, 1982). I like to think that as educators we can answer the call of the Second Vatican Council: 'We can justly consider that the future of humanity lies in the hands of those who are strong enough to provide coming generations with reasons for living and hoping' (*The*

Church in the Modern World, no. 31). We bring to this task our faith in Jesus Christ in whom we find the meaning and true significance of our lives in relationship to God — Father, Son and Spirit — and to each other.

A Variety of Situations

Our schools are involved with pupils, families and communities with a variety of experiences of life. They are affected by factors which include

- family relationships;
- social and economic conditions;
- culture;
- race; and
- religious commitment.

In my years in the Liverpool area the pupils in Catholic schools were almost entirely white and Catholic. Many were nominally Catholic: they had 'been done' in baptism with little contact with Church after that apart from attendance at a Catholic school. In the area of London where I am now based in many schools only about a third of the pupil intake is white. There is a great cultural mix. There is the same mix of nominal and more committed Catholics. About a third of the pupils come from practising, committed homes and are themselves committed. In other parts of the country there are a number of children from other Christian traditions and increasingly, especially in inner cities, a number from other faiths. Some of our schools work with children in areas of deprivation and poverty, others in affluent areas. While we seek to uphold and develop the 'Catholic' character of our schools we must do so in ways adapted to the needs of people and local circumstances.

Church documents reiterate the need for adaptation. The *General Catechetical Directory* is presented as 'general' because it 'is intended for countries which differ greatly in their conditions and pastoral needs'. The same point is made in *The Religious Dimension of Education in a Catholic School*: those involved in Catholic schools are asked 'to study these general guidelines and adapt them to their own local situation'. In their Low Week meeting of 1982 the bishops of England and Wales agreed to commission a revision of the Irish Veritas primary RE programme 'in order to be in tune with the multi-cultural and multi-faith background of our people'. Adaptation in this sense is an essential part of all pastoral work. It is necessary to bear this in mind when making judgments about schools and teachers.

Disquiet with Aspects of Recent Government Policy

Some aspects of recent government policy for education raise considerable disquiet particularly about the way schools are being evaluated and teachers assessed. Within the dual system in England and Wales Catholic schools are an integral part of the national system while enjoying particular rights as Church schools. The bishops and many others are now expressing fears that such rights may be eroded by some of the new legislation. Concerns are expressed not only about the rights of the Church within the national educational system but also about basic and fundamental principles of sound education which are in danger of being ignored. In July 1992 the Department for Education published a 'White paper' which was intended to carry forward its 'great programme of reform'. In their response the bishops were critical of the underlying philosophy: 'the only clear vision seems to be the centrality of individual autonomy exercised through competition and controlled by the market'. They suggest that over-stress on independence and autonomy endangers 'any sense of having a wider responsibility (the common good)'. In offering financial benefits to encourage schools to opt-out of Local Education Authorities and take up Grant Maintained Status the Government 'intensifies financial and curricular inequalities between schools and creates new inequalities'. Other legislation which sets out the National Curriculum and deals with the question of testing pupils at ages 7, 11, 14, and 16 may lead, in the opinion of some, to the neglect of the weaker and more vulnerable pupils. In order to be seen to achieve good published results schools may be reluctant to admit such pupils. For this and other reasons the bishops 'remain unconvinced that much of what is proposed is in the best interest of all pupils'.[1]

Crude and Incorrect Criteria for Judging

In the recent publication of the league tables of achievement for 16-year-olds who sat the GCSE examination my former school in Bootle came bottom of the league table in the area of Sefton which comprises such places as the reasonably affluent Southport, Formby and Crosby together with Bootle which, as I have mentioned, was designated one of the most deprived areas of Britain. We all know that there is more to a good school than academic standards set and measured nationally. However, this is not the message which many parents and others take from the publication of results. Such crude and incorrect comparisons ignore the very real progress made by pupils. It is necessary to consider their starting point, together with the background and back-up of the home and locality. It also ignores the courses which are not part of the GCSE but which for many of these pupils are more suited and more directed at their future prospects. It takes no account of the pastoral care within the school, of the chaplaincy, of liaison with families and the setting up of youth activities. Good teachers in such schools are demoralized: they feel badly treated and greatly misunderstood.

This is not simply a political issue. It is not unconnected with our faith vision of human life. For many of us there is the fear that market forces rather than Gospel, people-centred values may become the criteria for assessing what is a 'good' and 'successful' school, including Catholic schools. In the light of their beliefs Catholic educators should at the very least adopt a position of critical solidarity on these issues or, in the opinion of many, speak out with a more prophetic voice. In my view, some Catholic schools, in their attempts to keep up with all the latest requirements, appear to provide secular education with an appendage of religious education ('orthodox', of course, though often with fewer lessons in comparison with areas of the National Curriculum) and regular liturgy for all. These ingredients do not necessarily make a school 'Catholic'. They may ensure a certain amount of Catholic practices within the timetable but that does not necessarily add up to a good Catholic school. These considerations have relevance for religious education within the school. The Vatican document reminds us: 'religious instruction can become empty words falling on deaf ears, because the authentically Christian witness which reinforces it is absent from the school climate.' (RD 104).

Danger of Catholic League Tables and 'Spiritual Consumerism'

There is, I fear, the danger that when evaluating Catholic schools and the religious education which they provide we can fall into the same traps of league tables and a narrow success ethic. In this respect a school may be scored almost solely on the league table of 'knowledge and practice of the faith'. After all, if pupils do not know and practice the faith, are we getting our money's worth out of our schools? There is in this approach hints of a sort of 'spiritual consumerism': we want value for money. It all depends on what we see as real 'value' and what we mean by 'success'. Knowledge and faith practice are, of course, important features to be encouraged and fostered in Catholic schools and in religious education. The problem arises when, in the league table mentality, they are raised to THE criterion for judging success. This is, of course, to judge schools and religious education teaching too simplistically without giving due consideration to the wider and complex context in which they take place, without taking account of the people and their starting point, and the situations in which they find themselves.

School: One Partner among Several

As I have already indicated, there are pupils at a variety of levels of religious interest and commitment in our Catholic schools. Among the Catholics it is likely that about a third come from committed homes and are themselves committed. When I mentioned this in a group recently a priest expressed shock and suggested that it might be better to close schools. I asked him how many were in his parish. There were about 1,400. When I asked how many came to Mass on Sunday, the answer was about 450. 'Why not close the parish?', I questioned. Our schools mirror the reality outside. Nor can we expect the school to do the entire job of nurturing the faith of our children and young people. The school is one partner among several. Recent documents stress the partnership of home, parish and school. The time at school is only one part of the gradual, ongoing journey of faith.

> The religious formation offered by the school is inevitably influenced by the home background, and so it depends greatly on whether the home is co-operative or non co-operative . . . It needs to be recognised that the school is a relatively secondary influence in the religious search of young people. In terms of contact hours, this is obvious (and in terms of such measurement the school may be more central than the parish). (Gallagher, 1983, p. 88)

Different Levels, Different Needs

In pointing out the different levels of pupils in relation to faith and religious interest, I do not advocate that we look to the 'lowest common denominator'. We must care for *all* by recognizing and addressing their religious needs and potential. We do so with regard to other areas of the curriculum. Why should we not do so with regard to faith and religion? Schools can and should encourage the more committed to grow in the dimensions of Christian faith: experience of Church as community, knowledge and understanding of Catholic beliefs, celebration in liturgy and prayer, action in the service of others. At the same time care must be given to those with little experience of the Catholic way of life, to those who show apathy, lack of interest and little commitment. While these pupils may not be at home with Church and the language of formal religion, we have to ask ourselves whether this is the whole story. In the view of Michael Paul Gallagher to whose works I shall refer later, it is not the whole story: 'I think that apathy is often the face of hurt hope, or hidden hunger. My hunch is that what seems mere indifference can often disguise a real searching and new openness of religious horizons' (Gallagher, 1990, p. 78).

In what may seem a very radical passage the Vatican document *The Catholic School* states: 'First and foremost the Church offers its educational service to the poor or those who are deprived of family help and affection or to those who are far from the faith' (Congregation for Catholic Education, 1977). This is not the impression one gleans from many a school prospectus. How schools intend to accept and help these pupils should find expression in its mission statement and aims. Schools, of course, and legitimateley so, meet the needs of pupils in a variety of situations. The danger is that, in our present educational climate, those mentioned in the Vatican document may be less welcome. They may prevent a high score on the league table. They may end up in what are now known as 'sink schools'. With regard to 'those far from the faith', research undertaken by Dr Leslie Francis and others suggests that if we run our schools on the assumption that all are committed Catholics, or should be, we may fail to preserve the goodwill or enhance the religious development of less committed Catholic pupils and those from other Christian traditions and other faiths (Francis, 1986a, 1986b, 1986c).

Attention to All

In this connection I would like to quote some paragraphs of the mission statement and aims which we Salesians in Britain have recently outlined for our work in schools, parishes and youth centres. It is, I think, relevant.

> Fired by the spirit of Don Bosco we celebrate God's presence in the young and the poor . . . We witness to the love of God in all our attitudes and actions in a way that constantly invites ourselves and them to a commitment to Jesus and his Gospel, especially to the call to serve . . . We stand by the many young and poor who experience little dignity and worth and for whom Gospel and Church have little meaning.

In the 'knowledge and religious practice' league table approach, it is precisely the latter group whose needs can be ignored and little recognition given to the various ways in which teachers touch their lives and present 'reasons for living and hoping'. We have to recognize that each journey of faith is unique and we have to respect that each pupil has a different starting place and will have his or her own pace for the journey. We must be patient companions on that road. Reflection on the stages of the journey of the disciples in the Emmaus story will be of great help to all educators. We often tend to skip the first step of walking the road with people and taking time to ask 'What's the matter with you?' and to listen attentively to their story. We are anxious to rush on to the breaking of the Word and the Bread. A school in its general ethos, its pastoral care, its chaplaincy and its religious education, must look to and address the needs of all pupils. This calls for a fuller understanding of faith and its development and makes demands on time, finance and organization. For these reasons many schools short-circuit the process and burden RE teachers and lessons with the whole of the task.

Schools and Pupils in the Contemporary World

Another failing of the narrow league table approach with regard to faith and religion is the fact that it takes little or no account of the influence of contemporary culture on the faith and religious practice of young people. The first part of the 1988 Vatican document outlines an overview of the special situation of young people. It lists some of the positive and negative features of present day society which influence the religious lives of the young. John Paul II frequently calls for a 'new evangelization'. This does not suggest that we preach some new Gospel. It acknowledges that we preach the Gospel in a vastly changed environment and that those to whom it is addressed have new questions. Our message must be incarnated in this time and place. The Vatican document recognizes that 'for many young people, a critical look at the world they are living in leads to crucial questions on the religious plane' and that 'large numbers of them sincerely want to know how to deepen their faith and live a meaningful life'. It also accepts that 'perhaps some have become indifferent and insensitive' and goes on to say:

> With kindness and understanding, they [teachers] will accept the students as they are, helping them to see that doubt and indifference are common phenomena, and that the reasons for this are readily understandable. But they will invite students in a friendly manner to seek and discover together the message of the Gospel, the source of joy and peace.

When I was young doubt was quite definitely criticized, at least in apologetical theory. This shows scant appreciation of the living and dynamic process of coming to and growing in faith. In this respect I find meditation on Peter's journey very helpful and useful.

Young People in Relation to Faith

The Vatican document is somewhat optimistic when it says 'perhaps some have become indifferent and insensitive'. In a seminar held in the Lateran University in May of 1992, 'Rome's youth, between faith and indifference', it was accepted that indifference to the faith characterized most of Rome's young people. The figures speak for themselves: 60,000 of Rome's estimated 650,000 young people, i.e., less than 10 per cent are reckoned to have any sort of regular contact with Sunday Mass or parish associations. It was pointed out that although their links with Church were weak it does not mean that the 90 per cent are not in any way religious. The Church structures do not seem to provide adequate answers for these 'children of secularization' for whom God is 'superfluous and has no effect on their lives' (*Avenire*, 20 May 1992). This is certainly not only a Roman phenomenon. It is widespread. In the last general chapter of the Salesians at which I was present this was the central topic of our deliberations. Men dedicated to the aspirations and needs of young people from all over the world declared that when speaking of youth and faith 'the largest category is the young people who are untouched by the Church'. The committed 'form the smallest group but are a real sign of hope'. Speaking of Irish young people in relation to faith Michael Paul Gallagher suggests that those who remain active and involved in Church activities represent about 10 per cent. The embittered and hostile also represent about 10 per cent. The vast majority lies in the middle.[2] Within our schools and classrooms there is this mix of young people who need our presence and sensitive listening rather than, what may seem to them, a pre-packed panacea for all their ills. The Vatican document lists some qualities which should be found in the teacher of religion: 'affection, tact, understanding, serenity of spirit, a balanced judgement, patience in listening to others, and prudence in the way they respond and finally, availabilty for personal meetings and conversations with students'. (RD 96).

A New Environment of Faith

The Irish Jesuit, Michael Paul Gallagher, whose works I have already cited, has written widely on young people and their faith struggles. For me his works are essential reading for all involved in the education of young people. He lectured in modern literature at University College, Dublin, for twenty years. His contact with students gave him valuable insights into the nature of faith and unbelief in today's young. He has written several books which are evidence of a great pastoral sensitivity. In 1990 he moved to Rome to work with the Pontifical Council for Dialogue with non-believers. In one of his books he recounts the incident when counselling a student he began 'When I was your age' to which the student retorted 'Father, you were never my age'. He realized that what the student meant was 'You were never 20 in 1990'. There is great insight in the remark and we need to ponder on it. It is necessary to compare and contrast the situation of our children and young people with the time and environment in which we were their age. Much has changed. Like it or not, their world and the environment of faith is different. For Gallagher there is no point in bemoaning the situation, rather, 'it is essential to recognise that such factors create a drastically different environment for faith'. He frequently states that there is not so much a crisis of faith as a crisis of the language of faith: 'it is a problem of mutual communication, and the gaps widen between the world of every day and the churchy world' (Gallagher, 1990, op. cit., p. 46).

A Pastoral, Spiritual, Rather than an Apologetic, Doctrinal, Approach

In his essay *The New Agenda for Unbelief and Faith* Gallagher writes of the need to foster 'the wavelength of faith'. He tells of the time he came across an evangelist shouting his message through a loud-hailer in the Piazza Venezia which, in his view, was 'no doubt a well-intentioned effort of evangelisation, but one that seems sadly lacking in relationship, community, or in anything of pre-evangelisation'. While it was difficult to disagree with the content of the message, 'the tone made me cringe'. In our schools we must ensure relationships, community and attention to pre-evangelization. In the essay he describes 'a multi-faceted shift in the agenda of unbelief' and suggests a parallel shift is needed in the agenda of faith as pastorally presented. It involves a move from the concepts of culture, from doctrine to disposition, from apologetics about the 'existence' of God to a spiritual-cum-pastoral theology that ponders on how faith can be prepared and nourished today . . . The newer unbelief may call for a contrary image of God as radically present, hidden in the ordinary, in the grace-guided narrative of each person and people. (Gallagher, 1993, p. 133)

He stresses that 'the last thing the unbeliever needs is a fundamentalist and humanly insensitive language of faith'.

Much of this has relevance to the school and religious education. Speaking of religious education Gallagher upholds the vital importance of a competent understanding of faith in today's questioning world and the need for 'intellectual backbone' in religion classes. While appreciating that content is crucial, he considers 'relationship more important': 'the attitude to the class will count for more than the perfect theological synthesis' (Gallagher, 1983, op. cit., pp. 87–93). This makes considerable personal demands on the teacher. In this regard most of them need our support rather than our criticism.

Touching Lives as Jesus Did

It is my belief that my former school in Bootle is doing a much better job than is indicated by its position on the league table of success in examination results. It is my conviction that a Catholic school in which the array of values and beliefs of the Gospel and our tradition are actually lived, does immense good to all involved with the school, especially pupils and their families. I frequently quote the sentence from *The Catholic School* which says that in our schools we should provide a 'setting in which pupils experience their dignity as persons before they know its definition'. If this is seen as the heart of what we do in our schools, then they will be of immense value. Without meaning to sound too pious, in my view, such a school touches many lives with something of the love and compassion of Jesus. Many pupils whose lives they touch may never go to the parish and may come from unhappy home situations. In their attitude and relationships teachers can attempt to heal and make whole. For many in our schools this can be a first step towards faith: 'when self-worth is wounded, a whole language of faith — human and religious — may stutter or fall silent . . . unreadiness for revelation can have roots in this area of a person's life' (Gallagher, 1987, p. 94). To walk with people and to touch their lives in this way is a vocation open to teachers. Catholic schools should provide the setting in which this is made possible. Those who manage our schools should see to it that they are as well informed of Church documents on schools as they are of Government documents. The giving of 'self-worth' must surely rank as high as knowledge and practice of the faith or any academic success. Reflection on Jesus in the Gospels will give a truer understanding of 'success'. He touched many people's lives. Not all stayed and followed him, not all were grateful, yet all were richer for his presence and his touch. We can be over anxious about 'results', about getting our money's worth — evangelized, cat-echized, practising young people in numbers. Perhaps we should be more anxious about the quality of our evangelizing presence, touch and attitude.

The Twofold Fidelity: To the World and to People

I am conscious that I have made no attempt to discuss any religious education programme. I have focused more on the people, our pupils in the contempor-ary environment of faith. This is not to downgrade or ignore the need for a systematic study of the Catholic tradition (one which will include an ecumenical dimension and a respect for and an openness to other faiths). In England and Wales work is being done on drawing up an overview of what our pupils ought to know and understand in religious education during their years at school. This is urgent and essential work. Like the Catechism, it will be a tool and will provide a useful and necessary reference point for our work in schools. It will enable us to plan and evaluate what we do in religion lessons. However, in itself it will not do the job of religiously educating our pupils or of fostering faith. Even the Catechism of Trent acknowledges this fact:

> . . . age, capacity, manners and condition must be borne in mind . . . The priest must not imagine that those committed to his care are all on the same level, so that he can follow one fixed unvarying method of instruc-tion to lead all in the same way to knowledge and true piety. (McHugh and Callan, 1934, p. 7)

John Paul II in *Catechesis in Our Time* upholds the school's 'grave duty to offer religious education suited to the often widely varying religious situations of the pupils' (John Paul II, 1979). The document *Lay Catholics in Schools* calls for the greatest sensitivity in respecting conscience. It accepts that among Catholic pupils there will be 'many different levels of faith response' and states that 'the Christian vision of existence must be presented in such ways that it meets all these levels' (RD 66–70). How a school sets about meeting this challenge cannot be fully measured by or recorded in the over simple and misleading league tables of knowledge and practice of the faith, important as these may be. For a number of reasons, there can be an unreadiness for Revelation in many pupils for whom Gospel and Church may have little meaning. Yet if a Catholic school sets out to enable pupils 'to experience their dignity as persons before they know its definition', I feel sure that something of God's love will touch their lives and enhance their self-worth and personal dignity. They then may be more ready and able to know and understand 'its definition' as set out in our Christian faith and beliefs. We should not undervalue the powerful potential of our schools in this regard. At the same time, we must constantly inspire and challenge them to fulfil this tremendous vocation.

Notes

1 See *Choice and Diversity, a Framework of Schools*, HMSO, July 1992. The full text of the bishops' response can be found in *Briefing* 3 December 1992, Catholic Media Office.
2 See *Educating Young People to the Faith*, 23rd General Chapter of the Salesians of Don Bosco, Editrice SDB, Rome, 1990, pp. 52–7 and *Struggles of Faith*, p. 36.

References

CONGREGATION FOR CATHOLIC EDUCATION (1977) *The Catholic School.*

CONGREGATION FOR CATHOLIC EDUCATION (1982) *Lay Catholics in School, Witnesses to Faith* (LCS).

CONGREGATION FOR CATHOLIC EDUCATION (1988) *The Religious Dimension of Education in a Catholic School* (RD).

DWYER (1970) *The Renewal of the Education of Faith*, Italian Episcopal Conference, translated by the Australian Episcopal Conference.

FRANCIS, L. (1986a) 'Roman Catholic secondary schools: Falling rolls and pupil attitudes', *Educational Studies*, **12**, 2.

FRANCIS, L. (1986b) 'Are Catholic schools good for non-Catholics?', *The Tablet*, 15 February.

FRANCIS, L. (1986c) 'The choice of Catholic schools', *The Tablet*, 4 October.

GALLAGHER, J. (1986) *Guidelines*, London, Collins.

GALLAGHER, J. (1988) *Our Schools and Our Faith*, London, Collins.

GALLAGHER, J. (1991) 'Living and sharing our faith, a national project', *Priests and People*, August–September.

GALLAGHER, M.P. (1983) *Help My Unbelief*, Dublin, Veritas.

GALLAGHER, M.P. (1987) *Free to Believe*, London, Darton, Longman and Todd.

GALLAGHER, M.P. (1990) *Struggles of Faith*, Dublin, Columba Press.

GALLAGHER, M.P. (1993) 'The new agenda of unbelief and faith', in LANE, D.A. (Ed) *Religion and Culture in Dialogue*, Dublin, Columba Press.

HIRST, P.H. (1981) 'Education, catechesis and the Church school', *The British Journal of Religious Education*, **3**, 3.

JOHN PAUL II (1979) *Catechesis in Our Time*, St Paul.

McHUGH, J.A. and CALLAN, C.J. (1934) *Catechism of the Council of Trent for Parish Priests*, Herder.

RODGER, A.R. (1982) *Education and Faith in an Open Society*, London, The Handsel Press.

Chapter 21

Directions for Research in Catholic Education in the USA and the UK

Joseph O'Keefe S.J. and Bernadette O'Keeffe

Appropriate forms of research are essential to the future development and well being of Catholic schools on both sides of the Atlactic. In this chapter we offer a brief indication of the current state of research into Catholic schools in both contexts and an indication of issues requiring research effort.

The United States Perspective

In 1992 the National Catholic Education Association (NCEA) published a major compendium of research on Catholic schools (Convey, 1992). While inquiry took place on a wide range of topics, most empirical data came from national studies conducted by the United States Department of Education, notably the High School and Beyond Study [HS&B], the National Assessment of Educational Progress [NAEP] and the National Educational Longitudinal Study [NELS]. In reviewing the research to date, Convey identified two major lacunae, a comprehensive study of Catholic elementary schools and a comprehensive study of religious outcomes. Six other areas were identified as understudied: the school as community, leadership, values, parental choice, teachers, single-sex schools.

Since the publication of Convey's book, NCEA published Sebring and Cambrun's initial analysis of NELS (1988) data. Findings show that Catholic schools are successful in some subject areas, have a greater sense of community than their counterparts and provide a better educational environment for minorities. They also reveal that Catholic-school students come from more advantaged backgrounds and that they perform less well in social studies and science than their peers. *Catholic Schools and the Common Good* (Bryk, Lee and Holland, 1993) made a major appearance on the US stage; while the book poses important new questions, the empirical data date back to the 1980s. Finally, an ERIC search reveals 201 articles on Catholic education since 1992, eight are published reports of the NCEA and seventy-eight are in *Momentum*, the official journal of the NCEA.

Topics in *Momentum* are wide-ranging, from voluntarism and the law to religious education and children with disabilities, from computers to teacher recruitment and retention, from the organization of middle schools to multicul-tural students and special education, from marketing of schools to collaboration with universities, from partnerships with business to the need for ecumenism given changing student compositions, from financial reform to the role of inner-city schools, from serving the needs of single parent families to interdisciplinary studies in Catholic schools. In descending order, the most frequently mentioned themes are: computers, school choice, summaries of national congresses, inner-city schools, business partnerships, recruitment and retention of teachers, secur-ing the involvement of parents and organization of middle schools. Though authors employed a variety of methods in these pieces, they tend overall to be popular in tone.

Non-NCEA sponsored pieces include three AERA presentations and art-icles in a wide variety of journals, including *Urban Review, Educational Leader-ship, Religious Education, School Organization, Journal of Curriculum and Supervision, Educational Forum, American School Board Journal, Journal of Negro Education, Educational Policy, Teacher Magazine, American Educa-tor, Journal of Educational Administration, American Journal of Education, Education Foundations*, and *The International Journal of Education Research*. In descending order, the most frequently mentioned themes are the perform-ance of Catholic schools in comparison to public schools, school choice, Catholic schools and minorities, financing Catholic schools, caring communities and diversity, teachers and the law, religious education and women, parental involve-ment, technology, multi-cultural curriculum, symbolic leadership, volunteer programmes, and comparison of minority students in Catholic schools with their peers in public settings. While the research agenda will continue to be shaped to a large extent by the availability of federal-level statistical data, qualitative methods will figure prominently in forthcoming research initiatives.

In September 1994, NCEA gathered Catholic educators from around the country to discuss a research agenda for the future. In descending order of priority, the following themes were endorsed: a comprehensive study of ele-mentary schools; Catholic identity and formational issues; leadership training; collaboration between clergy and laity; spirituality; governance; leadership in the field, focusing on superintendents, pastors, school boards; the impact of schools on the local church; Catholic philanthropy directed at schools; creation of a national endowment for Catholic schools; marketing, development and parental choice; preparation and retention of teachers; cost-benefit analysis of Catholic schools; international studies of Catholic schools.

While the NCEA conference identified important areas for inquiry, many important questions were neglected. While the conference called for a com-prehensive study of Catholic elementary schools, scant attention was paid to schools in inner-city areas marked by urban blight. So called 'full-service' or 'integrated service schools' are responding to the needs of students by offering a range of social services, including health care and counselling psychology, as an integral part of the school experience. Are Catholic schools involved in this reform? Site-based management is being implemented in many public school districts. Are Catholic schools living laboratories of reform? In the public sector there is heated debate about extending the length of the school day as well as the length of the school year and many Catholic schools report extended care programmes. In what do they consist? Are they effective? While child care remains a national problem, preschool programmes have mushroomed in Catholic schools. Do they provide a model for a greater public? It is clear that the Latino population will grow in the United States and many have left the Catholic church. Are Latino children, who have the lowest educational attainment rate of any ethnic group in the US, adequately served by the Catholic educational establishment?

Technological advancement in travel and telecommunications has made the world much smaller, yet ethnocentrism is on the rise in many places. As a worldwide organization united in faith and mission, the Catholic Church can become the bridge between cultures and systems of schooling.

The England and Wales Perspective

Distinctiveness — a Faith Encounter

The 1981 report to the Catholic Bishops' Conference of England and Wales, *Signposts and Homecomings: The Educative Task of the Catholic Community*, speaks of four key elements which define a Catholic school — first, 'a perspective centred on faith in Christ as Saviour'; second, 'a deep respect for the individuality and integrity of all human beings'; 'third, a commitment to the pursuit of justice; and finally, 'the promotion of a sense of mission' which would enable individuals 'to renew the face of the earth'. The report maintains that when there is a balance between these four elements then the 'distinctiveness of Catholic education will be apparent' (ibid., pp. 119–21). Implicit in the working party's vision of Catholic education is the development of a school community which sustains and transmits the Christian faith, and nurtures and deepens faith and the spiritual lives of pupils. Catholic education posits a learning environment which permits pupils to grow, as they become morally mature, socially responsible persons who will endeavour to practise Christian virtues of compassion and justice and find their Christian vocation in the world.

The intervening years have seen the imposition of a series of major educational reforms in England and Wales instituted by law, not the least of which involves a system of school management at local level, side by side with an enlarged sphere of parental involvement. Suffice at this point to say that governors, teachers and staff are required to take decisions undreamed of just those few years ago. Opting out, performance league tables and pupil exclusions are only some of today's challenges. Thus the task facing us today of discerning the balance between the four elements clarified in *Signposts and Homecomings* takes on a fresh urgency.

An important focus for research is the ways in which Catholic schools in their daily lives seek to demonstrate the four elements outlined above which are perceived as distinctive of their character. The research of sociologists, Glock and Stark (1965) provides a research methodology for research on the effectiveness of Catholic schools in achieving their religious goals (O'Keeffe, 1992). Glock and Stark distinguish five dimensions of religiosity which provide a framework for measuring the 'religious development' of pupils. These dimensions are: the 'experiential' (subjective religious experiences and emotions, e.g., feelings of intimacy with the 'divine'); the 'ritualistic' (religious practices such as worship, prayer, the sacraments and Church services); the 'ideological' (the actual beliefs held by members of a religious group); the 'intellectual' (knowledge of basic tenets of beliefs and scripture); and the 'consequential' (the effects of religious belief experience and knowledge upon the individual's behaviour in all areas of involvement).

A more tangible defining aspect of the Catholic school, the learning environment itself, can in the opinion of some subvert the very nature of the school when the non-Catholic component of pupils or staff exceeds certain limits. The controversy surrounding St Philip's sixth form college in Birmingham throws into sharp focus the question of pupil admissions policies and their perceived impact on the distinctiveness of Catholic schools. As indicated in the chapter by Vince Murray in this volume, when the Oratorian Fathers, as trustees, proposed to close the school in 1992 they did so on the basis that the school could no longer claim to be 'Catholic' because Roman Catholics accounted for less than a third of the pupil population. In their view the Catholic character could not be maintained when Catholics constituted a minority in the school population. The Catholic staff in resisting the closure of the college argued that the measure of Catholicity 'cannot simply be confined to measures of religious practice, but must take into account the spiritual life of the school as a whole, witnessed to by the majority of those who come to it' (Walsh, 1992). They could not agree that the faith community is impaired by the presence of pupils who do not share the same beliefs. Sensitive and well conceived research is clearly needed in relation to this matter.

Diversity in the learning environment of Catholic schools is also evidenced by the relatively large number of non-Catholic teachers in some Catholic schools. The impact of large numbers of non-Catholic teaching staff is discussed in a survey carried out in 1991 on Catholic school provision in the Diocese of Arundel and Brighton which also reflects the changing context in which Catholic schools endeavour to pursue their educational role (1991). The committee's findings are of some importance for Catholic education in England and Wales generally. Dominant issues highlighted in the report include the increasing difficulties faced by Catholic schools in recruiting Catholic teachers and the decreasing numbers of Catholic pupils. The report concludes that the continuing trend in the reduction of Catholic teachers is potentially the greatest threat to the future of Catholic schools in the diocese and in the country.

These observations find confirmation in the main conclusions arrived at in *The Supply of Catholic Teachers to Catholic Schools*, based on research and analysis of teacher recruitment and the nature of teacher shortages in the Catholic school sector, compiled by the Catholic Education service. The difficulty in recruiting Catholic teachers is most apparent in the key posts for which the appointment of a Catholic is essential (Catholic Education Service, 1994, p. 53).

Findings reveal that in the Arundel and Brighton diocese the number of pupils who are not Catholic has risen by nearly 60 per cent in the past ten years, while the number of Catholic teachers in Catholic secondary schools is just under 50 per cent. Also recognized are instances where schools could not survive if admissions were restricted to a solely Catholic intake (Diocese of Arundel and Brighton, 1991, p. 32). The Committee makes a strong case for a national review of the radically altered circumstances faced by Catholic schools in the 1990s. A key question for the committee concerns 'the point at which a school ceases to be effective for the purposes for which it was founded'. The committee is challenged not so much by factors such as the academic record of the school as by the perceived threat to its distinctiveness.

The emergence of a less homogeneous school environment has seen a complementary upsurge of new hopes and fears for religious education. Debates flourish over how to approach, and what to teach in, religious education classes. The traditional catechetical instruction for so long a distinguishing feature of Catholic schools is called into question. Tensions are evident between those who want to engage in a more traditional catechetics and those other Catholic RE teachers who pursue a more pupil-centred approach to religious education. Those who see the need to reassess the place of catechesis in education do so generally in response to the reality of the many classrooms where it can no longer be taken for granted that pupils are part of a faith community supported by Catholic parents. They see the RE classroom as the anvil on which the defining character of the contemporary Catholic school will be forged.

The Catholic Education Service (CES) has produced a series of development materials to help staff and governors to define their role and to evaluate the 'specifically Catholic nature of the school and the curriculum it delivers', such as the pack *Evaluating the Distinctive Nature of a Catholic School* and also a work pack on producing a mission statement.

Research also has its part to play. Useful work has already been carried out in Australia and the US (Flynn, 1985; Fahy, 1991) on the evaluating of the effectiveness of Catholic schools. Additional measures are called for in Britain as the Catholic school is renewed and indeed transformed to face the challenges of the wider society. At a time when the Church school is having reform placed on its agenda by law, when its renewal is shaped in large part as conforming with societal norms and when the transformation of the whole school experience leads to *angst* and divisions it is pertinent to explore the role of research and the contribution of researchers. It seems certain that a major role for research will be to ascertain if the key elements of distinctiveness as proposed in 1981 for Catholic schools are commensurate with today's actual school practice and outcome.

Diversity and a Changing School Agenda

Under the auspices of the Roman Catholic Bishops of England and Wales a number of working parties were established to confront certain critical aspects of change in Catholic schools in England and Wales. The working parties were established against the backcloth of a growing acceptance that ours is a diverse society and a recognition that all schools have a role in relation to it. The working parties for the most part saw that shift in the school climate which involves governance, staff and pupils and which all schools were individually struggling to come to terms with. Anglican Church schools were also facing challenges of a similar kind.

In 1975, the then Commission for Racial Justice of the Catholic Bishops' Conference of England and Wales undertook a survey in twenty-eight Catholic schools in four multi-racial areas. Its published report *Where Creed and Colour Matter: A survey of Black children and Catholic schools* points out that despite the presence of a high percentage of 'immigrants' in many areas, Catholic schools 'seem to be making a very small contribution to the education of immigrants' (ibid., p. 8). It also points to the 'paradoxical situation of a near-white school in multi-racial areas, where children are being taught about the unity of man, on the one hand, and seeing division of races on the other' (ibid., p. 38). The report highlights the institutional inactivity on the part of some Catholic schools and their failure to respond positively to the aspirations of black parents for their children. It found little evidence of a commitment to teach pupils to understand and respect different faiths and cultures in the wider society. In schools, the notion that we 'treat all alike', thus concealing the presence of difference, was widely prevalent. Little concession was made to non-English cultural needs and beliefs' (p. 36). Little thought was seen to be given to the moral effect of 'a semi-segregated' school on white Catholic pupils. Overall, a picture emerged of a need for much greater effort and commitment to dismantling some of the barriers which existed between Catholic schools and their neighbourhoods.

Nine years later, a second Working Party on Catholic Education in a Multiracial, Multicultural Society was set up. This group had a two-fold aim — to examine and make recommendations concerning how Catholic education might better provide for;

> the education of all Catholics for life in a multi-racial, multi-cultural society, and the specific educational needs of Catholics who are members of racial or cultural minorities. (p. 8)

The Working Party visited fifty Catholic schools as well as all Catholic colleges of higher education and Seminaries in England and Wales over a period of two years. The research findings are published in its report *Learning from Diversity: A Challenge for Catholic Education* (1984). The working party found evidence of signs of a new openness among some Catholic institutions to new initiatives which seek to educate pupils for a multi-racial society. The level of positive response was higher in racially mixed schools. For others who saw multicultural education as relevant only in racially mixed schools and more specifically to black pupils direct involvement was not deemed to be necessary. Marked variations were also identified between schools in respect of their responses to racially, culturally and religiously diverse backgrounds of pupils. The working party found that because of the ways in which certain schools had evolved only some of them 'have adapted to the new presence in their midst or restructured themselves to take account of the wider variety of needs they must meet' in their response to pupils of other faiths (ibid., p. 65). Although there were many encouraging instances of good practice, the working party highlighted the fact that much remained to be achieved in this area. This was particularly so in predominantly white secondary schools where there were few new initiatives (ibid., p. 40). An issue of particular concern to the working party was schools' attitude to racism and the finding that many schools 'did not see dealing with racism as part of their task' (ibid., p. 47).

The Report of Cardinal Hume's Advisory Group on the Catholic Church's commitment to the black community *With You in Spirit* published in 1986 sought 'to develop awareness of the ways in which racism within the institutional structures of the Church and in the attitudes and practices of individual white Catholics militates against Black people' (ibid., p. ix). The opening paragraph of the report sets the context for this group. 'Racism permeates every part of British society' (ibid., p. ix). In its section on Catholic education the group reported the widespread misgivings among black parents in respect of 'the raw deal they get from the Church in education'. Black Catholics expressed concern about practices in Catholic schools which adversely affected their children's education (ibid., p. 24). They were 'outraged' by the failure of some schools to understand their aspirations for their children to succeed. Black pupils who 'rail against the system' that does not motivate them and express their frustration and disillusionment through forms of, protest, defiance and lack of motivation are labelled 'disruptive'. The advisory group put 'the defeat of racism' as a top priority for Catholic schools. The urgency of the task is expressed in the following way:

> There is an urgent need for those responsible in Catholic schools to put their house in order and to demonstrate to the black community that the system of education they are offering is fair and just for all God's people. (ibid., p. 28)

The research findings of the above working parties provide a window to the world on aspects of Catholic education. What emerges from the reports is the need for all schools to examine their policies and practices to enable them to make a greater contribution to the education they provide for a multiracial society. A theme running through all three reports and a central concern of the working parties is for a system of education, functioning in an environment characterized by diversity and difference, rooted in justice based on fairness.

The Institute of Race Relations (1994) voices deep concern that the number of black children excluded from schools is out of all proportion to their numbers in schools. Although it recognizes that any single factor explanation is unsatisfactory, institutional racism, teachers' attitudes, low expectations of many black pupils and stereotypical attitudes to black pupils play a significant part in the processes leading to pupil exclusions. Many of the cases documented by the Institute for Race Relations point to ignorance of teachers in respect of the backgrounds of pupils and their communities.

Drawing on case studies the report challenges Church schools to respond positively to the religious cultural, social, ethnic and racial backgrounds of pupils. It makes the following observation: 'denominational schools have a particularly poor record in this area, especially when dealing with children from different religious, cultural and racial backgrounds' (ibid., p. 45). It cites cases of a pupil temporarily excluded for growing a beard, and a girl for wearing a head scarf. Furthermore, it reports that 'denominational ones [schools] are punitive towards black children who fail to conform to the school's perception of "the norm"' (ibid., p. 29). It cites a case where a school threatened to exclude a 12-year-old African-Caribbean boy unless his mother sent him to school in 'simpler clothes'. The mother was reminded that she should 'be grateful that he is here at all because he is a non-Catholic' (ibid., p. 30).

The findings of the various working parties and the report published by the Institute of Race Relations make us aware of complexity within the school environment. As Kelly reminds us 'We are so ignorant of complexity we haven't yet asked the right question about what it is' (1994, p. 458). Research has a key role to play in locating that question which needs to be addressed. Kelly goes on to assert that 'we don't even have a good measure for diversity' (p. 459). Research will help us to translate our intuitive feelings into something very precise. Our pluralist society frequently displays values or visions which do not allow for a single common evaluation or agreed measure. Some form of arbitration is called for. Gellner (1995) argues that when two values or visions are incommensurate, no meaning can be attributed to the idea of rational choice between them. It is noteworthy that MacIntrye (1990), Aspin (1989) and Gellner arrive at a similar destination in the examination of the dilemma of incommensurate values. MacIntyre looks to a 'dialectical discourse', Aspin to 'talking together' and Gellner to 'haggle'. Gellner makes the pertinent observation that freefall 'pluralism' is not enough. The education system, including the Catholic school component, needs the idea of standards of criticism which are not under its control. Research has a key role to play in helping to develop acceptable standards and a new emergent awareness.

Disadvantaged Pupils and School Practice

The successive Education Acts in England and Wales and the accompanying legislation in the 1980s and 1990s are reshaping Catholic education. A brief sketch of the major changes includes the extended parental rights, the centralization of the National Curriculum, methods of assessment, attainment targets, the publication of league tables of public examination results, and the regular inspection of the quality of teaching and schools. As a result the autonomy of Catholic schools so closely protected and valued by the Catholic bishops, and financially supported by the Catholic community, in the negotiations leading to the 1944 Education Act is being threatened on all fronts.

The origin of the values and colour of contemporary educational reform to be found in the White Paper 'Choice and Diversity' is clear:

> Five great themes run through the story of educational change in England and Wales since 1979: quality, diversity, increasing parental choice, greater autonomy for schools and greater accountability. (par. 1.9)

These themes are intended to:

> provide a framework for the Government's aims and together define our goal for Britain's education system. (ibid., par. 1.20)

In consequence our schools are among the most competitive institutions in society today. The competitive climate in which Catholic schools function places self-interest, competition, success and the power of personal choice high on the agenda.

The social consequences of changes outlined above have received little attention in public debate. As Ball notes much of the literature on the education market concentrates on the demand side — on the centrality of choice, while 'strategies and the behaviour of the producers (schools) in the market' are neglected apart from the 'rather abstract notions about incentive and entrepreneurship' (Ball, 1993, p. 6). What gets neglected or 'glossed over' 'are the mechanisms of institutional survival in the market — more crucially competition. The research by Ball illustrates that, more often than not, decision making is financially led and rests upon the self-interest of the schools so as to ensure income maximization and to maximize the impact of resources on income. Furthermore there is 'a deliberate' empowering of certain individuals and groups over others (ibid.). Many schools go to endless lengths to attract 'good pupils'. These measures include greater selection procedures and the use of exclusions as a sanction to 'get rid' of difficult or disruptive pupils. As a result the market model of education in effect produces winning and losing schools together with pupils who are winners or losers.

The sharp increase in the numbers of excluded pupils is indicative of significant change which has taken place in the implementation of educational policy (O'Keeffe, 1995). The National Exclusions Reporting System (NERS) recorded that in 1992 there was an annual rise of almost 32 per cent in the number of pupils permanently excluded from schools. Birmingham Education Committee in its analysis of pupil exclusions (1994) noted that 'the most significant increase occurred when the governing bodies' powers were increased'.[1] The increasing recourse to exclusions evident in Church and County schools is affecting pupils at primary and secondary levels. The particular groups at risk include black children and children from stressed homes in the most deprived and neglected inner urban areas. In a collaborative report Barnardo's and Family Service Unit *Schools Out*, poverty, inadequate housing, over-crowding and family stress are identified as contributory factors which result in exclusion from school. The number of black pupils excluded is out of proportion to total school population (Bourne *et al.*, 1994). The Office for Standards in Education (1993) finds that 'there are no clear reasons' for the sharp rise in the numbers of exclusions. It lists possible reasons; increased family stress, giving rise to difficult behaviour in school; 'a form of punishment on tariff'; staffing difficulties; 'reduced levels of teacher tolerance' (p. 2). Evidence is emerging of an excessive recourse to the exclusion sanction as a disciplinary measure. The conflict between the needs of the school to perform in respect of league tables, attractiveness, school image, appeal to prospective 'clients' and the needs of disruptive or difficult pupils is becoming more apparent: 'Parents and professionals fear the market underpinning the education system . . . is leading to widespread exclusion of pupils for more trivial offences' (*Times Educational Supplement*, 1 July, 1994, 'Exclusion Bias' to be investigated'). For Newsam exclusion 'reflects an attitude of mind and it is that attitude of mind that is of crucial importance' (*Schools Out*, p. 101).

In a recent report on poverty and schooling *Education Divides* (1994) Smith and Noble point to an 'increasingly fragmented and divided educational service', with a strong shift away from the ideas of unified national educational system. The Government's pursuit of diversity of institutional provision, the report notes, is all too often translated into 'divisions and inequalities in provision' (ibid., p. 136). This observation of increasing educational inequalities is also echoed in a report published by Office for Standards in Education (Ofsted) (1993) *Access and Achievement in Urban Education*, a survey of seven urban areas characterized by significant levels of social and economic disadvantage. The report found people living in disadvantaged areas 'poorly served by the education system'. As a result most schools in these disadvantaged areas do not have within themselves the capacity for sustainable renewal. The rising tide of national educational change is not 'lifting these boats' (ibid., p. 45). The report's findings raise fundamental issues about multiple disadvantages in the wider society and the additional burdens which these children carry.

In an attempt to understand and respond to what is happening in Catholic schools in urban deprived areas the Committee for Community Relations has set in motion a 'Consultation on Catholic Secondary Schools in Urban Poverty Areas'. The consultation will have a research input from over twenty Catholic schools situated in some of the most deprived urban areas. The broad purpose of this initiative is to gain a clearer understanding of the plight of these schools and an exploration of the issues and challenges they face. The group will also be concerned with successful initiatives identified by headteachers which have helped to enhance pupil learning and increase self-esteem among pupils. Research in this area can enrich our educational work. However, we need to go a step further and involve the process of critical reflection.

Encountering Other Faiths

A recent consultation on *Catholic Schools and Other Faiths* turned its attention to areas of concern regarding religious pluralism and the Catholic school.[2] Three significant developments prompted the work of the consultative group. The first was the change in pupil composition seen by some as a threat to the Catholic character of the school as already outlined. The second relates to the controversies which surround approaches to, and content of religious education/catechesis in our schools. The third, schools looking for guidance in their developing relationships with children of other faith communities. The consultative group in its final deliberation has presented a combined theological and contextual appraisal for Roman Catholic relations with other faiths and particularly in respect of Catholic schools. However, the conclusions reached are by no means definitive. Why do parents of other faith traditions sometimes choose a Catholic school? What are their hopes and expectations for their children's education? What is the rationale for the admission of these pupils? Much work remains to be done with a key role for research as the complex inter-relationships of responsibilities to Catholic parents and children and the need to be responsive to religious and cultural diversity in the school community continue to be addressed. Are practical guidelines, appropriate teaching approaches and training of teachers which are reflective of the whole school environment a possibility for the future?

To what extent has the story of Catholic education today become no more than a subtext in the wider narrative of state education provision? The challenges are common to all schools, the initiatives and directives — all governmental in origin, common to all. Where is the social vision and whence will it emerge to contest the 'five great themes' of *Choice and Diversity*? The *raison d'être* of the Catholic school remains nebulous until the spiritual vision of *Signposts and Homecomings* with its outlined four key elements is brought into an equipoise with a social commentary which the body of Catholic social teaching seems at the present time ill-equipped to provide. The need therefore is pressing. Needed are all those philosophers, sociologists, educationalists and teachers who are willing to accept the challenge to provide cultural substance which is commensurate with Catholic spiritual or faith imperatives.

In forthcoming research initiatives there is a role for ethnographers to analyse schools and the communities in which they exist. In addition, there is considerable scope for historians to conduct studies of the institutions, especially in relation to current issues. The reflective scholarship of social scientists can help Catholics be more thoughtful about issues both micro and macro: psychological well-being among constituents, management of fiscal and human resources, implications of school choice, influencing public policy. There is much scope for theologians to reflect on the purpose of schools, the dynamics of community within schools, worship for young persons, creating faith communities among adults who work in education, always articulating how the teachings of the Church are operationalized institutionally. Philosophers must wonder aloud about inconsistencies between espoused mission and the exigencies of practice, the cultural milieu in which the schools exist, and reconciling the need for strong identity with the diversity of pupils who are to be served.

In qualitative methods, the researcher is himself or herself an instrument of research. Therefore, practitioners must work with scholars to bridge the chasm between theory and practice on an enormous range of issues such as instructional techniques, models of supervision and evaluation, assessment standards, and a list of others too long to mention here. Catholic universities and Catholic colleges of higher education can play a key role, especially in providing teams of researchers across local, diocesan and national boundaries. In all of these endeavours, the Catholic community must be vigilant to provide both the *emic* and the *etic* point of view. Catholic educators must welcome into their schools non-Catholic researchers to provide a richness of perspective and to lend credence, especially with respect to public–private comparisons. Schools in the US, Britain and other countries must welcome colleagues from outside the system to ask unheard-of questions and to share new paradigms.

Notes

1 Main provisions in The Education (No. 2) Act 1986 introduced reform of school governing bodies and articles and instruments of government. Provisions included the disciplinary responsibilities of headteachers including responsibility for discipline, and exclusions. The headteacher now has the legal power to exclude a pupil.
2 The consultation was requested by the Bishops Conference and was sponsored by the Department of Catholic Education and Formation, the Committee for Other Faiths, and the Committee for Community Relations.

References

ASPIN, D. (1989) 'Critical openness as a platform for diversity: Towards an ethic of belonging', in O'KEEFFE, B. (Ed) *Schools for Tomorrow: Building Walls or Building Bridges*, Lewes, Falmer Press.
BALL, S. (1993) 'Education markets, choice and social class: The market as a class strategy in the UK and the USA', *British Journal of Sociology of Education*, **14**, 1.
BISHOPS CONFERENCE OF ENGLAND and WALES (1984) *Learning from Diversity: A Challenge for Catholic Education*, Report of the working Party on Catholic Education in a Multiracial, Multicultural Society, Department for Christian Doctrine and Formation of the Bishops' Conference of England and Wales.
BOURNE, J., BRIDGES, L. and SEARLE, C. (1994) *Outcast England: How Schools Exclude Black Pupils*, London, Institute of Race Relations.

Bryk, A.S., Lee, V.E. and Holland, P.B. (1993) *Catholic Schools and the Common Good*, Cambridge, Harvard University Press.

Cardinal Basil Hume (1986) *With you in Spirit*, The Report of the Cardinal Hume's Advisory Group on the Catholic Church's Commitment to the Black Community.

Catholic Commission for Racial Justice (1975) *Where Creed and Colour Matter*.

Catholic Education Service (1994) *The Supply of Catholic Teachers to Catholic Schools*, *A Research Paper* (Researcher: Wells, D.), London, Catholic Education Service.

Cohen, R., Hughes, M., Ashworth, L. and Blair, M. (1994) *Schools Out: The Family Perspective on School Exclusion*, London, Barnardo's and Family Service Units.

Convey, J. (1992) *Catholic Schools Make a Difference: Twenty-five Years of Research*, Washington, DC, National Catholic Educational Association.

Department for Education (1993) *A New Deal for Out of School Pupils*, *Department for Education News 126/93, 23 April, 1993*, London, Department for Education.

Diocese of Arundel and Brighton (1991) *Report of the Special Committee on Catholic School Provision in the Diocese*.

Catholic Education Service (1990, 1994) *Evaluating the Distinctive Nature of the Catholic School*, London, Bishops Conference Department of Education and Formation.

Fahy, P. (1991) *Faith in Catholic Classrooms*, Homebush, St Paul.

Flynn, M. (1975) *Some Catholic Schools in Action*, Sydney, Catholic Education Office.

Flynn, M. (1985) *The Effectiveness of Catholic Schools*, Sydney, Society of St Paul.

Gellner, E. (1995) 'The Prophet Isaiah', *The Guardian*, 7 February.

Glock, C.Y. and Stark, R. (1965) *Religion and Society in Tension*, Chicago, Rand McNally.

Kelly, K. (1994) *Out of Control: The New Biology of Machines*, London, Fourth Estate.

McIntyre, A. (1990) *Three Rival Versions of Moral Enquiry: Encyclopaedia, Genealogy and Tradition*, London, Duckworth.

Office for Standards in Education (1993) *Education for Disaffected Pupils*, OFSTED.

O'Keeffe, B. (1992) 'A look at the Christian schools movement', in Watson, B. (Ed) *Priorities in Religious Education*, London, Falmer Press.

O'Keeffe, B. (1995) 'Fairness: A missing theme in education', in *Law and Justice* (The Christian law review), Hilary Easter No. 124/125, pp. 3–16.

Sebring, P.A. and Cambrun, E.M. (1992) *A Profile of Eighth Graders in Catholic Schools*, Washingtion, DC, National Catholic Educational Association.

Study Group of the Bishops Conference of England and Wales (1981) *Signposts and Homecomings: The Educative Task of the Catholic Community*, A Report to the Bishops of England and Wales, London, St Paul Publications.

Walsh, M. (1992) 'The Battle of St Philip's', in *The Tablet*, 10 October, pp. 1261–2.

Notes on Contributors

Michael Barnes S.J. is Lecturer in Theology and Religious Studies at Heythrop College, University of London. He is Director of the Westminster Interfaith Programme. Since 1984 he has been a member of the Committee for Other Faiths of the Catholic Bishops' Conference of England and Wales. He is the author of *Religions in Conversation*.

Anthony S. Bryk is Professor of Education at the University of Chicago. He is co-author (with Valerie E. Lee and Peter B. Holland) of *Catholic Schools and the Common Good* and is currently involved in efforts to promote school reform and improvement in the Chicago Public Schools.

Bruce S. Cooper is Professor of Administration, Policy and Urban Education in the Graduate School of Education, Fordham University. He is former President of Associates for Research on Private Education, a special interest group of the American Educational Research Association and has published on both public and private school issues and reforms.

James M. Day is currently Professor of Human Development and the Psychology of Religion in the Faculty of Psychology and Educational Sciences at the Catholic University of Louvain. He is currently working on a series of articles on the relationship between gender and religious experiences, and on relationships between religious development and moral development.

Jim Gallagher S.D.B. is Vice-Provincial of the Salesians of Don Bosco in Britain and Liberia. He was for eight years coordinator of the National Project for Catechesis and Religious Education of the Department of Christian Education and Formation of the Bishops' Conference of England and Wales. He formerly taught religious education in a secondary school and was a Senior Lecturer in Theology and Religious Education in Liverpool Institute of Higher Education. His books include *Guidelines* and *Our Schools and Our Faith*.

Gerald Grace is Professor of Education at Durham University. He is currently researching the changing nature of school leadership in England with particular reference to the position of teachers. His most recent book is *School Leadership: Beyond Education Management*.

Thomas Groome is Professor of Theology and Religious Education at Boston College. He has written widely in journals of religious education, pastoral ministry and theology. Recently published books include *Sharing Faith: A Comprehensive Approach to Religious Education* and *Pastoral Ministry* and *Language for a 'Catholic' Church*.

John Haldane is Professor of Philosophy in the University of St Andrews and Director of the Centre for Philosophy and Public Affairs. He has published widely in many areas of philosophy.

Peter Hastings was for twenty-one years head of the Trinity Roman Catholic Comprehensive School in Leamington Spa, Warwickshire (and a Catholic Grammar School from which it was created). He has been an Associate Fellow in the Department of Arts Education in the University of Warwick, and is currently writing a book on Catholic education.

David Hollenbach S.J. is Margaret O'Brien Flatley Professor of Catholic theology at Boston College, and an Associate Fellow at the Woodstock Theological Center, Georgetown University.

Mgr Paul A. Hypher is a parish priest in the Diocese of East Anglia. He Chaired the Catholic Bishops' Conference of England and Wales Consultation Group, 'Catholic Schools and Other Faiths'. From 1989 to 1993 he was Chairman of the Peterborough Interfaith Council. He is a member of the Committee for Other Faiths of the Catholic Bishops' Conference of England and Wales.

Catherine A. Lacey R.S.C.J. is a member of the Religious of the Sacred Heart, and a Programme Officer for the Spencer Foundation, which supports educational research. Her own research interests include the study of teaching, faculty development, women's education and narrative analysis.

V. Alan McClelland is Dean of the School of Education and Professor of Educational Studies at the University of Hull. His books include *English Roman Catholics and Higher Education 1830–1903* and (edited) *Christian Education in a Pluralist Society*.

Terence H. McLaughlin is a University Lecturer in education in the University of Cambridge and Fellow of St Edmund's College, Cambridge. He specializes in philosophy of education and has written widely on such topics as parents' rights in upbringing and education, common and separate schools, pastoral care, values in education and citizenship, diversity and education. He is editor (with David Bridges) of *Education and the Market Place* and is Secretary of the Philosophy of Education Society of Great Britain.

Vince Murray is Senior Lecturer in Newman College, Birmingham where he is responsible for the training of teachers of religious education in secondary schools. For five years he was a teacher of religious studies at St Philip's Roman Catholic Sixth Form College in Birmingham.

Joseph O'Keefe S.J. is Assistant Professor of Education at Boston College and programme coordinator for the Education Administration Programme. He is currently in receipt of a grant from the Jesuit Conference to do a national survey of inner-city Catholic elementary schools in the US, in conjunction with the National Catholic Educational Association.

Bernadette O'Keeffe is a sociologist who is Assistant Director of the Von Hügel Institute and a Fellow of St Edmund's College, Cambridge. As a Senior Research Fellow at King's College London, she wrote *Faith, Culture and the Dual System: A Comparative Study of Church and County Schools* and edited *Schools for Tomorrow: Building Walls or Building Bridges.*

Richard Pring is Professor of Educational studies at the University of Oxford and fellow of Green College, Oxford. He is editor of the *British Journal of Educational Studies* and has written extensively on many aspects of education.

Leela Ramdeen is currently a student at the College of Law, London. From 1993 to 1994 she was an education consultant. Formerly, she was deputy director of education for the London Borough of Haringey. Other appointments include inspector for multi-cultural education with Inner London Education Authority and director of Inner London Education Authority Project. In 1994 she was nominated Catholic Woman of the Year.

Richard Zipfel is secretary to the Committee for Community Relations of the Catholic Bishops' Conference of England and Wales. His books include *From Barriers to Community: The Challenge of the Gospel for a Divided Society* (with Mary Grey).

Index